Fourth Edition

Court Reporter's and CART Services Handbook

A Guide for All Realtime Reporters, Captioners, and CART Providers

Robert W. McCormick
Alfred State University

Mary H. Knapp

Prentice
Hall

Upper Saddle River, New Jersey 07458

Library of Congress Cataloging-in-Publication Data

McCormick, Robert W.
 Court reporter's and CART services handbook: a guide for all realtime reporters,
 captioners, and CART providers / Robert W. McCormick, Mary H. Knapp.—4th ed.
  p. cm.
  Rev. ed. of: Complete court reporter's handbook / Mary H. Knapp, Robert W.
 McCormick. 3rd ed. c1999.
  Includes index.
  ISBN 0-13-097634-2
   1. Law reporting—United States. 2. Computer-aided transcription. 3. Stenotypy.
 I. Knapp, Mary H. II. Knapp, Mary H. Complete court reporter's handbook. III. Title.

KF255 .M49 2003
347.73′16—dc21

2002066310

Publisher: Stephen Helba
Executive Editor: Elizabeth Sugg
Editorial Assistant: Anita Rhodes
Managing Editor: Mary Carnis
Production Management: Linda Zuk, WordCrafters Editorial Services, Inc.
Production Liaison: Brian Hyland
Director of Manufacturing and Production: Bruce Johnson
Manufacturing Manager: Ilene Sanford
Creative Director: Cheryl Asherman
Senior Design Coordinator: Miguel Ortiz
Formatting: BookMasters
Marketing Manager: Tim Peyton
Composition: BookMasters
Printer/Binder: Banta, Harrisonburg, VA
Cover Design: Christopher Weigand
Cover Printer: Phoenix Color Corp.

Pearson Education Ltd., *London*
Pearson Education Australia Pty. Limited, *Sydney*
Pearson Education Singapore Pte. Ltd.
Pearson Education North Asia Ltd., *Hong Kong*
Pearson Education Canada Ltd., *Toronto*
Pearson Educacion de Mexico, S.A. de C.V.
Pearson Education—Japan, *Tokyo*
Pearson Education Malaysia, Pte. Ltd.
Pearson Education, *Upper Saddle River, New Jersey*

10 9 8 7 6 5 4 3 2
ISBN 0-13-097634-2

The fourth edition of Court Reporter's and CART Services Handbook *is dedicated to the known court and realtime reporters who were present in the World Trade Center in New York City on September 11, 2001. They lost their lives helping others as members of a very noble and honorable profession. May their spirits live on forever.*

Contents

Preface

A lot has happened in the world of court and realtime reporting since the third edition of this textbook. The profession of court and realtime reporting has seen remarkable technological growth. There are more jobs paying higher salaries, but fewer people are going into the profession of court and realtime reporting. There is a need for competent reporters who will do the job of verbatim and assistive reporting in today's world.

The fourth edition of this handbook reflects these changes. Among other things, this new edition includes the following:

- Three sections to represent the three areas of reporting: officialships, freelancing, and captioning/CART

- An enhanced introductory section for those interested in the career of court and realtime reporting

- An entire section devoted to closed captioning and CART (communications and realtime translations) services, including a discussion on assistive technology

- Updated legislation that deals with television decoders, FCC regulations, and close captioning for the hearing impaired

- Updated ethics and professional guidelines, as well as the Procedures Manual for CART providers from the National Court Reporters Association

- Updated chapters dealing with research on the Internet and the World Wide Web

- Updated chapters dealing with the changing technology, including the use of voice writers

- Interviews with closed captioners and their views about what they do

- A complete revision and update of all material as it pertains to the field of court and realtime reporting, captioning, and CART providers

- New and improved supplemental material, including the Study Guide and a new Documents and Examples book

This textbook is meant to enhance the concept that the live-court and realtime reporter will always be needed and that the best, most reliable, and most dependable method still available for producing a quick, accurate, and honest transcript is the use of a court and realtime reporter, a captioner, or a CART provider.

Acknowledgments

The following individuals are to be commended for their dedication and spirit to the field of court and real-time reporting and captioning/CART services. Their input and insightful ideas were instrumental in updating the current edition of this textbook.

Chris Ales, Court Reporter
M. Monette Benoit, BA, RPR, CSR, RMR, CRI, CART Provider
Kelly DeVito, Stenocaptioner
Judy Miller, Official Court Reporter
Elizabeth (Cookie) Maki, CART Provider, Broadcast Captioner
SueLynn Morgan, BS, RPR
Ellen Oakes, Closed Captioner
Traci D. Walker, Realtime Captioner

Section A

General Information for Anyone Interested in Court and Realtime Reporting

Chapter 1

Considering Reporting as a Career

So You Want to Be a Reporter

Are you considering becoming a court or realtime reporter? If so, congratulations! You are thinking about joining one of the most exciting and challenging careers in the world. This decision could be the most important decision of your life. Reporting can be an interesting, rewarding, and challenging occupation in which your earnings will be limited only by your ability and your desire to work.

The reporting profession has many job opportunities for qualified workers. The term *court reporter* is a general terms that encompasses a number of specific job classifications within the reporting field. These job classifications are summarized in Table 1.1. The jobs listed are not all-inclusive and serve merely as examples.

This book will refer to all court, freelance, and captioning reporters with the general term *reporters* or *court and realtime reporters*. When necessary, specific terminology will be used to differentiate the various titles.

Court and realtime reporters are very happy at what they do. If you talk to working reporters you will find that the majority of them are very content with their career choice. In fact, if you were to ask a number of reporters whether they would choose a career in reporting again—that is, if they could start over—nine out of ten would respond with a resounding "Yes!"

The reasons for this occupational contentment and satisfaction are many. For some, the main reason is money. Court reporters can earn good incomes; but they also work hard and put in long hours. For others, the satisfaction of a job well done is enough. Some reporters enjoy the challenge of accomplishing what appears to others an awesome task. Finally, some enjoy reporting because it is fun!

Common Characteristics of Highly Effective Reporters

It is important to earmark some of the characteristics that make court and realtime reporters successful or "highly effective" at what they do. These basic attributes are ones that most reporters have in common. If you do not have all of them, do not be dismayed. Many successful people have overcome great obstacles to

TABLE 1.1   THE PROFESSION OF COURT AND REALTIME REPORTING

Official Court Reporting	*Freelance Reporting*	*Caption Reporting and CART*
Supreme Court	Deposition reporting	Broadcast reporting
County or family court	Negotiations or arbitrations	Web/Internet reporting
Hearing reporting	Conferences and conventions	Classroom reporting and CART

become what they wanted to become by substituting a missing characteristic with pure, unadulterated, 100 percent determination and motivation.

1. *Good physical and mental condition.* Without a doubt, the court and realtime reporter needs to be able to hear and see what goes on in a particular setting. In a very real sense, the reporter is the eyes and the ears of those who are not present. The reporter's responsibility is to capture what is said and done and then to share this information with others.

   Good health is important in many occupations, but probably more so in reporting. Occasionally, the workday may be long. Reporters will often travel a great deal. Working extra hours to finish a job that was due yesterday may be necessary. Reporters very often encounter stressful working conditions, deadlines to meet, and normal day-to-day pressures.

   Consequently, good physical and mental conditioning is important. The reporter should have reasonable hearing and sight, have good manual dexterity of both hands, and not be addicted or dependent on alcohol or drugs of any type.

2. *Knowledge of punctuation and grammar.* A reporter must have good English skills, which include vocabulary, spelling, grammar, and punctuation. The reporter is a "word processor" in the true sense of the phrase—the reporter processes words! A reporter's whole business is words—getting them down, reading them back, and producing an accurate transcript.

   Employers of court reporters rank good English skills as a top priority in hiring new reporters. The court reporter should enjoy words and be inquisitive enough to look up the definition of words that are unfamiliar. He or she should also make certain that the completed transcript contains correct punctuation, spelling, and format.

3. *Knowledge of world events.* If you are considering becoming a court reporter, you should enjoy reading. Most reporters like to read books, magazine articles, and newspapers. Reading keeps one's mind in tune with the happenings of the day. Just a half-hour a day reading a newspaper will have remarkable results for the student of court reporting. It increases your vocabulary; it makes you more aware of what is happening on a local, national, and international level; it entertains you; and it informs you about a variety of topics. A good knowledge of current and world events is helpful in understanding what is going on around you.

4. *Attitude.* Certain personal qualities that most successful reporters strive for or have acquired in their careers are needed. The first quality is a good attitude. You need a solid, positive feeling about yourself and what you are doing. Many people lose good jobs because they have negative attitudes. You can avoid this problem by developing a successful attitude while in school. You can begin by developing a friendly attitude with your fellow students and instructors and all types of people that you meet in everyday situations.

   In reporting you must display a positive, mature personality and exhibit a cheerful, pleasant demeanor under pressure. You must learn to accept and profit from criticism without becoming defensive. In court reporting, as in most professions, immature behavior is not acceptable. To feel good about what you are doing, you must first feel good about yourself. A good, healthy attitude about who and what you are is important. Accept yourself, with all your faults and shortcomings, as well as all your strong points. Above all, remember to think *positively* about your work, who you are, where you are going, and what you are doing with your life.

5. *Motivation.* Another necessary personal characteristic is motivation. Some people call this drive, determination, or perseverance. In reporting, motivation is vital. Real determination is needed to complete the course of study to become a court reporter and to overcome plateaus that may appear on the road to achieving a high machine shorthand speed.

   You will learn that you must devote time to the study of medical, legal, and technical terminologies, as well as other subject areas. You will learn that you will need to develop a writing speed in excess of 225 words a minute (wam) on testimony.

6. *Appearance.* Appearance is important. To be a successful reporter, you should look the part. Reporters should read current books and articles on proper dress, because they must create a favorable image of

themselves and the profession. As a reporter, you hold a very responsible position in our society. You are an officer of the court and therefore contribute to the layperson's respect for law and order. You will often be called on to transcribe cases involving large sums of money as well as people's lives. Your appearance should instill confidence in those who you meet; you must have an appearance that gives the impression that you can do the job and do it right!

Specifically, your clothing choices will depend on the custom and tradition of where you work. When on the job, look around you. If you see conservative attire, try to maintain the status quo. Talk to other reporters or court personnel to learn what is appropriate and what is not. Use common sense and good judgment.

7. *Confidentiality*. Another quality that is highly regarded among judges and lawyers is the ability of the court reporter to be confidential about legal matters. Confidentiality is essential. The slightest slip regarding something said or done in court or during a deposition or statement could cause serious harm to someone's life or affect a case adversely. Even an innocent remark to a juror could cause a mistrial. Therefore, reporters must learn to avoid discussing their work.

Confidentiality about the testimony extends to scopists, transcribers, binders, and everyone who works in the court or freelance office. Reporters must be very careful to guard the integrity of the record. Passwords should be used when working on transcripts, copies should not be left out in the open, new reporters should not be furnished with any information regarding a case, and copies of transcripts may not be sold or given to anyone without the authorization of the person who hired the reporter to take and transcribe them.

8. *Punctuality*. Professional people make it a point to be on time for any appointment or engagement. The court reporter who makes a success of himself or herself is the one who arrives early at a deposition or trial and makes sure that things are in order. In addition, the competent court reporter makes sure that transcripts are delivered on time, especially if a delivery date is promised. Punctuality, or being on time, is a personal quality that the beginning court reporter should strive to incorporate in his or her life.

9. *Respect*. Finally, reporters should strive to obey and respect the law. They should conduct themselves properly in social situations. Reporters should exercise courtesy toward judges and the diverse types of people that they meet every day.

Reporters are usually the only individuals present at a proceeding with whom no one is angry or upset. Therefore, they must remain unbiased. They should not show facial expressions or other actions that would suggest that they have an opinion regarding how a case is being handled. Reporters are expected to exhibit a calm, cool, and collected demeanor, which is sometimes very difficult to achieve.

Reporters must be loyal to judges, members of the bar, and their own profession. They should never speak adversely about any attorney or judge. Reporters must also be honest and forthright. The reporter's duty is to charge proper, uniform rates to all and do the best job that he or she possibly can for any client. Reporters should avoid unethical practices.

Mastering the Skill

The bottom line is this: To work as a court or realtime reporter, one has to be able to write accurately and transcribe quickly. In addition, having knowledge of grammar and punctuation, having an awareness of world events, dressing properly, working diligently, and being punctual and efficient are important qualities.

If you are considering a career as a court or realtime reporter, you have started in the right place. You are attempting to gather all the information you can about the profession so that you can make an informed decision. After you have read over the information contained in this book, your future is up to you. Only you can decide whether reporting is for you. We hope that you will decide that it is, because there is a shortage of good, competent court reporters. As long as court reporters can furnish quick, reliable, accurate, and dependable service and save consumers time and money, the future of the reporting profession is secure.

Court Reporting: Facts and Frequently Asked Questions (FAQs)

Facts

The student who begins to study reporting may know very little about what the profession really entails, what jobs exist, or how one goes about getting into the field. Somewhere he or she may have heard that court reporting is a job in which you can "make a lot of money!" What they have not heard is what they need to do to get to the point of earning money—how much schooling is required; nor are they aware of how much dedication is required to become a professional, well-paid court reporter.

The following list contains some facts about the field of court reporting. You will find that most of them are very positive; but others you may find a little difficult.

- *Fact 1: The initial cost of the education to enter the field is relatively low when compared to other professions.*

    You will find that you will need far less of an investment in time or money to enter the field of court reporting than to enter other professional fields. Doctors, lawyers, and engineers spend many years in preparation. Then, when they enter private practice, they work many years to build up the business.

    With the skills that you have developed and your computer-input machine, you will enter a high-paying field as a professional. You will have many opportunities to use your skills in various legal and nonlegal settings.

- *Fact 2: Reporting can be very exciting and fascinating work.*

    As a reporter, you will meet and learn from famous people, professionals, blue-collar workers, merchants, farmers, oil drillers, entrepreneurs, the highly literate, and the most illiterate—people from every type of background imaginable.

    In what other field of work could you ever absorb so much, perform such great service in our country's legal processes, be present during the making of history and record it being made, be of service in helping individuals who are hearing impaired, and have such a fascinating time doing it?

- *Fact 3: The profession of reporting is one of the few professions that does not discriminate.*

    Reporting is one profession in which women earn the same pay as men; and no discrimination exists as to race, color, creed, national origin, or sexual orientation. Within reason, as long as you can do the work that you are required to do, employers do not care if you are from Mars, Jupiter, or Venus! Keep in mind, though, the earlier comments about professional appearance and how important that is.

- *Fact 4: Court reporting is not a routine job.*

    A reporter is not tied to an 8:00 to 5:00 schedule. In the beginning, you may have to spend more than 8 hours a day; but if this profession is for you, you will love every interesting minute of it. How much more time the work will take depends on your own situation, how organized you are, and what talent you bring to the profession. Some reporting firms allow reporters to work a variety of hours during the day. Some days they will work for 10 or 12 hours, and other days they can take time off.

- *Fact 5: Not all reporting involves intriguing cases of murder and rape.*

    Perhaps your ideas of what a reporter does are founded mainly on what you have seen in courtroom-related television shows. Much of what reporters report will be exciting and dramatic, but remember that some material may be dull, such as condemnation suits for which the reporter will be writing figures and land descriptions over lengthy periods. Like any profession, every minute of the day is not all fun and excitement. Every profession has its dull moments; but, being a professional, you will take the good with the bad; you will take the excitement with the drudgery.

- *Fact 6: The schooling to become a court reporter can be very demanding.*

    Reporting is still a profession that can be entered on completion of a reasonable period of study. It has been said that the average length of time spent in school is 32 months. Studies have shown a very high dropout rate of students who start a court reporting program but never complete it.

The reasons for this high dropout rate are many: lack of motivation on the part of the student, lack of discipline, getting sidetracked into other areas, and personal problems. However, anyone who knows what he or she wants in life and sets out to achieve it in an orderly way should not have a problem. If you know that you want to become a reporter—just do it, but do it right!

You should select a reputable court and realtime reporting school where you can devote yourself to practicing. Ask a number of reporters which are the better schools. They will be more than happy to help you. The National Court Reporter's Association (NCRA) approves schools based on a standard of measurement. Check with the NCRA for a list of approved court and realtime reporting schools. You can contact the NCRA at www.ncraonline.com

- *Fact 7: Reporters can earn good money; however, only the competent reporters who work hard will earn high incomes.*

Avoid assuming that you are going to graduate from a court reporting school and immediately begin to make more money than a lawyer or judge. As in every profession, you must first prove yourself. If you are good at what you do, lawyers will request your services. If you are a good, competent reporter, you are going to be very busy. If you are mediocre, you will not be busy and will not be respected by members of the profession.

Remember also that you will earn money exactly in proportion to how hard you work. Hard work and diligence do pay off. You would not begrudge a doctor who charges for using the skills that he or she acquired in his or her years of training. Nor would you deny paying an engineer or lawyer their rightful income. So it may be true that good reporters earn a sizable income, but they work hard for it and, most importantly, they deserve it.

Frequently Asked Questions

Now that you have had an opportunity to learn some of the facts regarding the court reporting field, you may have some questions. The following are some of the most frequently asked questions about the field of court and realtime reporting:

Q: What is court reporting?

A: Court reporting is the art and skill of recording in shorthand what is said during a particular proceeding and then transcribing it into written form. Court reporting encompasses all forms of reporting the spoken word by manual, electronic, or computerized means.

Q: Is more than writing and transcribing involved in court reporting?

A: Yes. The court reporter also has certain responsibilities and duties in any given situation. For example, he or she may be responsible for swearing in the witnesses, marking and maintaining the exhibits, making sure that the proper signatures appear on a transcript, and so on.

Q: Is a court reporter also known as a *stenographer?*

A: Some people call court reporters *stenographers,* although that term usually applies more to a secretary. Court reporters have also been known as court recorders, shorthand reporters, verbatim reporters, realtime reporters, and captioners. Any of these terms are valid, and most people put them under the one title—court reporter.

Q: How does a court reporter record what is being said?

A: Most court reporters use a shorthand machine called a *steno machine* or *steno writer*. The keyboard on the steno writer has 24 keys and a number bar. When the keys are depressed, they produce English letters on a continuous-feeding paper tape. Some steno machines also record the letters electronically onto a cassette tape, a disk, or a microchip for immediate or later translation by a computer.

Q: How does a court reporter translate what is written on the paper tape or disk?

A: Three methods of transcription are typically used: First, reporters transcribe their own notes, either by dictating them for someone else to key or keying the notes themselves on a computer. Second, reporters can use a computer to translate the notes automatically and then edit the notes before final printing. Third, reporters can have their notes instantly translated onto a computer monitor by using a specialized software dictionary that recognizes the notes that the reporter has written. This method is known as *realtime writing and translation*.

Q: How are words written on the steno writer?

A: Words are basically written by sound, syllable, and spelling. For example, if you were to type the word *cat* on a typewriter, you would type *c*, then the *a*, then the *t*, a three-step process. On the steno machine, you would key *KAT* in one stroke.

Q: What does the steno writer keyboard look like?

A: Figure 1.1 shows you the steno writer keyboard. You will notice that the keyboard is arranged into three sections. The left section writes only initial sounds of words, the right section writes only final sounds of words, and the bottom-middle section writes all vowel sounds between the beginning and final sides. That is why you are able to write *KAT* in one stroke.

Q: How do you write the letters that are not on the keyboard?

A: Combinations of letters are used to represent letters that are not on the keyboard. The system is called *shorthand* because various shortcuts are used to write letters or words. For example, you notice that no vowel *I* is present on the keyboard. The combination of *E* and *U* together are used for the vowel *I*.

Q: How do you write numbers?

A: Numbers are written by striking a certain letter in the upper bank of keys along with the *number bar* located above the upper bank.

Q: Is the shorthand system hard to learn?

A: Yes and no. Learning the system is not difficult in the sense that you have a large amount to learn. It is difficult in the sense that many hours of practice are required. Without a doubt, study of the basic theory takes time, determination, and motivation. However, if you know that court reporting is what you want to do, you will enjoy every minute of it. When you think of the long-term benefits that you will derive from all your hard work and diligence, it is well worth it.

Q: What do the steno notes look like?

A: Figure 1.2 shows an example of what the notes look like after you have written them on the steno writer. The paper tape that the reporter writes on is approximately $8\frac{1}{2}$ inches long and about $2\frac{1}{4}$ inches wide. You will notice that all the letters written on the paper tape appear in the exact same spot every time they are written. The beginning *S-* is always written on the extreme left side and the final *-Z* is always written on the extreme right side.

FIGURE 1.1
The Steno Writer Keyboard

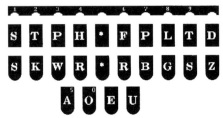

FIGURE 1.2
Steno Notes

```
STKPWHR
ST      A  EU        T
    K W R O   U R
    T P H A  EU  P L
    T P     O      R
                       T
         R O      R       D
                 FRPBLGTS
       P H          F P L
    T P H A  EU  P L
S
S K W R O        PB
         R        F P      D
S   P H    EU          TD
             A        PB     D
           AO EU
           HR   EU F B
               A            T
    2
             5  EU  7
         P H A  EU  PB
ST     RAO  E           T
STKPWHR
        WH A
    TK      O   U
    TK     AO
    T P     O      R
           A  EU
           HR   EU F  B  G
                     R B G S
S              EU  R
                   FRPBLGTS

           AO EU    P L
           A  EU
         K     O   U R    T
             R O      R   T
K W R    E    R
```

Q: Does a court reporter only work in a courtroom setting?

A: No. Court and realtime reporters can be divided into three general categories, as follows:

> *Official court reporters:* Reporters who work in a courtroom setting or do reporting for governmental agencies.
> *Freelance reporters:* Reporters who work for a deposition or freelance agency or are self-employed. Their work varies from day to day. One day they may be recording hearings for school boards or zoning commissions; the next day they may be taking depositions for lawyers.
> *Caption/CART:* Reporters who are employed to produce an instant record on a video screen. Caption/CART reporters are used in closed captioning for the hearing impaired. They may be used in classroom settings or board meetings where a *visual* record is required. These reporters may be referred to as *steno interpreters*. Both official and freelance reporters may use realtime technology.

Q: If I do not want to be a court reporter, can I still use my skills?

A: Definitely. Many new opportunities are opening for people who have the skill of writing words in shorthand and having their notes transcribed instantly by a computer. *Rapid text input* or *rapid data entry* is used by medical transcriptionists because this technology is quicker than typing from dictated notes. Any business, educational setting, industry, or service that requires fast input and transcription can use the skills of a realtime writer.

Q: How long does it usually take to become a court reporter?

A: That depends on many factors. If you attend a school that teaches you how to become a court reporter, you can expect to be in class a minimum of 2 years, full time. If you attend a private school on a part-time basis, it may be longer. Some people have a natural inclination for writing on a shorthand machine and can learn the theory much more quickly than others.

Q: What about tape recorders? Are tape recorders going to replace court reporters?

A: No. Although tape recorders do a fine job of recording music or "canned" speeches, live recording is best done by a live court reporter. The reason is that tape recorders not only pick up the voices, but also any other sounds that may go unnoticed, making the record, in some cases, inaudible and untranscribable. A great many studies have been done; and the ultimate conclusion is that the best technology for the money is the live court reporter coupled with the computer to produce an accurate, reliable, and rapid transcript.

Q: What about video recorders? Are video/audio tape recorders used to take depositions?

A: Yes. The video recorder works fine; but the fact is that, along with the video recorder, a written record is being made by a live court reporter. Most court reporting firms will offer video recording as a service. Video recording enhances what is called *litigation support,* those extra services offered to lawyers by court reporting firms.

Q: Where can I learn more about becoming a court reporter?

A: Your best source is a court reporter in your area. Most reporters are very friendly and open to talking to people who are interested in their career. Another source of information is the National Court Reporters Association (NCRA). Their toll-free number is 1-800-272-6272 (NCRA). The association can also be contacted via the Internet at www.ncraonline.com. It is a clearinghouse for information on the court reporting profession and will also give you information on schools that are approved by the association. You may also want to contact your local and state associations to learn about the reporting prospects in your area.

Chapter 2

A Self-Test to Determine Your Interest in Reporting

Perhaps you have seen in magazines self-interest quizzes that rate your ability to do certain things. Some of them are meant for pure entertainment, but some can help to determine whether you may have an interest in a particular field.

On the next few pages, you will have an opportunity to take such a quiz. Approach it with an open mind, with the idea that it may help you to decide whether to enter the court reporting field. However, do not let it be your sole determining factor. If you have doubts or questions, talk to a court reporter and get answers. This self-test is not meant to be a scientific calculation of your ability to do or not do court and realtime reporting. It is meant to give you an idea of some of the factors and qualifications that may go into considering reporting as a career.

What Are the Positives and the Negatives?

A series of statements that relate to court reporting are listed next. Rate each statement as a positive or negative statement. If a statement bothers you in any way or if you have difficulty with a statement, consider it a negative (−). If you have no problem with the statement or if it does not bother you in any way, consider it a positive (+). Circle the + or − after each statement. Directions for scoring your quiz appear at the end. Circle the first response that comes to your mind. Try to be honest as you respond.

Circle the + or − for each of the following statements.

1. Court reporting is a challenging career that will require a great deal of dedication on my part.   +   −

2. I will probably have to set some priorities if I want to learn court reporting.   +   −

3. Court reporting is more than the skill of recording what is being said. It requires learning other academic subjects, such as English, medical and legal terminology, and court procedures.   +   −

4. To become a competent court reporter, I will probably have to practice at least 3 hours a day for the next 2 years.   +   −

5. To learn how to become a court reporter, I may have to put some other plans on hold at this particular time.   +   −

6. When I become a court reporter, I probably will work for a freelance agency.   +   −

7. When I become a court reporter, I probably will work in a courtroom.   +   −

8. Court reporting requires a great deal of accuracy and concentration.   +   −

9. Court reporters sometimes work under a great deal of pressure and stress.   +   −

10. To complete a particular job, I may have to work beyond my normal working hours.   +   −

11. As a freelance reporter, I may be required to keep an account of all my expenses and pay self-employment taxes on my income.   +   −

12. As a court reporter, I am going to be responsible for producing an accurate transcript of whatever I record.   +   −

13. I will be responsible for making sure that the transcript is delivered on time.   +   −

14. I will be responsible for the accuracy of the entire record.   +   −

15. Occasionally, I will have to ask a witness to speak up or ask a lawyer to repeat what was said.   +   −

16. Some of the testimony that I will be required to record may be very graphic in nature.   +   −

17. Some testimony may be very emotional.   +   −

18. Some cases may involve murder, rape, incest, child abuse, spouse abuse, abandonment, pornography, prostitution, drug trafficking, and drug overdose.   +   −

19. Once I become a court reporter, I will have to keep up to date with changing technology.   +   −

20. I will benefit from joining a court reporting organization that offers seminars and workshops.   +   −

21. Court reporters earn a high income, but they work hard for it.   +   −

22. The amount of money that I earn will depend on my ability and experience.   +   −

23. Beginning reporters usually start at the bottom of the income ladder and climb up after years of gaining experience.   +   −

24. Only about one-third of those who study court reporting complete a program of study.   +   −

25. Although learning to become a court reporter may require a great deal of time, energy, and money, the effort will be worth it in the long run.   +   −

Now, count the number of + and − circled and enter here: ____   ____

Use the following chart to rate your interest in court reporting.

> If you had over 20 positives, you may be very interested in reporting.
> If you had 15 to 19 positives, you probably are somewhat interested in reporting.
> If you had 8 to 14 positives, you might have a little interest in reporting.
> If you had 0 to 7 positives, you probably have very little interest in reporting.

Should You Become a Reporter?

Do you think you should go into reporting? Only you can answer that question. If you are even slightly interested, we would implore you to investigate, ask questions, read books, conduct interviews, learn anything and everything that you can about the field, and then make your decision after thoroughly talking it over with those closest to you.

To help you to decide, you might consider the following questions. Respond to each question by circling Yes or No after the question.

1. Do you have a high school diploma or equivalency?   Yes   No

2. Do you have a college degree or any credit earned for attending college?   Yes   No

3. Are you able to spend at least 3 hours a day practicing and studying without interruption?   Yes   No

4. Can you keyboard, using the standard touch system, at 20 to 30 words a minute?   Yes   No

5. Are you able to punctuate simple and complex sentences by using commas, semicolons, periods, question marks, quotation marks, and the like?   Yes   No

6. Do you have a good basic vocabulary?   Yes   No

7. Do you understand most words that you hear or read?   Yes   No

8. Can you memorize simple definitions fairly well?   Yes   No

9. Do you take pride in your work?   Yes   No

10. Can you follow basic instructions?   Yes   No

11. Can you follow complex instructions, if you are allowed to ask questions?   Yes   No

12. Can you take criticism?   Yes   No

13. If someone said that you did something wrong, would you try to find out what you did wrong and correct it?   Yes   No

14. Do you have a basic grasp of computers and their operating systems?   Yes   No

15. Are you willing to learn?   Yes   No

16. Do you speak a foreign language?   Yes   No

17. Do you play a musical instrument?   Yes   No

18. Are you curious and inquisitive?   Yes   No

19. Are you patient?   Yes   No

20. Are you consistent?   Yes   No

21. Can you afford the schooling and other expenses of learning to become a court and realtime reporter at this time in your life?   Yes   No

22. Can you spend the time required to become a court reporter?   Yes   No

23. Do you have an active imagination?   Yes   No

24. Are you persistent?   Yes   No

25. Can you see yourself as a court or realtime reporter in the future?   Yes   No

Now, count the total number of Yes and No responses and enter here: ____   ____

Use the chart to help determine whether you should become a court and realtime reporter.

If you had 21 to 25 yes responses, you might consider studying immediately.
If you had 11 to 20 yes responses, you might consider beginning soon.
If you had 6 to 10 yes responses, you may or may not consider studying.
If you had 0 to 5 yes responses, you might reconsider your career goals.

Will You Succeed?

For fun, let's use your scores in the previous quizzes and apply them to an arbitrary "success scale." Use the following formula to determine your success score and then apply it to the success scale. Remember, this is not a scientific test and in no way predicts the success or failure of any one individual.

1. For every positive *and* yes response, give yourself 2 points.
   For every negative *and* no response, give yourself 1 point.

   number of positive *and* yes responses = _____ × 2 = _____
   number of negative *and* no responses = _____ × 1 = _____

2. Subtract your negative/no score from your positive/yes score to obtain your success score:

   positive/yes score = _____
   negative/no score = _____
   success score = _____

3. Apply your success score to the following success scale:

Score	Your Success Probability
90 or above	Super successful
76–90	Exceedingly successful
61–75	Very successful
46–60	Somewhat successful
31–45	Sort of successful
16–30	Maybe successful

   Will you succeed at becoming a court and realtime reporter? Many variables go into answering that question—your motivation, drive, enthusiasm, personal circumstances, and a myriad of other considerations. Only you can determine whether you will succeed.

Chapter 3

The Reporting Profession Defined

Who Are Court and Realtime Reporters?

Who is the person who sits in the front of the courtroom, usually between the judge and witness, furiously tapping his or her fingers on a strange looking keyboard? Who is the person who walks into a crowded room filled with lawyers and potential witnesses and calmly takes control of the situation? Who is the person who is responsible for having closed captioning appear at the bottom of millions of television screens across the nation? Who is the person upon whom the entire justice system depends for the preservation of a true and accurate record? Let us see who are the court and realtime reporters of the world today.

They Are Diverse

Court and realtime reporters come in a variety of shapes and sizes. They are both male and female; they are young and old; they represent a variety of nationalities, affiliations, and faiths. Court reporters are a diverse group of individuals who have many differences in appearance and demeanor; but they all have one thing in common: they record and transcribe in a professional and competent manner.

They Have a Positive Attitude

Usually, you will find that court and realtime reporters have an attitude to succeed. This quality is first exhibited when the reporter is in school, studying and practicing. Reporters do not give up. When things get tough and difficult, they usually find a way to accomplish monumental tasks. This attitude of success is not a domineering, overbearing, pretentious attitude that engulfs a person's whole being; but, rather, it is an attitude of "I know I can do it" and "I will do it."

They Persevere

Court and realtime reporters have a strong will to persevere and "hang in there." Their actions and what they choose to do with their lives will certainly depict their determination, grit, and perseverance. In a very real sense, they are a stubborn people, in the sense that they don't quit.

They Maintain Confidentiality

A sense of confidentiality accompanies the profession of court and realtime reporting. A universal rule among court reporters is that they never, ever mention what goes on in a courtroom when they are outside the courthouse. This same maxim holds true for all proceedings, legal or nonlegal. Reporters realize the ethics of not telling other people what transpires at a deposition, trial, or hearing. Even when the record is public, the reporter still maintains a sense of confidentiality about what happened. Furthermore, reporters remain impartial and unbiased, even in the most gruesome and heinous cases.

They Are Respectful

Court and realtime reporters exhibit a great deal of respect and courtesy toward the judge and the lawyers. The reason for this respect is not because it is demanded or required, but rather because it is a respect that has been earned by lawyers and judges. In the same sense, the legal profession has high regard for those dedicated professionals who work in the field of court reporting.

Reporters are willing to work with judges and lawyers in almost any type of environment. Although most working situations are compatible, sometimes personality conflicts and clashes arise. The reporter will always maintain a sense of decorum and courtesy toward the bar.

Court and realtime reporters also have very high regard for their employers and fellow employees. They know what is required to become a reporter and therefore respect and admire other people who have endured the stringent educational requirements in order to become a professional reporter.

They Know How to Use Tact and Diplomacy

Tact is the ability to handle a delicate situation. Court and realtime reporters possess a certain amount of tact when dealing with lawyers, judges, or clients. Their tactfulness and diplomacy imply a sense of self-control and discipline that most people do not possess.

They Possess a Sense of Loyalty and Pride

Most court and realtime reporters exhibit a deep sense of loyalty, both toward their profession and toward their employers. Reporters are a loyal bunch. This faithfulness is due, in part, to their keen sense of commitment and dedication; but there also exists a very strong comradeship and esprit de corps among reporters.

Court reporters pride themselves on giving a full and honest day's work for their pay. They also take great pride in their finished work product—the transcript.

They Are Punctual and Efficient

For the court reporter, being on time is being 30 minutes early. Reporters realize this rule and know that a great deal of preparatory work must be done before a deposition begins or a trial starts. A reporter will not walk in 2 minutes before the examination is to begin and start setting up his or her equipment; rather, an efficient reporter has already set up and started to gather some of the preliminary information that is essential to getting an accurate record.

They Are Trustworthy

Court and realtime reporters must be honest and possess a certain amount of integrity. Lawyers and judges know whom they can trust; and nine times out of ten, they are going to turn to the court reporter as a trusting and loyal companion in the judicial process.

Court and realtime reporters must be accepted as individuals who possess an honest and forthright disposition. If not, clients will have difficulty trusting the accuracy of the record. Of all the professions in the world, perhaps the most trusted and honored is the profession of court and realtime reporting.

They Earn Their Pay

So, who are court and realtime reporters? They are people who know what they want in life, work for it, and then do it! They are people who work hard at what they do and get paid well for it. They are professionals who take pride in a job well done. Court and realtime reporters are people who provide a valuable service to the judicial process and to humanity.

This brief description of who court and realtime reporters are may sound as though only super, extraordinary men and women need apply, but such is not the case. The most important thing to remember is that court reporters are ordinary, everyday human beings. Court and realtime reporters are people like you—you could be a court and realtime reporter!

What Does a Court and Realtime Reporter Do?

What exactly does a court and realtime reporter do? Well, to begin with, we know that he or she records what is being said and then transcribes it. Is this all that he or she does? Does this really describe the entire job of a court and realtime reporter? Yes and no.

True, the bottom line is to capture what is being said, using a shorthand system that will record notes on paper tape and, in some cases, onto a magnetic media, and then to produce an accurate transcript of what was said. However, few people realize what really goes into producing that accurate record.

Briefly, the job of a court reporter can be divided into two broad categories: writing and reading.

Writing: Capturing the Spoken Word

In being able to capture the spoken word, a court and realtime reporter must know a system of shorthand writing that he or she can use with confidence and assurance. A reporter must know the system thoroughly and be able to write words that he or she has never heard before by using a phonetic system of writing words. At the same time, a reporter must be aware that what he or she writes may be instantly transcribed; therefore, the pressures of error-free writing are constantly overshadowing the role of a reporter.

The Shorthand Theory   Most shorthand systems today are what are called *realtime ready* and *computer compatible*. Realtime ready means that the shorthand system writes each word or phrase in a separate and distinct way. The words and phrases are ready to be transcribed instantaneously on a computer for immediate reading. Computer compatible means that the shorthand system uses an electronic dictionary within a specialized computer program that will instantly transcribe notes that are put into a computer. This transcription of notes can be either immediate, in which case it is called *realtime translation* or *closed captioning,* or it can be saved for later transcription and editing. Most qualified court reporting schools teach a shorthand theory that is both computer compatible and realtime ready.

The Shorthand Machine   The shorthand writer that a reporter uses to capture the spoken word may be any one of the many different models that are available on the market. Basically, there are three types of writers: manual, electronic, and computerized.

Manual shorthand machines enable a person who writes on them to record everything that is being said onto a continuously fed paper tape. The alphabetic letters that make up the words are depressed on the keyboard by the court reporter, and the ink impression of the letters appears on the paper tape for later transcription. One negative aspect of this type of machine is that the writer must manually transcribe his or her notes by literally reading and translating them into a word processor or computer. The positive aspect of the manual writer is that the court reporter has a hard copy of the proceeding that can be filed away and referred to for years to come.

The electronic shorthand machine is much like the manual writer in that the notes are recorded onto a paper tape; however, in addition, the words that are written on the keyboard can also be recorded onto some sort of magnetic media, usually a 3.5-inch floppy disk. This disk can then be inserted into a computer, where it can be transcribed by the computer rather than by the reporter. The advantage of such a writer is, of course, the amount of time that is saved by the reporter. The reporter still has to edit the transcript before final printing and delivery; but, for the most part, a tremendous amount of time is saved in the transcription process.

Both the electronic and computerized shorthand writers use electricity as a power source; however, they can run on batteries for many hours of "plug-free" writing. The batteries can be recharged at night when the writer is not in use.

The only difference between the electronic shorthand writer and the computer shorthand writer is that the latter is hooked to a computer by cable, modem, or remote for instant translation. The writer still records onto paper tape and floppy disk, but an immediate transcript appears on the computer monitor— realtime writing.

Reading: Producing the Transcript

The ultimate goal of a court reporter is to produce an accurate transcript, and the accomplishment of this task can also be done in a variety of different ways. For purposes of discussion, let us divide the production of the transcript into the old method and the new method.

The old method of producing the transcript involved the court reporter taking his or her notes from the shorthand writer and then doing one of three things with those notes: (1) giving them to a notereader, who would then transcribe the notes for the reporter, (2) dictating the notes into a tape recorder and then giving the tape to a trained transcriptionist who would transcribe the notes, or (3) the reporter transcribing the notes by using a typewriter, word processor, or computer.

The new method of producing a transcript involves the use of the electronic or computerized writer, as previously described. The court reporter merely inserts the floppy disk into the computer and has the computer transcribe the notes; this process is referred to as *computer-aided transcription* or *CAT*. The written notes can also be instantly transcribed when the writer is hooked up to the computer; this process is referred to as *realtime writing*.

Some reporters will use the services of a *scopist,* who edits the transcript before the final printing. A scopist searches for any words that were not defined in the dictionary and defines them, corrects any punctuation or capitalization errors, and generally makes the transcript salable.

CAT and realtime writing involve the use of a specialized software program that is preinstalled on the reporter's computer. This specialized software has a built-in dictionary that recognizes the shorthand words that are written on the shorthand keyboard by the reporter. This dictionary can be individually adapted to a reporter's own theory and has the capacity to add new words as the court reporter writes and translates words that are not in the current dictionary.

This oversimplified view of what a court reporter does is expanded in later chapters that deal specifically with the job of a court reporter. For now, the bottom line is this: Court reporters write in shorthand and transcribe in English an accurate and verbatim transcript of what was said during various proceedings.

When Do Court and Realtime Reporters Do Their Jobs?

Now that we have seen who a court and realtime reporter is and what he or she does, the next logical question may be when and where do court reporters do their jobs. Let us now look at when the skill of the court reporter is needed.

Whenever an Accurate Record Is Needed

In almost every important trial or litigation in the history of the world, someone has always been there to record the events. The methods used to record may have changed over the years, but the fact that a human has always been responsible for recording the events is a remarkable feat.

In today's world of high technology, modern tape and video recording equipment, and computers, things have not changed! The fact is that the court and realtime reporter is still an integral part of the recording and transcription process. Study after study has proved that the most accurate and efficient method of producing a quick and accurate record is by using a live court reporter, coupled with a computer.

Whenever a Quick Transcript Is Needed

Court and realtime reporters pride themselves on the accuracy of the record and the production of the transcript within a reasonable time after the completion of the litigation or trial. Especially with the use of computer-aided transcription and realtime translation, transcripts are produced almost instantly on the spot.

Lawyers and judges appreciate the timeliness of a quick and accurate transcript. They do not have to put up with the hassle of having someone transcribe from an audio or visual tape, and they do not have to sit through many hours of viewing a video screen in order to find portions of a trial in which they may be interested.

Whenever a Permanent Record Is Necessary

The legal proceedings that court and realtime reporters are responsible for are preserved for many years. The presence of a court reporter assures that a responsible, trained professional has assumed the task of preserving the record.

With electronic audio and video recorders, the only method of preserving the record is by magnetic media. A court reporter always has the original printed notes, the transcript produced from the printed notes, and the floppy disk containing the original trial or deposition.

In addition, reporters are required by law to keep their notes on file for several years. The length of time depends on state laws and the nature of the case. Most reporters file their original notes and archive their computerized transcripts for many years.

Whenever Lawyers and Judges Want to Save Time and Money

Although some people contend that the cost of putting a tape recorder into a courtroom or deposition situation is cheaper than using a court reporter, the fact is that many hidden costs are involved in taping a litigation proceeding that are not included in the original cost.

For example, once the proceeding has been taped, the question arises of who will transcribe it. Lawyers have found that the transcription of audiotapes takes time, costs money, and is not reliable. Sometimes, complete audiotapes have been mistakenly erased or damaged. In other cases, the transcribed copy of an audiotape has been filled with inaccuracies and inaudibles.

Reporters are professionals who will guarantee the recording of the spoken word and the accuracy of the transcript. The reporting by a court reporter, coupled with a computer, is the most efficient method of producing an accurate and reliable transcript that has ever been used.

Whenever Assistive Reporting Is Needed

Assistive reporting can be defined as any type of reporting that serves as a help or an aid to someone in communicating. The best example of assistive reporting is, of course, closed captioning for the hearing impaired. The captioning reporter assists the hearing impaired community to effectively communicate. A service offered by realtime reporters is referred to as CART: Computer Access Realtime Translation. CART providers assist those with learning disabilities or speaking or hearing problems to communicate.

Where Do Court and Realtime Reporters Report?

The skill and art of court and realtime reporting are used in many different job situations. As we discussed in Chapter 1, *court reporting* is an all-encompassing term that can be broken down into the following categories: official court reporting, freelance reporting, and captioning/realtime reporting. Although these three categories will be discussed in greater detail in Sections B, C, and D, further delineation leads to the following applications of reporting within these categories.

Legal Reporting

Perhaps the largest deployment of court reporting activity can be found in the legal field. Court reporters are used in the courtroom situation for recording arraignments, sentencing procedures, parole hearings, jury and nonjury trials, appeals, and all other quasi-judicial proceedings that may be held before a magistrate, hearing officer, or judge. These reporters are usually referred to as *official court reporters*.

Reporters may also be used by lawyers to take *depositions* or *examinations before trial* (EBTs). Some reporters are called on to report arbitrations, negotiations, special hearings, and board hearings. These reporters are referred to as *freelance reporters*. The legal profession and the field of court reporting go hand in hand.

Medical Reporting

In the field of medicine, the skill of a reporter is being used for rapid text entry for producing a doctor's medical records, which would normally be dictated into a recorder and transcribed by a transcriptionist. A transcriptionist normally listens to a doctor's dictation and transcribes what he or she said at speeds of 90 to 100 words a minute using a word-processing package. A court and realtime reporter can record and edit the same material twice as fast, that is, at speeds of 180 to 200 words a minute. Obviously, the faster the output, the more work is accomplished and the lower the cost for the medical profession.

Entertainment Reporting

Perhaps the best-known example of entertainment reporting is in the field of closed captioning for the hearing impaired. Captioning/realtime reporters are employed by television broadcasting stations to use their skills to record the voices on various programs.

Captioning/realtime reporters record the dictation, much like they do in any court or legal situation; however, their writers may be hooked to a satellite broadcasting system via a modem that instantly broadcasts the transcript for immediate viewing. Closed captioning has been used by television networks for several years. The Americans with Disabilities Act (ADA) addresses closed captioning. The Television Decoder Circuitry Act of 1990 requires that all television sets sold in the United States be equipped with a caption decoder chip. In 1996, the Telecommunications Act was passed. It required all programs to be compatible with closed captioning by a certain date, following a phase-in period, after which 95 percent of all new programming must be captioned.

Educational Reporting

Some realtime reporters offer the service of closed captioning in schools and college classrooms where students of all ages have various levels of hearing deficiencies. These students can now participate in many classroom situations by "seeing" what is being said on a television monitor. Many students who did not have the ability to communicate in class have expressed how pleased they are to have the reporter present to interpret what is being said. Other names for this type of service are CART (computer-assisted realtime translation) and CART providers.

Business Reporting

Many businesses in the forefront of technology have used realtime writers to report their conventions and business meetings. The advantage of using the live reporter is twofold: (1) it addresses the need for those people who are hard of hearing to participate in the meeting, and (2) it offers an immediate copy, visual and printed, for use by the participants.

Business reporting includes the reporting of boards of director meetings, in-service workshops, conferences, conventions, and internal hearings or meetings. Some firms have employed captioning/realtime reporters to record business meetings that take place over the telephone. The reporter records what is being said and instantly sends it over the Internet for possible viewing by authorized personnel. Stockholders meetings can be "attended" by all shareholders via their own computer and the Internet.

The skill of a court and realtime reporter can be used in many other areas. The key to expanding the field lies in the spirit of innovation and imagination. The only limits to the use of your skill are the limits that you impose on yourself. You must explore new and even untried areas of court and realtime reporting using your skill.

Why Use Court and Realtime Reporters?

The following questions have been asked: Why use a court and realtime reporter? Why not plug in a tape recorder or videotape the proceedings? Aren't these methods just as good as using a court reporter? Can't you save money by using tape and video recorders? Let us address these questions and show why there will always be a need for a court reporter whenever a true, accurate, dependable, time-efficient, and cost-effective record is needed.

Here are some reasons why lawyers, judges, and anyone interested in getting a true and accurate record of a proceeding prefer the services of a professional, well-qualified court and realtime reporter.

Accuracy

Court and realtime reporters are highly trained individuals who, in most cases, meet minimum standards before being employed as reporters. In some states, official, freelance, and caption/realtime reporters have to pass examinations that attest to their ability to take down the spoken word and have it transcribed.

Most court reporting schools graduate only those students who are qualified to take high speeds of dictation at a minimum of 95 to 98 percent accuracy. This degree of accuracy is commendable when one thinks that the accuracy of a transcribed audiotape is probably in the 70 to 80 percent range.

The accuracy of the record is fundamental to preserving the justice system in America. Without the confidence that a record is going to be true, honest, and accurate, we lose all credibility as a democracy. The most accurate method of producing and preserving the transcript is by using a court reporter.

Reliability

Many stories of tape recorders and video cameras either losing their power or malfunctioning during an important legal proceeding abound in legal circles. In some instances, everything appeared to be working normally and yet, when the tapes were played back, nothing was there. In other instances the recording went well, but somehow what was recorded was lost before it could be transcribed.

Court and realtime reporters are reliable. Reporters have been reporting for many centuries and in many lands. Most shorthand writers that court and realtime reporters use have captured the spoken word both on disk and by stenographic notes. If for some reason a loss of power occurs, most shorthand writers can operate either on a battery or with the writer in a manual mode. If something should happen to the disk, the reporter always has his or her original notes that can be transcribed.

In addition, most lawyers, judges, defendants, and witnesses would rather trust the fate of a litigation proceeding to the hands of a human being than to a machine.

Time Efficiency and Cost-Effectiveness

Earlier we said that the bottom line of court and realtime reporting was the ability to write and read. When comparing the use of video or tape recording against a court reporter, most people tend to forget that what a recorder records must be transcribed. When people hear of the large savings that a tape recorder has over a court reporter, they fail to include the expense of transcribing the tapes.

Court and realtime reporters have the advantage of having an immediate transcript available in two different media: (1) as a viewable transcript on a computer monitor and (2) as a hard-copy printout that can be read at any time, any place.

Both the viewable transcript and the hard-copy transcript are easily transportable and easily accessible in terms of readability and finding certain parts of transcripts during the proceedings. This aspect of reporting is important, and it is one that is often overlooked by those who think that electronic recording devices can function just as well as court reporters.

People listening to tape recorders or a recording technician may have difficulty instantly finding a spot that may have to be read back or played back. Some recorders are digitally synchronized, but they do not work with the speed, efficiency, and reliability that a live court reporter does.

In addition, an audio or visual tape needs to be "viewed" in order to "read" the transcript. A person can read a printed transcript much easier than view a video or listen to an audiotape. As an example, if the infamous O. J. Simpson trial had been electronically recorded or videotaped in its entirety for court preservation, the months-long trial would have needed hundreds of videocassettes or audiotapes that would probably have filled a room. Sitting and viewing the entire trial would be an almost impossible task.

On the other hand, if one were to read the trial at one's leisure, it would be much easier and more efficient. Using a computer, a search for key words can be made and references made to only those pages that contain the key word. A realtime reporter offers the advantage of an immediate transcript plus a hard copy that can be ready at any time. The O. J. Simpson trial was recorded verbatim by professional court reporters using realtime technology.

Litigation Support

Litigation support services are those services that an individual court and realtime reporter or a reporting agency will offer to their clients in the way of extra services. Although you will learn more later about the ancillary services that the court and realtime reporter offers to their clients, here are just a few.

Instant viewing is the concept of realtime translation. When an attorney is at a legal proceeding, he or she has the advantage of seeing the transcript appear on a computer screen as the person is speaking.

This instant viewing concept leads to what might be called an *instant back-search* of the transcript for previous testimony. For example, if a witness is undergoing cross-examination by an attorney, the opposing attorney who is sitting at his or her desk behind a computer monitor can instantly look through the witnesses past testimony for words, phrases, and statements that were previously made.

In addition, this concept of instant back-search extends to *instant recall* of prior depositions or court transcripts from previous proceedings. In essence, the lawyers have a virtual library of past transcripts provided as a service by the court reporting firm.

One of the most frequently used litigation support services offered by court and realtime reporting firms to lawyers is the ability to have an *instant hard copy* of the day's proceedings in hand immediately after the close of the day. Lawyers are absolutely amazed at the fact that they do not have to wait two or three weeks to receive a transcript, but can have an immediate copy.

Some law offices prefer to have a copy of the proceedings sent to them electronically through a modem, or they can take an *ASCII disk* with them containing the proceedings. The American Standard Code for Information Interchange (ASCII), pronounced "ask kee," is a coding scheme used in many computers. An ASCII disk can be read by a variety of software programs.

Other litigation support services include what is called *keyword indexing*. Keyword indexing is the ability to have a running index appear at the beginning of a transcript that will list by page and line number the occurrences of a particular word or phrase within an entire transcript. For example, if an attorney wanted to see an index of every time the defendant used the words "blueberry popsicle," the reporter simply needs to "search and list" the occurrences.

Many attorneys like to mark or cue certain portions of testimony as it is being elicited. *Cue codes* can be inserted within an attorney's own copy of the transcript, along with any personal notes that he or she might write while the testimony is being given.

Many reporting firms offer what is called a *condensed transcript* as a litigation support service. The condensed transcript literally compresses the transcript into two or four smaller pages on one regular-sized piece of transcript paper. Some condensed versions offer as many as eight pages of transcript on one page, that is, four smaller pages on each side. You can imagine the space saving involved when an 800-page document can be condensed to 100 pages.

Reporting agencies and court reporters vary in the types of litigation support services that they offer, as well as in the amount of money that they charge for such services. These additional services are becoming an integral part of the litigation support that lawyers and court personnel are expecting from modern, up-to-date court and realtime reporters.

The Human Factor

Perhaps the most important reason why the majority of lawyers, judges, and court personnel prefer a live court and realtime reporter, rather than an electronic tape recorder or a video recorder, is what has been called *the human factor*.

The human factor is responsible for making sure that the proceedings are properly reported and preserved. The human factor is responsible for producing a quick and accurate transcript. The human factor controls the situation and helps to make sure that things go smoothly.

When all is said and done, the work of a live court reporter, coupled with CAT and realtime capabilities, is a service that is absolutely unparalleled in the history of recording the spoken word.

Section B

Official Court Reporting

Chapter 4

The Working Environment of the Official Court Reporter

This section of the handbook takes a detailed look at the official court reporter. Before delving into the specific types of jobs that the official reporter may be called upon to do, we will take a look at the working environment of the official reporter. By working environment is meant an overall picture of the reporter and what he or she does.

An official court reporter holds a position of high respect in the legal community, and any justice with a highly competent reporter will value that person. Official reporters work in a court, hearing, or administrative position that requires recording the spoken word for transcription. Local, county, or state court administrative bodies, as well as the federal court system, employ official court reporters.

Qualifying by Examination

An official court reporter is usually required to pass an examination to become a Certified Shorthand Reporter (CSR) and may, in addition, require years of experience. In some states, civil service dictates who shall be chosen for positions that are open. Appointments are made from a list, and eligible reporters work their way up the list. Testing may be required for various levels of reporting, and advancement comes through testing and seniority.

Where the CSR test alone is used to qualify reporters, the judge will appoint an official of his or her choice from among those eligible. Some states have certain certification tests that are given periodically; others have no CSR or certification requirement. In these states the judge has the exclusive power to appoint his or her court reporter. Frequently, judges insist that the reporter hold a testing certificate from the National Court Reporters Association (NCRA). The NCRA offers a variety of qualifying examinations to ensure that reporters adhere to certain minimum standards. One of the most accepted examinations offered by the NCRA is the Registered Professional Reporter (RPR) exam. Some people feel that all official and freelance court reporters should be required to pass a licensure examination before they can practice as reporters. Others feel that, as long as the reporters can perform and do their work well, a license or certificate is unnecessary.

In 1992 the National Court Reporters Association commissioned Hay Management Consultants in Washington, D.C., to conduct an analysis of the work of the official court reporter. Among other things, the report recommended that all official court reporters be classified according to their education, experience, and passage of NCRA examinations. The classifications, from lowest to highest, are as follows: Certified Court Reporter, Registered Court Reporter, Professional Court Reporter, Senior Professional Court Reporter, and Master Professional Court Reporter.

Will nationwide classification and certification eventually be required of all official court reporters? Some people feel that it is necessary to protect the integrity of the profession and to maintain an element of quality assurance. Should this certification and classification extend into the freelance area of reporting? These questions will be answered in time. The current method of classification and certification of official court reporters is left to the individual states.

Remuneration of an Official Reporter

Both men and women serve as official reporters. An officialship provides a good salary 12 months a year, a pension plan, health insurance, and an annual paid vacation and holidays. If an officialship involves traveling, the reporter will receive remuneration for mileage, meals, and lodging while away from home and, occasionally, a per diem (per day) fee if assigned to counties outside the regular district.

In addition, official reporters may be compensated for providing transcripts in addition to the copies provided to the court and immediate attorneys. Although most states do not allow official reporters to work as freelance reporters during their regular hours, some official reporters may have an interest in a freelance agency that will hire other reporters to do deposition work.

Transcript rates for official reporters are set clearly in each state's statutes, and the reporter may not overcharge for court transcripts. The salary of the court reporter is designed to compensate the hardworking reporter for his or her time, effort, and talent used to produce the accurate transcript. A reporter's salary is usually commensurate with the amount of education, training, background, and knowledge that he or she uses in producing the accurate record.

Job Considerations of an Official Reporter

The official reporter is an officer of the court and addresses attorneys, court clerks, and other court officers formally. The official reporter never speaks ill of the judge or allows others to do so in his or her presence. Even when the official reporter is on a first-name basis with the judge, he or she should always refer to the judge with the proper surname.

Each court has its own set of rules regarding proper dress, arrival and departure times, working arrangements with other reporters, whether outside work is permitted, whether the judge will expect everything to be reported, including opening and closing statements, all jury impaneling, motion, in camera conferences, and the like. Official reporters make an effort to become members of the entire team of reporters who make up the reporting environment.

Like any professional, the official court reporter must keep abreast of changes in technology. Therefore, the reporter should belong to a state or national organization that promotes the causes and efforts of the court reporting profession. These associations offer seminars and workshops that allow the practicing reporter to earn continuing education credits for maintaining certification. The classes are very timely and usually deal with changes in technology and job aspects of the working reporter.

An official reporter must be competent to report and transcribe at a speed of at least 225 words a minute (wam) on 5-minute testimony takes, 200 wam on jury charge, and 180 wam on literary material, all with less than a 5 percent error rate. These requirements may vary from state to state. The applicant must be a good citizen with no criminal record and a temperate individual whose behavior will never reflect poorly on the court. He or she must be punctual, efficient, and impartial at all times. The judge has the right to expect that his or her official reporter will use the initiative to produce timely records and transcripts with accurate spellings, correct punctuation, and exact word-for-word translation in an attractive format, complete in every way.

Cautions for the Official Reporter

The official reporter should not give advice to anyone concerning any matter in the court or that could end up in court. He or she should never purport to speak or act for the judge when judicial matters are involved.

Unless specifically authorized, he or she should never exercise the court's discretion, as in excusing jurors or setting hearings. He or she should not discuss the merits of any case with anyone.

An official reporter should never leave the impression with anyone that he or she could or would "talk to the judge" about a case or that he or she "knows what the judge is going to do." Nor should any official reporter ever express an opinion about how any case should be decided or what verdict a jury will return, thereby taking sides in a lawsuit.

An official reporter should never allow a lawyer to dictate anything into the record or change anything concerning any record out of the judge's presence. The official reporter must be courteous and fair to the bar and others, but not show favoritism. He or she should never improperly interpose himself or herself between the judge and others.

Court officials should never discuss politics or religion publicly and should avoid being identified with controversies that might reflect on the judge. If the official reporter is also an attorney, legal practice may not be done in the court in which he or she serves as reporter.

An official reporter may never neglect the work of the court in order to perform outside work. Of course, each official reporter will be required to take all criminal proceedings; and each reporter must be responsible for seeing that all notes, records, tapes, cassettes, disks, and so on, are placed in a permanent file, maintained for the statutory period, and then destroyed in a proper manner. If any official reporter's employment is terminated, he or she must promptly transcribe and deliver all notes and records as required by the Court.

Examples of Official Reporting Jobs

Official reporters work in federal court, in the trial level of the state courts, in county, surrogate, probate, and family courts, in grand jury investigations, and in some city and village courts. Official court reporters may also work as legislative reporters for a federal or state governmental body.

Pretrial Conference

A pretrial conference may take place before a trial begins. A pretrial conference is held in courts of record (those having a regularly assigned court reporter) to decrease the backlog of cases through settlement.

Once the court calendar is printed, a day is set down for pretrial conferences. On this day, lawyers representing both sides of each case, or their representatives, appear after receiving notice from the clerk, bringing all proof necessary to present a prima facie case. A *prima facie case* is a case that is legally sufficient; that is, it has legal merit to proceed.

In personal injury cases, a plaintiff's attorney is expected to bring all bills and proofs of damages, plus medical reports, so that the court and opposing counsel will be informed as to the extent of injuries, claims, and permanency of injuries.

The court reporter is usually required to record important parts of pretrial conferences. Some judges ask that the court reporter be present to report every matter to be discussed and to prepare a summary of each case for the court's consideration and information. The court clerk also maintains a record of what happened during these conferences and marks off the calendar those cases that are settled, stricken, or ordered continued by the judge.

A half-hour to an hour is usually required to complete each pretrial matter. A number of stipulations are often dictated. A *stipulation* is an agreement between counsel as to certain facts or matters that will not be argued. The reporter must record the stipulations and transcribe them for the record, although the judge often directs counsel to prepare stipulations and motions in printed form and present them for his or her signature within a stated time.

At this time, the judge may order depositions to be taken by one or both parties to a lawsuit at the pretrial conference. If the judge so orders, the depositions will be conducted between the pretrial conference and the date of trial. A freelance reporter is used to record and transcribe the depositions before the actual trial itself. For this reason, depositions are very often referred to as *examinations before trial* (EBT).

Many attorneys come to the pretrial conference held in a case and move for continuance. A *motion for continuance* is a request for more time for a specific reason. The trial judge must consider the reasons for such requests and decide whether stalling tactics are being used and then deny continuance when delay of the trial is not merited.

Once pretrial matters are disposed of, the judge will issue what is called a *pretrial order* for the particular case. This order, in effect, sets the date, time, and place of the trial and charges all parties with the responsibility to be present at the trial. A pretrial order is shown in Figure 4.1.

Thus begins the task of the official court reporter as he or she now marks on the calendar the date, time, and place of the trial. The descriptive outline of what takes place before, during, and after the trial is discussed in detail in later chapters.

Preliminary Examination

A *preliminary hearing* or *preliminary examination* is held in order to determine whether enough evidence is available to hold the accused person for trial. If sufficient evidence is presented by the prosecution that shows a probable cause to believe that the person who is the subject of the hearing committed the alleged crime, he or she is bound over to face trial

A jury is not present during a preliminary examination. In large municipal courts, assigned reporters regularly record and transcribe these proceedings. The hearing itself follows the regular trial procedures as far as direct examination and cross-examination of the prosecution's witnesses. The defendant seldom presents any witnesses.

FIGURE 4.1
Pretrial Order

PRETRIAL ORDER

Pretried by Judge _____
(type name)
on (date) _____

NOTE
First determine if the case is to be transferred to the County District Court as provided in Rule 4:3-4.

PRETRIAL CONFERENCE PROCEDURE

Recite specifically ALL of the following items, in sequence, identifying each subject by the numeral assigned below. If no statement is to be made upon a subject, type "NONE" after the identifying number.

1. A concise descriptive statement of the nature of the action.
2. The factual contention of plaintiff as to liability of defendant.
3. The factual contention of defendant as to non-liability and affirmative defenses.
4. The admissions or stipulations of the parties with respect to the cause of action pleaded.
5. All claims as to damages and the extent of the injury, and admissions or stipulations with respect thereto.
6. Any amendments to the pleading made at the conference or fixing the time within which amended pleadings shall be filed.
7. A specification of the legal issues raised by the pleadings, as amended to be determined at the trial.
8. A specification of the legal issues raised by the pleadings but now abandoned.
9. A list of exhibits marked in evidence by consent.
10. If leave is granted for further discovery by way of additional interrogatories, depositions or otherwise, state such fact and any time limit for completion thereof. Such leave at this stage is undesirable, and should be granted only in the most exceptional cases.
11. Any limitation on the number of expert witnesses.
12. Any directions for the filing of briefs.
13. State the order of opening and closing to jury, when a consolidated action or an action including third-party suit, counterclaim, cross-claim, or where there are several plaintiffs or defendants separately represented by counsel.
14. Any other matters which have been agreed upon to expedite disposition of the matter.
15. Estimated length of trial.
16. Weekly call or trial date.

_____COURT, _____COUNTY, _____DIVISION

Docket No. _____

Plaintiff

vs.

Defendant   Calendar No. _____

The parties to this action, by their attorneys, having appeared before the Court at a pretrial conference on the above date the following action was taken:

1.

Ordinarily, opening statements from both sides are given, and no jury instructions are given because no jury is present. Occasionally, defense counsel may make what may be called a *short closing argument in behalf of his or her client.*

At the end of the testimony, if the defendant is ordered held over to a higher court, the presiding officer will read a *holding order* naming the offense, the name of the defendant, and what the bail assessment is, if any. This order is kept in the file of the clerk of the court and may be secured by the reporter for comparison purposes. Sometimes, when such documents are read in open court, they are read very rapidly. The reporter may use the actual document to verify case numbers, dates, spellings of names, and so on. A sample preliminary examination is shown in Figure 4.2.

Grand Jury Investigation

Another type of hearing that may take place before the actual trial itself is called a *grand jury investigation.* This type of proceeding is also held to determine whether enough evidence exists to bring a person to trial; however, there are some important distinctions. First, no one has been arrested. There is no defendant, and therefore the information presented at the grand jury investigation is all ex parte, or one sided. Second, the grand jury hearing is held in secret behind closed doors.

A grand jury is selected from citizens of the community. The purpose of the grand jury is to investigate and determine whether sufficient evidence exists to charge a person with a criminal offense by means of an indictment and bring that person before the trial court.

The number making up a grand jury varies, but it is usually 23 jurors with 12 to 16 members required for a quorum. In large cities, several grand juries may be meeting at any given time. In some places a grand jury is chosen for an entire term of court, whereas in large metropolitan areas a given grand jury may serve for only one month. Grand jury members may be held over to complete any cases not finished at the end of their term.

The grand jury members consider all matters brought before them by a prosecuting attorney, who may be a state, city, or county attorney. The presiding judge administers the oath to the grand jury members in the courtroom and appoints one of their members as foreperson during their deliberations. The grand jury is then instructed as to the law and their duties and responsibilities by the judge, which is the reverse order of that followed in the trial courts. The court reporter normally will report the charge, but it is not usually transcribed. A page of grand jury transcript is shown in Figure 4.3.

Following the judge's charge, the jurors are taken to the grand jury room by the bailiff (in state court) or deputy marshal (in federal court) to hear the testimony regarding the case in which indictments are sought by the presiding official. The court reporter is sworn as the official reporter and sworn to secrecy by the secretary of the grand jury.

The prosecuting attorney usually opens with a brief statement about the case and the witnesses to be presented. The reporter will also report this proceeding, but usually does not transcribe it. The foreperson of the grand jury usually calls the witnesses by summoning the clerk from the outer room by a buzzer or bell. The foreperson or clerk will swear the witness, using the Bible as required in some states. Then the prosecuting officer will ask a number of questions regarding the matter under consideration, after which the grand jurors will question the witness. *Readbacks* may be requested when grand jurors do not understand testimony or when they wish to have a point reviewed to help them to understand something better.

When each witness is excused, the reporter may customarily leave the room with the witness so that discussion may occur secretly. In some places, however, the presiding officer will merely say, "off the record," and allow the reporter to remain present. Sometimes the court reporter will be called back in during deliberations of the grand jury to read testimony, in part or in whole, of any or all witnesses called for questioning.

At the end of a grand jury session, the reporter should request the exhibits and documents referred to during the proceedings to use for assistance in transcribing. He or she should also ask how many copies are needed and by whom.

FIGURE 4.2
Sample of Preliminary Examination

(a)

```
 1                    No. 366,890
                      No. 366,891
 2

 3   THE STATE OF TEXAS )              IN THE JUSTICE COURT
                       )
 4       -vs-          )              PRECINCT    NO.    ONE
                       )
 5   MICHAEL W. LEE and )             HARRIS COUNTY,  TEXAS
     ELMER A. LEE     )
 6

 7               A P P E A R A N C E S

 8   FOR THE STATE OF TEXAS:

 9           NATHAN MORTENSON, ESQUIRE
             Assistant District Attorney
10           Harris County, Texas

11   FOR THE DEFENDANTS:

12           HARVEY ATKINSON, ESQUIRE
             Attorney at Law
13           429 Vining Street
             Houston, Texas  77009
14
     PRELIMINARY EXAMINATION
15
            At an examining trial held on the 12th day
16
17   of December, A. D. 19__, in Houston, Texas, before the

18   Honorable Harry A. Irwin, Justice of the Peace, the following

19   proceedings were had and testimony adduced:

20                    H. R. WILSON

21   was called as a witness by the State and, having been first

22   duly sworn by the Court, testified as follows:

23                 DIRECT EXAMINATION

24   BY MR. MORTENSON:

25   Q    State your name, please, sir.
```

(b)

```
 1   A    H. R. Wilson.

 2   Q    How are you employed, Mr. Wilson?

 3   A    Houston Police Department.

 4   Q    And were you so employed on November 2nd of this year?

 5   A    Yes, I was.

 6   Q    About that time, on that date, did you meet two brothers

 7   named Michael Wayne Lee and Elmer A. Lee?

 8   A    Yes, sir, I did.

 9   Q    Do you recognize those men in Court today?

10   A    Yes, sir.  The gentlemen at the end of the table

11   (indicating).

12   Q    All right.  Where was it you met these men, Officer?

13   A    It was in the 5600 block of Yale.

14   Q    And what was the occasion on which you met them?

15   A    We were on routine patrol.  We observed their vehicle

16   northbound on Yale Street, and it appeared to have expired

17   dealer's tags.

18   Q    You stopped them and talked to them about the tags?

19   A    Yes, sir.

20   Q    Did anything unusual happen while you were talking?

21   A    Yes, sir.  As I approached the right side, one of the

22   defendants appeared to be stuffing a paper bag under his

23   seat.

24   Q    Under the seat that he was sitting on?

25   A    Yes, sir.
```

(c)

```
 1   Q    Would that be the passenger or the driver?

 2   A    Passenger.

 3   Q    Which one was the passenger?

 4   A    The gentleman in the brown coat.

 5   Q    That's Michael Lee?

 6   A    Yes, sir.

 7   Q    Did you make a search of the vehicle?

 8   A    Yes, sir, I did.

 9   Q    And what, if anything did you find?

10   A    I found inside the paper bag four plastic baggies

11   containing a green, plant-like substance which, in my opinion,

12    was marijuana.

13   Q    Did you place the defendants under arrest?

14   A    Yes, sir.

15   Q    Did you find anything else?

16   A    We found one glass pipe in the console of the vehicle.

17   Q    What kind of car was this?

18   A    If I'm not mistaken, a 1998 Chevrolet.

19   Q    You didn't charge them with paraphernalia or anything?

20   A    No, sir.

21   Q    Just marijuana?

22   A    Yes, sir.

23   Q    And you charged them with the marijuana that you found

24   under the seat of Michael Lee?

25   A    That's correct.
```

(d)

```
 1   Q    Did you search their persons?

 2   A    Yes, sir, I did.

 3   Q    Did you find anything on their persons?

 4   A    We placed Michael Lee in the vehicle after I found

 5   the marijuana in the bag.  He stated to me, "I have one bag

 6   in my pocket."

 7   Q    Did you check this out?

 8   A    He handed it to me.

 9   Q    Did you find anything on Elmer?

10   A    No, sir.

11   Q    Did you find any evidence to connect Elmer Lee any

12   closer than you've already testified?

13   A    Yes, sir.  He stated that he and his brother had bought

14   the marijuana together.

15   Q    Elmer did?

16   A    Yes, sir.

17            MR. MORTENSON:  Pass the witness.

18                 CROSS-EXAMINATION

19   BY MR. ATKINSON:

20   Q    Officer, with regard to the tags, how did you determine

21   that they were probably outdated?

22   A    They were faded and were too faint; you could barely read

23   the numbers.

24   Q    When you got out of the car, did you check that

25   first?
```

FIGURE 4.2
(continued)

(e)

1	A	My partner did.
2	Q	Were they outdated?
3	A	No, they were not.
4	Q	Had you already gotten to the side of the car?
5	A	Yes, sir, I had.
6	Q	In other words, when you got out, it was your main
7		objective to go check the dealer's tags, or was it to
8		check the occupants?
9	A	To approach the car, as the passenger of the vehicle
10		was making several movements.
11	Q	He started making these movements before you got out?
12	A	Yes, sir.
13	Q	Is it true, Officer, that the statement was made out
14		there by Michael Lee that he possessed the marijuana and not
15		his brother?
16	A	No. That's not true.
17	Q	You didn't find any marijuana, as you've earlier
18		testified, on Elmer Lee?
19	A	That's correct.
20	Q	Did either of the boys offer any resistance?
21	A	No, sir.
22	Q	They were courteous and polite, were they?
23	A	That's true.
24	Q	Evidently you didn't have to conduct a search? They
25		went ahead and gave the marijuana to you?

(f)

1	A	That's correct. I patted them down as they got out
2		of the car for weapons.
3	Q	Did you take them to the Houston Police Department?
4	A	Yes, sir.
5	Q	Did you search the boys there?
6	A	Yes, sir, we did. Upon placing them in jail, we
7		searched them.
8	Q	The marijuana that you had previously found was the
9		only marijuana found; is that correct?
10	A	That's correct.
11	Q	And all of this was under the right-hand side where
12		Michael had been sitting?
13	A	Four baggies were, and one was in his pocket.
14	Q	And Elmer didn't have any in his pocket?
15	A	No, sir.
16		MR. ATKINSON: That's all.
17		THE COURT: I find probable cause, and they
18		will be bound over.
19		(Whereupon, at 2:55 p.m., Court was in
20		recess in this matter.)
21		
22		
23		
24		
25		

(g)

```
 1                          No. 366,890
                            No. 366,891
 2
 3    THE STATE OF TEXAS §              IN THE JUSTICE COURT
                         §
 4        -vs-           §              PRECINCT  NO.  ONE
                         §
 5    MICHAEL W. LEE and §              HARRIS COUNTY,  TEXAS
      ELMER A. LEE       §
 6
 7
 8
 9         I, Justin Accurate, Official Court Reporter,
10    hereby certify that the foregoing _____ pages comprise a
11    true, complete, and correct transcript of the proceedings
12    at the Preliminary Examination in the above-styled
13    and numbered cause in said Court on the date stated
14    above and recorded in machine shorthand by me.
15         WITNESS MY HAND this the _____ day of December,
16    A.D. 19_ _.
17
18                              _____
                                JUSTIN ACCURATE
                                Official Court Reporter
19
20
21
22
23
24
25
```

FIGURE 4.3
A Page of Grand Jury Transcript

```
 1   Q    Did you have access to this information or not, or
 2   did Mr. Carr keep that information to himself?
 3   A    At one time we had a running account of the bank
 4   deposit for the payroll account; but, of course, during
 5   the last few days there wasn't any.
 6                MR. FREESE:  Are there any further questions
 7   of this witness?
 8   BY THE GRAND JURY:
 9   Q    Is the payroll week ended on a Saturday?
10   A    Yes.
11   Q    In other words, there was a work week, but they did
12   not get paid until the following week?
13   A    That's right.
14   Q    Both of these banks have a service charge for checks
15   returned.  Were those charges made for these returned checks?
16   A    Yes.
17   BY MR. FREESE:  Tell us how much Bob Carr was paid for his
18   salary.
19   A    I think it was $150 a week.
20                A GRAND JUROR:  Was Bob Carr authorized
21   to sign checks of the corporation?
22                THE WITNESS:  Not to my knowledge.
23                A GRAND JUROR:  Who did the typing of the
24   information on the checks?
25                THE WITNESS:  Most of it was done by hand.
```

Arraignments and Sentencings

An *arraignment* is a legal proceeding in which the person accused of a crime is brought before the Court to enter a plea. The accused may plead guilty, not guilty, or nolo contendere, which means "no contest." In a plea of nolo contendere, the defendant neither admits nor denies the charges, but throws himself or herself onto the mercy of the court. If any defendant does not enter a plea at the arraignment, the Court will enter a plea of not guilty.

When a defendant enters a guilty plea and is adjudged guilty by the Court, sentence may be pronounced immediately, or the case may be set for later hearing, and a presentence investigation may be ordered to allow for probation if the accused's background shows a clean criminal record. As the official reporter for a judge officiating over criminal matters, you will be responsible for recording in shorthand and transcribing pleas and sentences of the Court. Originals of arraignments, rearraignments, and sentencings are filed with the proper clerks of court, and copies are provided to the attorneys involved.

An example of a typical sentencing proceeding is included in Figure 4.4. Remember that the format will vary among different courts in different jurisdictions.

Ten Advantages of Official Reporting

1. The official reporter receives a steady, yearly salary with a paid vacation, pension plan, health insurance, and other benefits.

2. Reporters gain an excellent insight into the working of the legal system. They get a firsthand knowledge of the wheels of justice.

FIGURE 4.4
Sentence

```
 1                    COUNTY COURT OF NEW JERSEY
 2                    LAW DIVISION : JUSTICE COUNTY
                      INDICTMENT NO. I 173 M 80
 3
 4   STATE OF NEW JERSEY            :
 5         Complainant,             :
 6      -vs-                        :   S E N T E N C E
 7   ANGELO CAGGIATORE,             :
 8         Defendant.               :
     ----------------------------------------
 9                         Litigationville, New Jersey
10                         Thursday, August 31, 19___
11
12   B E F O R E :
13         HONORABLE SHOWING MERCIE
           Judge, County Court
14
15   A P P E A R A N C E S :
16         I, WRACKEN UPP, ESQ.,
           Prosecutor, Justice County, New Jersey.
17
18         HABEAS CORPUS, ESQ.,
           Attorney for the Defendant.
19
20
21
22
23
24                         TURNEM OUTTE ACCURATELY
                           Official Court Reporter
25
```
(a)

```
 1            THE COURT:  State of New Jersey
 2   versus Angelo Caggiatore.
 3            Mr. Caggiatore, do you have the
 4   services of an assigned counsel?
 5            THE DEFENDANT:  That is right, your
 6   Honor.
 7            THE COURT: Who is he?
 8            THE DEFENDANT:  Mr. Corpus, your
 9   Honor.
10            THE COURT: Are you satisfied with
11   the advice he has given you?
12            THE DEFENDANT:  Are you talking to
13   me?
14            THE COURT: Yes.
15            THE DEFENDANT:  Yes, sir.
16            THE COURT: You, of course, have had
17   explained to you your rights as to trial by
18   jury, have you not?
19            THE DEFENDANT:  Yes, sir.
20            THE COURT: And you have previously
21   waived your right of trial by jury?
22            THE DEFENDANT:  Yes, sir.
23            THE COURT: I will give you the right
24   of trial by jury if you desire it now.
25   Do you want it?
```
(b)

```
 1            THE DEFENDANT:  Sure.
 2            THE COURT:  Do you now want to
 3   have your case tried by the jury?
 4            THE DEFENDANT:  I am pretty sure I
 5   do.
 6            THE COURT:  I would suggest that we
 7   take a recess and you talk to your counsel.
 8                 (Recess taken.)
 9            THE COURT:  You are having a tough
10   time understanding me; is that right?
11            THE DEFENDANT:  Yes, sir.
12            THE COURT:  Do you want me to have
13   this matter brought before a jury?
14            THE DEFENDANT:  Well, I would like
15   to get it over with today, if I could.
16            THE COURT:  Has your attorney
17   explained every thing to you?
18            THE DEFENDANT:  Yes, sir.
19            THE COURT:  Are you satisfied with
20   the services which this attorney assigned by the
21   Court has rendered to you?
22            THE DEFENDANT:  Yes, sir.
23            THE COURT:  Mr. Caggiatore, I have
24   a report from the New Jersey State Diagnostic
25   Center.
```
(c)

```
 1            The sentence of this Court is that
 2   you, Angelo Caggiatore, be confined to New
 3   Jersey State Prison for a term of not less
 4   than one year and not more than two years.
 5            The sentence is hereby suspended,
 6   and you are hereby placed on probation for
 7   a period of three years.
 8            This action is subject to your
 9   agreeing to comply and your compliance with
10   the standard conditions of probation which
11   have been adopted by this Court and which
12   are on file with the Clerk of the Court,
13   and also with the special conditions of
14   probation which may be ordered by this Court
15   now or in the future.  A copy of the rules
16   and regulations of the Probation Office will
17   be provided you by the Probation Department
18   following this hearing.
19            In your case, the following special
20   conditions are imposed:
21            That you attend the Justice County
22   Guidance Clinic for treatment, and you are
23   to attend the Justice County Guidance Clinic
24   at such time or times as they will call you.
25            The Probation Officer will explain
```
(d)

FIGURE 4.4
(continued)

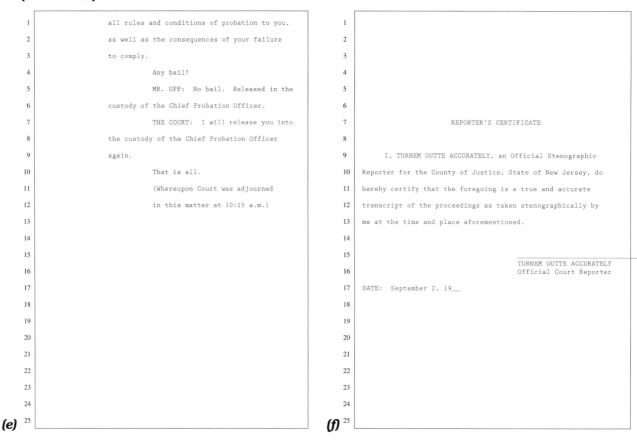

(e)
```
 1          all rules and conditions of probation to you,
 2          as well as the consequences of your failure
 3          to comply.
 4                  Any bail?
 5                  MR. UPP:  No bail.  Released in the
 6          custody of the Chief Probation Officer.
 7                  THE COURT:  I will release you into
 8          the custody of the Chief Probation Officer
 9          again.
10                  That is all.
11                  (Whereupon Court was adjourned
12                  in this matter at 10:15 a.m.)
```

(f)
```
 7                  REPORTER'S CERTIFICATE

 9          I, TURNEM OUTTE ACCURATELY, an Official Stenographic
10  Reporter for the County of Justice, State of New Jersey, do
11  hereby certify that the foregoing is a true and accurate
12  transcript of the proceedings as taken stenographically by
13  me at the time and place aforementioned.


                                    _____
15                                  TURNEM OUTTE ACCURATELY
16                                  Official Court Reporter

17  DATE:  September 2, 19__
```

3. A bond of trust exists between judges, lawyers, and court reporters that goes beyond the working environment.

4. Court reporting can be an exciting life, where one meets highly influential people and important celebrities.

5. The official reporter records many interesting, even history-making cases.

6. The official reporter usually has a well-furnished office and, in some cases, may have supplied all his or her equipment, including the computer and printer.

7. Court reporting is a very satisfying job in which one sees immediate results.

8. People respect your skill and talent and often are envious.

9. Appointments may be protected by civil service regulations.

10. Official reporting can be a very lucrative profession.

Ten Disadvantages of Official Reporting

1. In a large city, when a judge dies, resigns, or retires, the new judge may bring in another reporter, forcing the previous official reporter to seek other employment.

2. A judge who replaces a previous employer may be much different from the former judge. Working conditions may vary from judge to judge.

3. Some judges do not allow their official reporter to do any freelance work, believing that outside work may detract from their first responsibilities.

4. In some jurisdictions an official court reporter is also the judge's secretary. Sometimes, the reporter may be asked to perform menial, unchallenging, and demeaning tasks.

5. Travel and overnight accommodations might be required for judges who may be covering a different area, requiring the reporter to be away from home.

6. Official reporters may be required to take their vacation time at the same time that the judge does, whether this time is convenient or not.

7. Where a judge's jurisdiction is extended over a large territory, an official may be required to do a great deal of driving for the judge.

8. Some stress may be involved when working on a highly publicized case with many attorneys and witnesses.

9. More exhibits are usually marked in court actions than in freelance work. The reporter might be called on to keep all exhibits marked and maintained properly throughout the trial.

10. Unless the official is working on a computer or doing realtime reporting, acquiring a backlog of work that needs to be transcribed is easy to do. Reporting may be very demanding at times.

Chapter 5

Terminology of the Official Court Reporter

SECTION B

In the previous chapter a great many terms were introduced as they relate to the working environment of the official court reporter. This chapter will continue to help you to become familiar with the terminology of the official reporter.

In today's highly litigation prone society, it seems as though anyone can sue anybody at any time for anything! The important thing is whether the lawsuit has merit. Some suits are thrown out after the judge determines that they should never have been instigated, some are settled out of court in order to avoid lengthy trials, and some are drawn into that marvelous mechanism called *the American justice system*.

Parties to an Action

A person who is injured in any way is the one who has the right to sue, and this person must have the legal capacity to bring about an action. A minor's legal affairs must be handled by a parent or a guardian. In law, the word *person* may mean a company or a corporation, not just an individual. The litigants in a court case are called the *parties;* and the person who files the lawsuit is the *plaintiff,* sometimes known as the *petitioner*. The *defendant* is the party who is defending him- or herself against an action or specific criminal charges. In some cases, the defendant is also called the *respondent*. When a case is appealed, the party appealing is called the *appellant;* the party against whom the appeal is filed is known as the *respondent* or *appellee*.

Pleadings

Written statements are made by each side of a lawsuit stating the various claims made and defenses thereto. These written documents are called the *pleadings* of the case and are made up of the following legal documents:

The *complaint* is the legal document that begins a litigation proceeding. The complaint is filed by the plaintiff and lists the various charges brought against the defendant. In a civil action, the complaint and summons are required to be served on the defendant. In criminal matters, the complaint may be called the *information*.

The *answer* is the formal document that the defendant furnishes the plaintiff in response to the original complaint. The answer either admits or denies the charges made in the complaint and sets forth the defendant's defense to the allegations. One of the paragraphs of an answer might be a request for a more particularized account of the charges made, or a request for a *bill of particulars*.

The *demurrer* is a formal legal document made by a defendant to the plaintiff that admits the matters alleged in the complaint. However, it in effect says that the charges are insufficient and that the defendant cannot or will not answer the complaint. In essence, the demurrer disputes the sufficiency in law of the complaint. In some states the demurrer has been replaced by motions by counsel and court orders to clarify points of law before proceeding any further in the litigation process.

A *bill of particulars* is a formal document made by the plaintiff at the request of the *defendant,* which spells out in greater detail the charges set forth in the complaint. In essence, it helps the defendant to better answer the allegations made in the complaint. It is a motion for a more definite statement. A *petition* is a formal, written request to the court seeking judicial intervention or action on certain legal matters. To petition the court is to ask the court to do something.

A *summons* is the formal legal instrument used to notify a defendant that an action has been started against him or her. The summons is usually served on a person along with the complaint. It requires the person named therein to answer the complaint by appearing in court at the stated time and date.

The *subpoena* is the legal instrument served on a witness demanding that he or she appear in court to give testimony. Two types of subpoenas are used. A *subpoena ad testificandum* is an ordinary subpoena requiring one to appear and testify. A *subpoena duces tecum* requires a person to literally "bring with you" certain documents or records pertaining to the litigation.

An *affidavit* is a written statement of facts made voluntarily and sworn to under oath as to its authenticity. It can be made by any person who has any facts or knowledge concerning the litigation. An *affiant* is a person who makes an affidavit.

A *deposition* is the testimony of a person made under oath and given with notice to the opposing side for the purpose of cross-examination. It is a discovery device used to get information concerning the facts of a case. A *deponent* is the person who gives the deposition.

Upon receiving the first pleading in a case, the complaint, the court clerk will open a new file and issue a docket or case number. Fees are charged for filing papers with the court clerk, and, when these are paid, the documents are said to be *recorded* with the clerk of the court. A case is said to be *at issue* when the complaint and the answer have been filed. Then, *the issues have been joined,* which means that the parties have each presented their respective sides and are ready to proceed.

Jurisdiction

Jurisdiction is the authority or power of a court to hear a particular cause of action and to render a lawful and binding judgment against one or more defendants. Jurisdictions may be concurrent; that is, two or more courts may have jurisdiction over a particular cause of action, in which case the attorney may choose the best forum for the client's interests. A court must have jurisdiction over the subject matter of the litigation and over the person of the parties in order to hear a case and render a legal judgment.

Courts may have *original jurisdiction,* meaning that the court can hear the case for the first time; or they may have *appellate jurisdiction,* which empowers a court to hear a case on appeal. Some courts have both original and appellate jurisdiction. Jurisdiction may also be classified by the nature of the case; that is, whether it is *criminal* or *civil* or by the amount of money involved. Courts may also be classified as *juvenile, domestic,* or *probate.*

The Venue

The geographical location where a case is tried is called the *venue.* The venue may be a city, county, or district court. The venue is determined by statute and usually lies where the cause of action occurred. The venue may be changed at the request of the defendant for the following reasons: (1) an impartial trial cannot be heard in a particular location, (2) blatant prejudice or bias has been expressed by the judge or jury, (3) the convenience of the parties or witnesses is important, or (4) the interest of justice will be better served.

Discovery

In legal matters, the term *discovery* refers to the whole process of finding the facts relating to a particular lawsuit by various legal means afforded to the parties. A prime example of discovery is the taking of testimony during a deposition and using that testimony to gather facts about a lawsuit. The process of discovery follows strict rules of procedures.

Court Docket or Calendar

When a legal proceeding is filed with the clerk of the court, the docket or case number is assigned in either numerical order or divided into various subject matters. Some courts use a method that keeps track of the number of lawsuits filed in a particular category for each year. Docket numbers may be referred to in different jurisdictions in pleadings as Civil No. ____, Criminal No. ____, Index No. ____, or Case No. ____.

Officers of the Court

The *judge* is the presiding officer of the court. His or her major duties are to preside over hearings and trials in a case and to rule on issues that arise during a hearing or trial. He or she instructs the jury on matters of law in jury trials. The judge may be referred to as *the Court* or *the Bench*. During a trial, counsel may request permission to "approach the Bench," meaning that they wish to confer privately with the judge out of the hearing of the jury. This may also be referred to as *off-the-record discussion* or *sidebar*.

The *clerk of the court* is the administrator of the court and is responsible for the clerical details of the case. The court clerk is the custodian of all public records in most jurisdictions and is the ex officio recorder of conveyances and mortgages, keeping records of sales and mortgages on property and other documents.

Each judge in a court of record normally has a *court reporter* unless a pooling system is used. The judge's court reporter may also function as a secretary and assistant to the judge. The reporter will sit in the court while it is in session and record and transcribe the proceedings as required. The reporter may be responsible for the judge's calendar settings, file maintenance, and exhibits presented in lawsuits. Judges may also have law clerks, particularly in higher courts. The court reporter makes a verbatim record of all legal proceedings before the court.

The *bailiff* is the peace officer of the court and is responsible for keeping order. He or she is also responsible for the protection of everyone in the courtroom and for maintaining decorum during proceedings. In some jurisdictions, he or she may have charge of the jury.

The *sheriff* or *marshal* is the executive officer of the court who serves summonses and citations and carries out court orders. The sheriff is a county officer, and the marshal is a federal officer. The marshal transports federal prisoners. Some lower state courts also have *constables,* whose duties are the same as those of the sheriff. The sheriff not only deals with crime, but also plays an important part in civil proceedings by serving legal papers, making seizures to satisfy judgments, holding public auctions, and reporting back to the court regarding these matters. In some jurisdictions, the sheriff and bailiff may be the same person.

The *attorneys* for the respective sides are also officers of the court and, as such, they are obligated to uphold the dignity of the court and to abide by the rules of the court. The legal profession may be referred to as *the bar*. Attorneys are required to "pass the bar" or pass their licensure examination before they can practice before the bar.

The Jury

The *jury* is a body of ordinary citizens who are selected to hear a trial by jury. A jury pool may be selected from the tax rolls, voting registration, or motor vehicle registration. In most state courts, a jury is composed of 12 members who are selected after an initial screening process to determine their eligibility to hear a case. Some civil cases may only require 6 members on the jury panel. Most states require a three-fourths' or two-thirds' majority in civil cases, while in criminal actions a unanimous vote of the jurors is necessary for conviction.

Judgment

When a court issues a decision, it is called a *judgment*. The court's decision in a nonjury case is also referred to as a *finding*. Most courts give written reasons for judgment that set out the legal reasons for the decision. These are generally known as *findings of fact, conclusions of law,* and *order for judgment.*

The Verdict

In jury trials, the jury will deliberate the facts, apply the law given to it by the Court, and then reach a verdict based on the facts and law. The judge reviews the case and the jury's verdict and then pronounces the sentence.

Court Chambers and Open and Closed Court

Sometimes the judge may meet with attorneys and parties in his or her office, called *chambers,* for discussions outside the hearing of the jury or for decisions of motions. This session is also called a discussion *in camera,* which is Latin for *in chambers.* These sessions are usually more informal than open court hearings; however, the court reporter may bring his or her shorthand machine into the chambers and take down the verbatim discussion held in camera.

Hearings conducted in the courtroom at which visitors may be present are *open;* those from which spectators are barred are *closed.* Grand jury, juvenile hearings, adoptions, and some family court proceedings are usually closed by virtue of the law.

Ex Parte Hearings and Order to Show Cause

A judge may sometimes sign an order without hearing from both sides of a case when immediate action must be taken to stop something injurious to person or property, such as issuing a restraining order. *Ex parte* is Latin for *one side* or *one party.* An ex parte order might result from application to the judge for continuance of a hearing date or more time to file a legal brief.

An order granted ex parte normally provides for a date and time for the opposing party to appear to present arguments against the order. This order is designated as appearing to *show cause* why the order should not be granted permanently.

Chapter 6

A Typical Criminal Jury Trial

This chapter will take you through a step-by-step overview of a typical criminal jury trial. A *criminal matter* is one that deals with a person who breaks a law. He or she has committed a transgression against the laws of society and is held accountable for his or her actions. The difference between a criminal and civil matter is in terms of the parties to the action and the redress sought as a result of the litigation.

Generally, in *civil matters,* one person brings an action against another person for a wrong. In a criminal matter, a person who represents the people of a community, county, state, or nation brings an action against the person who wronged them by breaking the law. In a civil matter, the form of redress is financial, attempting to make the person who was wronged whole again by means of a monetary reward. In criminal matters, the form of redress is punishment and imprisonment for breaking the law.

The Constitution of the United States and the Bill of Rights protect a person's rights regarding criminal investigation and procedure. These protections include the following.

1. A person is protected from unreasonable search and seizure.
2. Persons accused of serious crime must be brought to trial only after an indictment by a grand jury, except in state prosecutions.
3. No persons shall be put into jeopardy twice for the same crime.
4. A defendant is not required to testify against himself or herself.
5. No one can be deprived of life, liberty, or property without due process of law.
6. Indicted persons are entitled to trial by jury and assistance of counsel and to be confronted by prosecution witnesses and to have witnesses in their favor.

Beginning of a Criminal Trial

The wheels of justice are put into motion when a person has committed a crime. The person who commits the crime may be arrested and then arraigned, after which a preliminary examination may result in holding the person over for trial court; or a grand jury may investigate facts surrounding accusations, resulting in an indictment.

Grand Jury Investigation

As noted previously, a *grand jury* is selected from the citizens of a community, usually a county within a state, for the purpose of investigating and determining whether sufficient evidence exists to charge a person with a criminal offense by means of an indictment.

The grand jury members consider all business brought before them by an elected public officer, who may be called the *prosecutor,* the *prosecuting attorney,* the *state's attorney,* the *city attorney,* or the *county attorney.* The presiding judge administers the oath to the grand jury members in the courtroom and appoints one of their members as foreperson, who acts as the presiding officer during their deliberations. The grand jury is then instructed as to the law and their duties and responsibilities by the judge. This *jury charge* or instruction to the jury is given at the beginning of the investigation rather than at the end. The court reporter normally reports this charge, but it is not usually transcribed.

Grand jury proceedings can be very formal occasions in cities where the presiding officer begins the questioning, which is followed by questioning by the grand jury members. Or they can be informal meetings in small places where jurors' questions are scattered throughout the testimony.

An example of grand jury testimony is given in Figure 6.1. Some reporters will note the questioning of grand jurors by placing the heading BY THE GRAND JURY: at the left margin, followed by the questions and answers. For example:

BY THE GRAND JURY:

Q: Where were you when you saw the man?

A: I was in my car.

When questioning by the jurors occurs throughout the interrogation, you can put the individual questions and responses in colloquy as follows:

A GRAND JUROR: Where were you when you saw the man?

THE WITNESS: I was in my car.

Grand jury reporters may be freelance reporters who have been hired by a local government, they may be official reporters appointed to grand juries, or they may be justice reporters. *Justice reporters* are hired by the prosecutor's office and are either pooled or assigned to a certain examiner for a given term. In a U.S. district court, they are often hired on a contract basis by the U.S. attorney.

When a grand jury decides that conclusive evidence of guilt is sufficient to try an individual, an indictment is issued. An *indictment* is the formal means of charging a defendant with a crime after an investigation by a grand jury. Another name for an indictment is a *true bill.* If the jurors find that sufficient evidence does not exist, an indictment is not issued. Very often, the grand jury sees fit to issue a series of sealed indictments that charge a person with a crime, but they do not release the name of the individual until the proper authorities have arrested him or her, at which time the indictment may be opened.

Preliminary Examination

A justice of the peace, a judge, or a magistrate presides over a *preliminary examination.* This is a hearing held to decide whether sufficient evidence exists to order an accused person to be held over for trial in a higher court within the jurisdiction.

If sufficient evidence is presented by the prosecution in a preliminary hearing to indicate a probable cause to believe that the person who is the subject of the hearing committed the alleged crime, he or she is bound over to face trial. If sufficient evidence does not exist, no crime occurred, and the person is released.

FIGURE 6.1
Grand Jury Testimony

(a)

```
 1                    JAMES E. ROBERTS,
 2   being first duly sworn by the Foreman of the Grand Jury as a
 3   witness, testified before the Grand Jury as follows:
 4                    DIRECT EXAMINATION
 5   BY MR. FLOWERS:
 6   Q    Mr. Roberts, you are the cashier of the Merchants Trust
 7   Company, is that right?
 8   A    The secretary-treasurer.
 9   Q    Where do you live?
10   A    134 Sunset Terrace, Brewster, New Jersey.
11   Q    Now, I believe the Star Printing and Publishing Company
12   had an account at your bank; is that right?
13   A    They had two; a regular account and a payroll account.
14   Q    Was there any difficulty in regard to the maintenance of
15   a balance in the payroll account with that company?
16   A    At times, there was.
17   Q    Do you recall when those times were, the dates?
18   A    (No response.)
19   Q    Let me ask it this way, and maybe this will simplify
20   things: On December 29th, 19_ _, can you tell me what the
21   balance was of this account in your bank?
22   A    I would have to go to the telephone to get that on the
23   payroll account.
24   Q    Let me show you a check dated December 29, 19_ _, Signed
25   by Frank Finelli, made payable to Ann Connors, for which
```

(b)

```
 1   at the date of presentation, the officer decides
 2   whether to overdraw the account or pay it.  A $2 charge
 3   is placed against the account.
 4          A GRAND JUROR:  You do send him a written
 5   notice?
 6          THE WITNESS:  It is a written notice on a form.
 7   Q    (By Mr. Flowers)  Did Mr. Finelli have any personal
 8   accounts in your bank?
 9   A    None at all.
10   Q    Did his wife have any accounts in your bank?
11   A    I don't think she did.  I am not sure.
12   Q    Who could draw checks on this account?
13   A    Frank Finelli.
14   Q    Was he the only one?
15   A    I don't know.  His son Ray was added to the account,
16   but I don't know at what time.  I can find out and give you
17   that information.
18          MR. FLOWERS:  That is all right.  Are there any
19   further questions of this witness?
20          THE GRAND JURY:  (No response.)
21          MR. FLOWERS:  Thank you very much, Mr. Roberts.
22   You are excused.
23          (The witness leaves the grand jury room.)
24          MR. FLOWERS:  Bring in the next witness, please.
25          (Witness sworn.)
```

Although a jury is not present, the rules of evidence are followed regarding the presentation of witnesses and exhibits in a preliminary examination. The procedure is much the same as a regular trial as far as direct examination and cross-examination of the prosecution's witnesses, and the defendant seldom presents any witnesses.

Court reporters are usually assigned to do preliminary examinations as a part of their duty as official reporters. The proceedings may or may not be transcribed, depending on whether the person is held over for trial. An example of a preliminary examination is found in Figure 6.2.

Coroner's Inquest

Reporters may also be called on to report other investigatory hearings that will result in the formal charging of a defendant with a crime. A *coroner's inquest* is called to determine the cause of death whenever foul play is suspected in the death of a person. In some states, the inquest is automatic when a person dies for no apparent reason.

The inquest revolves around the testimony of the doctor who did the autopsy on the dead person to determine the cause of death. The coroner, the jury, witnesses, a defense attorney, attorneys for other interested parties, and perhaps the district attorney will be present. The corpse is not present nor is it offered into evidence. The principal witness is the doctor who performed the autopsy.

The results of the inquest may lead to the formal arrest and charging of a person with murder. The inquest is transcribed only after a request is made by the judge or attorneys.

The Arraignment and Other Pretrial Matters

An *arraignment* is the hearing to which a person accused of a crime is brought before the Court to enter a plea to charges contained in the counts of an indictment or complaint. The purpose of the arraignment is to allow the defendant to enter a plea, to exercise his or her constitutional rights, and to be allowed to be set free on bail if the Court so deems.

The court reporter is responsible for recording what happens during the arraignment proceedings. If the accused pleads guilty, the Court sentences him or her, either immediately or at a later time. All pleas and sentences must be recorded by the reporter and transcribed.

Transcripts of pleas and sentences are normally set up as colloquy unless a prolonged examination by the Court takes place. If a lengthy examination occurs, the title EXAMINATION BY THE COURT: is used, followed by the normal Q and A format. Whenever the defendant speaks, the remarks are prefaced by THE DEFENDANT: instead of the name.

The title page is similar to the title page used for the trial transcript. It contains the venue, indictment or information number, style of the case, and designation of the case such as ARRAIGNMENT or SENTENCE. The location and date are keyed under the title box. The judge presiding is listed, and the appearances of counsel are placed on the title page. The reporter's name and title are shown at the bottom of the title page. An example of a sentencing proceeding is found in Figure 6.3.

Sentences are reported verbatim, making sure that different sentences for different counts are recorded properly. Record whether a sentence is to be served concurrently or consecutively with other charges. *Concurrent sentences* are served at the same time, whereas *consecutive sentences* are served one after another.

FIGURE 6.2
Preliminary Examination

(a)

```
 1                        No. 369,984
 2   THE STATE OF TEXAS    }        IN THE JUSTICE COURT
                           }
 3        -vs-             }        PRECINCT NUMBER TWO
                           }
 4   LAWRENCE D. MALCOLM   }        HARRIS COUNTY, TEXAS
 5
 6                        APPEARANCES
 7   FOR THE STATE OF TEXAS:
 8          JAMES GUNTHER, ESQUIRE
            Assistant District Attorney
            Harris County, Texas
 9   FOR THE DEFENDANT:
10          THOMAS E. BARTLETT, ESQUIRE
            Attorney at Law
11          509 Fannin Street
12          Houston, Texas
13                        PROCEEDINGS
14          At an examining trial held on the 7th day of
15   March, A.D. 20__, in Houston, Texas, before the Honorable
16   Hearem N. Weepe, Justice of the Peace, the following
17   proceedings were had and testimony adduced:
18
19                      RAE ALICE JONES
20   was called as a witness by the State and, having been first
21   duly sworn by the Court, testified as follows:
22                    DIRECT EXAMINATION
23   BY MR. GUNTHER:
24   Q     Would you state your name please?
25   A     Rae Alice Jones.
```

(b)

```
 1   Q     Where do you live, Mrs. Jones?
 2   A     1506 Gennessee.
 3   Q     I'd like to direct your attention back to around
 4   the 22nd day of January of 19__ and ask you: Do you recall
 5   whether or not you were at 3874 Oxford Street?
 6   A     Yes, I was.
 7   Q     Did you live there at that time?
 8   A     Yes, I did.
 9   Q     What was your apartment number at that time?
10   A     I think it was 211.
11   Q     All right. Were you present at that location on or
12   about the 22nd day of January of 19__?
13   A     Uh-huh.
14   Q     Did you live there alone or with somebody?
15   A     I had a roommate.
16   Q     Do you know the defendant seated here, Lawrence D.
17   Malcolm?
18   A     No.
19   Q     I said do you know him now?
20   A     I know him now.
21   Q     Did you see him out there on Oxford Street about
22   January 22nd?
23   A     I don't know the date, but I seen him.
24   Q     Was he out at your apartment?
25   A     Yes.
```

FIGURE 6.2
(continued)

```
 1                          No. 369,984
 2   THE STATE OF TEXAS    §              IN THE JUSTICE COURT
                           §
 3         -vs-            §              PRECINCT NUMBER TWO
                           §
 4   LAWRENCE D. MALCOLM   §              HARRIS COUNTY, TEXAS
 5
 6
 7
 8
 9                    I, Hardy Harhar, Official Court Reporter,
10   hereby certify that the foregoing _____ pages comprise a true,
11   complete, and correct transcript of the proceedings had at the
12   examining trial in the above-styled and numbered cause had in
13   said Court on the date stated above and recorded in machine
14   shorthand by me.
15                    WITNESS BY HAND this the _____ day of March
16   A.D. 20__.
17
18                                    _____
19                                    HARDY HARHAR, CSR
                                      Official Court Reporter
20
21
22
23
24
25
```
(c)

If the defendant pleads not guilty, a trial date is set, and the prisoner is either kept in jail, released on bail, or released on personal recognizance. To be released on bail, the defendant must raise money or provide a property bond and leave it with the court to assure that he or she will return to stand trial. To be *released on one's own recognizance* is to be released with the assurance that he or she will return to stand trial. Sometimes, as in the case of a minor defendant, the person may be released in the custody of another person, a parent or guardian.

In some courts, before the trial is to be held, a pretrial hearing or pretrial conference may be held. This hearing helps to simplify the issues, amend the pleadings, obtain admissions of fact, limit the number of expert witnesses, make motions, or otherwise settle the case and agree on damages. A report of the pretrial hearing becomes a part of the official record of the case, and it may be read to the jury at the time of the trial.

Selection of the Jury

Every person has a right to a trial by jury. In civil matters that right may be waived, and in criminal cases the defendant may waive his or her right only in some states. Some states require that all defendants in felony prosecutions be tried before a jury.

The first step in a trial by jury is the selection of the individuals who will make up the jury. Usually, the process begins with a panel of jurors who convene in the Court in which the case is to be tried. Prospective jurors are selected according to statutory and constitutional provisions within each jurisdiction. In general, all jurors must be citizens of the United States, a local resident within the jurisdiction, of majority age, of approved integrity, and of reasonable intelligence. Some localities use the lists garnered from the voting registration as a list of prospective jurors, while others use motor vehicle registration or tax records.

Attorneys will examine the prospective jurors as to their qualifications, lack of prejudice, and general knowledge and understanding, which is called *voir dire examination. Voir dire* is a French term that means to *speak the truth*. The attorney may challenge or excuse the prospective jury members either for cause or *peremptorily,* that is, without cause. Depending on the matter, the first 12 persons who are accepted as satisfactory by both sides constitute the jury.

In some jurisdictions, court reporters must report everything that occurs during voir dire examination. In most other states, the judge will call for the court reporter only when required. In capital cases the official reporter reports everything. The official reporter should always check with the judge in a particular jurisdiction about what should be reported before the trial. Some reporters will take the voir dire as a preliminary warm-up, although they may not be required to do so.

If the matter is a felony offense, a reporter will usually be requested to take the voir dire examination, which must be completely accurate. After a verdict is reached, counsel on either side has the right to subpoena the entire jury and have them return to court. At this time, questions are asked about what happened in the jury room. Attorneys will request that the official reporter transcribe the voir dire examination to see whether any irregularities occurred in what was answered under voir dire. If a juror was not honest in his or her answers or failed to divulge something that might have been important or had an impact on his or her acceptance as a juror, the court may rule that an injustice has occurred and grant a motion for a new trial. An example of a transcript containing voir dire examination is shown in Figure 6.4.

FIGURE 6.3
Sentencing

(a)

```
 1                      COUNTY COURT OF NEW JERSEY
                        LAW DIVISION : JUSTICE COUNTY
 2                      INDICTMENT NO. I 173 M 80

 3

 4   STATE OF NEW JERSEY,       :

 5            Complainant,      :

 6        -vs-                  :          SENTENCE

 7   ANGELO CAGGIATORE,         :

 8            Defendant.        :

 9   - - - - - - - - - - - - - - - - - - - - - - - - - -

10                               Litigationville, New Jersey
                                 Thursday, August 31, 20_ _
11

12   BEFORE:

13            HONORABLE SHOWING MERCIE
              Judge, County Court
14

15   APPEARANCES:

16            I, WRACKEM UPP, ESQUIRE,
              Prosecutor, Justice County, New Jersey.
17
              HABEAS CORPUS, ESQUIRE,
18            Attorney for the Defendant.

19

20

21

22

23

24                          TURNEM OUTTE ACCURATELY
                            Official Court Reporter
25
```

(b)

```
 1            THE COURT:  State of New Jersey

 2   versus Angelo Caggiatore.

 3            Mr. Caggiatore, do you have the

 4   services of an assigned counsel?

 5            THE DEFENDANT:  That is right, your

 6   honor.

 7            THE COURT:  Who is he?

 8            THE DEFENDANT:  Mr. Corpus, your

 9   Honor.

10            THE COURT:  Are you satisfied with

11   the advice he has given you?

12            THE DEFENDANT:  Are you talking to

13   me?

14            THE COURT:  Yes.

15            THE DEFENDANT:  Yes, sir.

16            THE COURT:  You, of course, have had

17   explained to you your rights as to trial by

18   jury, have you not?

19            THE DEFENDANT:  Yes, sir.

20            THE COURT:  And you have previously

21   waived your right of trial by jury?

22            THE DEFENDANT:  Yes, sir.

23            THE COURT:  I will give you the

24   right of trial by jury if you desire it now.

25   Do you want it?
```

FIGURE 6.3
(continued)

1	THE DEFENDANT: Sure.
2	THE COURT: Do you now want to have
3	your case tried by the jury?
4	THE DEFENDANT: I am pretty sure I
5	do.
6	THE COURT: I would suggest that we
7	take a recess and you talk to your counsel.
8	(Recess taken.)
9	THE COURT: You are having a tough
10	time understanding me; is that right?
11	THE DEFENDANT: Yes, sir.
12	THE COURT: Do you want me to have
13	this matter brought before a jury?
14	THE DEFENDANT: Well, I would like
15	to get it over with today, if I could.
16	THE COURT: Has your attorney
17	explained everything to you?
18	THE DEFENDANT: Yes, sir.
19	THE COURT: Are you satisfied with
20	the services which this attorney assigned by
21	the Court has rendered to you?
22	THE DEFENDANT: Yes, sir.
23	THE COURT: Mr. Caggiatore, I have
24	a report from the New Jersey State Diagnostic
25	Center.

(c)

1	The sentence of this court is that
2	you, Angelo Caggiatore, be confined to New
3	Jersey State Prison for a term of not less
4	than one year and not more than two years.
5	The sentence is hereby suspended,
6	and you are hereby placed on probation for
7	a period of three years.
8	This action is subject to your
9	agreeing to comply and your compliance with
10	the standard conditions of probation which
11	have been adopted by this Court and which
12	are on file with the Clerk of the Court,
13	and also with the special conditions of
14	probation which may be ordered by this Court
15	now or in the future. A copy of the rules
16	and regulations of the Probation Office will
17	be provided you by the Probation Department
18	following this hearing.
19	In your case, the following special
20	conditions are imposed:
21	That you attend the Justice County
22	Guidance Clinic for treatment, and you are
23	to attend the Justice County Guidance Clinic
24	at such time or times as they will call you.
25	The Probation Officer will explain

(d)

Before the attorneys begin questioning the *veniremen,* the prospective members of the jury, they often make a few introductory remarks. These remarks are not the opening statements of the attorneys.

Sometimes the entire jury panel is seated in the courtroom, and questions are asked of the whole group, with responses from one or a few prospective jurors being given. In this case, the reporter often has no way of identifying the particular jurors unless the attorney calls them by name or the reporter knows them. Therefore, if the reporter is taking down the voir dire examination, the jury members will be designated as "A Prospective Juror" or, more preferably, by the number assigned to them when they were called forward, as in "Prospective Juror No. 3." Another option is to use the straight Q and A format after the attorney has designated the juror by name in his or her question.

Generally, as each juror is called to the jury box to be examined, the clerk will read his or her name and address. Usually, before interrogation begins, the first 18 chairs are filled. If a juror is excused, he or she will leave the box, and a new juror will be called forward to take that place.

The attorneys for either side can excuse prospective jurors. Jurors are excused by the exercise of a peremptory challenge or a challenge for cause. Each party is allowed an unlimited number of *challenges for cause,* which are challenges for which some reason is stated. For example, if a prospective jury member turns out to be related to one of the parties to the action, he or she would be excused for cause.

The number of peremptory challenges is set by statute depending on whether it is a civil or criminal matter and depending on the number of jurors to be selected. A *peremptory challenge* is a challenge for which no reason has to be given for excusing the juror. The reporter should keep track of the challenges made and chart the jury as it is seated.

FIGURE 6.3
(continued)

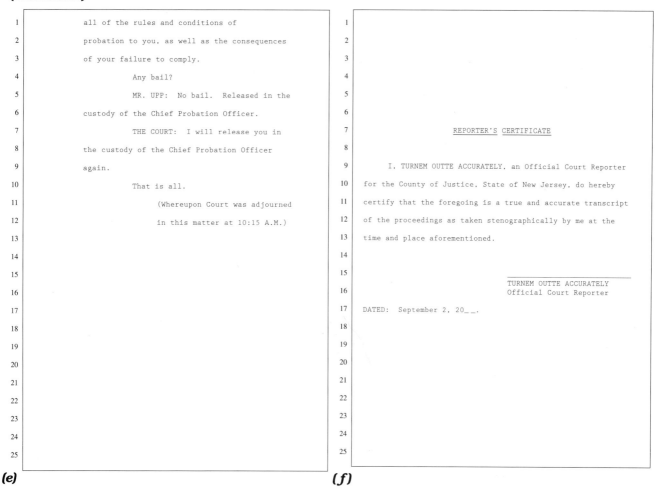

1 all of the rules and conditions of	1
2 probation to you, as well as the consequences	2
3 of your failure to comply.	3
4 Any bail?	4
5 MR. UPP: No bail. Released in the	5
6 custody of the Chief Probation Officer.	6
7 THE COURT: I will release you in	7 REPORTER'S CERTIFICATE
8 the custody of the Chief Probation Officer	8
9 again.	9 I, TURNEM OUTTE ACCURATELY, an Official Court Reporter
10 That is all.	10 for the County of Justice, State of New Jersey, do hereby
11 (Whereupon Court was adjourned	11 certify that the foregoing is a true and accurate transcript
12 in this matter at 10:15 A.M.)	12 of the proceedings as taken stenographically by me at the
13	13 time and place aforementioned.
14	14
15	15 _____
16	16 TURNEM OUTTE ACCURATELY
17	17 DATED: September 2, 20__. Official Court Reporter
18	18
19	19
20	20
21	21
22	22
23	23
24	24
25	25
(e)	**(f)**

Another type of challenge occurs when an attorney makes an objection to the entire panel of prospective jurors. This challenge is called a *challenge to the array* and asks that the entire panel be excused and that a new panel who more closely represents a group of peers be selected. For example, an attorney representing a Native American or an African American person may challenge an entire panel if no members of her or his particular ancestry or heritage are on the panel.

After a satisfactory jury has been selected, the jury is sworn and the trial proceeds. In general, during the trial the Court determines all questions of law, and the jurors determine the questions of fact.

At times the jury may be *sequestered,* or secluded in hotel rooms overnight. To sequester is to isolate or segregate from the public. Sequestering is usually the case in highly publicized cases in which the jury may be swayed by events that occur outside the courtroom, for example, the television or radio coverage of the trial. During the trial the Court may admonish the jury panel, instructing them not to talk to anyone about the case, not to read newspapers, and not to watch television or listen to the radio.

The Trial

A chronological order of events that occur during a jury trial after the preliminary investigations or a grand jury investigation, the pretrial matters, the arraignment, and the selection of the jury is presented in this section.

FIGURE 6.4
Voir Dire Jury Selection

(a)

```
1        IN THE DISTRICT COURT OF HARRIS COUNTY, TEXAS
2                    122ND JUDICIAL DISTRICT
3    STATE OF TEXAS,        )
                            )     CR. NO. 127,780
4              Plaintiff    )
                            )     VOIR DIRE EXAMINATION OF
5        -vs-               )
                            )     PROSPECTIVE JURORS
6    HARVEY GEORGE LAMARE,   )
                            )
7              Defendant.   )
8    APPEARANCES:
9    For the Plaintiff,
     The State of Texas:          ROBERT C. BENNETT, ESQUIRE
10                                and RAY MONTGOMERY, ESQUIRE
                                  Assistant District Attorneys
11
     For the Defendant,
12
     Harvey George LaMare:        MURRAY L. LISTERMAN
13                                Attorney at Law
14       BE IT REMEMBERED that upon this, the 28th day of
15   October, A.D. 20__, the above entitled and numbered cause
16   came on for trial before the Honorable Robert A. Harley,
17   Judge of the 122nd Judicial District Court of the State
18   of Texas, and a jury; and both the Plaintiff and the
19   Defendant appearing in person and/or by Counsel, announced
20   ready for trial; and all preliminary matters having been
21   disposed of, the selection of a jury commenced, and the
22   following Voir Dire Examination of Prospective Jurors
23   was had and made of record, commencing on the 28th day of
24   October, A.D. 20__, vis:
25
```

(b)

```
1                    P R O C E E D I N G S
2                      October 28, 20__
3                          9:30 a.m.
4                           - - -
5        (In open Court.)
6        MR. BENNETT:  Members of the jury, the case
7    before this court this morning is the case of The State of
8    Texas versus Harvey George LaMare.
9        THE COURT:  (To Mr. Listerman)  Do you have
10   your client here?
11       MR. LISTERMAN:  Yes, your Honor.
12       THE COURT:  Please come around here, sir.
13       (The defendant complies.)
14       THE COURT:  Mr. LaMare is represented by the
15   attorney of his choice, Mr. Murray L. Listerman.  The State
16   will be represented in this case by two Assistant District
17   Attorneys:  Mr. Robert C. Bennett and Mr. Ray Montgomery.
18       It is alleged by the Indictment, ladies and
19   gentlemen of the jury, that this defendant, Harvey George
20   LaMare, on or about the 16th day of October of 20__, made an
21   assault upon one Willie Merkle and by that assault and by
22   violence took from the possession of this Willie Merkle
23   certain personal property, it allegedly occurred here in
24   Harris County, Texas.
25       Does anyone of you happen to know anything
```

Opening Statements by Counsel

After the jury has been impaneled and sworn, the attorneys for both sides of the case may make an opening statement to the jury. The purpose of the opening statement is to outline their theory of the case and tell the members of the jury what they should expect the evidence to show. The reporter is not allowed to interrupt counsel during their opening statements. Most attorneys will use a speaker's stand and a microphone to present their case, but some may stroll around the courtroom, approaching the jury box, and generally turning away from the reporter. The reporter must make sure that he or she can hear the attorney and get an accurate record of what is said. Some reporters move their chairs next to the jury box to hear better.

The plaintiff's attorney presents his or her case first. The plaintiff has the option of waiving the opening statement. After the plaintiff's opening statement, the defendant may give his or her opening argument or wait until the plaintiff rests his or her case. If more than one defendant is involved, each counsel will be given a chance to make an opening statement on behalf of his or her client. The amount of time allowed for each opening statement may be set in advance by agreement of Court and counsel. Some judges require officials to report opening statements, even though they are not transcribed. Statements given at trials for first-degree felonies are always transcribed and put into the record. Some attorneys request that the opening statement be transcribed and put into the transcript of the statement of facts.

In any event, opening statements are a good way for the reporter to warm up for the dictation at the trial. Because the reporter needs to record all objections made during the opening statements, the entire statement should be recorded.

FIGURE 6.4
(continued)

(c)

```
 1              MR. BENNETT:  Thank you, Mr. Boyd.
 2              Mr. Zettle -- is that the way you pronounce
 3   your name?
 4              PJ ZETTLE:  Yes, sir.
 5              MR. BENNETT:  Who do you work for?
 6              PJ ZETTLE:  Matco Pipe Company.
 7              MR. BENNETT:  What kind of work do you do
 8   for them?
 9              PJ ZETTLE:  I am a helper.
10              MR. BENNETT:  Have you ever had a personal
11   interest in the outcome of a trial case?
12              PJ ZETTLE:  Yes sir.  I was convicted of
13   burglary about five years ago.
14              MR. BENNETT:  We will excuse Mr. Zettle, your
15   Honor.
16              THE COURT:  Mr. Zettle, you will be excused
17   from service on this jury.  You will be notified when to
18   appear again.
19      (The same questions are propounded with slight variance
20   to other jurors:  Mr. Deforges, Mr. Brunsen, Mr. Cole, Mrs.
21   Gigstad, Mr. McBridge, Mr. Moore, Mrs. Adkins, and Mr. Bocek.
22   Following this, Mr. Listerman asks the jury panel his
23   questions, and strikes are then taken.)
24              THE COURT:  Ladies and gentlemen, I want those
25   of you who have been selected as jurors to sit up here
```

(d)

```
 1   in the jury box and listen objectively to the testimony
 2   that is give here.  Do not draw any conclusions or
 3   make up your minds before the entire evidence that we
 4   hope to present is laid out before you, so that your minds
 5   will be open to all evidence, either that of the State
 6   or that of the defense.
 7              You must form your final conclusion
 8   strictly upon the evidence that we present to you and
 9   not upon your feelings.  Try to set those aside if they
10   hamper you in any way and, upon the evidence that we
11   present to you in this reasonable doubt as to the guilt
12   of the defendant.  If there does, we ask that you acquit
13   this defendant.
14              Thank you.
```

Attorneys may tell the jury in their opening statements that the judge will instruct them in a certain way concerning the law later in the case, but what an attorney says about the law does not govern. Opening statements of the attorneys are not evidence, and trial lawyers usually make no attempt to discuss the law in any detail during the opening statements.

If the official reporter is requested to record and transcribe the opening statements, they are transcribed as part of the record. Observe the protocol for your jurisdiction and use an acceptable format when transcribing the opening statements.

When opening statements are not ordered in a transcript, an appropriate parenthetical should be placed in the transcript. For example:

(Mr. Attorney made an opening statement on behalf of the plaintiff.)

or

(Ms. Attorney waived making an opening statement on behalf of the defendant.)

or

(Mrs. Attorney reserved making an opening statement on behalf of the respondent.)

Plaintiff's Case in Chief

After selection of a jury, preliminary motions, and the opening statements have been disposed of, the plaintiff's attorney will present all witnesses on whom he or she will rely to establish the facts of his or her case and all physical evidence or exhibits that will support the allegations.

Witnesses are called by the plaintiff's attorney. When witnesses are called, they are set up according to the previous chapter regarding the proper setup of witnesses. The attorney who called the witness conducts the direct examination of that witness, and it is so noted in the setup. For example:

> JOHN O. HUNTSKI, a witness called on behalf of the plaintiff, having been duly sworn by the Clerk of the Court, testified as follows:

DIRECT EXAMINATION

BY MS. ATTORNEY:

Q: What is your full name, for the record, please?

A: My name is John Oliver Huntski.

Each witness brought forward by the plaintiff is first questioned by plaintiff's counsel on direct examination and is then cross-examined by the defense counsel. The direct examination and cross-examination are followed by redirect examination and recross-examination. If the questioning goes beyond direct, cross, redirect, and recross, it is designated as further redirect examination and further recross-examination.

The testimony of a witness may be interrupted by various motions or objections by opposing counsel. It may also be interrupted by a hearing conducted by the Court on another matter or by lunch or adjournment for the day.

During examination of a witness, opposing counsel may ask to conduct voir dire examination to establish competency or qualification of the witness to testify concerning some subject or exhibit to prevent improper evidence from being placed in the record. This type of examination is designated as follows:

VOIR DIRE EXAMINATION

BY MRS. ATTORNEY:

Q: Now, please explain to the court and jury how you knew. . . .

Physical evidence is presented in the form of exhibits. Exhibits may be documents or business records, or they may be actual objects that have a direct link to the case at hand, such as an item of clothing or a weapon. Evidence is usually marked for identification first, then discussed, then if appropriate, received into evidence. For a thorough discussion about exhibits, see Chapter 13.

When all plaintiff's witnesses have been called to testify and all exhibits have been marked and received, the plaintiff's attorney rests the case. Include this fact in the record and transcribe it properly. As soon as the plaintiff rests, in many instances, a motion to dismiss the case is made by the defendant's attorney. The attorney may make a motion for a directed verdict, that is, ask the Court to find in favor of the defendant without giving the case to the jury.

If the motion is granted, the case is ended, and the defendant will not have to present any evidence. If the motion is denied, the case will continue with the presentation of evidence by the defendant.

Defendant's Case in Chief

Assuming that the judge denies the motion to dismiss the case, the defendant now presents all witnesses and exhibits to support his or her side of the case. At this time the defendant produces evidence not only to deny the plaintiff's claim, but also in support of any affirmative defense that the defendant has pleaded.

If defense counsel did not present an opening statement at the beginning of the trial, he or she may do so at this time or waive it altogether.

Witnesses presented by the defendant's attorney are called on direct examination by the defense and cross-examination by plaintiff's counsel. The same is true of redirect examination by the defendant's attorney and recross-examination by the plaintiff's attorney. Additional testimony is called *further redirect* and *further recross-examination.*

When the defendant has completed the presentation of his or her proof, the defendant rests, and it is so noted in the record.

Prosecution Rebuttal and Defense Surrebuttal

At this point, the plaintiff may now present his or her case in rebuttal. *Rebuttal* is confined to presenting testimony that will refute the evidence of the defendant. The evidence presented during rebuttal must truly rebut evidence produced by the defense. New evidence is not permitted without permission from the Court. Witnesses called in rebuttal undergo direct, cross, redirect, and recross-examination in rebuttal.

When the plaintiff's case in rebuttal is finished, he or she closes his or her case. If new points are brought out by plaintiff's rebuttal evidence, the defendant may present evidence in rejoinder. The defendant's presentation follows rebuttal and is called *surrebuttal.* Witnesses undergo direct, cross, redirect, and recross-examination as in rebuttal. At the conclusion of the defendant's case in surrebuttal, the defendant rests.

Testimony by Deposition

The deposition of a witness may be read into the record by the attorney who conducted the original deposition. The reporter may be furnished with a copy of the deposition, and the Court may tell the reporter to record only objections and rulings concerning the deposition. When objections or colloquy occur, the reporter writes the material before the objection, the resulting colloquy, and the judge's ruling.

If a copy of the deposition is not furnished to the reporter, at the judge's discretion the reporter may or may not be requested to record the reading of the deposition. Parentheticals may be used to indicate the reading of the deposition into the record.

Bench Conferences or Sidebars

The reporter may be called to the bench to take material outside the hearing of the jury. Such bench conferences or sidebars may or may not be included in the record. Whether a sidebar discussion is recorded is up to the judge, the reporter must ask the judge when to go "on the record."

Jury Visits

The court, on motion of counsel, may direct that the jury be escorted by court officers to inspect the locality of an alleged accident or crime or to view a large piece of heavy equipment. The court reporter may be taken along to report testimony at the scene. In a sense, the court is in session at the scene of the jury visit and all material taken down and reported should be included in the transcript of the trial in the proper sequence of events.

Closing Arguments

After both sides have completed their respective presentations of evidence, the summation to the jury or closing statements or final arguments are presented. The prosecution must deliver the first closing argument. It should cover all evidence and issues raised during the trial. The final arguments will include analysis of the evidence and discussion as to the credibility of witnesses and application of the rules of law that will be given by the judge in his or her charge to the jury.

The defense's closing argument follows the prosecution's. In like manner, the argument covers the points brought out during the trial and the defenses presented by counsel. The closing argument is the defendant's final opportunity to address the jury.

The prosecution has the final word and may opt to present a rebuttal argument. No new issues can be raised; only those issues mentioned in the defense's closing statement can be addressed.

The reporter may not be required to report closing arguments. It depends on the court, the jurisdiction, and the matter being tried. Reporters should always ask what the judge wishes in this regard. The trend is more to have the reporter record everything that occurs from the very start of a case to its completion.

The Court's Instruction to the Jury

After the closing arguments, the judge delivers his or her charge to the jury. The *jury charge,* also called *jury instructions,* sets forth the principles of law governing the case being heard and the application of these principles in reaching a verdict in the case.

The judge ordinarily prepares his or her charge, and the lawyers provide the Court with instructions that they would like to have included within the charge. The Court then meets with the attorneys in chambers before presenting the charge to discuss those instructions proposed by each side.

The jury charge must be reported verbatim by the reporter. It includes any exceptions of counsel to any part of the charge as given by the Court and any further requests made by the attorneys after the charge. If an attorney makes a specific request for an addition to the charge, the Court will rule on that request, either adding it or denying it.

The exceptions made by attorneys during the charge are a vital part of the transcript. Note parenthetically whether the jury is present when discussion involving the charge takes place. Discussions regarding exceptions to the charge out of the presence of the jury may take place in chambers, although the judge will often send the jury out and call the attorneys and reporter to the sidebar or bench to report all exceptions and his or her rulings on them.

The official reporter is usually asked to transcribe a copy of the jury charge for the judge's files. The instructions may or may not be included within the transcript, depending on the request of counsel.

The jury charge is important because more appeals are made from the instructions given to the jury by the Court than from anything that occurred during the trial itself. For this reason, the official reporter must always record the charge exactly as read, not as he or she may think it should be read, because an error or an omitted or added word may reverse a case in the appeals court.

Occasionally, the judge may need to give a supplementary charge because the jury may have sent a note requesting further clarification, or they may indicate that they are deadlocked. If the jury cannot agree and so inform the Court, the judge may give what is known as an *Allen charge,* or *dynamite charge,* which asks that the jurors continue deliberations and try to reach a verdict if they can conscientiously do so.

Jury Deliberations and Verdict

The reporter must note carefully the time when the jury begins its deliberations. Also, record each time that the jury comes back into the courtroom and leaves it again. A proper parenthetical expression must be inserted into the record where appropriate. For example:

(At 3:30 p.m., the jury retired to deliberate on a verdict.)

or

(At 2:00 p.m., the jury retired to commence deliberations.)

Each note sent by the jury is marked as an exhibit, and proper parenthetical expressions must be included in the transcript. While the jury is deliberating, the court reporter must be on call and readily available to read requested material and to report additional instruction or the verdict.

If the official is asked to read to the jury one or several days' testimony of a witness or witnesses, the jury will be brought back into the courtroom. The testimony is read back, but objections, rulings, and material objected to are omitted in reading at this time.

The jury may find for the defendant not guilty in a criminal case or no cause of action in a civil case. Or the jury may find for the plaintiff. If they are unable to reach a verdict, the jury is called a *hung jury* and a mistrial is declared. The case must then be tried again before a new jury.

When the jury reaches a verdict, it is returned to the courtroom to have the verdict announced or *published*. The jury may announce the verdict through its foreperson, or the clerk of the court may read the written and signed verdict of the jury. Sometimes the verdict is sealed and opened at a later session of court in the presence of the parties, counsel, the jurors, the judge, and the reporter. This situation may occur when the verdict is reached at a very late hour at night.

The reporter must record the verdict and the *polling of the jury* if this is requested. The polling of the jury means that each juror is asked whether he or she individually agrees that the final verdict is his or her verdict.

Directed Verdicts and Special Issues

After the plaintiff has rested and again after both sides have rested, either party to a lawsuit may move for a directed verdict if it feels that the case is so one-sided that the judge should make the decision instead of the jury or that only questions of law remain, and the judge should decide them. If the motion is granted for a directed verdict, the Court will dismiss the jury and make the decision based on the evidence.

Sometimes a case is decided on special issues, and a directed or instructed verdict in the lawsuit is based on these issues. In this event, the jury is given a series of questions to answer, and only one decision can result from the answers. Counsel may bring in prepared special issue questions, but the judge may call in the reporter and dictate the special issues to be resolved by the jury.

Reporting the Verdict

All verdicts are reported verbatim by the official reporter and are transcribed as a part of the record. Any comments made by the Court involving sentencing or further action must also be reported, as well as any exceptions made by the attorneys and any requests or motions made by the losing party. Sentencing may follow the decision of the jury immediately or, most likely, it will be postponed until a later date.

Chapter 7

A Typical Civil Jury Trial

Reporting a civil trial is much the same as for a criminal trial, except, of course, the nature of the trial is much different. In a criminal trial, an individual is being tried for a crime he or she committed against society; in a civil trial, one individual sues another individual for a violation of his or her civil rights.

The Pleadings in a Civil Trial

A civil trial begins with the filing of a complaint in an action. The *complaint* is the first pleading filed in a lawsuit. When pleadings are the formal documents that make up the litigation, the complaint is the document that outlines the allegations made by the plaintiff against the defendant. In most states, the complaint and summons must be served on the defendant before a lawsuit commences.

The complaint must contain a statement of jurisdiction, a statement of claim against the defendant showing that the plaintiff is entitled to relief, and a demand for judgment for the relief sought. The *summons* is the legal document that accompanies the complaint and literally "summons" the defendant into court to answer the charges contained in the complaint. The summons usually states that, if the defendant fails to file an answer in the allotted time, a default judgment will be entered against him or her. Once the complaint and summons have been served on the defendant, he or she is given the opportunity to file an answer to the complaint. The answer is a legal document that makes up part of the pleadings.

The defendant's attorney may make a motion to dismiss the complaint. Motions may also request a more definite complaint or a motion to strike certain allegations from the complaint.

The *answer* is the formal written statement in which the defendant states the grounds of his or her defense against the allegations made in the complaint. By law, the defendant must address every issue made in the complaint by either denying or admitting the allegations.

Counterclaims and Cross-Claims

Sometimes the issues revolving around claims, counterclaims, and cross-claims can become confusing. The court reporter must have an appreciation of the differences among them.

A claim is filed by a plaintiff against a defendant for a civil wrong. The defendant, in his or her answer to the complaint, may file a counterclaim against the plaintiff. The *counterclaim* by the defendant alleges that he or she is not at fault, but, in fact, the plaintiff is at fault. The counterclaim involves the original parties to the suit, suing each other around the original litigation.

The original defendant may also file a cross-claim against another party who, by implication, may be called a *codefendant* or *coplaintiff*. In essence, when a claim and counterclaim involve the original parties, the cross-claim involves coparties who may be involved in the original litigation.

If a new party is brought into a lawsuit, he or she is referred to as a *third-party plaintiff* or *defendant*. The third-party plaintiff files a third-party complaint against a third-party defendant. Another name for third-party lawsuits is *impleader*.

Pretrial Activities

A great deal of activity takes place before the plaintiff and defendant have their day in court. Included in these activities are various motions that will be made by either party, the discovery of facts concerning the suit, and maybe even attempts to arbitrate or settle the litigation before trial.

Motions Made before Trial

Before trial proceeds in a civil action, various motions may be made by the plaintiff and defendants. The purpose of these motions is to terminate the litigation before trial in favor of one side over another.

If a defendant fails to answer a complaint within the required time limit as set by statute, the plaintiff may make a motion for default judgment against the defendant. A *motion for judgment on the pleadings* is made by either party for the judge to decide the case based only on the allegations or defenses in the pleadings. A *motion for a summary judgment* is for disposition of the matter, asking the court to rule in favor of a party on the basis that no genuine issues of material fact exist and that the moving party is entitled to judgment as a matter of law.

Discovery

The process of gathering information for trial is called *discovery*. Discovery helps to clarify the factual and legal issues and preserve the testimony of a witness for trial. Basically, five different methods of discovery are used in courts of law: by deposition, by interrogatories, by requests for production of documents, by requests for admission, and by a request for physical and mental examinations of a person. The court reporter is usually involved in the first two methods, deposition and interrogatories.

Pretrial Conferences and Pretrial Orders

When a case is not settled outside court and is ready to proceed to trial, a pretrial conference may be held between the parties to the litigation in order to make certain that all information is correct and that both parties are ready to proceed to the trial stage.

In federal court, actions may include an initial pretrial conference that is held early in the litigation process to set the ground rules by which the litigation will proceed. The final pretrial conference occurs when all parties are ready to proceed with trial.

The final pretrial conference is usually held several weeks before the trial itself. The procedures followed at the pretrial conference differ among jurisdictions. Among the activities that occur during the pretrial conference are stipulations between counsel as to the authenticity of documents, the narrowing of issues, and the exchange of information so that the trial may go smoothly. All questions concerning the admissibility of evidence can be taken care of during pretrial conferences.

Some states require that both sides to a litigation bring to the pretrial conference a statement of their client's contentions, suggested stipulations, a list of exhibits, a list of witnesses, and a list of issues for trial. The attorneys will exchange this information with one another.

The court reporter is usually required to record important parts of the pretrial conferences. Some judges ask that the court reporter be present to report each matter to be discussed and prepare a summary of each case for the Court's consideration and information. The court clerk also maintains a record of what occurred during these conferences and marks off the cases that are settled, stricken, or ordered continued for trial by the judge.

The result of the pretrial conference is the issuance of the pretrial order that sets the trial date, after which the litigation proceeds to trial.

The Civil Trial

The first step in the civil jury trial is similar to the first step in the criminal jury trial, the selection of the jury. The process of selecting the jury from a panel of possible veniremen is the same; however, the number of jurors may vary, depending on whether the trial is in state or federal court and on the local rules of practice.

For example, although 12 jurors are the numbers traditionally required, many districts require only 6 jurors in civil matters. One or two alternate jurors are usually picked in case a member of the original jury becomes sick or is unable to complete his or her duty.

Once the jury has been selected and sworn in, the trial proceeds in the same fashion as a criminal trial. The following is a summary of a typical jury trial:

1. Jury selection
2. Opening statement by plaintiff
3. Opening statement by defendant (or wait until presentation of case)
4. Presentation of plaintiff's case in chief
   a. Calling of witnesses
      direct examination
      cross-examination
      redirect examination
      recross-examination
      further redirect
      further recross
   b. Presentation of physical evidence
      marked for identification
      received into evidence
5. Plaintiff rests
6. Defendant's motion for a directed verdict (in favor of defendant)
7. Presentation of defendant's case in chief
   a. Opening statement if waived at beginning of trial
   b. Calling of witnesses (same as above)
   c. Presentation of physical evidence (same as above)
8. Defendant rests
9. Plaintiff's rebuttal evidence
10. Defendant's surrebuttal evidence
11. Motion for directed verdict by either party
12. Closing argument by plaintiff
13. Closing argument by defendant
14. Plaintiff's argument in rebuttal (if desired)

15. Jury instructions

16. Jury deliberation and verdict

17. Entry of judgment

As in a criminal trial, the court reporter is required to record all statements, motions, objections, rulings, orders, testimony, and colloquy that occur during the trial. In addition, the court reporter is responsible for marking the exhibits and parenthetically noting important activities during the trial.

Posttrial Activities

Two motions that may occur after a trial by jury are a motion for judgment notwithstanding the verdict and a motion for a new trial. These motions must be filed within the time requirements as established by the statutes.

A *motion for a judgment notwithstanding the verdict* is a request by the losing party to set aside the verdict of the jury and to have the judge rule in favor of the losing party. To make a motion for a judgment NOV, the attorney must have made a motion for a directed verdict at the close of all the evidence.

A *motion for a new trial* is made upon the assertion that something occurred during the trial that requires the matter to be tried again. Some examples of grounds for a new trial include the awarding of damages by a jury that are too large or too small, misconduct of an attorney during a trial, failure of the jury to follow the Court's instructions, and newly discovered evidence.

The losing party may also file an appeal to the Court's ruling, provided that the proper time requirements are followed. In an appeal, the original losing party tries to convince the appellate court that the trial court committed a reversible error that entitled the party to a new trial. The *appellant* is the party who files the appeal and seeks to overturn the judgment of the trial court. The party who defends the appeal is the *appellee* or *respondent*.

Chapter 8

Things to Consider before a Trial Begins

Although great amounts of time and energy are exerted in physically recording the spoken word, the reporter still must complete a great deal of work to produce a complete and accurate transcript of the proceedings. The following chapters of this section of the handbook deal with some of those things that court reporters are responsible for doing in putting together a complete transcript.

One might ask how a court reporter knows where his or her job is going to take place. Surely, official and freelance reporters must have some sort of system that will let them know where they have to be and at what time they have to be there.

Preliminary to a case going to trial, a variety of events may or may not occur that would involve official and freelance reporters. A preliminary hearing or a grand jury investigation, both of which are used to determine whether enough evidence exists before the actual trial itself, may occur. Official court reporters may be used to report these matters. In addition, various hearings on motions may be held in court to determine the validity or legality of some matters pertinent to the case. Arraignment proceedings are held when a person is accused of committing a crime. All these preliminary investigatory matters were discussed in previous chapters dealing with the specific jobs that official and freelance reporters might be called on to do.

Now, to get to the matter at hand, how are all these various hearings, trials, examinations, and inquests scheduled?

The Court Calendar

The parties to an action and their attorneys, the judge who hears the particular matter, and the court reporter all have something that they share in common that brings them together on the assigned day, at the assigned time, in the assigned place. The court calendar is used to place cases on the docket for trial. Once placed on the docket, all parties adhere to the schedule.

An official reporter, while assigned to a specific court, may find that he or she will not be in court every day. Preparing transcripts, conducting research, editing, and performing other activities will occupy a reporter's time. Most court reporters have a large wall-sized calendar or desk calendar that corresponds to the court calendar. The court reporter pencils in days when he or she must be in court, as well as other assignments that come up in the daily routine of a court reporter.

Some court reporters work from as many as three different calendars. The large wall-type calendar with large blocks for each day of the month is usually the *master calendar* from which all court assignments can be called. A *desk calendar* might serve as a reminder for daily appointments or important telephone calls that need to be made. A *pocket calendar* might be used for personal or on-the-spot dates, which will later be transferred to the master calendar if needed. At the beginning of each week, and again at the end of each day, an official reporter verifies his or her presence for the next day and makes sure that he or she is in the right place at the right time.

How to Complete the Worksheet

No reporter should ever enter a hearing room, courtroom, or deposition-examining room without a worksheet to record the information required to produce the transcript. The worksheet serves as an essential link between what occurred and what is transcribed. The *worksheet* is a preprinted form that is filled in at the time of the proceeding when everyone is present. Other names for the worksheet are the *information sheet*, *dog sheet*, *dope sheet*, *poop sheet*, and *control sheet*.

No matter what type of reporter and no matter what the reporting job is—a freelancer reporting a deposition or an official reporting a jury trial—a worksheet is needed to help to keep track of what happened during the proceeding.

Different types of worksheets may be used in different circumstances, but they all share certain items in common. Although some reporters use a separate worksheet for depositions and hearings, we will discuss an all-purpose worksheet that can be used in every situation. An example of a worksheet is found in Figure 8.1.

FIGURE 8.1
Worksheet

WORKSHEET

No. ________ Date ________ Term ________ Judge ________

Title ________________________________

APPEARANCES

Plaintiff	Defendant

EXHIBITS

Plaintiff	Ident.	Evd.	Defendant	Ident.	Evd.
P-1			D-1		
P-2			D-2		
P-3			D-3		
P-4			D-4		
P-5			D-5		
P-6			D-6		
P-7			D-7		
P-8			D-8		
P-9			D-9		
P-10			D-10		
P-11			D-11		
P-12			D-12		

WITNESSES

Plaintiff	Direct	Cross	Red.	Rec.	Defendant	Direct	Cross	Red.	Rec.
1.					1.				
2.					2.				
3.					3.				
4.					4.				
5.					5.				
6.					6.				
7.					7.				
8.					8.				
9.					9.				
10.					10.				
11.					11.				
12.					12.				
13.					13.				
14.					14.				
15.					15.				

Arbitrary Abbreviations and Spellings ________________________________

Basic Parts of a Reporter's Worksheet

Each reporter may design a worksheet to meet his or her needs. However, each worksheet contains common elements, which are presented next.

Heading

The top portion of the worksheet should contain spaces for the case number, the date of the examination, the term and judge if it is a trial, the venue, and the title of the case. The *title* of the case is also called the *caption, style*, or *heading*. This information will be necessary to complete the title page of the transcript. Any missing information will lead to a loss of time in getting out the transcript, and any loss of time eventually is a loss of income.

Your name, that is, the name of the reporter, and the date should also be written at the top of the page.

Appearances

Appearances mean the actual presence of the attorneys representing their clients. Appearances are "noted"; that is, they are written on the worksheet and then transferred to the appearances page of the transcript.

Ask each attorney for his or her proper name and law firm. You cannot assume that an attorney listed in the pleadings will be the same attorney who will be present at the proceeding. For this reason, ask each attorney for his or her business card and, in addition, make sure that you know who is his or her client.

A plaintiff or defendant may have more than one attorney present, and insurance carriers or noninterested parties may have attorneys present during a deposition or hearing. Their appearance must also be noted.

Exhibits

You will notice on the worksheet in Figure 8.1 that a place is available for recording plaintiff's and defendant's exhibits. Evidence is usually marked for identification and then received into evidence, although not always. Some exhibits may be marked for identification and never received into evidence. Check off what happens to the exhibits as they are marked, introduced, talked about, and either received or disposed of. Deposition exhibits may be marked for deposition purposes only.

Write a brief description of the exhibits in the space provided and check off when each is marked for identification and received into evidence. In Chapter 13, the different types of exhibits and how to handle them are discussed.

Witnesses

Plaintiffs and defendants call witnesses for their particular side of an issue. In a court trial, the person who called the witness begins with direct examination, followed by cross-examination by the opposing attorney. This examination, in turn, may be followed by redirect and recross and, if necessary, further redirect and further recross examination. In addition, some witnesses may be taken on what is called *voir dire examination*. This type of examination takes place outside of normal direct or cross-examination and is used to clarify a point or prove the expertise of a witness or exhibit.

In depositions the plaintiff, defendant, or witnesses are sworn in and examined by the attorney who called them, followed by examination by the opposing attorney. Some agencies will transcribe all testimony at a deposition as "Examination by Ms. Attorney" and "Examination by Mr. Attorney."

Local Abbreviations

During a particular hearing or deposition, a proper name of a city, company, event, or person may occur over and over again. For example, continual reference may be made to the Houston Rapid Transit. A good reporter will instantly create what is called a *local abbreviation* for the phrase and use that abbreviation instead of writing the entire phrase each time that it is used. For example, the local abbreviation H-RT may be used for Houston Rapid Transit.

Most computer programs allow a reporter to define any abbreviations immediately or whenever he or she has a break in the proceedings. After defining the abbreviation, the word is transcribed the next time it is written. However, if the word is not defined in a dictionary, a notation needs to be made on the worksheet. A notation should be made for all abbreviations that were used by the reporter that are not common or familiar.

Technical terms used during dictation may require using the reporter's creative instinct to make a *short form* for the term. For example, if an expert witness is talking about the "binomial nomenclature" of plants, the abbreviation BI/NOEM might be used instead.

The listing of abbreviations on the worksheet is important for the reporter who may have to report notes that have been in storage for a number of months. A scopist or editor who may be required to edit these notes will find such a listing helpful.

Spelling of Proper Nouns

The correct spelling for all proper nouns, technical terms, unusual terms, and so on, should be included on the worksheet. For example, spell out the surname, street name, and city name for James Gargiloia, 231 Reisenhower Court, Mescalero, New Mexico. Also include the proper spellings for all witnesses, lawyers, and other persons mentioned by name within the matter.

Designation of Counsel and Court

Because someone other than the reporter may transcribe the notes, or they may be transcribed at a later date, all designations that are used for counsel should be noted. This is true even for those transcribing using computer-aided transcription. A place on the worksheet is reserved for such designations that include the shorthand and the name of the person that the designation stands for. This *legend of designations* includes arbitrary abbreviations that the reporter uses. It is important to have so that the software program or the transcriptionist can transcribe the correct name for the person speaking.

Special Instructions and Comments

This portion of the worksheet is where any special instructions that need to be given to a scopist or transcriptionist are written. Also, make any notes to remind you that an attorney has requested something. Some examples of special instructions might be a notation that the transcript needs to be completed before a certain date, that an attorney wants a keyword search throughout the transcript, or that an ASCII disk is to be included along with the printed copy.

Number of Copies and Billing

The final portion of the information sheet may contain information concerning the number of copies that are needed, where they will be sent, and who will be billed for what portion of the invoice. This information is more relevant for depositions and other matters that are held outside the duties of an official reporter.

A freelance reporter needs to know the number of copies to be produced and who will pay for the questioning during a deposition or hearing. This information is normally secured at the end of the deposition before the parties leave.

Official reporters do not charge the Court for the production of the transcript, because that is their job in being employed by the Court. However, attorneys may request copies of the transcript, in which case a statutory fee is charged. This information will be helpful for the person who is responsible for sending out the invoices for the reporter or agency.

Trial Stipulations

Stipulations are agreements between counsel or between counsel and the court as to certain things that occur at the beginning of a trial or during the litigation process. *Trial stipulations* are different from deposition stipulations in the sense that they can occur at any given moment during the trial itself. They are also different in the sense that a stipulation usually pertains to a witness, an exhibit, or some other form of evidence. Usually, trial stipulations can be classified as *stipulations of fact* or *stipulations of evidence*.

Stipulations of Fact

Whenever something is so factual or so obvious that it cannot be disputed, it may be agreed to by all parties as a *stipulation of fact*. The agreement between the attorneys that something is a fact means that no further proof would be required to prove or disprove it.

For example, if an accident occurred on December 24, one party may contend that a snow blizzard occurred on that day. If the opposing party knows that one of the city's worst blizzards occurred on that day, he or she may stipulate to the fact that snow did in fact fall on that day. Such stipulation would mean that no further proof would be necessary.

The stipulation of fact is a spoken statement from the opposing counsel in the form of dialogue that occurs outside the normal question and answer format. This dialogue is called *colloquy*. For example:

BY MS. ATTORNEY:

Q: Please tell us the weather conditions on the day of the accident, December 24.

A: Well, it was snowing.

Q: How much snow fell?

> MR. ATTORNEY: We will stipulate to the fact that a snow blizzard occurred on the day of the accident.
>
> THE COURT: So stipulated.
>
> MS. ATTORNEY: Thank you, your Honor.

BY MS. ATTORNEY:

Q: How fast were you driving?

Stipulations of Evidence

Stipulations of evidence are similar to stipulations of fact, except they might not be as obvious. An example is the stipulation that the credentials of an expert witness who is about to testify are adequate and that testimony does not have to go into why the witness is versed in his or her particular field. If an opposing attorney has prior knowledge about the qualifications of a person testifying, he or she may stipulate as to that person's education and background.

Other stipulations of evidence may occur throughout the trial. For example, stipulations may be made in accepting copies of documents rather than their originals; agreements may be made that certain witnesses will be excused during portions of testimony; or the parties to both sides may stipulate that a deposition or document may be read into the record.

The occurrence and transcription of the stipulation of evidence are similar to stipulations of fact. For example:

BY MR. ATTORNEY:

Q: Please state your name and occupation for the record.

A: My name is Dr. John Hopkins. I'm a licensed doctor of medicine.

Q: And will you be so kind as to go into your education and background, Doctor?

MS. ATTORNEY: That won't be necessary, your Honor. I am quite familiar with the qualifications of Dr. Hopkins because I have been involved in a number of cases where he has been called as a witness. We will stipulate to the good doctor's qualifications.

THE COURT: So stipulated.

BY MR. ATTORNEY:

Q: Doctor, when were you called in on this case?

Chapter 9

How to Administer the Oath, Witness Setup, and Speaker and Examination Identification

The Oath

The use of an oath to attest to one's honesty and integrity goes back to ancient times. People would swear on their lives that they were telling the truth; and if a person went against his word and lied, he would lose his life.

The oath is used in today's society in much the same way. A person who swears to tell the truth is taking an oath that he or she cannot or should not break. An *oath* is a solemn or formal calling on a person's god to witness to the truth of what one says. If a person refuses to take the oath because of a religious belief that prohibits this, then an affirmation is given. An *affirmation* is much like an oath, except that all reference to a god is omitted.

In a court of record, the clerk of the court will usually administer the oath to the witness. Sometimes the judge may administer the oath, or he or she may ask the court reporter to swear in the witness. A freelance reporter will administer the oath during interrogatories, statements, depositions, and some hearings.

How to Administer the Oath of a Witness

The oath is always administered to the witness before any questioning begins. The reporter must know who is responsible for giving the oath. In courts of law, the clerk of the court usually administers the oath. After the bailiff or clerk of the court calls a witness to the stand, he or she stands before the person administering the oath, places his or her left hand on the Bible, raises the right hand, and responds to the question. If the Bible is not used, the witness simply raises his or her right hand and repeats what the administering officer says.

A typical trial oath might be "Do you solemnly swear that the testimony that you shall give in the cause now pending before this Court shall be the truth, the whole truth, and nothing but the truth, so help you God? Then, upon securing an affirmative answer, the clerk of the court may request the witness to be seated and to state his or her name for the record.

If a person refuses to take an oath in court because of religious beliefs, the person affirms that he or she will speak the truth by answering "I do" to the following affirmation: "Do you solemnly affirm that the testimony you are about to offer regarding the cause herein under consideration shall be the truth, the whole truth, and nothing but the truth? This you do under the pains and penalties of perjury?"

How to Show the Oath in the Transcript

The proper transcription of the name of a witness as it appears within the transcript is referred to as the *witness setup*. It refers to the information that appears between the time that a witness is called and when he or she begins testimony. The witness setup includes the calling of the witness, the oath if transcribed, his or her name keyed in spread-heading format, and who the witness was called for or whether he or she is the plaintiff or defendant. The setup may also include asking the witness to state his or her name and address for the record.

Calling forth the witness is usually done by the attorney who has subpoenaed the witness to come to court, but it may also be done by the clerk of the court. The oath or affirmation given to the witness may or may not be transcribed. If it is transcribed, the reporter records what the clerk says and the response by the witness. If the oath is not transcribed, the swearing in of the witness is referred to in the setup.

The name of the witness is indented from the left margin and appears in all capital letters with a space between each letter and three spaces between each word. A comma follows the name, as follows:

J O H N   S.   F L I N T R O C K,

The words that follow the name of the witness clearly define whom the witness was called by or whether he or she is the plaintiff or defendant appearing on his or her own behalf. If the oath was not transcribed, reference is made to the fact that the witness was "duly sworn and testified as follows:" The address of the witness may also be included in the setup.

The dialogue that follows the setup may include the clerk or the attorney requesting the witness to state his or her name and address for the record. The following are examples of setups for witnesses in different situations. Remember, setups may vary from state to state.

Transcription of Oath and Setup for Witness Called by the People

MR. ATTORNEY: People call Roberta R. Roberts.
THE CLERK: Please raise your right hand.
Do you solemnly swear that the testimony you may give in the cause now pending before this court shall be the truth, the whole truth, and nothing but the truth, so help you God?
THE WITNESS: I do.
R O B E R T A   R.   R O B E R T S, called as a witness by the people, testified as follows:
THE CLERK: State your name, please.
THE WITNESS: Roberta R. Roberts

DIRECT EXAMINATION

BY MR. ATTORNEY:

Q: Is it Miss or Mrs. Roberts?

Oath Not Transcribed for Plaintiff as Witness

MS. ATTORNEY: We call as our first witness Mrs. Margaret Crosby. Please take the witness stand.
M A R G A R E T   S.   C R O S B Y, the plaintiff herein, called as a witness on her own behalf, having been duly sworn, testified as follows:
THE CLERK: State your full name, please, ma'am.
THE WITNESS: Margaret Sharon Crosby.

BY MS. ATTORNEY:

Q: Now, Mrs. Crosby, you are the plaintiff in this action, are you not?

Resumption of Witness after Recess

Q: Now, Mr. Black, have you seen Exhibit 8 before?
A: No, sir, I have not.
Q: Would you please. . .

> THE COURT: Excuse me, Ms. Attorney, but if there is no objection, we will take our morning recess. We have been here all morning, and the jury needs to have a break.

> (Whereupon a short recess was taken.)

> THE COURT: You may resume, Ms. Attorney.
> B E R N A R D B. B L A C K, having already been duly sworn, resumed the witness stand and testified further as follows:

CROSS-EXAMINATION *(continued)*

BY MS. ATTORNEY:

Q: Now, before we took our recess, you stated you had not seen Exhibit 8; is that correct, sir?

Transcription of Affirmation for Witness Called by Defendant

> MR. ATTORNEY: We call Mr. Penn.
> THE CLERK: Do you solemnly affirm that the testimony you may give in the cause now pending before this Court shall be the truth, the whole truth, and nothing but the truth, this you do under the pain and penalty of perjury?
> THE WITNESS: I do.
> A D A M W. P E N N, called as a witness by the defendant, testified as follows:
> THE CLERK: Please be seated and state your name and address for the record.
> THE WITNESS: Adam Walter Penn, and I live at 275 Main Street, right here in Centerville.

DIRECT EXAMINATION

BY MR. ATTORNEY:

Q: Are you the brother of the defendant in this case?

A Final Note Concerning the Setup of Witnesses

You will notice that the reporter records what is said by the attorneys, the clerk, the judge, the witness, and so on. What is said may vary from one case to another, but the information is essentially the same. The important consideration is that the reporter record the information and then set up the witness appropriately.

How to Designate Speakers and Note the Types of Examinations

One of the main capacities that differentiates a court reporter from an electronic recording device is the fact that a court reporter has the ability to designate who is speaking at any given time. Tape recorders record all voices, noises, and sounds that are within the vicinity of the microphone. Whatever sound happens to be loudest is going to be recorded over that which has the lowest volume. Thus the sudden movement of a chair over a bare floor at the same time that a crucial answer is given may mean that what gets recorded is the sound that the chair made.

A court reporter has the capacity, if he or she does not hear the witness, to stop the proceedings and ask the witness to repeat what was said. When using a tape recorder, no one would realize that the answer was missing on the tape until it was transcribed. A court reporter makes sure that he or she hears correctly. A court reporter designates between different speaking voices by using a special shorthand outline that stands out clearly in the notes. For example, the shorthand outline STPHAO is used to designate the attorney for the plaintiff.

It is essential that the court reporter identify counsel properly at all times in the record. When the reporter enters the deposition or hearing room, he or she should obtain a business card from each attorney and mark on each whom it represents. These cards should then be used to write the appearances on the information sheet together with their address and phone number. The designation that will be used for each counsel should also be put on the information sheet.

Some reporters find it helpful to keep a small pad of paper on the top of the shorthand machine to write in the designations that are being used for the different attorneys. If the reporter has a sudden lapse of memory, he or she can glance down at the sheet and strike the proper designation for the attorney who is speaking.

Probably, more than one or two attorneys will be present at a deposition or hearing, and you must get the correct names of those who speak into the record for proper transcription. To do this, you need to have a good set of designations with which you are comfortable.

A court reporter needs to be concerned with three different types of designations: (1) the symbols used for questions and answers, (2) the symbols used for speaker identification, and (3) the designations used to identify the type of examination.

Remember, when you read back in court or when you transcribe, you *always* say "question" or "answer" for the symbols and substitute the proper names for the designations in your notes.

Question and Answer Designations

The symbols used to designate the question and the answer are almost universal. The reasons that most reporters use them are because they are easy to write, they stand out in the notes so that they cannot be confused for anything else, and they are easy to transcribe.

STKPWHR-

The symbol for the *question* is the entire left bank of upper and lower keys without any vowels: STKPWHR-. This symbol represents the question that is asked by the lawyer, and it is translated as *Q* along with the proper spacing.

If the question is more than one sentence long, include all punctuation within the question. An ending question mark at the end of the question is not necessary because, if you are using a computer program, it will automatically insert the question mark when it reads the next answer. If you are not using CAT or realtime, you must key the question mark at the end of the question in your transcription. If a question ends in a statement and requires a period, -FPLT for the period needs to be written on the shorthand machine so that it can be correctly transcribed.

-FRPBLGTS

The symbol for the *answer* is the entire right bank of the upper and lower keys without any vowels: -FRPBLGTS. This symbol represents the answer given by the witness and is translated as *A* along with the proper spacing.

If the answer is more than one sentence long, include all punctuation within the answer. An ending period at the end of the answer is not necessary because, if you are using a computer program, it will automatically insert the period when it reads the next question. If you are not using CAT or realtime, you must key the period at the end of the answer in your transcription. If an answer is in the form of a question, you must key the question symbol on the shorthand machine to have it correctly translated.

Speaker Identification Symbols for Colloquy

Speaker identification symbols vary from reporter to reporter. Some reporters prefer one method to another. No matter what system of designation is used, it should stand out very clearly in the notes and be easy to read back and transcribe. Designations used for speaker identification can be classified into three main types: alphabetic, numeric, and syllabic.

Alphabetic Designations

A standard procedure for designating attorneys, the court, and the witness when they speak in colloquy or outside of testimony is to use either the upper or lower bank of keys on the left or right side, together with the vowels. The following are the most common designations:

Shorthand Designation	Represents
STPHAO (upper left + vowels)	Attorney for plaintiff/petitioner/claimant
SKWRAO (lower left + vowels)	Attorney for defendant/respondent/state
EU-FPLT (vowels + upper right)	The court
EU-RBGS (vowels + lower right)	The witness

In addition to these standard designations, the following adaptations can be made for additional counsel who are present or other officers of the court who speak during a proceeding.

Shorthand Designation	Represents
STPHAOE (upper right + long e)	Second attorney for plaintiff/other attorney
STPHAOEU (upper right + long I)	Third attorney for plaintiff/other attorney
SKWRAOE (lower left + long e)	Second attorney for defendant/other attorney
SKWRAOEU (lower left + long i)	Third attorney for defendant/other attorney
STKPWHR-K (question + -K)	Comments by the clerk
STKPWHR-D (question + -D)	Comments by the defendant
STKPWHR-B (questions + -B)	Comments by the bailiff

Numeric Designations

The numeric system of designating counsel in colloquy is very similar to the alphabetic system, except that the number bar is used. The following designations use numeric symbols. Keep in mind that these are only suggestions and that many other suitable combinations can be used.

Shorthand Designation	Represents
1234-6	Attorney for plaintiff/petitioner/claimant
1234-7	Attorney for defendant/respondent
1234-8	The court
1234-9	The witness

In addition to these standard designations, the following adaptations can be made for additional counsel who are present or other officers of the court who speak during a proceeding.

Shorthand Designation	Represents
1-6789	Second attorney for plaintiff/other attorney
2-6789	Third attorney for plaintiff/other attorney
3-6789	Second attorney for defendant/other attorney
4-6789	Third attorney for defendant/other attorney
1234-R	Comments by the clerk
1234-B	Comments by the defendant
1234-G	Comments by the bailiff

In the last three examples given, the letter combinations with the number will only work when you use the bottom bank of keys. Other combinations can be developed from these suggestions.

Syllabic Designations

Some reporters use the first syllable of an attorney's last name to designate whenever that person speaks. The syllable is struck twice on the machine so that it stands out and cannot be confused with any other words or short forms. To use this system, you have to know the attorneys' names.

When transcribing, the proper name for the designation is substituted in the transcript. Caution has to be made for two attorneys who have the same or similar names. For example, if you use the syllabic designation MAK/MAK for Mr. McCormick, you cannot use the same designation for Mr. McConnell. Some reporters will go to the second syllable KON/KON to make the distinction between similar names. Striking the designation twice makes it stand out and defines it as a dictionary entry peculiar to that outline.

The following are examples of syllabic designations:

Shorthand Designation	Represents
FRAOER/FRAOER	Mrs. Freer
FRAIZ/FRAIZ	Ms. Frazier
GOELD/GOELD	Mr. Goldenstein
KLERK/KLERK	The clerk
WI/WI	The witness
DEFT/DEFT	The defendant

One final standby method deserves mentioning. Some reporters designate attorneys by their physical characteristics when all else fails. For example, writing BALD/BALD for the bald-headed lawyer who suddenly starts to interject something during the proceedings, or RED/RED for the attorney dressed in red, and so on. In all cases, caution must be used to substitute the person's name correctly for the designation.

If a number of people are sitting around a conference table, each person can arbitrarily be assigned a number starting from left to right. Each time number 8 speaks, you write 8 to designate the fact that he or she is talking; when number 1 speaks, strike the number 1, and so on. Caution must be used when numbers appear in the transcript.

In all cases, whether you are using the alphabetic, numeric, syllabic, or another method, you must create a legend listing the designations and their proper names. This legend should be placed on the worksheet so that anyone reading or transcribing your notes can determine who is talking.

Examination Designations

After colloquy and before testimony begins, you must designate the type of examination that the witness is undergoing. This usually takes place right after the witness setup. Types of examination and a short description follow:

Examination Type	Conducted By:
Direct examination	Attorney who called witness
Cross-examination	Opposing attorney

Examination Type	Conducted By:
Redirect examination	Attorney who called witness, after cross
Recross-examination	Opposing attorney, after redirect
Further redirect	Attorney who called witness, after recross
Further recross	Opposing attorney, after further redirect
Voir dire examination	Attorney for plaintiff on defendant
Examination	Court or used for noncourt proceedings

Some reporters have their own designations for each type of examination and then follow that designation by the alphabetic, numeric, or syllabic designation for the attorney. An easier way of designating the examination and the speaker is to combine the two into one designation.

The following tables illustrate examples of designations that can be used for combining attorneys with the types of examination that they are conducting. Notice that these designations use -X, -V, and -Q. Some shorthand theories do not have -X, -V, and -Q. If your shorthand theory does not, the following combinations can be used: use -FRPB for -X; use -FB for -V; and use -LGTS for -Q.

Type of Examination by Attorney	Designation
Examination by attorney for plaintiff	STPHAO-X
Direct examination by attorney for plaintiff	STPHAO-D
Cross-examination by attorney for plaintiff	STPHAO-K
Redirect examination by attorney for plaintiff	STPHAO-RD
Recross-examination by attorney for plaintiff	STPHAO-RK
Further redirect examination by attorney for plaintiff	STPHAO-FRD
Further recross-examination by attorney for plaintiff	STPHAO-FRK
Voir dire examination by attorney for plaintiff	STPHAO-V
Return to Q & A mode after colloquy	STPHAO-Q

The same pattern can be followed for the attorney for the defendant, as follows:

Type of Examination by Attorney	Designation
Examination by attorney for defendant	SKWRAO-X
Direct examination by attorney for defendant	SKWRAO-D
Cross-examination by attorney for defendant	SKWRAO-K
Redirect examination by attorney for defendant	SKWRAO-RD
Recross-examination by attorney for defendant	SKWRAO-RK
Further redirect examination by attorney for defendant	SKWRAO-FRD
Further recross-examination by attorney for defendant	SKWRAO-FRK
Voir dire examination by attorney for defendant	SKWRAO-V
Return to Q & A mode after colloquy	SKWRAO-Q

The court's examination can be designated as follows:

Type of Examination by the Court	Designation
Examination	X-EUFPLT
Voir dire	V-EUFPLT
Return to Q & A mode after colloquy	Q-EUFPLT

Reporters who use computer-aided transcription and realtime can program their dictionaries to transcribe these designations with proper line and tabulation spacing, capitalization, and punctuation. The designations can then be job-defined with the proper names for the attorneys.

Chapter 10

How to Report Parentheticals

A *parenthetical,* as used in the English language, is any words included between parentheses or explanatory information interjected, as in a parenthetical expression.

In courtroom reporting, a *parenthetical* is also an expression or a statement that gives more information or explains a situation. Parentheticals are seldom dictated, but they are added by court reporters as directions, explanations, or movements that occur during proceedings. In a very real sense, parentheticals add explanatory notes to transcripts that are necessary to create an entire picture for those who were not physically present at the proceeding.

A court reporter can be compared to a photographer; that is, he or she produces a picture of everything important that occurs during any proceeding that is reported, verbal as well as visual. Not everything in the record will be spoken words. A complete transcript of any proceeding contains not only the verbatim record of the spoken words, but also such parenthetical notations that are necessary to complete the total picture of what happened. These entries are just as essential to the record as any other part of the transcript and sometimes more so.

Parentheticals can be divided into two broad categories: parenthetical directions or notations and question-and-answer parentheticals. *Parenthetical notations* are statements or explanations that are complete sentences. They begin with a capital letter, have a subject and predicate, and end in terminal punctuation or a colon included within the parentheses. All lines are indented from the left margin at least two or three tabs or 10 to 15 spaces; the right margin may also be indented.

On the other hand, a *question-and-answer parenthetical* is considered a part of a question or answer and falls within the verbatim question or answer. It may be one or two words that indicate or clarify an answer. It does not begin with a capital letter and does not end in terminal punctuation, because it is considered a part of the question or answer itself.

Parenthetical Notations

The following paragraphs list various parenthetical notations that should be included in transcripts and describe how they should be indicated.

Noting the Presence of the Defendant

In criminal matters, a court reporter should note on the record the fact that the defendant is present with counsel. The notation should read as follows:

(The defendant was personally present, together with counsel.)

73

In addition, the record should always begin with the fact that the proceeding is held in open court; that is, in the presence of the jury and attorneys.

> (The matter was heard in open court.)

Voir Dire Parenthetical

When a jury trial is required, the entire jury panel is sworn. After swearing in, the attorneys and judge may ask questions of the panel to select the men and women who will sit on the jury. This examination of prospective jury members is known as *voir dire examination.*

The oath that is given by the clerk of the court reads something like this: "You, and each of you, do solemnly swear that you will well and truly answer such questions as may be asked of you touching upon your qualifications to serve as trial jurors in the case now pending before this Court, so help you God." This statement may not be reported verbatim, but may be noted by the following parenthetical:

> (The jurors were duly sworn for voir dire examination.)

After the voir dire examination and the exercise of various challenges, the jury is selected along with the alternates. The clerk of the court will again swear in the jury and alternates using words similar to these: "You, and each of you, do solemnly swear that you will well and truly try the cause now pending before this Court and a true verdict render therein according to the evidence and the instructions of the Court, so help you God." A proper parenthetical might be the following:

> (The jurors and alternates were duly sworn to try this case.)

In some instances, the voir dire examination may be required to be reported and transcribed. The reporter needs to verify the custom of the court to determine the standard protocol to follow in terms of jury selection. If it is transcribed, the questions and answers will be reported and transcribed. If the jury selection is not reported and transcribed, the transcript will start with a parenthetical similar to this one:

> (A jury was impaneled and sworn.)

Invoking the Rule

At any time during a trial of a case, either party may ask that a witness be sequestered or removed from the courtroom so that he or she will not hear the testimony of other witnesses. This request to have a witness sequestered is known as "invoking the rule." The rule is invoked to prevent witnesses from changing their testimony because of what they hear others testify. The parenthetical may read like any of the following examples:

> (The rule was invoked, and the Court instructed the witness as follows:)

or

> (The rule having been invoked, the Court gave the following instructions:)

or

> (The witness having been ordered sequestered, the Court gave the following instructions:)

After the Court's instructions to the witnesses explaining what it means to invoke the rule or sequester the witnesses, the following parenthetical will be added:

> (The witness left the courtroom.)

Reading of the Indictment

In a criminal case, when the defendant does not waive the reading of the indictment, the parenthetical may read:

(The indictment was read in open court.)

At an arraignment proceeding where the indictment is read and the defendant enters a plea, if the court reporter is not required in his or her jurisdiction to transcribe all the proceedings, the parenthetical may read like the following:

(The indictment was read and the defendant entered his/her plea of guilty/not guilty.)

If the defendant waives the reading of the indictment, the parenthetical may read:

(The defendant waived the reading of the indictment and entered his/her plea of guilty/not guilty.)

Opening and Closing Statements

Counsels on each side of a case are entitled to make opening statements detailing what they intend to prove and closing statements summing up what they believe the evidence has shown relative to their sides of the case.

In some jurisdictions and in some cases, the reporter may be required to report and transcribe the opening and closing statements. In others, the reporter may record them but not transcribe them. Whatever the custom in your court, make sure that you understand it and follow it.

If opening and closing statement transcriptions are ordered as a part of the transcript, transcribe them in their entirety. However, a lawyer who orders an appeal transcript usually omits these unless they are germane to the appeal.

If the opening statements and closing arguments are to be omitted from the transcript, a parenthetical may be included as follows:

(Mr. Attorney made an opening statement on behalf of the plaintiff/government/state/petitioner.)

and

(Ms. Attorney made an opening statement on behalf of the defendant/respondent.)

or

(Mr. Attorney made a closing statement on behalf of the plaintiff/government/state/petitioner.)

and

(Ms. Attorney made a closing statement on behalf of the defendant.)

Bench Conferences or Sidebars

An attorney will often make the following request: "May we approach the bench, your Honor?" The judge will grant permission, and the lawyers will approach the bench. The judge and the attorneys will decide whether they wish to have this *sidebar* or other *bench conferences* reported. The reporter customarily takes his or her shorthand machine up to the bench and reports what is said among the judges and lawyers, but be prepared for the judge to say that the reporter does not need to record what is being said.

The purpose of a bench conference is usually to clarify a legal point or to discuss something outside the hearing of the jury. Some court reporters have a second machine located near the bench. Some use a tripod that allows them to stand while recording the conference, and others set the shorthand machine right on the bench and record the conference while standing. If the reporter is recording on disk, he or she will have to use the same machine, being careful not to unplug or trip over cords, extensions, or computer cables. Real-time writers will have to consider sidebars and bench conferences in terms of what to include in the real-time transcript.

The reporting of an *on-the-record bench conference* or *sidebar* can be difficult because most people are speaking in a lower than normal tone. In addition, some speakers may have their backs or sides to the reporter. If necessary, have attorneys and the judge repeat what you do not hear because the conferences are very important.

The following parentheticals may be used for reporting an on-the-record sidebar:

(A conference was held at the bench without the hearing of the jury as follows:)

or

(The following proceedings were had at the bench by Court and counsel out of the hearing of the jury:)
THE COURT: State your motion.
MR. ATTORNEY: I move to strike the testimony on the ground that it is immaterial.
THE COURT: Overruled.

Following this ruling, a proper parenthetical would be:

(Thereupon, the following proceedings continued within the hearing of the jury:)

or

(The following took place within the presence and hearing of the jury:)

If the conference was not reported, a simple parenthetical noting the fact that a discussion occurred may be used as follows:

(A conference was held at the sidebar between counsel and the Court.)

or

(A conference was held at the bench between counsel and the Court.)

Parentheticals Relating to the Jury

A reporter must note the presence or absence of the jury during the trial proceedings. Many conferences, motions, voir dire questioning by the Court and counsel, discussions as to legal points and admissibility of evidence, considerations of requested jury instructions, and so on, require hearings outside open court. Many of these items must be reported by a court reporter, but they could be grounds for appeal if the jury is present during the discussion.

The record should contain the proper parentheticals at the start of each session and at such times throughout the proceedings as required. Examples of proper parentheticals follow:

(The following took place within the presence and hearing of the jury:)

or

(The following took place without the presence and hearing of the jury:)

or

(The jury left the courtroom, after which the following proceedings were had:)

or

(The jury returned to the courtroom, after which the following proceedings were had:)

The judge may excuse the jury upon motion of either counsel or of his or her own volition. If the jury leaves the courtroom, a proper parenthetical should be used, along with one indicating their return and the continuation of the proceedings.

(The jury left the courtroom.)

and

> (The jury returned to the courtroom, after which the following proceedings were had before the Court and jury:)

Sometimes the judge will hear legal arguments toward the end of the day or will wish to discuss points of law with counsel that will be reported on the record but outside the hearing of the jury. Your parenthetical should be similar to the following:

> (The jury was excused for the day, after which the following proceedings were had before the Court in this matter:)

If the jury is excused so that other proceedings may be held or other matters settled, a parenthetical may read as follows:

> (The jury was excused, and another matter was heard before the Court.)

When a jury is excused for lunch or dinner or if they are excused at the end of the day, proper parentheticals may be the following:

> (At 6:15 p.m., the jurors were escorted to dinner, after which they returned to the jury room and continued deliberating.)

and

> (At 5:45 p.m., the jury was excused for the day.)

Sometimes the jury will send a note to the Court requesting clarification on a legal matter or the reading of testimony. They will be ushered into the courtroom, and the following parentheticals may be used:

> (In open court, in the presence of the jury, the following occurred:)

or

> (Upon the request of the jury, the direct examination of Mr. Witness was read to the jury.)

When the jury returns to their deliberations, the following form of parenthetical may be used:

> (At 5:45 p.m., the jury returned to the jury room to deliberate.)

If no episodes intervene between the retiring of the jury to deliberate and the rendering of the verdict, the parenthetical used would be condensed into one statement as follows:

> (Thereupon, the jury retired to the jury room to consider their verdict. Thereafter, and on the 12th day of November, 1999, the jury returned into court at 9:00 a.m., and the following proceedings were had:)

Polling the Jury

Once the jury returns a verdict, the losing party may request that each jury member be polled. This *polling of the jury* is a formal question to each jury member as to whether he or she agrees with the verdict, which requires a verbal response on the part of each juror.

The reporter records all conversation surrounding the verdict and, if the defense counsel requests polling of the jury, the reporter may transcribe the entire polling if required by the Court to do so, but usually the following parenthetical is used:

> (Each juror, upon being asked by the Court, "Is that your verdict?" answered in the affirmative.)

Excusing the Jury

At the end of each jury case, the Court thanks the jury for their dedication and service to the judicial process. The jury is then excused and the following parenthetical may be used:

> (The jury was excused.)

or

> (The jury was dismissed from duty.)

In Chambers Hearings

Many legal matters are heard in the judge's chambers. These *in camera* hearings are important and may require the presence of a court reporter to record and transcribe what occurs. A parenthetical should indicate that the hearing was held in the judge's chambers. A proper parenthetical may be as follows:

> (The following proceedings were had in chambers:)

or

> (The following proceedings were had in chambers, the defendant being personally present:)

Identifying Recesses

Most courts take a midmorning or midafternoon recess. Short recesses may be noted by using any of the following parentheticals:

> (A recess was taken, after which the following proceedings were had:)

or

> (A recess was taken.)

The times may be noted, especially if the recess is a noon recess, which may be longer than the midmorning or midafternoon recess.

> At 12:30 p.m., the noon recess was taken, after which the following proceedings were had:)

or

> (At 10:35 a.m., a 20-minute recess was taken.)

and

> (At 10:55 a.m., the court was reconvened.)

When court is adjourned for the day, such adjournment may be noted with any of the following parentheticals:

> (On Tuesday, March 22, 1999, at 5:30 p.m., Court was recessed until Wednesday, March 23, 1999, at 9:30 a.m., and after such recess the following proceedings were had before the Court and jury:)

or

> (Thereupon, the proceedings were adjourned at 5:00 p.m. until the following day, June 9, 1999, at 9:00 a.m.)

or

> (At 5:30 p.m., Court was adjourned until the following day, May 16, 1999, at 9:30 a.m.)

or

(Court adjourned at 6:15 p.m.)

Following a recess or adjournment, a witness who has not completed his or her testimony may be required to resume the stand to testify. The transcript should show that this is the case, as follows:

(After a short recess, the witness resumed the stand and testified as follows within the hearing of the jury:)

or

(Court adjourned for the day.)

(Court reconvened in the presence of the jury.)

(The witness resumed the stand and testified as follows:)

Off-the-Record Discussions

During depositions and court cases, frequent off-the-record discussions are held. These are not recorded by the court reporter, although he or she should remain alert and ready to go back on the record. Sometimes an attorney may assume that the reporter knows that they are back on the record and begin talking, thinking that what he or she says is being reported. If the reporter is in doubt, he or she should ask, "Is this discussion for the record?"

The following forms of parentheticals may be used:

(An off-the-record discussion was held.)

or

(A discussion was held off the record.)

Any discussion requested to be on the record should be recorded during the recess with a notation that the jury was not present and that recess was being held.

Parentheticals Relating to Marking and Receiving Exhibits

All exhibits are usually marked for identification; that is, they are marked and then testimony revolves around the exhibit. Once it proves to be beneficial to the case, the attorney who had the exhibit marked for identification will ask that it be marked and received into evidence. An exhibit may be marked for identification and never received into evidence, but very seldom is it received into evidence without first being marked for identification. Deposition exhibits are usually marked for identification purposes only and then re-marked when they are reintroduced at the time of trial.

The general rule to follow in marking exhibits is to put a parenthetical immediately after the request to mark or receive it. The parenthetical contains complete sentences that include the party offering the exhibit, the number of the exhibit, a brief description of the exhibit, and whether it is being marked or received into evidence.

In Chapter 13 you will learn how to physically mark various exhibits. As a rule, plaintiff's exhibits are usually numbered, and defendant's exhibits use capital letters. Multipage exhibits or pages within a file may be marked with a number and letter as in Plaintiff's Exhibit No. 1-A through 1-H. If more than 26 defendant's exhibits are used, double letters may be used as in Defendant's Exhibit A-A or Defendant's Exhibit A-D.

Some reporters use an initial that corresponds to the party introducing the exhibit, followed by a number. For example, Plaintiff's exhibits would be P-1, P-2, and so on; Defendant's exhibits would be D-1, D-2; and Government's exhibits would be G-1, G-2, and so on.

Be sure to put into your transcribed record the correct parenthetical expression for State's Exhibit, Government's Exhibit, Plaintiff's Exhibit, Defendant's Exhibit, Appellant's Exhibit, Respondent's Exhibit, and so on.

The normal punctuation for exhibit markings is to capitalize the identification, use the possessive form, and use the abbreviation No. for number; for example, Plaintiff's Exhibit No. 456. If the exhibit identification is a letter, it is usually referred to by letter only; for example, Defendant's Exhibit C. These standards may vary from court to court; therefore, the reporter must verify the local protocol within the court jurisdiction.

The following are examples of proper parentheticals for exhibits:

(Plaintiff's Exhibit No. 1, a lease dated May 1, 1999, was marked for identification.)

(The following exhibits were marked for identification: Plaintiff's Exhibit No. 16, a check dated June 30, 1999; and Plaintiff's Exhibit No. 17, an envelope addressed to Martin Company, postmarked June 30, 1999.)

(Defendant's Exhibit C, a ledger sheet for the May Company, was received into evidence, and a copy of the same appears in this record at the page shown in the index.)

(The following exhibits were received into evidence: Defendant's Exhibit A, an itemized sheet showing the assets of the defendant; Defendant's Exhibit B, a liability sheet; and Defendant's Exhibit C, a balance sheet for the defendant's company.)

Sometimes photocopies of original documents are substituted by agreement for original exhibits. This substitution occurs in the case of official documents, licenses, or certificates. A proper notation should be made as follows:

(The original of Plaintiff's Exhibit No. 4, a divorce decree dated August 16, 1999, was withdrawn by agreement, and a copy of same was substituted and identified as Plaintiff's Exhibit No. 4-A.)

Remembering the purpose of exhibits, that is, to paint an entire picture of the proceedings, a parenthetical notation is usually made whenever the exhibits are handed between counsel, judge, and jury. Some examples follow:

(Defendant's Exhibit A-G, a photograph of the intersection involved in the accident, was circulated among the jurors for their examination.)

or

(Plaintiff's Exhibit Nos. 1 and 2, accident photographs, were handed to the jury for their examination.)

or

(The exhibits were handed to the jury.)

Sometimes, listing and defining the exhibits in the parenthetical are not feasible. However, they are always listed in the index. The parenthetical may look something like this:

(Government's Exhibits 12 through 64, previously marked for identification, were received into evidence.)

Parentheticals Showing Action

At times, parentheticals regarding actions of counsel such as the following are needed:

(Counsel conferred briefly.)

(Counsel examined the exhibit.)

(Counsel handed the exhibit to the witness.)

(Counsel read the document.)

(Counsel handed the document to the Court.)

(Mr. Attorney read to the jury from Defendant's Exhibit A as follows:)

When a witness is asked to mark an × on a map or plat or some similar request is made, an appropriate parenthetical would be:

(The witness complied.)

(The witness indicated on the map.)

Frequently, the witness is asked to step down from the witness stand to illustrate some point on a map, chart, blackboard, or for some other similar purpose. The following parentheticals would be appropriate:

(The witness left the stand and went to the blackboard.)

(The witness left the stand and stepped over to the plat.)

After a witness completes a request away from the stand and he or she returns to the stand, the following notation should be made:

(The witness returned to the stand.)

When a witness's testimony is interrupted to allow another legal matter to be considered or some other testimony given, the following parenthetical is considered proper:

(The witness was excused temporarily.)

When the witness completes his or her testimony, the parenthetical would read:

(Witness excused.)

or

(The witness left the stand.)

Parentheticals Indicating the Use of Videos or Slides

Videos or color slides are often presented during the course of a trial, requiring the use of a video playback unit and monitor or a projector and screen. You should note its usage as follows:

(A VCR and monitor were set up in the courtroom, and Plaintiff's Exhibit No. 5 was played for the Court and jury.)

Parentheticals in Interpreted Proceedings

Non-English-speaking witnesses may testify through an interpreter who is sworn first by the clerk. The oath for the interpreter says that the interpreter will truly interpret the testimony for the person. The clerk then administers the oath to the witness through the interpreter. Your record will show:

(José Jiminez Gonzales was sworn as the Spanish interpreter by the clerk of the court. The witness was duly sworn through the Spanish interpreter.)

The transcript would then continue as usual with the understanding that all answers made by the witness and all questions put to the witness were through the interpreter. If the witness's answers are in English or broken English, it is noted on the record with a parenthetical within the answer. An example of this type of parenthetical is given in the section entitled Question-and-Answer Parentheticals.

Depositions Read into the Record

Depositions are read into the record when witnesses are unavailable or deceased. The reading of the deposition may be done by the original attorneys who made the depositions. Ordinarily, the reporter merely notes the reading with a parenthetical; however, if an interruption, objection, colloquy, or ruling occurs during the reading, it must be noted by the reporter.

Some attorneys may indicate that they want the entire reading in the record, in which case the judge will ask that it be included and transcribed. An example of a deposition being read and noted parenthetically would be the following:

> (Mr. Attorney read the deposition of Mrs. Witness to the jury.)

or

> (Mr. A. Attorney and Ms. B. Attorney read to the jury the direct- and cross-examination from the deposition of Dr. Witness.)

A notation of an objection might be handled in the following manner:

> (Mr. A. Attorney read to the jury from page 4, line 9, to page 56, line 2, of the deposition of Mrs. Witness.)
> MR. B. ATTORNEY: That last question is objected to as immaterial to the issues in this case.
> THE COURT: Sustained.
> (Mr. A. Attorney continued reading from page 56, line 3, to page 102, line 14.)

Readback Parentheticals

Whenever an attorney or judge asks a court reporter to read back questions and answers, it is called a *readback*. Readbacks are requested during depositions and hearings to a great extent. Technically, any readback situation is at the discretion of the Court and should receive his or her permission. Some judges insist that the attorneys make all requests for readbacks directly to them; and they, in turn, direct the reporter to read. Follow the procedures used in your court jurisdiction.

Questions and answers that are read back immediately can use a parenthetical similar to the following:

> (The last question and answer were read by the reporter.)

or

> (The last question was read back by the reporter.)

or

> (The last answer was read back by the reporter.)

In most cases, you do not report what you read back verbatim in the parenthetical, but merely report the fact that you read the requested material and then continue with the testimony. When a portion of the record that is not immediate is read back, a definite reference to the material read must be made in the transcript so that no misunderstanding about what occurred and what was read back is possible. One way of handling the readback is by direct reference to the page and line number, but this information can only be filled in after the transcript is completed and you know where the questions are located.

Another way of handling a readback is to literally insert the question or answer within the parenthetical. Of course, this method presents a problem if the material is lengthy.

The following are examples of parentheticals that might be used:

> (The questions and answers on page 52 of this transcript, beginning on line 21 and ending on page 54, line 13, were read back.)

or

> (The question was read by the reporter as follows: "What did you see on the second occasion that you encountered the defendant on the night of May 24, 1999?")

or

> (The first six questions and answers contained in the direct testimony of John W. Witness were read back by the reporter.)

Sometimes the reporter will be requested to read back objections or rulings, in which case the record will read as follows:

> (The objection was read by the reporter.)

or

> (The ruling of the Court was read back by the reporter.)

Jury Deliberations and Readbacks

After all evidence and arguments have been presented, the judge will send the jury to a jury room to deliberate and arrive at a verdict. In federal court, the custom is to swear in marshals who escort the jury members to their room. An appropriate parenthetical would read:

> (Two marshals were duly sworn.)

When the jury retires to make their deliberations, it is noted as follows:

> (At 3:30 p.m., the jury retired to deliberate on a verdict.)

or

> (At 3:30 p.m., the jury retired to commence deliberations.)

When a portion of a witness's testimony is read to the jury during their deliberations, a parenthetical will be used to note that fact. When reading back to the jury, the reporter will read back only the questions and answers that are germane to the jury. You will leave out objections and rulings, questions to which objections were sustained, and questions and answers that were ordered stricken from the record. In most cases, you will have time to "prepare" your notes for readback to the jury. Parentheticals that may be used for readback to the jury include the following:

> (The testimony of Mary W. Witness was read to the jury by the reporter.)

or

> (The cross-examination of John W. Witness was read to the jury by the reporter.)

or

> (Portions of the testimony of Mary W. Witness were read to the jury by the reporter.)

or

> (The requested material was read.)

In some cases, when the transcript has already been completed, as in the case of realtime translation, the reporter may read from the transcript. An appropriate parenthetical would be the following:

> (The reporter read to the jury from the transcript of May 3, 1999, page 2, line 3, through page 28, line 14, inclusive.)

When a note is written by the foreperson of the jury and sent to the court requesting certain pieces of evidence, the reporter will make a parenthetical within the transcript when the event occurred and mark the note as a Court exhibit:

> (A note from the jury was marked as Court Exhibit No. 1.)

Question and Answer Parentheticals

Whenever a parenthetical is considered a part of a question or answer, it becomes a part of that question or answer and is not keyed on a separate line. The following are examples of these types of parentheticals:

Descriptive One-Word Parentheticals

A one-word parenthetical that describes some sort of activity or action is included within the question or answer. It is not capitalized, and any punctuation falls outside the parentheses. Examples of these parentheticals and how they are used follow:

Q: Where does it hurt you?

A: Right here (indicating).

or

Q: How did you push the papers off the desk?

A: Like this (demonstrating).

or

Q: Please read the last paragraph.

A: Okay (reading).

or

Q: Will you please draw a line showing your movement?

A: Yes, sir (drawing).

The reporter must be careful to assure that these parentheticals are not too descriptive; that is, the reporter is not to put in his or her own interpretation about what the person is doing. The reporter should not write (indicating the left side of his or her face) or (demonstrating a quick movement of the left hand). Such descriptions are judgments on the part of the reporter. If clarification is needed, and it usually is, the attorney or judge will clarify the activity in a series of questions or statements. For example, the attorney may make a statement such as, "Let the record show that the witness is indicating the left side of his face."

Phonetic Spellings

Occasionally, a court reporter is unable to verify the spelling of a proper name or a technical word. Customarily, a parenthetical is inserted after the name or term that indicates that the word is spelled phonetically, that is, according to how it sounds. This method is not to be used as an excuse for not researching names or terms; it is reserved only for those words or names for which you honestly cannot find a spelling.

For example, a witness may say, "I believe his name was Boris Vanitschlewski." When asked for the spelling, the witness may not know, the attorney may not, and the name is not listed in a local telephone directory. In such a case, the transcription would appear as follows:

Q: What is his name, please?

A: I believe his name was Boris Vanitschlewski (phonetic).

The Use of [sic]

Sometimes an attorney may make a mistake in stating a person's name or using a date that is so blatant that anyone who looks at the record will know what it should be. For example, if a witness has identified himself as John Doe and the attorney directs the first few questions to "Mr. Doe," but then suddenly addresses him as "Mr. Roe," the error is obvious; the reporter knows what the attorney meant. Some reporters may correct the obvious error of an attorney because she is not under oath. Others will place the expression [sic] within brackets after the obvious error. Check with the protocol for your particular court jurisdiction.

The word [sic] is the Latin word for *thus* or *so*. It is used to indicate that the word or phrase preceding the parentheses is not a mistake and is to be read as it stands.

Caution must be used to transcribe exactly what a witness says. Because a witness has sworn to tell the truth, a witness's answer must never be changed. However, the response of a witness may occasionally require the use of the bracketed [sic]. For example, when a witness uses a totally different word from what he or she means, transcribe what was said, but use [sic] as follows:

Q: What did your wife do when she saw the body of the man lying in her bed?

A: Well, she began to scream louder and louder, she began ranting and raving and became very historical [sic].

Speaker Identification

Some courts and freelance agencies, as a standard practice, will indicate in parentheses who is doing the questioning after a lengthy break has occurred within an examination. In other words, if the testimony is interrupted by an objection, discussion, ruling, or further discussion and the testimony resumes, the reporter will indicate who is asking the questions. Some reporters indicate the name of the examiner in all capital letters at the left margin as follows:

BY MR. ATTORNEY:

Q: Now, I will ask you that question once more. Were you present during the signing of Mr. Lee's will?

A: Yes, sir.

Other reporters will use the parenthetical as follows:

Q: (By Mr. Attorney) Now, I will ask you that question once more. Were you present during the signing of Mr. Lee's will?

A: Yes, sir.

A final example of a parenthetical used for speaker identification is the following:

Q: BY MR. ATTORNEY: Where were you when you heard the noise?

A: I was on the back porch, watering the flowers.

English Answers in Interpreted Proceedings

At times, a witness testifying through an interpreter answers in English rather than in her or his native language. Some reporters put an asterisk before or after the *A* in which the witness responds in English. At the bottom of the page, they place an asterisk followed by the words "Answers of the witness in English."

Other reporters denote answers in English or through an interpreter by using a parenthetical phrase within the answer as follows:

Q: Have you ever been involved in any other maritime accidents?

A: (In English) Five times. (Through the interpreter) I slipped on the dunnage in a stow twice, was in a chain fall accident once, and fell myself twice.

Answers That Have No Response

Sometimes witnesses reply to a question by physically nodding or shaking the head yes or no. The court reporter never makes a determination as to whether a person shakes his or her head in the negative or nods his or her head in the affirmative. It is up to the attorney to question the witness as to whether he or she means yes or no. Some lawyers say something to the effect, "Let the record show that the witness is shaking her head in the negative." Other attorneys will instruct the witness to give an audible response. For example:

Q: Where did you go next?

A: (No audible response.)

or

Q: Did you participate in the riot?

A: (Witness nods head).

>   MR. ATTORNEY: Mr. Witness, the reporter cannot record the nodding of your head, you'll have to answer the question with a yes or no.

>   THE WITNESS: Yes.

BY MR. ATTORNEY:

Q: Thank you. Now, how did you participate in the riot?

A Final Word of Caution about Parentheticals

Another type of parenthetical should be mentioned, because you may be called on to use these during the course of your career. These parentheticals seldom, if ever, appear in court and deposition work. They are restricted almost entirely to transcripts of public addresses, speeches, convention proceedings, conferences, and meetings. In addition, they are used in closed captioning and reporting proceedings for the hearing impaired when it is necessary to capture events that would add to the total picture of the occurrence.

These parenthetical expressions consist of a word or phrase immediately following a transcribed sentence, but within a paragraph. The most frequently used words of this nature are (*laughter*) and (*applause*). For example:

>   "I am very happy to announce the winner of the sales contest, Harry Bascom (*applause*)."

You will find that other parenthetical remarks will be required from time to time to suit particular circumstances. With common sense and a little forethought, you will be able to devise these as required, keeping in mind that each parenthetical comment should be clear, concise, and essential to the understanding of what occurred during a proceeding.

If in doubt, the best thing to do is to ask an experienced court reporter. He or she likely has already faced the exact situation that you are facing and will be able to give you a quick and precise answer.

Chapter 11

How to Report Motions

In legal terminology, a *motion* is a request by an attorney for the judge to make a specific ruling or take some sort of action regarding the request. Motions are the "mode and method" of conducting business in the world of litigation.

Some judges will hold a regularly scheduled *motion day* for the purpose of hearing general motions. A motion may be either written or verbal. In court proceedings, the motions are usually spontaneous and verbal. Other motions made before or after a trial may be written motions.

Motions will be argued by having both sides present their case for granting or not granting the request. Many motions and their arguments are presented during recesses or in chambers before court begins. In some cases, the judge may dismiss the jury so that motions can be argued outside the presence of the jury.

Motions have to be reported *verbatim* (word for word), and all arguments by opposing counsel and rulings by the judge are important matters that need to be recorded and transcribed accurately. The reporter may obtain a copy of the motion, as well as the briefs that each attorney has prepared in arguing his or her case, to verify the transcript.

Different Types of Motions

Some of the most common motions that the court reporter should be familiar with are discussed in this section.

Motion in Limine

The Latin phrase *in limine* means "at the beginning." A *motion in limine* is a motion made at the outset of a trial in an attempt to suppress damaging or inadmissible evidence that the other side may want to use. Such motions ask the Court to prevent opposing parties, their counsel, and their witnesses from presenting some evidence until its admissibility is decided on outside the hearing of the jury.

Motion for a Bill of Particulars

A *bill of particulars* is a document made by the plaintiff at the request of the defendant. It is a detailed account of the charges made against the defendant. A defendant's attorney frequently makes a motion for a bill of particulars when the plaintiff in a civil or criminal case has claimed the cause of action in a vague, general, or indefinite manner.

Motion to Have Claimant Medically Examined

Defense attorneys often make a motion to have a claimant examined by an impartial medical expert in a personal injury case, because many cases can be settled as a result of such an examination. Even if the case is not settled, the defense attorney can prepare more adequately to refute the medical testimony presented by the plaintiff.

Motion for Change of Venue

Motions for a change of venue are routine when a case has had widespread publicity, and the defendant's attorney does not believe that the defendant can receive a fair trial in the place of original jurisdiction. The *venue* is the place where the case is tried, that is, the geographical location of the court.

Motion to Disqualify a Judge

A judge may disqualify himself or herself from a case, or a lawyer may make a motion to have the judge disqualified. Disqualification usually occurs because the judge may have knowledge of the case or may have even represented one of the parties in previous cases. The disqualification of a judge is done in the interest of fairness and justice.

Motion for Continuance of Case

A motion for a *continuance of case* is simply a request to postpone the trial until a later date or court session. A motion for continuance is made for a variety of reasons, including the substitution of counsel, unavailability of witnesses, military services of parties or witnesses, absence of material evidence that can be obtained in the future, and so on. Sometimes continuances are set by the Court's own motion.

Motion for Amendment of the Pleadings

Either counsel may make motions for an *amendment of the pleadings*, including addition or deletion of parties to an action or severance of defendants from jointly tried cases.

Motion for Summary Judgment

If, during preparation of a case, either party decides that no real issue of fact is to be decided at trial, a motion for *summary judgment* may be made requesting the Court to grant judgment in favor of the party filing the motion. The motion is usually accompanied by affidavits or answers to discovery, stating undisputed facts that entitle the party to a judgment in his or her favor.

The party filing such a motion has the burden of proving that no genuine issue of fact is in dispute, and the opposing party has time to respond. The Court usually holds a hearing on such a motion and if the Court determines that no fact issue exists, judgment is granted for the moving party. If the motion is not granted, the case is then tried on its merits; that is, the case will be tried in the normal sequence of litigation events.

Motion to Dismiss for Want of Jurisdiction

If a defendant feels as though the Court does not have the proper authority to hear or decide a case, the attorney for the defendant will make a motion to *dismiss for want of jurisdiction*.

Motion to Dismiss for Lack of Prosecution

After a case has been on file for a long period with no action by the plaintiff's attorney to prepare for trial, the defendant's attorney may make a motion to dismiss for lack of prosecution.

Motion for Nonsuit

A plaintiff's motion requesting the Court to dismiss the case either with prejudice or without prejudice is referred to as a *motion for nonsuit*. In some jurisdictions, this motion is referred to as a *voluntary dismissal*. When such a motion is granted without prejudice, the plaintiff may later refile the same action; but if the case is dismissed with prejudice, the plaintiff cannot again file the same cause of action. In federal court, this motion is called a *motion for dismissal pursuant to Rule 41 of the Federal Rules of Civil Procedure*.

Motion for Protective Order

A *motion for protective order* asks the Court to allow one side to hold back temporarily from showing the other side certain documents or other things about the case. This type of motion also asks for court protection for a person from harassment, service of process, or other similar situations. Such a motion can be filed regarding a notice to take a deposition. If the distance involved for travel or the shortness of time of the notice makes appearing at the time and place scheduled difficult or impossible for a deponent or attorney, a motion for protective order can be requested. It may also be used when interrogatories are oppressive or when requests for production are unduly burdensome.

Motion to Compel

A *motion to compel* is filed to require the opposing party to perform some act, such as to answer interrogatories or produce documents in accordance with a motion for production. If this motion is not responded to or action performed, it is set for hearing, and the Court may impose sanctions, including an order that the act be performed. If the order is not obeyed, the disobedient attorney may be held in contempt of court or his or her pleadings may be wholly or partially stricken or removed by the Court, and money penalties may be assessed.

Counsel may make a motion, at any time before a case comes to trial, requesting a party to produce such items as medical or hospital reports, letters, correspondence, documents, plats, charts, diagrams, sketches, surveys, insurance policies, photographs, accounting records, and testimony from previous trials.

Motions are also made to secure a list of planned witnesses, acquisition of confessions, transcripts of grand jury testimony, police reports, and statements of witnesses. Likewise, motions are made to suppress materials obtained in an illegal search and seizure, confessions illegally obtained, and other improper evidence.

Motion for Writ of Habeas Corpus

A *writ of habeas corpus* as a judicial order to someone holding a person to bring that person to court. It is used to get a person out of unlawful imprisonment or confinement by forcing the person in custody to bring that person to court for a decision on the legality of the imprisonment. A motion for a writ of habeas corpus may be made, inquiring into the reason for detention of a defendant and obtaining his or her release if it is deemed illegal.

Motion to Dismiss Complaint

At the end of the plaintiff's case, and again at the end of the entire case, the defendant's attorney may make a *motion to dismiss the complaint*. Examples of arguments for requesting such a motion include the following: (1) The plaintiff has failed to establish negligence on the part of the defendant, (2) contributory negligence was exhibited on the part of the plaintiff, (3) the accident complained of was not the proximate cause of the alleged injuries, (4) the evidence is insufficient to base the complaint on, and (5) the indictment is incorrectly worded. Usually, these motions are denied, and the case continues to its completion.

FIGURE 11.1
Motion for a Mistrial

(a)

```
 1                    NO.  837,458
 2   WILLIAM J. McNAMARA, I          IN THE DISTRICT COURT OF
                          I
 3           Plaintiff, I           HARRIS COUNTY, T E X A S
                          I
 4       -vs-             I           174TH JUDICIAL DISTRICT
                          I
 5   JOHNSON CORPORATION, I
                          I
 6           Defendant. I
 7
              DEFENDANT'S MOTION FOR MISTRIAL
 8
 9       Comes now defendant at approximately 10:00 a.m.
10   on the morning of Wednesday, the 22d of October, 19__,
11   and following receipt from the jury of their third note
12   indicating irreconcilable conflict, respectfully moves the
13   Court to discharge the jury herein and respectfully states
14   that in the light of the statements contained in the three
15   notes that have previously been sent in by the jury, the
16   first one having been sent in at approximately 2:50 P.M.
17   on Tuesday afternoon, in which the jury indicated they
18   were eleven to one on Issue No. 6 and unable to resolve
19   that issue (reference hereby being made to the first note
20   for its contents); thereafter the jury, at approximately
21   4:15 P.M. on Tuesday afternoon, sent in their second note
22   stating that they were eleven to one on Issue No. 7 and
23   ten to two on Issue No. 12, and stating that they had
24   considered the evidence and had repeatedly been over the
25   Court's instructions, and they could not seem to resolve
```

(b)

```
 1   the issues (reference being made to such note of the jury
 2   for its full contents); and the jury having now sent in
 3   their third note to the Court on Wednesday morning at
 4   approximately 9:45 A.M., in which they advise that they
 5   are still eleven to one on Issue No. 7 and ten to two on
 6   Issue No. 12 and advise that they have considered all the
 7   evidence and have been over the Court's instructions many
 8   times and are unable to resolve the issues (reference
 9   hereby being made to the contents of such third note from
10   the jury for the contents thereof); and the jury having
11   started their deliberations at 10:00 A.M. on the morning
12   of Tuesday, after having briefly retired following the
13   submission of arguments on Monday afternoon, and having
14   deliberated all day Tuesday, and now being in their second
15   day of deliberations; and in the light of the clear and
16   unequivocal statements that there is a conflict or impasse
17   in the jury as to Issue No. 7 and Issue No. 12, which
18   cannot be resolved although they have reviewed the
19   evidence and the Court's charge many times in an attempt
20   to do so, it is respectfully urged and submitted to the
21   Court that any further requirement that such jury
22   deliberate or any further instructions that they continue
23   to do so would, in effect, constitute coercion of the jury
24   and an indication of a compulsion that they must resolve
25   such conflict even though they have clearly indicated on
```

Motion for Mistrial

A *mistrial* occurs when the judge ends the trial and declares that it will have no legal effect on either party. A mistrial occurs whenever a major defect in procedure occurs, such as counsel being guilty of misconduct, the inability of a material witness or party to continue on the witness stand, or the death or sickness of a juror with no alternate appointed. Mention of insurance may cause a motion for mistrial. A motion for a mistrial is shown in Figure 11.1.

Motion to View Premises

During a trial a request may be made by either counsel to have the jury view a scene where an alleged criminal offense has taken place, for example, at an arson scene or a hazardous intersection where a collision occurred. If the motion is granted, the court reporter may be required to accompany the Court and record questions asked by jury members.

```
 1   three occasions that they cannot do so.

 2        WHEREFORE, defendant respectfully moves the Court to

 3   discharge the jury herein and not compel them to remain in

 4   deliberation when they have made it clear on three separate

 5   occasions that they cannot resolve such differences after

 6   repeated efforts and studies of the evidence and the Court's

 7   charge.

 8

 9

10

11

12

13

14

15

16

17

18

19

20

21

22

23

24

(c)  25
```

Motion for a New Trial

After a case has been tried and a verdict is reached, defense counsel will usually make motions requesting a new trial. If the losing party feels as though the verdict is excessive or not supported by the facts, the motion may be made requesting a setting aside of the verdict. These motions are almost always denied unless the judge is convinced that a gross miscarriage of justice has taken place. Motions are either granted or denied by the judge. Official and freelance court reporters are responsible for recording all motions made, all arguments in support or against the motion, and all rulings by the Court. A motion for a judgment or a new trial is shown in Figure 11.2.

Motion to Strike

A *motion to strike* certain evidence may be made for any of the following reasons: (1) when evidence presented was apparently proper when received, but later shown to be objectionable, (2) when evidence is admitted subject to the understanding that it will be ruled on later in the trial, (3) when a witness makes a voluntary statement or testifies when no question is pending, and (4) when an answer is not responsive to a question. When an attorney promises to connect objectionable matter later, the Court may permit a question and answer, subject to later connection.

The court reporter writes all testimony included and all discussion concerning the striking of matter from the record. This material includes, the motion, the ruling by the Court, and all conversation between counsel and the Court. In addition, all testimony and discussion are included in the transcript. The Court's ruling that certain matter "may be stricken from the record" or "may go out" means that the jury should disregard it in their consideration of the facts.

In actuality, the only items a court reporter omits from the transcript are off-the-record discussions and matter that has been ruled to be physically expunged, that is, ordered to be removed from the record by the Court.

FIGURE 11.2
Motion for a Judgment NOV (non obstante veredicto) (notwithstanding the verdict)

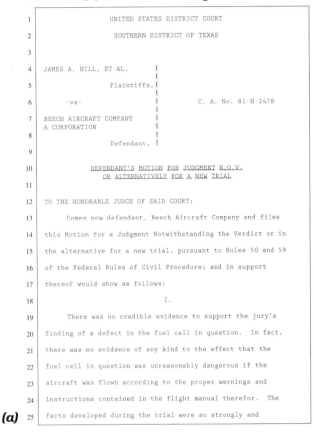

(a)

```
 1              UNITED STATES DISTRICT COURT

 2               SOUTHERN DISTRICT OF TEXAS

 3

 4   JAMES A. HILL, ET AL.       I
                                 I
 5              Plaintiffs, I
                                 I
 6       -vs-                I        C. A. No. 81-H-2478
                                 I
 7   BEECH AIRCRAFT COMPANY    I
     A CORPORATION             I
 8                             I
                Defendant, I
 9

10        DEFENDANT'S MOTION FOR JUDGMENT N.O.V.
             OR ALTERNATIVELY FOR A NEW TRIAL
11

12   TO THE HONORABLE JUDGE OF SAID COURT:

13        Comes now defendant, Beech Aircraft Company and files

14   this Motion for a Judgment Notwithstanding the Verdict or in

15   the alternative for a new trial, pursuant to Rules 50 and 59

16   of the Federal Rules of Civil Procedure; and in support

17   thereof would show as follows:

18                        I.

19        There was no credible evidence to support the jury's

20   finding of a defect in the fuel cell in question.  In fact,

21   there was no evidence of any kind to the effect that the

22   fuel cell in question was unreasonably dangerous if the

23   aircraft was flown according to the proper warnings and

24   instructions contained in the flight manual therefor.  The

25   facts developed during the trial were so strongly and
```

(b)

```
 1   overwhelmingly in favor of defendant on this issue that

 2   reasonable men should not arrive at a verdict of "defect" in

 3   this case.  Under those circumstances, a judgment in favor of

 4   the defendant notwithstanding the jury verdict should be

 5   entered herein.

 6                       II.

 7        There was no credible evidence to support a finding

 8   that the design of the fuel cells in question was the cause

 9   of the accident in this case.  The only evidence introduced

10   on this issue which specifically related to the facts of this

11   case demonstrated that the fuel in the fuel cells will not

12   unport under the flight conditions as testified to by the

13   pilot.  Under these circumstances, the evidence is of such

14   quality and weight that reasonable and fair-minded men in the

15   exercise of impartial judgment could only reach the

16   conclusion that a defect as alleged by plaintiffs was not the

17   cause of this accident, and the Court should enter a judgment

18   notwithstanding the verdict of the jury hereon.

19                       III.

20        Even if the Court were to find that there was

21   sufficient evidence in the record to permit an inference to

22   support the jury's findings, the verdict is against the clear

23   weight and preponderance of the evidence and would result in

24   a miscarriage of justice if permitted to stand.  Under these

25   circumstances, the Court should grant a new trial on the
```

```
 1   issues of defect and causation, as well as the defensive
 2   issue asserted thereto.
 3       Wherefore, premises considered, defendant urges this
 4   Court to grant its motion for a judgment notwithstanding
 5   the verdict or in the alternative to grant a new trial in
 6   the above case.
 7
 8
 9
10
11
12
13
14
15
16
17
18
19
20
21
22
23
24
(c) 25
```

Chapter 12

How to Report Objections

One way that lawyers protect the interests of their clients is through the use of the rules of evidence. The *rules of evidence* are procedural guidelines by which attorneys and the judge conduct the litigation processes.

The rules of evidence fill many books and state what is allowed and what is not allowed in the presentation of a case. They serve to keep issues within the frame of the case and limit testimony to direct facts seen or heard by the witnesses. These rules of evidence have been developed over many years to determine what procedures will best help the Court and the jury decide the issues in lawsuits. *Evidence* includes all the means by which any alleged matter of fact, the truth of which is submitted to investigation, is established or disproved. Evidence includes both oral testimony and physical objects, such as exhibits introduced in a case.

Attorneys are expected to *protect their record* by making timely use of objections and motions to strike during legal proceedings. These objections are essential to preserve the rights of the litigants. When one party attempts to offer evidence that is not admissible under the rules of evidence, the other party must object, giving a precise reason, if he or she wishes to keep such evidence out of the case. Objections should be made to questions immediately before an answer is made, because once testimony is heard by the jury, they cannot lightly dismiss it from their minds, even though the judge may rule that they must ignore such testimony.

A lawyer who fails to object to evidence ordinarily waives claim as to its inadmissibility. The judge will rule on all objections, sustaining proper ones and overruling improper ones. Sometimes objections are stated as motions, in which case the judge will grant or deny the motion.

In some states, opposing counsel is considered to have an automatic exception to court rulings adverse to his or her side of the case. In other states, attorneys must note their exception (disagreement) with the ruling by so noting on the record. Such notification is done by using any combination of the following: "I respectfully except to the Court's ruling," "Exception," or "I take an exception." This procedure is referred to by the Court and counsel as *protecting the record*. The purpose of taking an exception is to put the trial judge on notice that an attorney does not agree with the Court's ruling and may use that if an appeal is made.

Anticipating and Marking Objections

Most court reporters learn to sense immediately when an objection is going to occur. They can tell by the nature of the question or by the response given by the witness. This anticipation makes the reporter ready for the ensuing exchange of words that will usually follow a pattern of objection by one attorney, response by the other attorney, an exchange between counsel, eventual ruling by the Court, and possible exception to the ruling by the attorney.

Most reporters also realize that the questions and answers that were given right before the objection will probably have to be read back to the court as a point of reference. As a result, good reporters mark the spot in their notes where the objection began and then quickly go back to that spot to find the correct place to read back.

Various methods are used by reporters to mark their notes. Some reporters use a device connected to their cover plate that, when pushed on the left or right side, will automatically put a small ink spot on the extreme left or right side of their notes. Other reporters draw a line on their paper tape using a pen, and still others use a paper clip or a colored tab of paper in their notes that indicates the fold to which the reporter needs to return.

SECTION B

How to Handle Objections

When a question is asked and the opposing attorney interjects an objection, the discussion that follows may get pretty "hot and heavy." The attorneys, in the heat of argument, may speak very quickly and, in some cases, both attorneys may speak at the same time, with the judge trying to interpose a ruling.

If a tape recorder were taping what occurred, you would have a garbled mess to untangle that would be very difficult, if not impossible, to decipher. A court reporter has the advantage of stopping the attorneys before they get out of hand and reminding them that only one person should speak at a time. Discretion must be used in stopping attorneys. They do not like to be interrupted while they are arguing their points. If possible, avoid stopping attorneys while they are arguing objections unless it is absolutely necessary to the preservation of the record.

During these periods of objections, always record the question and answer because they are essential. If you can, mark them somehow because they may have to be read back. Then, record the fact that an objection occurred and record as much of the grounds for the objection as you possibly can, preferably verbatim. You will have preserved the record in case the matter is appealed.

Next, be sure to record the ruling of the Court. If the objection is sustained and an answer already had been given to the question, the opposing attorney will make a motion to have the answer stricken from the record. If this situation occurs, the motion and response by the Court are recorded verbatim, but nothing is ever removed from the record. If the objection was overruled and the witness had not answered, the attorney who asked the question may request that it be read back so that the witness can answer it.

Grounds for Objections

When objecting, attorneys may voice general or specific grounds. The *grounds for an objection* are the reason that the attorney gives in support for raising the objection in the first place. When attorneys say "objection" or "we object" or state that they object to the form of the question, they are making a general objection. When an attorney gives a reason for the objection, he or she is making a specific objection.

The following pages contain some more frequently used forms of objections, along with a brief explanation of each. A court reporter must understand why objections are made by counsel.

Incompetent, Irrelevant, and Immaterial

Perhaps the most common form of objection is to object to evidence on the grounds that it is incompetent, irrelevant, and immaterial. It is called a *blanket objection* and may include other grounds to make the objection more specific, such as the fact that the question has no relevancy to the matter under consideration.

The words of this objection are similar in meaning, but not identical. The word *incompetent* means not proper to be received, *irrelevant* means not relating to or applicable to the matter at issue, and *immaterial* means not important or pertinent.

Examples of this type of objection are as follows:

Q: To your knowledge, is Samantha Smith a prostitute?

> MR. ATTORNEY: I object to that as incompetent, irrelevant, and immaterial. How could her profession matter in a robbery case, Your Honor?

———————

Q: In your work with polygraphs, have you ever determined results that have led to dismissal of charges against any defendant?

> MS. ATTORNEY: I object to that as incompetent, irrelevant, and immaterial. Previous cases have absolutely no relevancy to the case at hand.

———————

Q: Was the apprehension of Dale Morgan in Wyoming reported in the newspapers, to your knowledge?

> MR. ATTORNEY: I object, Your Honor. Newspaper reports in Wyoming are not relevant to this hearing and have nothing to do with this matter at all.

———————

Q: You have given us your professional qualifications and experience, Doctor, but did you mention anything about your experience in testifying in other cases?

> MS. ATTORNEY: I don't think that is relevant, Your Honor; and I object to the implication contained therein.

———————

Leading and Suggestive Questions

Another very common objection is to object to a question that is leading and suggestive. This type of objection may be preceded by the words "I object to the form of the question."

Questions are leading when they clearly *suggest* to the witness the answer desired by counsel. In other words, the attorney is telling the witness what to say by giving him or her the answer in the question.

For example, a leading and suggestive question might be the following:

Q: You knew your wife was going to meet this man at eight o'clock on the night of March 23 at Carmelita's Corner, didn't you?

> MR. ATTORNEY: I object to the question as being leading and suggestive, your Honor.

———————

The question might more properly be asked as follows:

Q: Do you have any knowledge of where your wife was going on the night of March 23?

———————

Leading questions may be allowed when a witness is elderly and infirm, a young child, an illiterate person, or one suffering from a language barrier. Leading questions may also be proper on cross-examination. The Court may ask leading questions of a witness to bring about the truth in a case. The Court may also allow leading questions to be asked by counsel on direct examination when a witness becomes hostile or appears evasive. As with all objections, the judge may sustain or overrule them.

Nonresponsive Answers

When a witness does not clearly respond to the question asked, counsel may object to the answer as not responsive and ask the Court to strike the nonresponsive matter. An answer that is *nonresponsive* goes beyond the scope of the question and includes subject matter not called for by the original question. Usually, the attorney who asked the question will invoke the objection. Voluntary statements by witnesses are considered as nonresponsive answers.

Q: What is your name?

A: Well, my mother, rest her soul, used to call me Tiby. My father still calls me Libby. My husband, well, I won't say what my husband calls me; but when I was growing up my little cousin, Joe, couldn't pronounce my name, so he called me Lizzy. . . .

> MR. ATTORNEY: Your Honor, I object to the answer as nonresponsive and move to have it stricken from the record.
> THE COURT: Sustained. It may be stricken from the record. Mrs. Smith, please listen to the question and just answer the question the best you can. Please don't volunteer anything until it is asked of you.

Lack of Proper Foundation

Sometimes attorneys will object to a question because no proper foundation has been laid for the question. Evidence should proceed logically, and a foundation must be laid step by step.

Ordinarily, witnesses are asked their names, addresses, businesses, and qualifications, if experts. Then their connection with the matter at hand is established before they tell what they have seen or heard regarding the matter. An attorney cannot elicit that a man saw another murdered until he or she establishes that the person was at the spot where the incident took place.

Part of the foundation for facts may be the marking of evidence, such as papers, documents, photographs, and X-rays, for identification. Once marked for identification, the evidence is talked about and may later be received into evidence.

Q: Do I understand, then, that the only way you advertise is by brochures sent to customers?

> MS. ATTORNEY: I object. No foundation has been laid to show that the company had any brochures or has ever sent any to prospective customers.

Facts Not in Evidence

This type of objection is often used when an attorney assumes facts that are not in evidence. A hypothetical question that does not parallel the case at hand will be objected to on the grounds that it assumes facts not in evidence.

Q: Did you see Mr. Stone in the same car in which you saw the stolen lawn mower?

> MR. ATTORNEY: Your Honor, I object. He has not testified that he ever saw either him or the lawn mower in any car. He is assuming a fact not yet in evidence.

Repetitious Questioning (Asked and Answered)

Questions that are repeated over and over again are objectionable because they take up the valuable time of the Court, the litigants, the jury, and their witnesses, in addition to being an expense for taxpayers.

Q: Do you know why the engineer determined that the backflow preventer should not be put on this system?

> MS. ATTORNEY: I object to this question as repetitious, Your Honor. That is the third or fourth time that the question has been asked and answered in some form or other.

Hearsay Evidence

Hearsay evidence is frequently objected to by counsel. *Hearsay* is a term given to testimony offered by witnesses who testify not to what they know personally, but to what others have told them or what they have heard said by others. It is secondhand information.

Hearsay evidence is permissible in some instances, but each case has to be ruled on its own merits, given its own set of circumstances. The following may be admissible hearsay evidence: dying declarations, confessions, admissions, statements against interest, business entries, public records, former testimony, reputations, statements about physical condition or mental state, and res gestae or statements that are part of an occurrence that has already been shown to have existed. In some courts this is known as the *best evidence rule*.

Hearsay statements usually begin with the witness using any of the following beginnings: "I understand," "I understood," "It is my understanding," "I was informed," "I was notified," "It was reported to me," "I have heard," or "I was told." Witnesses may ordinarily testify only to what they have direct knowledge of through their own senses and not what others have told them.

If a lawyer objects to a hearsay answer given by a witness, the lawyer will make a motion to strike the answer, upon which the judge, if he or she agrees with counsel, will sustain the motion.

Q: When was the first time you saw Mrs. Johnson that day?

A: Someone called from Room 39 and reported that she was there.

> MR. ATTORNEY: Excuse me, Your Honor. I object to what was reported as hearsay and ask that the answer be stricken from the record.
>
> THE COURT: The objection is sustained.

Q: Did the girl say anything at that point?

A: Well, she said someone told her that John broke the glass to get in.

> MS. ATTORNEY: I will object to the answer as hearsay and move to strike the answer.

Self-Serving Answers

Self-serving statements and *self-serving documents* are objectionable because they serve no purpose other than to bolster the person's case who offers them. Often during the trial of a case, the plaintiff or the defendant will try to justify his or her actions or try to explain a matter in greater detail. During this explanation or justification, the witness will tend to add extraneous matter that will only help his or her own cause.

Q: When you came to the hospital, you told them that Mr. Hanson ran you down, didn't you?

A: Yes, I certainly did. He did it on purpose.

> MS. ATTORNEY: I object to the question and answer as self-serving.

––––––––––––

Q: Did you notice that considerable business activity was occurring in my client's store at the time you were in there?

> MR. ATTORNEY: I object on the grounds that the question calls for a self-serving answer. The amount of business can't be shown by this witness.

––––––––––––

Compound and Complex Questions

Questions that are difficult to understand or call for long, involved answers can be objected to by the opposing attorney. This type of question is very often asked by attorneys who are trying to elicit all the facts that they can by putting several questions together. The answers to such questions are often an attempt by the witness to respond to each part of the question. Breaking down the question into different components and asking each separately is much better for the record. Usually, upon objection to such questions, the judge will ask the counsel to rephrase the question.

As the court reporter, you may be asked to read back such questions by the Court or questioning attorney, particularly when the witness did not understand the question. Usually, the attorney, after hearing his or her original question, will concede to restate the question in a clearer manner.

A question that requires more than one answer is objected to on the grounds that it is a compound question.

Q: Did you remove the article from the car that was parked on the corner at the time that the man who said he saw you near the gas station ran into the street yelling for you to stop, or did you just sit there in your patrol car and observe the men who came out of the terminal because the whistle had blown?

> MS. ATTORNEY: Your Honor, I object to the question as compound and complex and ask the Court to instruct the witness not to answer the question until it is understood by everyone.

––––––––––––

Q: Do you know when they were tested, and do you know why they were picked up to be tested?

> MR. ATTORNEY: I object to that question as a double question.

––––––––––––

Ambiguous Questions

Vague, uncertain, and ambiguous questions are also objected to because an indefinite and uncertain question cannot elicit an intelligible answer. Ordinarily, upon objection the Court will request that such questions be rephrased by the attorney who asked the original question.

Q: Would you say that there is a great likelihood of assuming that if small particles of sand or other debris gets into the system, that there would be a fairly good possibility of the valves wedging closed? Would you say that a very, very, remote possibility exists?

> MS. ATTORNEY: I object to the form of the question. It is broad, vague, and indefinite. The witness would have to know the location of the material, the exact size of the material, and under what conditions the valve was operating at the time.

———————

Q: Did you ever, in your lifetime, talk to Mr. Anderson at all?

> MR. ATTORNEY: I object to this question as too vague, Your Honor. My client is not expected to remember every single conversation he has had in his lifetime; and in addition, which Mr. Anderson is he asking about? Three Mr. Andersons are involved in this case: John, John, Jr., and William. Which one are you referring to?

———————

Other Than the Best Evidence

Sometimes attorneys will present copies of letters or instruments or photocopies of checks and documents as exhibits when the originals could be made available. Also, counsel will sometimes bring in a secondary witness to testify to a matter when a different witness may better testify as to the facts of a case. Opposing counsel will object to such presentations as not the best evidence.

Q: I am going to show you what has been marked as Defendant's Exhibit A for identification, a rental schedule of the building in question, and ask you to tell us what Mr. Jay's rent was during January of last year.

> MS. ATTORNEY: We object to this line of questioning pertaining to the rental schedule as not being the best evidence, Your Honor. If counsel wishes to know the amount of rent, why doesn't he produce the actual signed lease between the landlord and the tenant as the best possible evidence.

Q: I show you a photocopy of the contract before it was signed by all parties.

> MR. ATTORNEY: To which I object as not the best evidence.

———————

Call for Conclusions or Opinions

Objections are commonly made to questions that call for conclusions, opinions, or speculation on the part of a witness who is not an expert. *Opinions* are inferences or conclusions that are drawn by a witness from the facts. Ordinarily, witnesses may give only the facts and not their opinions or any conclusions that they may draw from the facts. When a witness states what he thought, what he concluded, or what he assumed, the answers are objectionable.

Q: What do you see in this photograph, Ms. Smith?

A: To me, it shows evidence of a bloodstain on the front seat of the car.

> MR. ATTORNEY: I object to that answer as a conclusion on the part of the witness. That spot could be anything, and from the photograph she could not possibly tell whether it was blood or not.

Q: All you are saying is that a possibility exists that the gas could have been in that lower bottle and that this gas could possibly have escaped through the top?

> MS. ATTORNEY: I object to this line of questioning as being highly speculative, Your Honor.

Illegally Obtained Evidence

A valid objection is often made concerning evidence that is illegally obtained and therefore not admissible. This objection is frequently made against the inclusion of confessions that may have been obtained under circumstances where doubt exists about whether the accused were properly advised of their rights.

Q: I show you now your statement that has been marked as State's Exhibit No. 1 and ask you if you can identify it.

> MS. ATTORNEY: Your Honor, I object to the introduction of this exhibit because it was illegally obtained. My client was not properly advised of his constitutional rights prior to this interrogation, and he gave that statement not knowing that he was entitled to the services of an attorney before he said anything and that an attorney would be provided for him if he could not afford one.

Self-Incriminating Testimony

When a person makes a statement or gives testimony that may be damaging to himself or herself, he or she is incriminating himself or herself. Under the Fifth Amendment of the United States Constitution, a person does not have to give incriminating testimony against himself or herself and can claim privilege against this self-incrimination. A client's attorney will quickly object to any question calling for the individual to testify against his or her self-interest.

Q: Did you run an illegal bookmaking scheme for the purpose of procuring bets on horses?

> MR. ATTORNEY: My client refuses to answer that question on the grounds that it might tend to incriminate him.

Cross-Examination beyond the Scope of Direct Examination

A frequently used objection on cross-examination is that the testimony goes beyond or outside the scope of the direct examination or that the question is improper cross-examination. An attorney who cross-examines may cover only the subject matter already covered on direct examination. New subject matter may not be developed on cross-examination except in the case of an adverse witness or one who shows prejudice or hostility to the side that called the witness.

Q: Are you able, Doctor, to form an opinion of your own, based on the reports of the latest laboratory examinations, as to the need for more tests?

> MS. ATTORNEY: I object to this question as going beyond the scope of direct examination.

The Question Calls for Expert Testimony

Questions may be asked of a witness who is not an expert (lay witness) that call for more than factual answers. These questions will be objected to by counsel as calling for expert testimony. If the witness on the stand can be qualified as an expert, an answer may be allowed. Otherwise, the objection will be sustained.

Q: What is the value of this property next to your home?

> MS. ATTORNEY: I am going to object because the witness has not been qualified as an expert in the matter of appraisals.

Counsel Is Taking Witness on a Fishing Expedition

The loose, scattered questioning of a witness that goes beyond the scope of the lawsuit is often called a *fishing trip* or *fishing expedition*. The use of the term means that the attorney is grasping for anything and everything that may or may not bring about damaging information. The opposing counsel immediately recognizes this line of questioning for what it is worth and will object.

Q: Why were you married six times before this marriage, and each previous marriage was to someone whose last name started with the letter T?

> MS. ATTORNEY: Objection, your Honor. Counsel is taking the witness on a fishing expedition. The question is not germane to the subject matter at hand.

Badgering the Witness

Attorneys are not allowed to argue with a witness because it tends to produce inferences, not facts. Attorneys also are not allowed to badger a witness nor demean any person who is testifying in any way. To *badger* is to pester or nag a witness. Counsel are quick to object to such treatment of witnesses by an opposing attorney.

Q: Your answer is you think so? Is that all you can say? You think so. Come on, now. You're not a stupid person. You can answer my question better than that, can't you? Or is it because you don't want to answer my question?

> MS. ATTORNEY: Your Honor, I object to counsel's arguing with the witness and badgering him in this manner. The witness has answered the question.

Evidence Speaks for Itself

A common objection is that the evidence speaks for itself. This objection is used when a counsel may try to adduce lengthy explanations concerning material that is readily discernible from documents or photographs.

Q: What does the scene depict other than the roadway itself?

> MR. ATTORNEY: I will object to that, if the Court please. The picture speaks for itself.

Q: I am going to show you the contract in question and ask you whether contained therein is a provision for locking block valves in this installation.

> MS. ATTORNEY: I object to the question because the document speaks for itself and is the best evidence of what it contains.

Privileged Information

Certain information is considered as *privileged* between husband and wife, attorney and client, clergy and confessor, and physician and patient. The objection regarding privileged information is made by the counsel for the person who made the confidential communications.

Q: What did your husband tell you as to his plan to commit this bank robbery?

> MR. ATTORNEY: I object. The question is asking for privileged matter between husband and wife.

Q: Have you discussed with your attorney whether either one of these tests was made in this case?

> MS. ATTORNEY: Counsel is asking for privileged matter in an attorney–client relationship. Don't answer that question. I object, Your Honor.

Narrative Form of Testimony

An attorney may object to rambling, narrative-type testimony, which many times will get into inadmissible matter. This type of objection is similar to the objection used when an answer is not responsive to the question.

Q: Please tell us where you were at 6 p.m. on the evening of the murder.

A: Well, you see, I always like to relax a little before I go out for the evening. I picked up this habit when I was a small child. My mother always used to make me take a nap after school, especially when I had had a hard day at school. I remember one teacher I had in kindergarten who used to make us work all day long. One day when she was teaching us how to glue paper, I got some glue on my new blue dress.

> MS. ATTORNEY: Your Honor, I object to the answer as not responsive to the question and ask the Court to instruct the witness to answer the question. The witness tends to go beyond the scope of the question and answer in narrative form.

Objections to Expert Witness

If an expert witness testifies about his or her qualifications and they are found not to be sufficient to establish his or her expertise, the Court may rule that the witness is not qualified to speak as an expert. On the other hand, if a particularly world renowned expert is placed on the witness stand, counsel may stipulate or agree as to the qualifications of the witness, meaning that he or she will not have to list his or her training, experience, and accomplishments.

Q: Please state your experience as a dog trainer.

A: Well, to tell you the truth, I have had no prior experience; but I have raised two dogs for my brother-in-law.

> MS. ATTORNEY: Your Honor, I object to this witness as not being qualified to testify as an expert in the field of dog obedience and ask that he be excused immediately.

> MR. ATTORNEY: Your Honor, I call Mr. Ronald McDonald as an expert in the cooking of hamburgers.

> MS. ATTORNEY: We will stipulate as to the qualification of Mr. McDonald in the fast-food industry. His reputation speaks for itself.

Mention of Insurance

During certain proceedings, if an insurance company is mentioned or any reference is made to an insurance policy, defense counsel may object. The reason is that knowledge of a third party who may be responsible for payment of all damages may prejudice the jury in favor of the plaintiff. The jury may decide to give an excessive amount to the plaintiff as compared to the figure they would decide on if it were assessed against an individual.

Q: Where did you keep your insurance policy for the house that was burned down?

> MS. ATTORNEY: I object, Your Honor. Counsel knows very well that any reference to insurance will prejudice the jury. I ask the Court to declare a mistrial.

Objections as a Result of Surprise

An interesting objection is the claim of *surprise* on the part of an attorney. This claim means that one of their own witnesses has changed his or her story or introduced material not previously known to the attorneys, contrary to what they were led to believe that the testimony would be. As a result of this surprise information, they are forced to plan a whole new line of strategy and attack, which may require asking the Court to adjourn the matter to allow preparation time.

Q: You are a fine, outstanding citizen, aren't you, Mr. Jones. You have never been arrested, have you?

A: Well, I was arrested twice on a weapons violation; and last year I was arrested for a felony DUI. This year I've only been arrested six times for check fraud. Other than that, I have not been arrested, no.

> MR. ATTORNEY: Your Honor, in light of this new information, I would request that our star witness be excused, and we hereby request a continuance of the matter to allow us enough time to plan our defense.

Attempt to Impeach One's Own Witness

To *impeach* a witness is to show that he or she is untruthful and has lied either in past statements or in immediate testimony. If an attorney tries to impeach a witness he or she has called to testify, opposing counsel will object. Attorneys are supposed to bring in witnesses who are favorable to their own sides to strengthen their cases. They are expected to be familiar with the testimony that the witnesses will give.

Q: Didn't you just tell me you weren't near the scene of the crime?

A: Yes, but I didn't understand the question.

Q: And didn't you tell us yesterday that you saw everything because you live near the scene?

A: Yes. I thought you meant something else.

Q: And didn't you tell your boss that you were going to change your answer because you didn't like the way you were treated on the stand yesterday?

A: No, I mean yes. I mean, I don't understand what you mean.

> MR. ATTORNEY: Your Honor, counsel is trying to impeach his own witness. I object to this line of questioning and question the motives of counsel in calling this witness in the first place.

Objections to Exhibits

Anytime that exhibits are introduced by one side, either for identification or to be received as evidence, the opposing side has an opportunity to challenge the exhibit by objecting. Various grounds may be used for objecting to exhibits, including their relevancy, clarity, accuracy, and so on. Such objections will be noted and, as a result of the objection, the exhibits will either be admitted or not admitted into evidence.

> MS. ATTORNEY: Your Honor, at this time I offer Defendant's Exhibit D that has been marked for identification into evidence.

MR. ATTORNEY: I object to the admissibility of the document as evidence because no testimony has been given as to where or when this document was originally made. For all we know, Your Honor, it could have been made this morning.

THE COURT: The objection is sustained. The exhibit will not be received at this time. Counsel, can you clarify when this document was made?

Counsel may use other types of objections during the proceedings. You, as a court reporter, must have an understanding of what each objection means so that you can adequately report and transcribe what happened.

When dealing with objections, remember to remain calm, do not panic, and do a good job in recording the proper information so that you can produce an accurate transcript.

Chapter 13

How to Mark Exhibits

The marking of exhibits is an art and skill in and of itself that requires common sense and practice. *Exhibits* are material items of physical evidence introduced by attorneys to corroborate and confirm oral testimony or to introduce new evidence based on an exhibit, all for the purpose of helping the presenting side to prove their cause.

Exhibits are usually marked for identification so that they can be discussed. After testimony is elicited to bring out the validity of an exhibit, it may be received into evidence. At depositions, exhibits are marked for identification only. They may or may not be introduced during the trial of a case.

Generally, most exhibits in a case are identified and received into evidence in court by the party bringing suit. The exhibits are offered in court first for identification and then are shown to opposing counsel and the Court. Objections and rulings may be made, after which questioning proceeds regarding an exhibit. Then an exhibit is offered as evidence. Objections may be raised again, and the exhibit is either received or not received into evidence.

What Constitutes an Exhibit

Physical evidence may include guns, bullets, medical records, marriage certificates, soil and quicksand samples, tapes or slides, videos, stamps, charred rugs and furniture in arson cases, chemicals, X-rays, statements, confessions, clothing, hospital records, drugs, machinery, rubber tires, accounting records, mortality tables, city ordinances, bloodstained items, blood samples, letters—and even the kitchen sink! In essence, the list of what can make up an exhibit is endless.

Some exhibits are large; some are small. Where bringing a large exhibit into the courtroom is physically impossible, photographs may be submitted. Complete files containing hundreds of pages of textual material may be admitted as well.

In short, almost anything imaginable can and will be marked for identification and offered into evidence in order to help a lawyer to win a case. The reporter has to be ready to mark the exhibits appropriately and keep a record of the exhibits for the transcript.

Marking Exhibits

To mark exhibits properly, a reporter should have a variety of supplies on hand. These supplies may include an exhibit stamp, a stamp pad, and other marking materials.

Exhibit Stamp

An *exhibit stamp* is probably one of the most useful and universal methods of marking exhibits used by reporters. The exhibit stamp can be used in a variety of situations to mark all kinds of exhibits. Even when a physical exhibit cannot be stamped directly, a sticker or tag can be stamped and placed on the exhibit.

A stamp for marking exhibits should have blank lines for information concerning variables that will change from case to case. The exhibit stamp should have a blank line for the party presenting the exhibit, a blank line followed by the initials ID and EVD that can be filled in with a number or letter, and a blank line for indicating whether the exhibit is marked for identification or received into evidence. The next line should contain a place to insert the date, and the last lines should contain the name and title of the court reporter. An example of this all-encompassing stamp might look like this:

_____ID _____EVD

Date: _____

Mary H. Knapp, CSR

Official Court Reporter

This particular exhibit stamp provides for marking exhibits both for identification and for received into evidence, as well as for exhibits from any party to the litigation.

A Well-Inked Stamp Pad

If your exhibit stamp requires the use of a stamp pad, make sure that you keep it well inked and have it readily available. Most reporters will have a stamp and pad right on their desk or work area in the court and, in addition, carry an extra stamp and pad in their briefcases.

Miscellaneous Marking Materials

Among the paraphernalia that one might use in marking exhibits might be felt-tip pens, variously sized self-sticking labels, paper clips, stapler and staples, tags with ties, variously sized envelopes into which to insert exhibits, and so on. Court reporting supply companies offer a variety of preprinted labels and stamps that can be used for marking exhibits. These labels are available in different colors and are clearly marked as Plaintiff's, Defendant's, or other party's exhibits.

As a reporter gains experience in marking exhibits, he or she soon realizes that sometimes the imagination has to be used to mark exhibits.

Where to Mark Exhibits

Physically marking exhibits requires placing identifying information somewhere on the exhibit. If it is a large, cumbersome exhibit, the exhibit information should be placed on a tag and then tied to the exhibit. If it is a document or photograph, markings can be placed in the upper-right corner, lower bottom portion, or, if necessary, on the back of the exhibit. Follow the protocol for your court jurisdiction regarding where exhibits may and may not be physically marked.

Avoid marking exhibits in places that would cover any writing or material part of the exhibit. Nothing is worse than having a photograph or document marked for identification and then pasting a large label over the portion that needs to be discussed.

Check carefully as to an attorney's preference when marking exhibits consisting of more than one page or more than one unit. Some lawyers will distinctly inform you of how they want exhibits marked. Follow their suggestions, unless you know that the numbering they suggest is erroneous or will cause confusion.

Some lawyers, realizing that they have a bundle of exhibits to be marked, will ask the Court for permission for you to premark them. If premarking is allowed, make sure that you keep a careful listing of what each exhibit is and the numbering system that you use.

What to Mark on the Exhibit

At the very least, the marking of an exhibit should contain the party who is introducing the evidence, the exhibit number, the date, and the reporter's name or initials. Usually, all plaintiff's exhibits are marked with a number, and all defendant's exhibits are marked with a letter, although most reporters now use a letter representing the party introducing the exhibit followed by a number. For example, State's Exhibit No. 234 would be marked S-234, and Respondent's Exhibit No. 2 would be marked R-2.

To reduce confusion at the time of trial, most deposition exhibits are marked as Deposition Exhibit No. 1 and so on. At the time of trial, the marking may be changed to correspond to the plaintiff's or defendant's trial exhibit markings.

In some courts, letters are used as markings for exhibits in depositions, and numbers are used when the exhibits are marked during a court trial. Often, trial exhibits are marked at the pretrial hearing, at which time the reporter lists them on a worksheet and identifies them by description. In some places, the known exhibits are offered and received into evidence at that time, often with no objection from either side. If the trial exhibits are marked and received at the pretrial hearing, they are already in evidence before the trial begins.

The bottom line is to check with court personnel as to the proper procedure that is used in your particular jurisdiction.

Procedures for Marking Exhibits

Exhibits are clearly marked in such a way that the exhibit markings will not be erased, smudged, or fall off. During a deposition or trial, the attorney presenting the exhibit will usually ask the Court for permission to have the exhibit marked. If no one objects, the Court will agree. This permission is the signal for the court reporter to stop recording dictation and to mark the exhibit with the proper materials: stamp, label, tag, or the like.

The court reporter must take the time to mark all exhibits properly and with the proper number. If the Court or attorneys do not mention the number or letter, the reporter must know what the proper marking should be. You will keep track of all exhibits on an information sheet or worksheet that you keep in your work area. This information sheet is discussed in Chapter 8.

Once an exhibit has been marked properly, do not hand it back to the attorney who gave it to you until you have clearly marked it on your worksheet. The reason is that once you give it back to the attorney he or she will begin asking questions about it, and you will want to be ready to begin writing on your machine.

In a very real sense, you are in control of the situation. You must properly mark the exhibits, make the proper notation on your worksheet, hand the exhibits back to the attorney, and make a parenthetical notation in your notes. During this process, the attorneys cannot ask questions nor expect answers from witnesses, because you are marking the exhibits. Sometimes attorneys will forget and start to talk while they are waiting for the exhibit to be marked. The judge will usually remind the attorney to wait until the exhibits have been marked.

Marking Different Objects

You may have to be creative in marking some exhibits, and certain precautions may need to be taken. For the most part, exhibits can be marked with labels or tags; but some unusual objects may require additional consideration. These objects are discussed in this section.

Marking Papers That Are Clipped Together

When a group of papers is presented as one exhibit, make sure that they are stapled together and not paper clipped. Paper clips become loose, and papers can be lost. A staple will guarantee that the papers remain as one unit. If in doubt about stapling them together, ask the Court or the attorney whether you may staple them together.

Because the exhibit is considered as one exhibit, your marking will reflect the different pages within the exhibit. For example, if the plaintiff offers Exhibit No. 26 and it contains 17 pages stapled together, your exhibit number will be P-26-1 through P-26-17, the last number signifying the page number. Mark each sheet to prevent any sheets from being taken out and others inserted.

Marking Envelopes or Bags Containing Various Items of Evidence

Items that are so small that they cannot be physically marked are often placed in envelopes or small clear plastic baggies. A sticker is then placed on the outside of the bag. For example, small bullets, fragments, nails and screws, marijuana plants, drugs, and so on, may be placed in envelopes or baggies. If the baggie or envelope contains more than one item, note the quantity in the description and, in some cases, by numbering and letter. For example, an envelope containing three broken bolts from a suspected wheel involved in an accident may be marked as P-1-a, P-1-b, and P-1-c. Or the entire envelope may be marked as Plaintiff's Exhibit No. 1-a through 1-c and then, within the description, will be words to the effect that "the envelope containing three broken wheel bolts" was marked for identification.

Marking Substitutes for Original Exhibits

Attorneys often request the substitution of a copy of a document in place of the original, especially in the case of an expert witness's license, diploma, or certificate, or other official documents that may be required to be returned to their owner.

When an original is introduced as an exhibit, it is marked appropriately; for example, State's Exhibit No. 8 would be marked S-8. Then, if the original is withdrawn and a copy is substituted in the record, it is marked as S-8-a, and a parenthetical is inserted within the transcript referring to the substitution.

Marking Dry Erase Board or Blackboard Drawings as Exhibits

Very often, a witness will be requested to draw a picture of a scene, location, accident, or the like. The drawings may be made on a blackboard using chalk or on a large dry erase board using an erasable felt-tip marker. After the drawing is made by the witness, the attorney may offer the drawing as an exhibit, either to be marked for identification or to receive it into evidence.

The drawing is marked, using a label, chalk, or a felt-tip marker, in one corner. Then the attorney who introduced the exhibit must verbally put into the record that a photograph will be substituted for the actual drawing.

In a criminal case, the sheriff's department or bailiff of the court arranges to have a photograph of the drawing taken. In civil matters, the attorneys usually stipulate that a photograph will be taken and that they will make the appropriate arrangements. Some court reporters have a camera that makes instant photographs readily available in their desk for such circumstances.

Marking Bulky Items as Exhibits

Large, bulky items are often introduced as evidence in a trial. In such a case, photographs are often used to depict the actual evidence being introduced. In the case of an automobile, a locomotive, a burned building, or the like, photographs are used to tell the story, and the photographs are marked for identification and received into evidence.

In addition, for items seized in a large drug seizure, for example, the Court and the prosecutor will usually agree to introduce only a sample and photographs of the total quantity. The bulky exhibits are introduced and received into evidence, and pictures are made by the sheriff's department or other court personnel. On the record, the attorneys will agree that all except a small sample will be withdrawn from court and the photographs substituted.

Exhibit Parentheticals

The parenthetical that you use in your shorthand notes can be a very quick notation that can be filled in at the time of edit; it can be a computer-generated "include" command that will automatically insert a predefined parenthetical; or it can be written in its entirety. The parenthetical should contain the information mentioned in Chapter 10; that is, the identifying name and number of the exhibit, as well as a brief description of the exhibit. For example:

> (The documents referred to were marked for identification as State's Exhibit Nos. 5 through 15.)

or

> (The pistol referred to was marked for identification as State's Exhibit No. 1.)

All exhibit markings should correspond to the worksheet that you keep near your work area, and these in turn have to correlate to the index of exhibits that will be included within your transcript. The index is discussed in Chapter 15.

Who Marks Exhibits and What Happens to Them?

During depositions, exhibits are marked by the court reporter when requested by the attorneys to do so. The attorney providing the exhibit may request the reporter to retain the exhibits and file them as a part of the original deposition. If the exhibits are made a part of the deposition, the original exhibits are usually placed in the back of the original of the deposition and copies are placed in the back of the attorneys' copies.

In the federal courts, exhibits are marked and maintained by the clerk of the court and often precede the reporter's transcript to the court of appeals. In state district courts and county courts, the reporter usually marks the exhibits and may be required to keep control over them until the case is disposed of, returning them finally to the counsel who presented them during the case.

In most of these courts, however, the exhibits are maintained by the clerk of the court and transmitted by him or her to the proper appellate court with the other records. Later, they are returned to the attorneys by the clerk of the court when the matter has been finally settled.

In courts not of record, the judge or clerk may mark the exhibits and retain them, even though an attorney may have brought a reporter to produce a verbatim record in case of appeal. Because each court in each jurisdiction differs in terms of who marks exhibits and who retains them, you must follow the protocol for the court jurisdiction in which you are working.

If the court reporter is responsible for marking and keeping exhibits, he or she should check carefully at every recess and adjournment to ensure that all exhibits are in his or her possession. The reporter should never let any exhibits lie around where they may be picked up by anyone or inadvertently destroyed.

Sometimes, in the normal, everyday confusion of a court situation, exhibits thought to be received into evidence may not have actually been received. Usually, the last thing an official reporter does at a trial is to check over the exhibits with the worksheet to separate those offered and received. Only those exhibits offered and received into evidence are allowed to go to the jury. If, by mistake, other exhibits go to the jury room, it could result in a mistrial.

Some reporters always return exhibits that have been marked for identification but have not been received in evidence to the attorneys offering them at the end of the day. The reporter and attorneys then know that the exhibit is not considered part of the record.

At the end of the day, put all exhibits into numerical order and check carefully to make sure that all of them are in your possession. Sometimes the judge will ask the attorneys to wait for this task to be done. Retrieve any missing exhibits from the attorneys' files. If the reporter is charged with the care and custody of the exhibits and they are to be kept by the bailiff or sheriff in the evidence room, request a receipt for the exhibits and note the fact that they have been given to the proper authority for safekeeping. Examples of exhibit receipts are shown in Figures 13.1 and 13.2.

Some official reporters always go over with the judge and attorneys the exhibits that are and are not in evidence before the parties rest their cases. Some exhibits may be withheld while attorneys are waiting for a ruling by the Court.

Some judges always send exhibits directly to the jury; others wait until they specifically request all exhibits or some of them.

In some jurisdictions, the reporter charged with the responsibility for exhibits is required to store small valuables in safe-deposit boxes at a bank or within the confines of the courthouse. In other jurisdictions, the marshal, sheriff, or other court personnel have a specific evidence room where exhibits are securely locked and, in some cases, guarded under 24-hour watch.

The reporter must keep records of all exhibits and what happens to them. Most attorneys or judges will turn to the court reporter and ask him or her where exhibits are located, even though the reporter may not have the responsibility of keeping them.

A Final Note about Exhibits

As the guardian of the record, the court reporter is ultimately responsible for keeping track of all exhibits, how they were marked, and who has them. Therefore, the court reporter keeps a good record of the exhibits on his or her information sheet, marks the exhibits using an appropriate sequential numbering system, places proper parentheticals within the transcribed record, and knows exactly where any given exhibit is at any given moment.

FIGURE 13.1
Form of Receipt for Exhibits

```
                        No._____


THE STATE OF TEXAS            IN THE 158TH DISTRICT COURT

        Plaintiff.            OF HARRIS COUNTY. TEXAS

    -vs-                      _____ TERM. A.D. 19__

    Received of:








the above items introduced into evidence and kept in
possession of the court reporter.


Date: _____
                              _____
                              WRITING PRETELY
                              Official Court Reporter
                              158th District Court
```

FIGURE 13.2
Form of Receipt for Exhibits

```
                        No._____


THE STATE OF TEXAS            IN THE 158TH DISTRICT COURT

        Plaintiff.            OF HARRIS COUNTY. TEXAS

    -vs-                      _____ TERM. A.D. 19__


    The evidence in the above entitled and numbered cause
being:





was released to me this date by the Court Reporter of the
158th District Court of Harris County. Texas.

Date: _____        _____
                              Name

                              _____
                              Title

                              _____
                              Address
```

Although keeping track of exhibits may seem like a big responsibility for the court reporter, it is one of the things that judges and lawyers rely on the reporter to know how to do. Always check with court personnel within your court to see how different situations are handled. When you take a new job, you will not always have someone to ask for answers to all the little questions that arise. A good reference will be previous transcripts of depositions and trials that can be found in the files of court clerks and other places of public records. Most clerks will cooperate willingly if you explain to them what you are doing. Another valuable source is veteran court reporters who have handled similar situations.

Of course, the judge is the ultimate authority for the official court reporter. If you have an important question as to how to handle something, ask the judge.

Chapter 14

How to Read Back and Testify

One of the most important responsibilities of the court reporter is to read back portions of the record upon request. With the arrival of realtime reporting and modern machines that have instant playback for all previous questions, this task has become much easier. However, court reporters may be asked to take their notes and read large portions of testimony to the jury.

Reading Back

Sometimes whole court sessions will go by without anyone asking for a single readback. Then again, during depositions or hearings, requests to review testimony seem to be endless as attorneys object or witnesses fail to speak loudly. You may be asked to read an entire day's testimony or a long statement by counsel to the jury or to the Court and counsel in chambers.

Although in realtime courtrooms the judge and attorneys do not require a court reporter to read back because they can view their screen, it is important for the court reporter to know what to do in a readback situation. Basic principles should be followed in any readback situation that will make the situation easier. These principles are presented in this section.

Practice Reading Back

The first principle is literally to practice reading back. As a student of court reporting, you should have spent hours and hours of reading back either in class or in your practice. This reading back exercise has given you experience and allowed you to hear the sound of your voice as you read back.

Develop a Readback Voice

Succinctly, a *readback voice* is a voice that can be heard by everyone present in the room. You should not have to shout to be heard, but you should project your voice outward. Most new court reporters make the mistake of reading back to their notes. As a result, their voice is absorbed by the machine and notes directly in front of them.

When seasoned reporters read back, they place the notes in front of them, but they raise their heads so that the words that they utter go out and beyond their notes. They are literally reading to the entire room.

Take Time to Read

Perhaps one of the most important things to remember when reading back is to take your time. Remember, you are in control of the situation. Never begin reading back until you are 100 percent sure of yourself. Carefully find the place that you were requested to read, then read slowly, deliberately, and loudly. When you think that you are reading loud enough, increase the intensity of your voice a little more and project your voice out and beyond your notes. This technique helps to keep your reading speed slow enough to enable you to look ahead constantly in your notes so that you can see trouble spots and decipher them in advance. When you use this technique, you will have very few pauses as you read along. On the other hand, if you read rapidly and then stop suddenly, you may appear to be having trouble with your notes.

Remember these basic rules and read back slowly, deliberately, and loudly. If you follow these rules, you will have few problems.

Why Readback Situations Occur

Readbacks usually occur for specific reasons. The original question may have become so garbled that it needs to be rephrased, and to rephrase it, the attorney who asked the question needs to know what he or she said. Some attorneys may begin again by simply saying, "strike that," and then continue with a rewording of the question. Other attorneys may ask you to repeat the questions.

Sometimes a witness may not hear the question or, in thinking about the question, wish to have it read back in order to give him or her more time to formulate a proper response.

Sometimes the witness will give an answer, but he or she speaks so softly that only the court reporter who is intent on listening hears the answer. In this case, the judge or the attorneys may ask that the answer or the last question and answer be read back.

Sometimes an immediate objection is made to the question asked by the opposing counsel. If the objection to the question is overruled, the witness must answer the question. The attorney who asked the question will usually ask the reporter to read back the last question.

In other cases, a certain point may come out during testimony that relates to a previous section of testimony. Attorneys may ask the court reporter to go back and find that portion of the testimony and read it back. Such testimony may have even occurred during a previous day's testimony. Most attorneys will ask for and receive a recess from the court to allow the court reporter to find the notes and then read back when the court is reconvened.

During statements and depositions, the questioner and even sometimes the witness may ask for something to be read back.

Other readback situations occur during jury deliberation or during the arguing of a legal point in the judge's chambers. A court reporter may be asked to read to the jury the entire testimony of a defendant or witness. Usually, the court reporter will have time to prepare his or her notes for readback to the jury.

Many judges conduct a formal court and insist that attorneys address all requests for readback to the judge, who, in turn, directs the court reporter to read. In other courts, the rules of procedures may not be as strict, and the attorneys or witnesses may simply ask the court reporter to read back a question or answer.

How to Read Back

In reading back, read only what is in your notes. If you come to a difficult section of your notes, read it back as best you can. Lawyers and witnesses often speak in broken sentences. Read back broken and "dashed" sentences just as they were spoken. Do not make up words or phrases that are not part of the record.

If you stumble on a word or phrase, remember that it is not the end of the world. An occasional error may occur; and if an attorney or judge corrects you, thank them politely and then continue reading slowly, deliberately, and loudly.

Try to cultivate a pleasant, well-modulated voice with just enough expression to make sure that everyone understands the words that you speak. If a witness has been highly dramatic in giving testimony, do not try to mimic the witness and read back dramatically. Simply read the material in the same matter-of-fact way that you read anything else.

If off-color language or slang is used in a courtroom, the reporter should not act ill at ease or make any remarks or gestures that might reflect an opinion of such words. The reporter should act as naturally as possible and should read back such material just as he or she would any other testimony. Some court reporters have only the notes for the current day's session in the courtroom with them, keeping all other notes in their office. If an attorney asks for a readback from a previous day's session, the reporter has an opportunity for a recess and a chance to go back to his or her office, get the notes, and find the proper spot.

Finding and Marking Readback Spots

Court reporters need to devise a good method of finding a certain place in their notes for instant readback. You can be almost certain that a readback will be called for after an objection and the colloquy that follows. Some reporters use the marker located on top of their shorthand machines, some insert a colored piece of paper into the notes where an objection begins, and others use a rubber band or paper clip, anything to identify where an objection started and where you will ultimately have to return to when the attorney or judge asks for the previous question to be read.

Keep your mind on what is happening, and you will usually remember the general vicinity of any passage that may be requested. You will soon develop a sixth sense that warns you that a readback is imminent regarding testimony or a controversial argument.

When readbacks that have long preliminary statements are requested, try to read only the questions; on the other hand, if counsel asks for a question to be read back and the last question is only one word or does not make sense by itself, read the preceding question and answer also.

The court reporter must record who requested the readback in the notes. Some reporters draw a straight line across their notes at the beginning of the portion read back and at the end so that they can insert the proper parenthetical in their transcripts. Some reporters have developed their own shorthand for material read back. For example, KWERD is used for "question read," and KWARD is used for "question and answer read." Realtime and CAT writers have the outlines defined in their dictionary so that the appropriate parenthetical will appear in the transcript.

Reading Back to the Jury

Juries often forget what a witness said during testimony, or they cannot remember which witness said a certain thing. Sometimes, too, they think they heard a certain thing said, but their memories are faulty. In such cases, the reporter is called on to read portions of the transcript back to the jury. In some cases, one or two questions and answers may be read; in other cases, the entire testimony might be read back.

In the case of a readback for the jury, the jury sends a note to the judge through the bailiff or matron in charge of the jury. The note states that they want to have the reporter read back something from the trial. The judge and the attorneys must agree that what is asked for was actually testified to and is part of the record. The reporter will first have to search through the notes (or pull them up on a laptop computer in the case of realtime or CAT).

Depending on what material the jury wants read back, the readback may take place in open court with all parties present and the reporter seated in the witness stand, reading back the requested portion. Sometimes the reporter will read right from his or her normal place in the courtroom. Occasionally, the reporter will go to the jury room to read back.

When reading back to the jury, the reporter should face the jury, use a microphone if one is provided, and read slowly, because jurors may want to take notes. Many times reporters will not have an opportunity to review their notes before reading back. They will need to look ahead in their notes to see whether objections are coming up and, if they are sustained, skip the question, ruling, and discussion.

The advantage of having time to prepare for a readback situation is the opportunity to go through your notes and mark the areas that should not be read. When you are reading testimony to the jury, do not read questions that were objected to, objections that were sustained, the colloquy that followed, and places where witnesses were not allowed to answer. In addition, bench conferences or sidebars are not read back to the jury.

Marking portions that are to be omitted on readback with a pen or paper clips helps when you begin the actual reading. As you review your notes, clean up any trouble spots and punctuate where necessary to make sense of a long, confusing question or answer.

If you are reading back to the jury in the jury deliberation room without having counsel and the judge present, you should read back only what has been requested. If the jury wishes additional testimony read, have the foreperson make a request in writing to the judge.

When you are called on to read long portions of material, state to the jury, "I will now read to you the testimony of John Witness, which was heard on Wednesday, March 15, 1999. I will start with the direct examination by the district attorney, Mr. Attorney." Always, always read back the words "question" and "answer" for each Q and A as it appears in your notes.

Your reading must be totally verbatim, that is, word for word, as the outcome of the case may hinge on the matter requested to be read. Read fluently, clearly, and loudly so that you can be heard by all. Do not show emotion, because you might have an influence over the jury in doing so; you must be impartial at all times.

If you come to a poor spot in your notes that may take some time to translate and you have been reading a lengthy portion of the record, it has been suggested that you ask the question "Have I read the part that you wished to hear?" or something similar. If the requesting party says yes, you need read no more.

Good reporters read back with authority, vigor, and clarity so that there is seldom any question as to the accuracy of what is being read back.

When you have concluded reading back to the jury, excuse yourself and leave the courtroom or jury room. Do not converse with the jury about anything related to the trial. You should not be present during any of the deliberations of the jury. If they begin to discuss anything about the case before you have completed your readback in the jury room, remind them of your duty and ask the foreperson if you should leave or continue reading. If you leave without concluding the readback, mark in your notes where you stopped and advise the judge and counsel of what occurred.

Most reporters enjoy the break in the normal routine of writing all day when they are called on to read. Some reporters also enjoy the challenge of being able to show everyone what a good job they do. In a very real sense, being able to record the dictation and read it back in proper form is what reporting is all about.

Testifying in Open Court

Sometimes court reporters are required to take the witness stand and testify as to the contents of their transcripts and the accuracy of their notes. Although this type of questioning may seem unusual and may appear to be questioning the integrity of the court reporter's work, this is not always the case.

Attorneys request reporters to testify in order to impeach witnesses, to resolve contradictory facts, to inquire as to circumstances surrounding the taking of matter, such as the mental or physical capacity of the witness as it appears to the reporter, or even to try to prove the incompetency of a court reporter who may not have a good reputation for accuracy.

What to Do When Testifying

If you are called to testify regarding a matter that you have reported, take your original notes to court with you. Arrive early so that you have an opportunity to discuss your testimony with the attorney who requested your presence.

Some attorneys who see notes that contain other markings may question why the notes are marked up. You merely need to explain that the marks are part of the editing process and that the notes are cleaned up for transcription; editing does not change the accuracy of the notes nor their reliability. The attorney may ask you to read portions of your notes while he or she is holding the transcript that you produced. If this is the case, read calmly and coolly. Usually, the attorneys reserve their questioning to the portion in controversy, but some attorneys may ask you to read other portions. The opposing counsel should be alert to this tactic and object.

Answer all questions honestly and courteously. If attorneys become rude or seem to question your ability, do not become defensive and retaliate. You should pride yourself on the work that you do and always act professionally in these types of situations.

Your appearance will be very important on such an occasion. Dress appropriately in conservative business attire. In a very real sense, you are being called as an expert witness, and you should dress as an expert witness would dress.

Types of Questions to Expect

After you are placed under oath, you will be asked to state your name, address, and business or profession. Next you will be questioned about your education, qualifications, and experience as a court reporter. Be totally honest, but not so modest that you do not prove that you are capable of doing your job and doing it well. Tell about the months of training that you had to undergo to get to where you are, any tests you have passed, awards, and so on.

The attorney doing the questioning may ask you how much experience you have had as a reporter. If you have had a great deal of experience, the answer to this question will be easy. If you have not had much experience, stress your fine training and the fact that you have reported many mock trials or had an extensive internship with practicing reporters while you were in training.

If you have passed any qualifying tests such as CSR or RPR, they should be mentioned. Also, mention any continuing education courses, workshops, or seminars that you may have attended through your state organization or the National Court Reporters Association. Do not be meek or modest here, but let everyone present know that much work is required to become a professional court reporter.

Once this preliminary information is put into the record, the attorney may ask you to explain what a court reporter does, what the shorthand machine is, and how you can read the coded letters on the notes and translate them into English. Be concise but clear in your answers. You may even be asked if you or your transcribers or scopists ever make any mistakes. You should assure them that all work is proofread carefully to be sure that no material errors occur.

The attorney may ask about your percentage of accuracy and your percentage of error. Be totally honest and explain that you always attempt to achieve a level of 100 percent accuracy. You may be asked whether an error has ever been brought to your attention in any transcript that you produced. If none have been pointed out, then answer honestly and state that no material error has ever been brought to your attention. An error may have occurred, but it was not brought to your attention and, therefore, was probably insignificant.

One of the most common questions that the attorney will ask the reporter who is testifying is whether witnesses sometimes speak so rapidly that you cannot keep up with them. A good answer would reflect the fact that you stop witnesses when they speak too rapidly and ask them to repeat the testimony and that you have enough reserve speed due to your training that stopping a witness almost never happens.

Attorneys will want to know what you do when three or four people speak at the same time. Your answer would reflect the fact that you ask them to speak one at a time and have them repeat anything that you could not hear because of overlapping. Because you can record well over 225 words a minute, this speed allows you to record most overlapping comments without interrupting.

After your qualifications as a reporter have been established and the attorney has given the jury an idea of what the court reporter does, the attorneys will turn their attention to the matter at hand. You will be asked whether you were the court reporter involved in the matter at hand and whether you were the one who took the notes and produced the transcript. You may be asked if you recall all the questions asked by counsel and all the answers of the witnesses. Of course, your answer would be no.

At some point you will be asked to turn to the relevant portions of your notes and answer questions as to whether the witness was sworn and how he or she testified. Your notes may be marked for identification as an exhibit, and you may be asked to read from your notes in some instances at this point.

The attorney may ask whether you prepared the transcript of your own notes or had another person under your direction do so and when the transcription was done. The transcript will normally be marked for identification as an exhibit at this point.

You will be asked whether the transcript you have identified as your work is a true and correct translation of your original notes and, specifically, the particular portion in question. Some discussion and questions regarding how a transcript is produced and, in particular, how you produced your transcript may occur. If you used a scopist or proofreader, questions may arise as to their qualifications and whether they are competent. Undoubtedly, you will be asked whether the witness testified certain things in response to certain questions.

You may be asked to read from your transcript or from your notes. Always arrive prepared with your notes. The attorney asking the questions may feel that your reading from the notes is much more effective than your being questioned concerning the transcript. An objection may be made by some attorneys that the transcript is not the best evidence, but that the testimony should be elicited from the original notes. However, the Court has ruled in *People v. Colon, 119 NYS. 2d 503,* that a court reporter may use a transcript instead of his or her notes.

Reporting and Testifying

At some point in your career, you may be called on to testify about your own notes, and because you are the only court reporter in the area, you may have to take your own testimony. Although this situation does not happen very often, as a rule you would write the question posed by the person asking the question and then write your answer without saying anything verbally. After writing your answer, you would read your answer from what you wrote.

Although this method seems cumbersome, it is much easier than trying to write what you say at the same time. This method will assure that your testimony is recorded in a verbatim manner and that questions are not asked before you have completed writing your answers in the record.

General Guidelines

Always be totally honest in all your answers. If you do not remember something, say so. If other witnesses were to testify differently, you would have a credibility problem. Testify forthrightly and confidently.

Always keep in mind that judges, attorneys, juries, and the public want to believe that you, as a court reporter, do a fine job day after day. You must do your part to help them believe in you by being a good witness when called on to testify.

Treat testifying about your notes as a routine part of your job. You read back every day, and testifying about your notes is no different, except that your notes are usually much older. Remember, people in court often try to change their stories to help their own causes. Lying is often easy for such individuals. Your testimony will help to bring out the truth. If you have completed your education in a good school and worked diligently, you have nothing to fear when you are called on to testify regarding your notes and transcripts.

Chapter 15

How to Produce the Transcript

The ultimate goal of the court and realtime reporter is to produce an accurate transcript that is satisfactory to the judge, the attorneys, and all parties involved. The transcript is the culmination of all the skills and abilities of the reporter.

While the specific format of a transcript may vary from court to court or agency to agency, the general format is basically the same. Transcripts also vary in size, from one or two pages in length to hundred and even thousands of pages. This chapter will deal with some of the main parts of the transcript and how to produce them.

Preliminaries

Most reporters will follow standards when producing a transcript. Most of these standards follow the basic guidelines as set forth by the National Court Reporters Association. In addition, most court reporting firms or state agencies add their own guidelines to follow in producing a transcript.

The most commonly observed rules in producing transcripts include the following:

1. Transcripts should contain 25 numbered lines per page.

2. The body of the transcript should be double-spaced. Some items appearing on the front pages and certificate page may be single-spaced.

3. The *Q* and *A* for *question* and *answer* should be keyed at the first tab (5 spaces) from the left margin; the actual question and answer should be at the second tab (10 spaces) from the left margin; second and subsequent lines should be word-wrapped to the left margin.

4. Colloquy should be keyed at the third tab (15 spaces) from the left margin, with second and subsequent lines at the left margin using word-wrap.

5. Each type of examination should be centered and keyed in all caps, and the examining attorney should be keyed in all caps at the left margin.

6. Acceptable margins include a $1\frac{1}{2}$ left margin, $\frac{1}{2}$ right margin, and 1-inch top and bottom margins.

7. Transcripts should be bound at the left in an appropriate secure binder.

8. A standard 10-pitch font that allows for 10 characters per inch should be used on typewriters, word processors, or computer printers.

9. Transcript paper should clearly depict the name of the reporter or firm at the bottom of the paper. Boxed transcript paper is acceptable.

10. Pages should be numbered consecutively in the upper-right corner of each page, and all page references in the indexes should refer to the appropriate page numbers.

Several blank or lined, unnumbered pages may appear at the back of a transcript for lawyer's notes. An example of a page for lawyer's notes is found in Figure 15.1. The final transcript should be proofread to correct all errors and should be neat and presentable.

Title Page

The first page of the transcript is the *title page*. Normally, it is not numbered, although some CAT programs may automatically number the first page of the transcript. Although many different formats may be used for setting up title pages, each title page has certain items that are similar to all transcript title pages.

The first element to be keyed on the title page is the venue or geographical location where the matter is being held, usually keyed in all capital letters. The next material appearing on the title page is the title or style of the case, often set off in a box format. The names of the parties are usually keyed in all capital letters, and the descriptive words are in lowercase.

FIGURE 15.1
Page for Lawyer's Notes

LAWYER'S NOTES

Page	Line	

The spacing on each title page varies according to the information contained on the page itself. For example, if several plaintiffs or defendants are involved, you would not leave as much space as if only one were involved.

After the title and case number, a description of what the matter pertains to may be included, that is, whether it is a deposition or hearing, a jury trial, a special hearing, and so on. Also, a paragraph stating who the deponent or witnesses are, where the matter was held, and so on, may be included. A title page for a court case is shown in Figure 15.2.

Appearance Page

The next page of the transcript may be an appearance page. The *appearances* are a listing of the attorneys who are present for the action and the parties that they represent. Although some reporters prefer to put the appearances on a separate page, they may begin on the title page and carry over to a second page.

The appearances of attorneys on behalf of the plaintiffs are always listed first, followed by the appearances on behalf of the defendants. If more than one plaintiff and more than one defendant are involved, you must specify which plaintiff and defendant each attorney is representing.

Place the title *Esquire* after an attorney's name, abbreviating it *Esq.* Traditionally, the title was reserved for male attorneys; however, current interpretation favors the use of the title for both male and female attorneys. Whenever the title is used, the personal titles, *Mr., Mrs., Ms.,* or *Miss,* are never used.

FIGURE 15.2
Title Page for Deposition

```
 1         IN THE DISTRICT COURT OF HARRIS COUNTY, TEXAS
 2                    113TH JUDICIAL DISTRICT
 3
 4   I.M. LITIGATING,        |
 5          Plaintiff.       |
 6          -vs-             |          CIVIL FILE NO. 34,958
 7   URA GONNA LOSE,         |
 8          Defendant.       |
 9
10         DEPOSITION OF URA GONNA LOSE
11         On the _____ day of _____, A.D. 20__, beginning
12   at _____ p.m. in the offices of HITTEMM HARDE, ESQ., of the
13   law firm of Harde, Nails & Tax, 558 Disputatious Boulevard,
14   Houston, Harris County, TX 77036, before me, _____,
15   a court reporter and notary public in and for Harris County,
16   Texas, appeared URA GONNA LOSE, who being by me first duly
17   sworn, gave his oral deposition in said cause pursuant to
18   agreement of Counsel for the respective parties as
19   hereinafter set forth.
20
21
22
23
24
25
```

FIGURE 15.3
Appearance Page

```
 1
 2
 3
 4
 5                         APPEARANCES
 6
 7   REPRESENTING THE PLAINTIFF,
     I. M. LITIGATING:
 8
 9              MS. HOLLIE GOLIGHTLY
                Treading, Softly & Golightly
                Attorneys at Law
10              327 Stepping Stone Lane
                Houston, TX  77002
11
12   REPRESENTING THE DEFENDANT,
     URA GONNA LOSE:
13
14              HITTEMM HARDE, ESQ.
                Harde, Nails & Tax
                558 Disputatious Boulevard
15              Houston, TX  77036
16
17
18
19
20
21
22
23
24
25
```

If more than one attorney represents a party, include this information. Always list any other people who might be present at the proceedings, whether they are insurance adjusters, interested parties, or the like.

Spell each attorney's name correctly and list his or her address properly. If an attorney is representing a firm, list the complete name of the firm and address. Sometimes an attorney is hired by a firm to represent it, sometimes they are in-house attorneys, and sometimes they are employees of the firm. The best way to solve the problem is to use the name, address, and firm on the business card that you receive from each attorney. An appearance page is shown in Figure 15.3.

Index Page

The *index* is a very important part of the transcript because it shows the person looking at the text exactly where to go to find references to the examination of witnesses, the marking of exhibits, and so on. An index page is shown in Figure 15.4.

The index refers to the page where the witness was called and on what page he or she underwent each type of examination. It also lists the page numbers where each exhibit was first introduced and marked for identification, as well as the page where it was received into evidence. An index of exhibits is shown in Figure 15.5. The trial index contains references to opening statements, closing arguments, and motions and is generally much more comprehensive than the deposition index. Two examples of indexes are shown in Figures 15.6 and 15.7.

FIGURE 15.4
Index Page

	INDEX			
	Direct	Cross	Redirect	Recross
Jury impaneled and sworn	3			
Plaintiff's opening	5			
Defendant's opening	16			
Plaintiff's witnesses				
Tunis Willingham	24	36	40,48	46,50
Iva Hadditt	56	60	72	81
Ura Coldnotes	85	88	91	93
Plaintiff rests	96			
Motion and ruling	96			
Defendant's witnesses				
Eukelia Kubes	97	103	109	137
Also A. Square	195	199	207	222
Ima Deere	245	298		
(Deposition)				
Defendant rests	335			
Plaintiff's rebuttal witness				
Harry Lee	335	367		
Defendant's surrebuttal witness				
Summitt Upp	367	378		
Motion and ruling	387			
Plaintiff's summation	388			
Defendant's summation	401			
Charge to the jury	459			
Verdict and motions	491			
Adjournment	494			

FIGURE 15.5
Index of Exhibits

INDEX OF EXHIBITS

PLAINTIFF'S EXHIBITS

Exhibit Number	Description	Page Ident.	Page Rec'd.
P-1 - P-6	Photographs of Finishing Room at Marvco Film Company	8	9
P-7	Invoice for Medical Expenses of Sarah Long	15	15
P-8 - P-9	Work Records of Sarah Long	109	122
P-10	Autopsy Report of Sarah Long	146	147

* * * * *
* * *
*

DEFENDANT'S EXHIBITS

Exhibit Number	Description	Page Ident.	Page Rec'd.
D-1 — D-2	Adding Machine Tapes Run in Computing Sarah Long's Time and Wages	272	274
D-3	Death Certificate of Sarah Long	282	
D-4 — D-6	Photographs of Interior of Finishing Room of Marvco Film Company	326	326

* * * * *
* * *
*

Figure 15.8 is an example of an index of witnesses and an index of exhibits appearing on the same page. Figure 15.9 is another example of an Index of Exhibits used for a trial transcript.

Stipulations Page

Transcripts for trials or hearings may not contain any stipulations before the trial. *Stipulations pages* are usually used in deposition transcripts when attorneys agree before the testimony about certain matters regarding the way that the matter will be conducted. The stipulations may be lifted from a reporter's file of "usual stips" and inserted into the transcript, or they may be dictated during the proceeding. How to do the deposition stipulation page is covered in Chapter 21.

Body of the Transcript

The body of the transcript can be divided into those pages that contain either colloquy or testimony. Usually, the body of the transcript will begin with some preliminary colloquy or exchange between the counsel present or the counsel and the Court. This opening colloquy is very important as it sets the tone for the entire matter.

Colloquy is defined as any spoken matter that falls outside the normal realm of testimony. For example, whenever counsels talk to one another during a proceeding, have a conversation with the judge, make requests for exhibits to be marked or received, make objections to questions and rulings on the objections, and make motions and rulings on the motions are all considered colloquy.

Colloquy is normally keyed at the third tab or 15 spaces from the left margin. Colloquy always begins with the name of the speaker in all capital letters, followed by a colon. If the judge speaks, he or she is referred to as THE COURT. If the witness speaks, all references are made to THE WITNESS. The proper title MR., or MS., or MRS. is used with the attorney's last name, or use the first and last name if more than one attorney share the same name.

When a witness first appears in a transcript, he or she is usually sworn in and his or her name will appear in the proper setup for a witness. The witness setup begins with his or her full name keyed in all caps and may use a spread-heading format. The address may follow the name of the witness. The next portion of the setup is descriptive in nature in that it takes into account whether the witness is the plaintiff or defendant, who called the witness, and the fact that he or she was duly sworn. A witness setup is shown in Figure 15.10.

Following the witness setup, the type of examination and who is doing the questioning are included. The examination is usually keyed in all capital letters at the center point, followed by a return to the left margin for the name of the examining attorney. For example:

<u>DIRECT EXAMINATION</u>

BY MR. ATTORNEY:

The questions asked by the attorney and the answers given by the witnesses are reported as testimony. Although the Qs and As and their placement may vary from agency to agency and court to court, generally, they are keyed at the first tab with the actual question and answer keyed at the second tab, using word-wrap to return to the left margin.

Lengthy questions and answers in testimony or colloquy should be paragraphed at logical points or at least every four or five lines for ease of reading. Sample testimony with colloquy is shown in Figure 15.11.

Reporter's Certificate

The last page to appear within a transcript is a certificate, dated and signed by the court reporter who took the matter. This certificate attests to the fact that the transcript is a true and accurate translation of the material recorded by the reporter on the dates set forth. The certification page is not the same as pages that

FIGURE 15.6
Partial Trial Index A

I N D E X — Page

Docket Call 4
Selection of Jury 11
Jury Sworn 59
Motion for Severance by Mr. Hugo 61
Motion for Severance Denied by the Court 71
Witnesses Sworn 72
Rule Invoked 72
Rearraignment 75
Opening Statement by Mr. Rheem 88

STATE'S WITNESSES

Gerald R. Fondren
Direct Examination by Mr. Rheem 93

Michael E. Russo
Direct Examination by Mr. Rheem 100
Cross-Examination by Mr. Hugo 125
Redirect Examination by Mr. Rheem 150

STATE RESTS 168

DEFENDANT'S WITNESSES

G. Arthur Maynard
Direct Examination by Mr. Hugo 168
Cross-Examination by Mr. Rheem 192

DEFENDANT RESTS 238
Summation by Mr. Hugo on Behalf of Defendant 239
Summation by Mr. Rheem on Behalf of the Government . . . 250
Court's Charge to Jury 274
Reporter's Certificate 301
Order and Agreement on Settled Record 302

FIGURE 15.7
Partial Trial Index B

I N D E X — Page

CAPTION 1

PLAINTIFF'S EVIDENCE

WITNESSES:

ANNA KITTMAN
Direct Examination by Mr. Marco 2
Cross-Examination by Mr. Norman 16
Redirect Examination by Mr. Marco 27
Recross-Examination by Mr. Norman 28
Redirect Examination by Mr. Marco 29

JOHN W. FINDLAY
Direct Examination by Mr. Marco 39
Cross-Examination by Mr. Norman 61
Redirect Examination by Mr. Marco 91
Recross-Examination by Mr. Norman 94

HAROLD GRAYCO (by written interrogatory)
Offered by Mr. Marco 107

OREN J. KINCAID
Direct Examination by Mr. Marco 141
Cross-Examination by Mr. Norman 142
Redirect Examination by Mr. Marco 143

PLAINTIFF RESTS 143
MOTION FOR DISMISSAL by Mr. Norman 143
RULING by the Court 144

****
*****
***
*

DEFENDANT'S EVIDENCE

WITNESSES:

ANNANELLA CHENEY
Direct Examination by Mr. Norman 145
Cross-Examination by Mr. Marco 179
Redirect Examination by Mr. Norman 185

I N D E X (cont.) — Page

DEFENDANT'S EVIDENCE (con't.)

GEORGE O. MIRANDA
Direct Examination by Mr. Norman 186
Cross-Examination by Mr. Marco 209

ANGELINA DEAN
Direct Examination by Mr. Norman 212
Cross-Examination by Mr. Marco 238
Redirect Examination by Mr. Norman 256

WESLEY BRUCE
Direct Examination by Mr. Norman 268
Cross-Examination by Mr. Marco 285
Redirect Examination by Mr. Norman 294
Recross-Examination by Mr. Marco 301

DEFENDANT RESTS 302

****
*****
***
*

PLAINTIFF'S REBUTTAL EVIDENCE

WITNESSES:

ANNA KITTMAN
Direct Examination by Mr. Marco 303

EVIDENCE CLOSED 305
REPORTER'S CERTIFICATE 306
Agreement of Counsel and Order for Settled Record 307

FIGURE 15.8
Index of Witnesses and Exhibits

```
 1                      I N D E X

 2

 3

 4   STATE'S WITNESSES    Direct   Cross    Redirect  Recross

 5   Louis Nigra            2       16        48        59

 6   Albert Strysko        60       69        73

 7   Sophie Strysko        74       78

 8   Peter Ventimiglia     90       96

 9   Frank Colvin         102

10   Det. Anthony Ignoffo 105      109

11   Phillip Perrone      115      122

12   George Hickman       127      151       175       179

13   Theodore Strysko     210

14

15                  INDEX OF EXHIBITS

16
                                 Marked for   Received in
17   Exhibit No.   Description   Identification  Evidence

18     S-1         Rifle              7           94

19     S-1         Bullets (3)      120          121

20

21

22

23

24

25
```

FIGURE 15.9
Index of Exhibits

```
 1                INDEX OF EXHIBITS

 2

 3   PLAINTIFF'S EXHIBITS
                                                 Received
 4   Exhibit                      Marked for        in
 5   Number        Description    Identification  Evidence

 6   P-1           Invoice dated 2/14/__    9

 7   P-2           Original Invoice dated
                   2/11/__               11          11
 8
     P-3, P-4      Ledger Sheets of Winston
 9                 Salem Company          43          45

10

11   DEFENDANT'S EXHIBITS

12   D-1           Original Invoice dated
                   3/15/__               92          95
13
     D-2           Driver's License Receipt
14                 dated 4/7/__          105        107

15   D-3           Check dated 5/3/__     114        114

16   D-4           Handwriting Specimen   187        201

17   D-5, D-6      Photographs dated 5/19/__  225    287

18   D-7           Employment Application
                   dated 6/14/__          289
19

20

21

22

23

24

25
```

contain questions that were certified. Certified questions are keyed separately from the transcript, but may be included with the front pages for ruling by a judge. A reporter's certificate is shown in Figure 15.12.

A Final Word about Transcripts

Remember, the transcript is the only means by which your clients can measure your effectiveness as a reporter. It should be a good, accurate, and neat transcript that is delivered in a reasonable length of time and for which the client pays a fair and reasonable charge for your services. Every transcript you produce is a reflection on your ability. You should take pride in every transcript produced and delivered from your office, agency, or court.

FIGURE 15.10
Witness Setup

```
 1                          URA GONNA LOSE,
 2    called as a witness on his own behalf, having been duly
 3    sworn, was examined and testified on his oath as follows:
 4
 5                          EXAMINATION
 6    BY MS. GOLIGHTLY:
 7    Q     Would you please state your name, sir?
 8    A     Ura Gonna Lose.
 9    Q     Could you spell your last name, please?
10    A     L-o-s-e.
11    Q     Where do you live?
12    A     2 Winners Circle, Houston, TX  77066
13    Q     Now, Mr. Lose, have you talked to Mr. Harde, your
14          attorney, about what we are going to do here today?
15    A     Yes, ma'am.
16    Q     Do you understand what a deposition is?  Has he
17          explained that to you?
18    A     Yes, ma'am.
19    Q     Has he told you that you are under oath and I'm going
20          to ask you some questions, and you are, hopefully, to
21          give me the best answers you can, to the best of your
22          knowledge and recollection?
23    A     Yes, ma'am.
24    Q     And if there is anything you don't understand, would you
25          tell me, and I will try to explain it, as far as my
```

FIGURE 15.11
Testimony and Colloquy

```
 1          questions are concerned?
 2    A     Yes, ma'am.
 3    Q     Then I will be able to assume after you have given me an
 4          answer that the answer that you have given is the best
 5          answer you can offer and that it is foursquare and
 6          correct in every way; is that correct?
 7    A     Yes, ma'am.
 8    Q     Can we have that agreement?
 9    A     (Witness nods head affirmatively.)
10              MR. HARDE:  Don't nod your head
11            because the Court Reporter can't take
12            that down.
13    Q     At the time that you loaned you brother the vehicle on
14          October 13, 1999, was the automobile in good working
15          condition --
16    A     Yes, ma'am.
17    Q     -- to your knowledge?
18    A     Uh-huh.
19    Q     Have you ever had any conversation with anyone concerning
20          this accident except your lawyer and an investigator to
21          whom you gave a statement on October 15, 1999?
22    A     No, ma'am.
23              MS. GOLIGHTLY:  I would like to have
24            the reporter mark this as Plaintiff's Exhibit
25            No. 3 for identification.  It is the map drawn
```

FIGURE 15.12
Reporter's Certificate

```
 1   THE STATE OF TEXAS Ï

 2   COUNTY OF HARRIS    Ï

 3        I, Lightning Digits, a court reporter and notary public

 4   in and for Harris County, Texas, hereby certify that the

 5   matters set forth in the caption to the foregoing deposition

 6   are true and correct; that the witness, URA GONNA LOSE,

 7   appeared before me at the time and place set forth; that said

 8   witness was first duly sworn by me to tell the truth, the

 9   whole truth, and nothing but the truth, and thereupon proceed

10   to testify in said cause; that the questions of Counsel and

11   the answers of said witness were taken down in machine

12   shorthand by me and thereafter reduced to typewriting under my

13   direction; and that the foregoing 7 pages comprise a true,

14   complete, and correct transcript of the testimony given and

15   proceedings had during the taking of said deposition.

16        I further certify that I am not a relative or employee or

17   attorney or counsel of any of the parties hereto, nor a

18   relative or employee of such attorney or counsel, nor do I

19   have any interest in the outcome or events of the action.

20        WITNESS MY HAND AND SEAL OF OFFICE, this the ____ day of

21   _____, A.D. 20__.

22

23                    _____

24                    LIGHTNING DIGITS (or other name)
                      Notary Public in and for
                      Harris County, Texas
25                    My Commission Expires _____
```

Chapter 16

How to Invoice and Deliver the Transcript

When a transcript is completed, the court reporter is responsible for making sure that it gets into the hands of the court or the client who ordered it. In deposition or freelance reporting, an office manager may take care of the assembly, invoicing, and delivery of the transcript, but the reporter must make sure that everything is proper.

Court transcripts are usually delivered to the clerk of the court, who will handle the distribution to the judge and attorneys involved, although extra copies of transcripts will have to be billed and delivered by the individual reporter.

This chapter discusses some concerns that reporters may have when putting together a transcript and delivering it to their client.

Assembling the Transcript

One of the most rewarding aspects of being a court reporter is to hold in your hands the completed transcript of a job that you recorded—to watch it progress from its very inception until the day that it is signed, sealed, and delivered! Perhaps even more rewarding, of course, is the day you hold in your hands the paycheck, your financial remuneration for a job well done.

After the transcript has been created, edited, proofread, and printed, the next logical step is to put it all together and bind it for invoicing and delivery. Transcripts are now printed on letter-quality, high-speed laser printers on good quality transcript paper. For most reporting firms, printing an original copy of the transcript and then making as many photocopies of the original as needed is more economical.

Some states allow the insertion of exhibits within the bound transcript, while others use a separate binding for exhibits. Inserting exhibits within the bound transcript can be done either by including the original exhibit or scanning the exhibit so that it becomes a permanent part of the printed and saved record. Of course, the size and nature of the exhibit will dictate whether it can be included within the transcript. In any event, check with the court or agency that you are working with to determine their normal procedure and follow that procedure.

Transcript paper can be ordered in a variety of formats for binding at the left. Transcripts can be bound in many different ways. A new reporter should obtain a catalog from one or more of the manufacturers and suppliers of court reporting office supplies; their addresses and telephone numbers can be found in *The Court Reporting Journal*, the professional magazine published by the National Court Reporters Association.

Some reporters use prepunched paper that contains three holes for placement between a transparent plastic front cover and a stiff backing. Metal brads are used to hold the transcript, cover, and backing together. Another method of binding is to use a specially designed machine that will fuse plastic prongs at the left. Other reporters prefer to use a plastic spiral binding at the left that requires a special machine for binding.

Some transcripts may be several hundreds of pages in length, and the method of binding will dictate the number of pages that can be bound together to produce one transcript. If a transcript requires two or more bindings, they are referred to as *volumes*. Normally, a volume consists of 300 pages of transcript, although this number may vary among agencies and courts.

A good transcript has three essential qualities:

1. The transcript should have a professional appearance: use a good paper with your name or the name of your court or agency imprinted on it, a good quality printer and copier, and a professional-appearing binding system.

2. The transcript should be neat and clean, and it should be error free. All errors discovered after proofreading should have been corrected, and a final proofreading should reveal absolutely no errors in content or form.

3. The binding method used should be permanent, and the transcript should not come apart when someone reads it or when it is handled by many different people.

Court Transcripts

Court transcripts are handled in the same way as deposition transcripts, with a few minor differences. Sometimes an attorney on either side of a court case may request a partial transcript before the trial has ended. As a trial progresses, attorneys may request excerpted testimony, motions, objected portions, and so on.

The percentage of trials transcribed in their entirety is less than the percentage of depositions that are transcribed. However, the number of transcripts for trials is increasing, as is evidenced by the increase in the number of cases on appeal. Usually, the person most interested in obtaining a copy of a transcript is the losing party, because he or she will base an appeal on the record.

In case of a mistrial, attorneys may order a transcript of the proceedings to better retry the case the next time. Attorneys may also have transcripts prepared in a case because companion cases are yet to be filed, and a study of the complete case record will assist in representing other clients.

The record is most often ordered from an official reporter because an appeal is to be taken or the losing party may feel that the verdict was excessive or contrary to justice. In some states, an appeal is mandatory in criminal felony cases.

Any requests for copies of trial transcripts should be made in writing to the court reporter. Most reporters will complete the transcript and then bill the attorney; in some jurisdictions, the reporter has the right to ask for a deposit of the estimated cost of a transcript before beginning to transcribe. In other places, the money for the estimated cost may be required to be placed on deposit with the clerk of the court before the reporter begins work. Make sure that you check the protocol for your jurisdiction.

When the official court reporter receives a letter ordering a transcript, some reporters respond with a letter to the attorney confirming the order and stating that, on receipt of the estimated sum, the transcription of the case will begin and that delivery can be anticipated on a stated date that is before the appeal. Monies received before completing the transcript should be kept in a separate account or trust account set up for the purpose of helping to produce the transcript.

In the case of an indigent person who cannot afford to pay a court reporter, most states allow for payment under the Pauper's Oath, by which the reporter is paid at the statute rate by the county or court jurisdiction. In other states, these transcripts are produced by the official reporter as pro bono work or free of charge. Attorneys very often take cases pro bono in the case of a person who cannot afford a lawyer.

Estimating the Cost of a Transcript

The following are easy rules for estimating the cost of a transcript:

1. Take the first 100 pages of four or five completed transcripts.
2. Find the accompanying notes that correspond to the first 100 pages and measure their depth in inches using a ruler.
3. Average the four or five notes you measured to arrive at one figure.

In this way, you can look at your notes and compare them to the measurement that corresponds to 100 pages of transcript.

Another method is to measure 1 inch of notes for four or five transcripts and find the page on which 1 inch of notes will end; then average the numbers to arrive at the number of completed transcript pages per inch of notes.

Other reporters have adapted this method to the number of kilobytes contained in a file; that is, so many kilobytes on a disk equals so many pages of completed transcript.

Either method is fine for ordinary cases, but keep in mind that technical cases, medical Q and A, or heavy solid matter will result in fewer pages per inch. Because of the multisyllabic words that are used, you are writing fewer words per fold. Conversely, light material like negligence cases or matrimonial cases normally yield more pages to the inch of notes than technical or medical material.

Really short cases may require you to use the manual method of estimating transcript costs. The *manual method* involves counting the total number of folds in your notes and dividing by two. The two flaps of steno paper that form a natural fold are considered one fold. The total number of folds divided by 2 is equal to your approximate number of pages. Keep in mind that you have to allow for the type of case and your system of shorthand—do you use numerous short forms and phrases or do you write everything out? Also, how close the spacing is on your shorthand machine will make a difference.

Occasionally, measure an entire pad of notes and compare that figure with the number of pages in the transcript. If you do this with a number of pads and transcripts, you will get a fairly good average.

Remember to multiply the number of pages of transcript by the cost per page in order to arrive at a total estimate for the transcript. In giving the estimate, most reporters use a figure that is liberal rather than conservative. In this way, if the estimate was high, you will have the pleasure of refunding money along with the delivered transcript, but if the figure was low, you may not receive the additional money for some time.

A Final Word about Transcripts

Follow the proper procedure for the court or agency within your jurisdiction regarding reading and signing of depositions and the delivery of the original transcripts to the clerk of the court. When in doubt, ask another reporter from your firm or an official reporter who has had experience. Never leave to chance matters that deal with the life and liberty of individuals. You are being paid for doing a job, and that job should be completed to the best of your ability. Your transcript reflects you; make sure that it is neat, attractive, accurate, and professional.

Chapter 17

How a Trial Transcript Looks

Included in this chapter are 10 pages of a trial transcript. Note that a break in the transcript is noted in the page numbering for the transcript.

Notice the setup of the Q and A in relation to the colloquy. Also, notice the placement of the title page, appearances, index, and certificate in relation to the entire transcript.

Remember, transcripts vary from court to court and agency to agency, but they generally follow basic guidelines.

```
 1   STATE OF NEW YORK

 2   SUPREME COURT        :        COUNTY OF ALLEGANY

 3   ---------------------------------------X
                                      :
 4   ROGER T. AMIDON,                 :
                                      :
 5                     Plaintiff,     :
                                      :
 6            -against-               :  Index No. SC2000875
                                      :
 7   MICHAEL THOMAS RIGBY,            :
     Mayor, City of Hartwell         :
 8                                    :
                      Defendant.      :
 9                                    |
     ---------------------------------------X

10

11   Jury Trial proceedings held in the above-captioned

12   matter at the county courthouse, in Alfred, New York,

13   Commencing at 10:00 A.M. on Monday, September 27, 20__,

14   Before the HONORABLE WILMA W. WILLIAMS, Supreme Court

15   Justice, and a jury.

16

17

18

19

20   REPORTED BY:    Corena Tinsdale, CSR
                      Official Reporter
21

22

23

24

25
```

EXPERT REPORTING SERVICE
Alfred, NY

```
 1              A P P E A R A N C E S

 2    For the Plaintiff, Amidon

 3                    BARNEY & ERICSON
                      Attorneys at Law
 4                    By Jeff Anson, Esq.
                      721 Washington Towers
 5                    Alfred, NY 14802

 6    For the Defendant, City of Hartwell

 7                    SMITH, SMITH, SMITH & FLINT
                      Attorneys at Law
 8                    By Omar Wheate, Esq.
                      Liberty Bank Building, Suite 1300
 9                    Alfred, NY 14802

10

11

12

13

14

15

16

17

18

19

20

21

22

23

24

25
```

EXPERT REPORTING SERVICE
Alfred, NY

```
 1                              INDEX

 2    Plaintiff's Witnesses       Direct    Cross    Redirect    Recross

 3    Roger T. Amidon                6        11         14         16

 4    Teresa Fields, M.D.           17        20

 5    Debbie Jenson, M.D.           22        26

 6    Bryon T. Lent                 28        31

 7    Plaintiff rests               32

 8    Motion                        32

 9    Defendant's Witnesses

10    Michael Thomas Rigby          33        35

11    Henry S. Teninson, M.D.       36        38
      (Deposition)
12
      Defendant rests              41
13
      Plaintiff's Witnesses
14    in Rebuttal

15    Bryon T. Lent                 41        42

16    Defendant's Witnesses
      in Surrebuttal
17
      Michael Thomas Rigby         43
18
      Motion                       44
19
      Verdict and motions          45
20

21

22

23

24

25
```

SECTION B

EXPERT REPORTING SERVICE
Alfred, NY

```
 1                              EXHIBITS

 2                                   Identification   Evidence

 3   Plaintiff's Exhibit No. P-1 (X-ray)       24          25

 4   Plaintiff's Exhibit No. P-2 (X-ray)       24          25

 5   Plaintiff's Exhibit No. P-3 (X-ray)       24          25

 6   Plaintiff's Exhibit No. P-4 (X-ray)       24          25

 7   Plaintiff's Exhibit No. P-5 (report)      30          31

 8

 9   Defendant's Exhibit No. D-1 (X-ray)       26          26

10   Defendant's Exhibit No. D-2 (X-ray)       26          26

11   Defendant's Exhibit No. D-3 (X-ray)       26          26

12   Defendant's Exhibit No. D-4 (X-ray)       26          26

13   Defendant's Exhibit No. D-5 (X-ray)       26          26

14   Defendant's Exhibit No. D-6 (X-ray)       26          26

15

16

17

18

19

20

21

22

23

24

25
```

EXPERT REPORTING SERVICE
Alfred, NY

1   (A jury was duly impaneled and sworn.)

2   THE COURT: Now, that the jury has been

3 impaneled and sworn, let me introduce the counsel who are

4 present in this case.

5   My name is Judge Williams; Mr. Anson is

6 representing the plaintiff, Roger Amidon; and Mr. Wheate is

7 representing the defendant, the City of Hartwell.

8   Any opening statements, gentlemen?

9   MR. ANSON: Yes, Your Honor, thank you.

10   (Mr. Anson opened to the jury in behalf of

11   the plaintiff.)

12   THE COURT: Mr. Wheate?

13   (Mr. Wheate opened to the jury in behalf of

14   the defendant.)

15   THE COURT: We are now ready. Mr. Anson,

16 will you please call your first witness?

17   MR. ANSON: Your Honor, I call the plaintiff,

18 Roger Amidon.

19   R O G E R T. A M I D O N, the plaintiff

20 herein, called as a witness in his own behalf, being duly

21 sworn, testified as follows:

22   THE CLERK: State your full name and address

23 for the record.

24   THE WITNESS: Roger Timothy Amidon.

25   MR. ANSON: And your address, Mr. Amidon?

```
 1              THE WITNESS: 21 West Main Street, Buffalo,

 2    New York.

 3                       DIRECT EXAMINATION

 4    BY MR. ANSON:

 5         Q    Mr. Amidon, are you the plaintiff in this case?

 6         A    Yes, sir.

 7         Q    And how old are you?

 8         A    24 years of age.

 9         Q    On the day this accident happened to you, the 20th

10    of October of last year, where were you employed?

11         A    Well, at that time I was working for McDonald's.

12         Q    And at the time of this accident, had you been

13    employed by McDonald's for some time?

14         A    Yes, sir. About a year.

15         Q    Was that your usual occupation?

16         A    No, sir.

17         Q    What is your usual vocation?

18         A    I am a professional disc jockey for a local radio

19    station.

20         Q    And for a year or so you have been working at

21    McDonald's?

22         A    Yes, sir.

23         Q    What was the wage you earned while working at

24    McDonald's?

25         A    Well, I had paychecks for $500, depending on what
```

EXPERT REPORTING SERVICE
Alfred, NY

SECTION B

```
 1     A     Yes, sir.

 2     Q     What doctor was that?

 3     A     Dr. Wright.

 4            THE COURT: That clears that up, doesn't it?

 5            MR. ANSON: That's all I have at this time.

 6            THE COURT: Any recross Mr. Wheate?

 7            MR. WHEATE: Yes, Your Honor.

 8                   RECROSS-EXAMINATION

 9     BY MR. WHEATE:

10       Q    Mr. Amidon, was there any damage to your car after

11     the accident?

12       A    No, sir.

13       Q    Did you notice whether the large Santa Claus that

14     hit you on the head was broken or not?   Did you see whether

15     it broke after it fell to the ground?

16       A    No, it was not broken.

17            THE COURT:  Okay, anything else? You may

18     step down.  Mr. Anson call your next witness.

19            MR. ANSON:  Your Honor, at this time I call

20     Dr. Fields.

21            T E R E S A   F I E L D S, M.D., called as

22     a witness on behalf of the plaintiff, being duly sworn,

23     testified as follows:

24            THE CLERK:  State your full name and address

25     for the record.
```

EXPERT REPORTING SERVICE
Alfred, NY

1   MR. WHEATE: I object to that as leading and

2   suggestive.

3   THE COURT: I will sustain the objection.

4   BY MR. ANSON:

5   Q   Then based upon his statement, did you make this

6   report of your investigation?

7   A   From his information, I made the report out.

8   MR. ANSON: I'll offer this into evidence, the

9   report into evidence, Your Honor.

10   MR. WHEATE: No objection.

11   THE COURT: It will be so marked.

12   (Plaintiff's Exhibit No. P-5, the police

13   report, was recieved into evidence.)

14   MR ANSON: You may examine counselor.

15   MR. WHEATE: Thank you, counselor.

16   CROSS-EXAMINATION

17   BY MR. WHEATE:

18   Q   Officer, do you recognize the man whom you just

19   said you had the conversation with?

20   A   No, I wouldn't recognize him, I only spoke to him

21   for a few minutes.

22   THE COURT: Your answer is, "No, I wouldn't

23   recognize him."

24   THE WITNESS: That's correct, Your Honor.

25   BY MR. WHEATE:

EXPERT REPORTING SERVICE
Alfred, NY

1 in favor of the plaintiff, Roger T. Amidon, and against the

2 defendant, the City of Hartwell, in the amount of $400,000.

3   MR. WHEATE: May it please the Court,

4 defendant moves to set aside the verdict, on the ground that

5 it is against the evidence, against the weight of the

6 evidence, contrary to the law and on all the grounds set

7 forth in the Civil Practice Act, except inadequacy; on the

8 further ground that on the proof in this case, the verdict

9 is grossly excessive.

10   THE COURT: I will deny the motion at this

11 time.

12   MR. WHEATE: Will Your Honor give me thirty

13 days' stay?

14   THE COURT: Thirty and sixty.

15   MR. WHEATE: Thank you, Your Honor.

16   (The Court adjourned at 5:40 P.M.)

17

18

19

20

21

22

23

24

25

EXPERT REPORTING SERVICE
Alfred, NY

SECTION B

```
 1              C E R T I F I C A T I O N
 2        I, CORENA TINSDALE, a Certified Shorthand Reporter and
 3    Notary Public within and for the County of Allegany, State
 4    of New York, do hereby certify:
 5        That the foregoing transcript is a true and accurate
 6    account of the stenographic notes taken by me in the matter
 7    of Roger T. Amidon against the City of Hartwell and Michael
 8    Thomas Rigby, Mayor, to the best of my ability.
 9        I further certify that the foregoing 46 pages of
10    testimony are a true and accurate computer-generated record
11    of my stenographic notes taken at the above mentioned
12    proceeding.
13        And I further certify that I am not related to any of
14    the parties to this action by blood or marriage, and that I
15    am in no way interested in the outcome of this matter.
16        Dated this _____day of _____, 20__.
17
18
19        _____
20        CORENA TINSDALE
          Certified Shorthand Reporter
21
22
23
24
25
```

EXPERT REPORTING SERVICE
Alfred, NY

Section C

Freelance Reporting

Chapter 18

The Working Environment of the Freelance Reporter

One of the most popular places of employment for students who graduate from court reporting schools is to be hired as a *freelance reporter* working for a *freelance agency*. Let us begin by defining a *freelance court reporting agency*.

Freelance Agencies

A *freelance reporting agency* is a company that hires individual court reporters to do assigned work for the firm. Basically, people who need the services of a court reporter contact the agency, the agency then contacts the reporters, and the reporters do the job. The people who contacted the agency pay the firm, and the firm pays the reporter, taking a percentage of the money as a fee for finding the job and, in some cases, offering their facilities and equipment. Freelance agencies are large and small. Some agencies employ hundreds of reporters; others are as small as one or two employees. In addition, freelance agencies offer a variety of fringe benefits and employment incentives.

Prospective reporters who may want to work for a freelance court reporting agency should weigh the merits of working for a particular firm. Most freelance agencies can be measured by comparing the following characteristics.

Employee Status

A reporter working with an agency needs to know whether he or she is considered an *employee* or an *independent contractor*. Employees who are hired directly by the freelance agency enter into an employer–employee relationship. In this case the employer is required to deduct all federal, state, and local taxes pertaining to income tax and Social Security.

If the person is hired as an independent contractor, the agency does not deduct anything for taxes or Social Security, and the individual reporter is responsible for paying all required taxes. A reporter may have to file a quarterly statement with the state or federal income tax departments and pay the estimated amount of taxes required by law.

Being hired as an employee has several advantages; for example, job security, Social Security and retirement benefits, as well as medical and vacation benefits. On the other hand, working as an independent contractor also has advantages. These advantages include being able to work for more than one company, being your own boss, owning your own equipment, working when you want to, and so on.

Working as an independent contractor also has disadvantages. Because independent contractors are required to pay taxes on the money that they earn, they must keep good financial records, including a mileage log in their cars. The routine of a 9-to-5 job where one has to go to an office in order to transcribe work is a disadvantage for some reporters.

Employee Benefits

Another important distinguishing characteristic between working as an employee or an independent contractor is the benefits that a company or agency offers those who work for them. Freelance agencies vary widely on the type of fringe benefits that they offer their employees. Some offer great benefit packages, while others offer very little other than job security. Independent contractors, on the other hand, receive no employee benefits because they are not considered employed by the firm.

The following list includes some of the benefits that reporting agencies may offer their employees:

- Financial interest in the agency as a partner or shareholder
- Retirement account or tax savings annuity programs
- Paid holidays and vacation time
- Medical and dental insurance
- Straight salary plus commission on work produced
- Liability insurance and malpractice insurance
- Use of company equipment, including computers and writers
- Company supplies all steno paper, printer paper, disks, ribbons, and the like
- Use of company reference books
- Use of company services: proofers, scopists, editors, and other office staff

Keep in mind that not all freelance agencies offer these benefits. As a general rule, the more benefits that an agency offers its employees, the greater the percentage that the firm will keep as their "split" for work that you do for the company.

Reporter–Agency Fee Split

The *reporter–agency split* refers to the ratio of what a freelance firm keeps and what they give to the reporter. In other words, if a firm charges $4.00 per page and a reporter does a 1000-page transcript, the reporter brought $4,000 into the company. An agency will keep a percentage of that $4,000 in order to pay for its overhead expenses, taxes, rent, employee expenses, equipment, and so on.

Like the benefits, the splits vary from agency to agency, depending on whether one is considered an employee or an independent contractor. In a recent national study of reporting firms, over one-third reported that their split was 30/70. That is, the company receives 30 percent; the reporter, 70 percent. Another one-third estimated the split to be 40/60. When independent contractors were considered in the statistics, almost two-thirds said that reporters kept between 70 and 75 percent of the fees charged.

Place of Work

Most employees of a freelance agency will work in an office environment; that is, they will report to the home office of the agency, wherever that may be. Some agencies have very elaborate downtown suites located in large office buildings; other freelance agencies operate out of a private home. In addition, most employees are required to be physically present at the office when they are not taking dictation. While present in the office, they are transcribing, scoping, editing, copying, and otherwise preparing transcripts for delivery to their clients.

On the other hand, independent contractors work out of their own homes. The method of operation may be to telephone the agency a day or two in advance to find out what jobs have been assigned and then to go to the job site on their own. After recording the dictation, they return to their homes and complete the transcription process using their own equipment. After finishing the transcripts, they deliver them to the agency, who in turn will mail them to the clients, along with the company invoices. Payment is usually made directly to the freelance agency by the clients, and the agency in turn pays the independent contractor on a job-by-job basis, based on the agency split.

Equipment and Supplies

Freelance reporting agencies also vary greatly in terms of the equipment and supplies that they offer their employees or independent contractors. As a general rule, most agencies offer a place to work, a computer station, and a printer. Beyond the basics, some agencies may also supply all the paper for the shorthand machine and printer, business cards, stationery, and other office supplies. They usually do not supply the steno writer nor pay for the general maintenance of the writer. Whether an agency offers equipment and supplies to its employees should be a consideration in selecting employment with an agency.

Examples of Freelance Agencies

Taking into consideration the different characteristics by which agencies can be measured, one needs to weigh the different aspects of each freelance firm and determine for oneself which is the best place of employment. Three examples of agencies that present different circumstances are discussed in this section.

Agency A

Agency A is a reporting firm located in a downtown office in a large city. The agency has three owners, all of whom are official reporters who do not do any freelance reporting themselves. They own the agency and employ reporters to do the freelance work. The agency has an office manager who assigns reporters to jobs on a regular rotation basis. Currently, 20 reporters are working for the agency, but they could use an additional 5 reporters or more.

The firm hires its reporters after an interview process, trains them for a period of six months, and then eventually works them into the reporting environment by giving them the smaller, less complicated matters first. They find jobs for their reporters and seem to care about their general well-being, not wishing to overwork them.

The firm offers a week's paid vacation after one year, two weeks' paid vacation after two years, and a maximum three weeks' paid vacation after three years with the firm. They offer bonuses for professional development and workshops and seminars attended. In addition, full medical and dental coverage is offered, as well as an individual retirement account and a tax-deferred annuity.

The firm also gives its reporters all paper and supplies and allows reporters to use the computers in the office. The only thing the firm does not supply is the shorthand writers, maintaining that reporters are responsible for purchasing and maintaining their own writers.

The split for the agency is 60/40; that is, the reporting agency keeps 60 percent of what its reporters bring in, and the reporters get 40 percent.

Agency B

Agency B is a medium-sized firm, employing seven reporters, located in the same city as Agency A. They could use an additional two or three reporters. They offer no medical or dental benefits, but they do have liability insurance. Their vacation period is one week, fully paid, for all employees. The agency has a small office where reporters can work if they choose. The agency provides transcript paper and steno paper, but reporters must supply everything else. If a reporter chooses to work on a computer, he or she must pay for the initial software license as well as the equipment.

The agency does not care how the reporters produce transcripts; in other words, the reporter could hire their own note readers, scopists, or transcriptionists, as long as they get the work to the agency in proper format. Basically, the agency's only responsibility is to find the jobs, deliver the transcripts, and bill the clients. Reporters get paid after the clients pay the firm. The agency split is 25/75; that is, the agency keeps 25 percent of what it brings in, and the reporter gets 75 percent.

Agency C

Agency C is located in the same city as A and B, but it is considered a small firm, employing only two reporters. The reporters are partners in the firm and are considering hiring one additional reporter to handle their overflow. The agency will offer no benefits at all and would consider a reporter as an independent contractor. In essence, a reporter would work out of his or her home, using his or her own equipment and supplies. The owners may consider allowing the reporter to become a partner in the business after working for them for at least two years. The agency split is 10/90; that is, the firm takes 10 percent of what reporters bring in, and reporters keep 90 percent.

Choosing the Best Agency

As a future court reporter, you may be faced with the choice of having to decide which agency you will want to work for. A large agency that has a great many employees is much different from a small agency where you may be one of only two or three reporters. You should list all the good and bad points for each position and make your decision only after carefully looking over and considering all the facts.

Ten Advantages of Freelance Reporting

1. How much a reporter earns is commensurate with how much he or she wants to work—the more pages produced, the more money earned. Freelancing can be very lucrative, or it can be a source of a little extra income for a family.

2. The freelance reporter may have more freedom in terms of time; it is not strictly a 9-to-5 job.

3. Another reporter is usually available to appear for an assignment if the scheduled reporter becomes ill or desires to take a vacation at any particular time.

4. Freelance reporters often have opportunities to specialize in a particular field of work that they enjoy, such as medical malpractice, patent infringement, or maritime reporting.

5. Many opportunities are available for travel to other states or countries to do reporting jobs.

6. There is a great variety of cases to be heard and people to meet on freelance assignments.

7. Reporting assignments are usually screened so that the more seasoned reporters will get the most difficult jobs, and beginning reporters progress in terms of the degree of difficulty of the work involved.

8. A great deal of experience can be acquired working in a freelance agency. Seasoned reporters will help train novices. Standard forms books will teach reporters proper formatting and reporting methods.

9. Some freelancers have their offices at home and have the advantage of transcribing, editing, proofing, and printing whenever convenient for the individual or family.

10. Usually, the freelance reporter can find a job wherever he or she moves. Most large cities have freelance agencies with opportunities for good reporters with experience.

Ten Disadvantages of Freelance Reporting

1. Many freelance companies do not provide any fringe benefits, such as health insurance, tax withholding, or retirement benefits.

2. The reporter may be hired as an independent contractor and have to keep track of all expenses for proper deductions, as well as withhold all FICA and Social Security payments.

3. Because most freelance reporters are paid for pages produced, most reporters will have to take time off or vacations without pay. When you do not work, you do not get paid.

4. Some firms cannot screen all assignments at all times, and reporters may find themselves in situations that may be a little above their heads.

5. Friction may develop among reporters within an agency because some may feel that work is being unevenly distributed. An uncomfortable working environment may result.

6. Freelance work may be "feast or famine." At times a reporter may have too much work to handle; at others, there may be too little work to go around for everyone. A large paycheck may have to be spread out over a long period to cover smaller paychecks.

7. Some firms may require that a reporter sign a contract to work for them. The contract may require a person to work for a certain time with the promise that he or she will not work for anyone else nor freelance in the same general area if he or she leaves the company.

8. Some people consider working at home a disadvantage; they would prefer to have an office location where they can concentrate on the work at hand.

9. Freelance reporters may be required to purchase all their own equipment, including the shorthand writer, computer, printer, and software. These purchases could mean a large investment of funds and a long period before they are paid off.

10. Once in a freelance position, very few opportunities for promotion may occur within the agency, unless the reporter becomes a shareholder or partner of the company.

Reporting as a Self-Employed Freelancer

Some court reporters do freelance reporting on their own, without the many advantages that agency reporting has to offer. After a few years of hard work, dedication, and experience, the promising individual may begin to employ other reporters and open his or her own agency.

Self-employment is not for everyone. Some reporters need the structure of a job to motivate them, and some reporters enjoy the security of working for someone else. However, some reporters appreciate the challenges offered by operating their own business.

The work of the independent freelance reporter is much the same as the agency freelance reporter; however, the advantages and disadvantages should be considered carefully.

Ten Advantages of Independent Freelance Reporting

1. You are your own boss. You do not have to answer to anyone except yourself.

2. A certain amount of prestige, as well as a certain amount of accomplishment and self-satisfaction, results when working for oneself.

3. You can, to a certain extent, determine your own hours and work whenever and wherever you want to, bearing in mind that jobs turned down once or twice will probably mean that the client will look elsewhere.

4. You do not have to pay an agency a portion of the amount of money you earn. What you get paid by your client is yours, minus the normal business expenses.

5. You may be able to qualify for certain Small Business Administration or minority loans for beginning businesses.

6. Certain tax advantages result from incorporating your business.

7. If you do a good job, your reputation will quickly spread among the legal community as one who is well qualified and competent.

8. You can have people working for you.

9. To a certain extent, you can choose the jobs that you do.

10. If you work hard and do a good job, you can earn a good income.

Ten Disadvantages of Independent Freelance Reporting

1. A large amount of time, energy, and money are required to begin working on your own. The expense of purchasing all the equipment and office supplies may require a sizable business loan to begin your work.

2. You may not be able to obtain many jobs, because most clients remain loyal to a freelance agency that does a good job.

3. You will be in direct competition with well-established reporting firms that have been operating for a number of years.

4. You will have no experience in handling some of the major problems that may occur with clients that a typical agency would handle for you. For example, collecting fees, obtaining signatures of deponents, delivering transcripts, and so on.

5. If you do a poor job for one client, your bad reputation as an incompetent reporter will quickly spread among lawyers and firms.

6. You will have to keep track of all accounts, income received, expenses, taxable deductions, withholding fees, and so on. In addition, you will be responsible for every aspect of each job, from making the appointment to delivering the finished transcript.

7. You may have to work all hours of the day and sometimes night to complete transcripts that are due.

8. You will have to reinvest a certain portion of your profits into the business to keep abreast of the changes in technology.

9. If you do not have good business sense, you risk the chance of losing your time, effort, money, and reputation if you cannot make a success of the business.

10. Pressures and stress are involved in handling all the responsibilities of owning one's own business. You may not be able to deal effectively with the stress and pressure.

Working for an Agency or Working on Your Own

Should you work for a freelance agency or should you venture forth and work on your own as a freelance court reporter? The question is not easily answered. Many considerations need to be weighed in each individual circumstance. However, wisdom dictates that the beginning reporter should thoroughly research all avenues of employment and accept the position that is best suited for him or her and, most importantly, work at the job that gives the most satisfaction.

Chapter 19

Terminology of the Freelance Reporter

This chapter includes some definitions of basic terminology that the freelance reporter should be familiar with. These are terms that the agency or independent freelancer will come across in the normal working environment of the freelance reporter.

Deposition Reporting

Usually, a freelance reporter is called on to take the depositions in a litigation. This chapter discusses the initial stages of a deposition. A closer look at depositions is presented in the following chapters.

To begin with, a deposition is usually instigated by attorneys who wish to gather information regarding a civil or criminal litigation. A deposition may also be called an *examination before trial,* which is abbreviated with the initials *EBT* or *XBT*. It is the testimony of parties or witnesses in the form of questions and answers, taken in writing, under oath or affirmation, before a legally designated judicial officer. Almost all depositions are taken for the purpose of producing a printed transcript. The parties appear for the deposition as a result of a Notice, a Dedimus (Commission), or an Order of the Court.

Depositions make up the majority of the daily activity for most reporting firms. They are essential in the judicial process to bring a trial to a speedy and fair conclusion. Without them, litigation in the United States would be hopelessly deadlocked.

Two types of depositions are used: those taken on oral examination and those taken on written questions. Depositions taken on oral examination are those in which the witness or witnesses appear with their attorney or attorneys and testify under a direct- and cross-examination format.

De Bene Esse Deposition

De bene esse literally means "for the good of the record" or "for perpetuation of testimony." A *de bene esse deposition* may be used at the time of trial when the person testifying is not available for the trial. Such depositions are used in the case of the impending death of a witness, a maritime or military person who is overseas, an individual who becomes too ill to testify, or a person who resides at a great distance from the place of trial. Doctors, important businesspeople, and heads of government may give their depositions, de bene esse. Counsel who request a deposition de bene esse must be able to prove these facts to the Court's satisfaction before they are taken.

Discovery Deposition

Most oral depositions are taken for the purpose of discovery. *Discovery depositions* are reported before a trial begins to elicit evidence that will give information concerning the facts surrounding the litigation. These depositions act as a settlement device wherever possible, thus saving the court time and money. They also serve as a preparation aid for counsel in conducting the trial itself. They prevent witnesses and parties from changing their testimony at the time of trial. They can also serve as the basis for the impeachment of a witness at trial. To *impeach a witness* is to prove that he or she has lied or changed the original facts given by the witness.

Discovery depositions narrow the issues of a case and allow opposing counsel to determine their adversary's theory of the case. Depositions may be taken for all parties to a case. A *deponent* is one who gives a deposition. Deponents include expert witnesses such as doctors, police officers, investigators, or eyewitnesses who saw or heard and can testify to the facts surrounding the case.

The plaintiff, the person who brings the action, and the defendant, the person who is defending himself or herself in the action, may also be required to give their depositions. Most pretrial depositions are taken with counsel for both sides being present.

More and more criminal cases are using discovery depositions to bring out important facts surrounding an investigation. Criminal depositions must adhere to certain restrictions; for example, the work product of law enforcement officers may not be secured through deposition questioning. Also, privileged matter or self-incriminating material cannot be obtained through a deposition.

Discovery depositions serve to lessen the possibility of a surprise during the suit in court. They may not be used as a fishing expedition in which irrelevant and immaterial questions are asked in the hope that something of importance will come out in any of the answers given by the deponent.

In Aid of Execution Deposition

Depositions in aid of execution may be taken after a case is completed and the Court has ordered a money judgment against a party. This type of deposition is used to list the assets of the losing party so that a determination can be made about how and when a judgment should be paid. This type of deposition is also called a *disclosure deposition,* because it is used to reveal financial information.

Deposition on Written Questions

Depositions on written questions are similar to written interrogatories with one important distinction: the person answering the questions is required to appear by subpoena. The written questions must be served to the answering party along with notification of where and before whom the questions are to be answered. Some states offer the opportunity for cross-questions and, if necessary, redirect and recross questions.

Depositions on written questions are interrogatories in which the witness is compelled to answer the questions before a designated officer, usually in the presence of a court reporter. A notice of taking depositions on written questions is shown in Figure 19.1.

Calling of the Deposition

When statutes do not require written notice of taking depositions, many are set up by friendly telephone calls between counsel, who agree on the time, place, and the witnesses to be deposed. The freelance agency is called and asked to send a reporter to the scheduled deposition. The reporting firm is responsible for making sure that a court reporter is assigned to the particular deposition.

All reporting firms maintain an appointment book or computer-generated calendar. The calendar lists the date, time, place, name of reporter assigned, and any other pertinent information that may be necessary.

FIGURE 19.1
Notice of Taking Depositions on Written Questions

FIGURE 19.2
Written Notice to Take Deposition

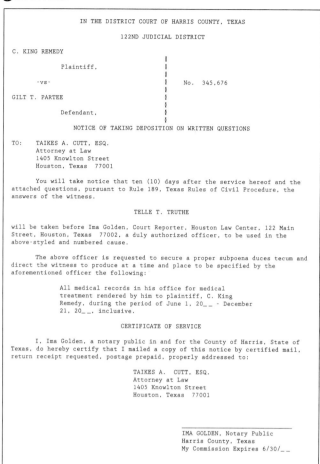

```
          IN THE DISTRICT COURT OF HARRIS COUNTY, TEXAS

                     122ND JUDICIAL DISTRICT

C. KING REMEDY                    I
                                  I
          Plaintiff,              I
                                  I
     -vs-                         I    No. 345,676
                                  I
GILT T. PARTEE                    I
                                  I
          Defendant.              I

          NOTICE OF TAKING DEPOSITION ON WRITTEN QUESTIONS

TO:    TAIKES A. CUTT, ESQ.
       Attorney at Law
       1405 Knowlton Street
       Houston, Texas  77001

       You will take notice that ten (10) days after the service hereof and the
attached questions, pursuant to Rule 189, Texas Rules of Civil Procedure, the
answers of the witness,

                         TELLE T. TRUTHE

will be taken before Ima Golden, Court Reporter, Houston Law Center, 122 Main
Street, Houston, Texas  77002, a duly authorized officer, to be used in the
above-styled and numbered cause.

       The above officer is requested to secure a proper subpoena duces tecum and
direct the witness to produce at a time and place to be specified by the
aforementioned officer the following:

          All medical records in his office for medical
          treatment rendered by him to plaintiff, C. King
          Remedy, during the period of June 1, 20__ - December
          21, 20__, inclusive.

                    CERTIFICATE OF SERVICE

     I, Ima Golden, a notary public in and for the County of Harris, State of
Texas, do hereby certify that I mailed a copy of this notice by certified mail,
return receipt requested, postage prepaid, properly addressed to:

                    TAIKES A.  CUTT, ESQ.
                    Attorney at Law
                    1405 Knowlton Street
                    Houston, Texas  77001


                    _____
                    IMA GOLDEN, Notary Public
                    Harris County, Texas
                    My Commission Expires 6/30/__
```

```
 1    24TH JUDICIAL DISTRICT COURT FOR THE PARISH OF JEFFERSON

 2                     STATE OF LOUISIANA

 3                         DIVISION E

 4    NO.  138-495

 5    HAGGLING FUTELY,        I
                             I
 6           Plaintiff.I
                             I
 7        -vs-               I
                             I
 8    REE SISTING,           I

 9           Defendant.

10    FILED: _____ DEPUTY CLERK: _____

11              NOTICE TO TAKE DEPOSITION

12    TO:  LITIGATIOUS DAILY, ESQ.
           Contentious Building
13         411 Lawsuit Avenue
           New Orleans, LA 70130
14
           PLEASE TAKE NOTICE that undersigned counsel for defendant
15
      REE SISTING will take the oral deposition of the following
16
      named person before an authorized officer on July 22, 20__,
17
      at 3:00 p.m., at 1024 Legal Lane, New Orleans, Louisiana:
18                      Miss Mary M. Contrary
                        4243 Seesitall Road
19                      Metairie, LA 70132

20    Dated this 17th day of June, 20__.

21
                        _____
22                      LYKE LEE WINNER
                        Attorney for Defendant
23                      1024 Legal Lane
                        New Orleans, LA 70130
24

25
```

To avoid any deposition appointment not being met, most agencies make provisions to ensure a quick replacement for the original reporter in cases of illness, absence, or lengthy prior assignments.

If a written Notice of Deposition is required, it must state the title and venue of the action, the name and address of the person giving the notice, the person before whom the testimony will be taken, the time and place of the deposition, the name or names of those who will give testimony, and the matters on which each person will testify. A written notice to take Deposition is shown in Figure 19.2.

Attendance of witnesses for depositions can be ordered by subpoenas. In the case of a *subpoena duces tecum,* the required books, records, or other objects demanded must be brought by the witness to the deposition room. Copies of a subpoena and a subpoena duces tecum are shown in Figures 19.3 and 19.4.

The reporter may be required to prepare these forms and arrange for proper service. Care must be taken to prepare the forms properly and to follow all required procedures in accordance with each state's requirements to prevent a witness from failing to appear at the proper time and place. Freelance reporters may be called on to report pretrial matters, preliminary investigations, and grand jury examinations when the official reporter is on sick leave or vacation.

In some large cities the prosecutor's office hires a number of reporters who are classified as *justice reporters*. These reporters are either pooled or assigned to a certain examiner for a given term. In a U.S. district court, they are often hired on a contract basis by the U.S. attorney. The method of payment under these circumstances varies widely, being on a per diem basis in some instances and a salary basis in others. Those paid on a per diem basis are paid either "by the job" or "by the day."

FIGURE 19.3
Subpoena

```
                IN THE DISTRICT COURT OF HARRIS COUNTY, TEXAS

                         159TH JUDICIAL DISTRICT

CLOUDEE OUTLOOK,              §
                             §
            Plaintiff,       §
     -vs-                    §              No. 800.475
                             §
SUE DOFFEN,                  §              SUBPOENA
                             §
            Defendant.       §

TO ANY SHERIFF OR CONSTABLE OF THE STATE OF TEXAS, GREETING:

        You are hereby commanded to summon CUSTODIAN OF MEDICAL RECORDS for Dr.
Jacob Gray, 555 Montrose Boulevard, Houston, Texas, a resident of Harris County,
Texas, to be and appear before me, a notary public in and for the County of
Harris, State of Texas, or any other person authorized to administer oaths in
Harris County, Texas, at 11:00 a.m. on the 14th day of January 20__, in the
offices of said Custodian, then and there to make answers under oath to written
questions now in my possession; said Custodian being summoned at the instance of
the Defendant's Attorney, and that she bring with her and produce at said time
and place the following:

        Any and all office records, reports, or other writing
        in the custody or subject to the control of said
        custodian pertaining to treatment or examination of
        Cloudee Outlook by Dr. Jacob Gray,

and that said witness continue in attendance from day to day until discharged by
me.

        Herein fail not, but make due return to me on or before the 14th day of
January 20__, showing how you have executed the same.

        Given and issued under my official hand and seal of office on this 1st day
of January, 20__, acting under and pursuant to Notice served on the 30th day of
December, 20__.

                                    _____
                                    EZEE WRITER, Notary Public
                                    Harris County, Texas
                                    My Commission Expires 3/2/__.

                        OFFICER'S RETURN

        Came to hand the ____ day of _____, 20__, and executed the ____
day of _____, 20__, by handing the above-named a true copy of this
subpoena and by tendering the above-named witness fee of $1.00, which he
accepted.

        Returned this ____ day of _____, 20__.

Mileage _____         C. V. "BUSTER" KERN,
Sheriff                              Harris County, Texas
Service _____
Total              $_____     BY:_____
                                    Deputy Sheriff

Make Return to:  Ezee Writer
                 Ace Reporting, Inc.
                 1411 Westheimer Street
                 Houston, TX  77036
```

FIGURE 19.4
Subpoena Duces Tecum

```
                      THE STATE OF TEXAS

TO THE SHERIFF OR ANY CONSTABLE OF HARRIS COUNTY, TEXAS, GREETING:

        You are hereby commanded that you summon JANE HOUGH to be and
appear before me, Lightning Digits, Notary Public in and for Harris
County, Texas, or any Notary Public of my designation, in the offices
of Dr. Robert E. Dahl, 1348 Essex, Houston, TX  77001, on the 25th day
of July, A.D. 20__, at 2:00 p.m., and there to make answers under oath
to certain written Interrogatories to be propounded to her at the
instance of the defendant, Janet Reim, in a certain suit now pending
in the 145th Judicial District Court, wherein Patsy E. Costain, et al.,
Plaintiffs and Kamet Reim, Defendant, appear, being No. 461,397 on the
docket of said Court, and that she bring with her and produce at said
time and place the following, to-wit:

        All records in the office of Dr. Robert E. Dahl pertaining
        to care and treatment of Patsy R. Costain from the very
        earliest to the most recent one;

and that she continue in attendance before me from day to day until
discharged by me.

        This Subpoena is issued under and by virtue of authority of a
Commission issued out of the Honorable 145th Judicial District Court
of Harris County, Texas, and now in my possession.

        Herein fail not, but have you then and there before me at said
time and place this Writ, with your return thereon, showing how you
have executed the same.

        WITNESS MY HAND AND SEAL OF OFFICE at Houston, Texas, County of
Harris, on this the 14th day of July, A.D. 20__.

                                    _____
                                    LIGHTNING DIGITS, Notary Public
                                    in and for Harris County, Texas
                                    My Commission Expires 6/30/__

                        OFFICER'S RETURN

Came to hand on this the 14th day of July, A. D. 20__, at 10:00 a.m.,
and executed the 14th day of July, A.D. 20__, at 11:00 a.m., by
reading the within Subpoena to the said Jane Hough at 1384 Essex,
Houston, TX  77002, the said _____ accepting the tender
of $1.00.

Fees:  Service Writ _____
```

Interrogatories

Interrogatories are a type of examination or method of discovery by which questions are already written and sent to the examining party. The written questions are then answered either in writing or orally. In some states the written interrogatories are served to the defendant along with the complaint and summons. The defendant is then required to answer the interrogatories within a given amount of time.

In the case of a deposition-type interrogatory, the answering party usually responds to the questions in front of a lawyer who has called a freelance agency to use the services of a court reporter. The lawyer reads the questions and the witness responds. The court reporter then produces a transcript that is signed and filed as a deposition.

Interrogatories may be taken for the purpose of securing records from a medical custodian or other person entrusted with the care, custody, and control of the record. The questions may also be a set of standard questions used over and over again to secure information regarding frequently occurring situations, for example, automobile accidents, pedestrian mishaps, falls, customer–restaurant complaints, and passenger claims. Interrogatories also may involve questions asked of medical or other expert witnesses regarding specialized situations.

Interrogatories may not be answered, there may be a motion to "quash" or end the questions, or there may be cross-questions to the interrogatories to be answered by the initial party. Costs are usually paid by the attorney who initiated the direct interrogatories.

Sometimes a court reporter is not required to answer interrogatories, because they may be answered in writing by the responding party. The secretary for the attorney may receive the responses from the witness, transcribe them, and then mail them back to the lawyer who sent them originally.

Written interrogatories are often directed to securing records, to assessing the value of a case, and to settling without costly litigation. Scheduling interrogatories may be less expensive than setting up depositions. For many cases, they provide a valuable evaluation tool that will show the strengths and weaknesses of a case.

Written interrogatories are also useful for impeachment purposes if a witness changes his or her answers at the time of trial. Answers to interrogatories are almost universally considered as prior admissions by a party against his or her interest, so they are an exception to the hearsay rule. Therefore, they may be admitted into evidence and referred to during the closing arguments, thus serving as a very important piece of evidence for consideration by the jury during their deliberations. A transcript of a written interrogatory is shown in Figure 19.5.

The lawyer requesting the interrogatory may handle all preliminaries. Methods and forms vary widely from state to state; therefore, reporters must know the procedures and forms for their particular state.

FIGURE 19.5
Written Interrogatory

```
 1                    No.   461,397
 2
 3
 4    PATSY R. COSTAIN, ET AL.,  §        IN THE DISTRICT COURT OF
                                 §
 5                  Plaintiffs, §        HARRIS COUNTY, T E X A S
                                 §
 6          -vs-                 §        145TH JUDICIAL DISTRICT
                                 §
 7    JANET REIM                 §
                                 §
 8                  Defendant,  §
 9
10          ANSWERS TO DIRECT WRITTEN INTERROGATORIES
11                            of
                           JANE HOUGH
12
13        The following deposition was taken before the undersigned
14    at the offices of Dr. Robert E. Dahl, 1384 Essex, Houston, Texas
15    77001, on the 27th day of July, A.D. 20__, the same being taken
16    upon interrogatories duly certified by the Clerk of the Court in
17    which said cause is pending.
18
19        Said witness, having been duly sworn by me before the
20    examination, deposed as follows:
21
22
23
24
25
```

(a)

```
 1                    JANET HOUGH,
 2    being first duly cautioned and sworn to testify the truth,
 3    the whole truth and nothing but the truth in answer to the
 4    direct questions as hereinafter indicated, deposes and says
 5    as follows:
 6    Direct Interrogatory No. 1:
 7        Please state your name.
 8    A    Jane Hough.
 9    Direct Interrogatory No. 2:
10        Please state whether you have under your care and
11        custody any and all records in your office pertaining
12        to the care and treatment of Patsy R. Costain.
13    A    Yes.
14    Direct Interrogatory No. 3:
15        Please state whether these records have been under the
16        care, custody and control of any other individual since
17        October 1, 20__.
18    A    No.  I have been the sole custodian of these records at
19        all times since that date.
20    Direct Interrogatory No. 4:
21        If you have stated that you have such records, please
22        pass all records, from the very earliest to the most
23        recent one to the court reporter taking this
24        deposition.
25    A    (Complied)
```

(b)

FIGURE 19.5
(continued)

```
 1                        (Copies of records are attached
 2                        hereto and made a part of this
 3                        deposition.)
 4
 5                        _____
 6                        JANE HOUGH
 7   STATE OF TEXAS    Ï
                       Ï
 8   COUNTY OF HARRIS Ï
 9       Subscribed and sworn to before me, the undersigned
10   authority, on this the 27th day of July, 20_ _.
11
12                        _____
13                        LIGHTNING DIGITS, Notary Public
                          in and for Harris County, Texas
14                        My commission Expires 6/30/_ _
15
16
17
18
19
20
21
22
23
24
25
```
(c)

```
 1
 2   THE STATE OF TEXAS Ï
                        Ï
 3   COUNTY OF HARRIS   Ï
 4        I, Lightning Digits, a notary public in and for
 5   the County of Harris, State of Texas, do hereby certify
 6   that I took in shorthand the foregoing testimony of the
 7   witness, JANE HOUGH, and that it was reduced to a printed copy
 8   under my direction.
 9        I further certify that I am not, in any capacity,
10   a regular employee of the party in whose behalf this
11   deposition is taken, nor in the regular employ of his attorney;
12   and I certify that I am not interested in the cause, nor of kin
13   or counsel to either of the parties.
14        I further certify that I sealed said deposition
15   and delivered it to the Clerk of the Court in which said
16   cause is pending without it having been out of my possession
17   or altered after the transcript was prepared and it was
18   read and approved by the witness in my presence on this
19   27th day of July, 20_ _.
20
21
22                        _____
                          LIGHTNING DIGITS, Notary Public
23                        in and for Harris County, Texas
                          My commission Expires 6/30/_ _
24
25
```
(d)

Statement Reporting

In addition to deposition reporting, reporters employed by a freelance agency may be called on to report statements. Generally, freelance reporters report statements about accidents: automobile, industrial, marine, pedestrian, and so on. Some police departments hire freelance reporters to report criminal confessions and statements. The first page of a sworn statement is shown in Figure 19.6.

In most states a freelance reporter must be a notary public in order to swear in witnesses and to add validity to the statement that he or she will report and transcribe. Statement reporting is often easier than deposition or courtroom reporting because the only questions asked are those of the examiner, who is usually an attorney, insurance adjuster, or other investigator.

Most statements follow a general pattern as follows:

1. The questioner identifies the witness and gets the location where the statement is taken on the record.

2. The reason for taking the statement is discussed.

3. The qualification of the witness to give his or her statement is put into the record. For example, was the person an eyewitness? Was he or she present at the scene?

4. The person giving the statement will give his or her story, prodded by questions from the examiner.

5. The witness will verify that the statements were given freely and voluntarily and that the witness was not under the influence of alcohol or drugs. The witness may also state that he or she understood the questions and answered them truthfully and to the best of his or her ability.

6. The witness may also be asked whether he or she cares to state any additions.

Statements do not carry the force of a deposition, but they are helpful for impeachment purposes. Sometimes a person will give a statement, but at the time of trial he or she will forget or purposely tell a different story. When that person is confronted with the testimony that they gave in their statement, he or she has been *impeached*.

Many times the reporter will ride with the interviewer to the location where the statements are to be taken, although sometimes the reporter will be instructed to meet him or her at a designated place. The reporter must arrange in advance with the interviewer whether he or she is to swear in the witness. Although most statements require that a witness be sworn in, some statements do not require an oath. Whether an oath is necessary or not depends on the subject matter, who is giving the statement, and what it will be used for. The first page of an unsworn statement is shown in Figure 19.7. A statement certificate such as the one shown in Figure 19.8 accompanies sworn and unsworn statements.

Statements are taken in a variety of places and at all times of the day and night. Sometimes the reporter has to remain standing while taking dictation. Sometimes no place is available for the reporter to set his or her machine. Special tripods and other equipment can be used for such situations. Most court reporting supply companies offer extended tripods that can be used while standing or shoulder harnesses that allow the reporter to strap the machine in front of him or her and literally take dictation while standing or walking.

FIGURE 19.6
First Page of Sworn Statement

```
 1                      SWORN STATEMENT
                             OF
 2                      TELLING WILLINGLY

 3

 4   TAKEN AT:                   609 Seeall Avenue
                                 Erie, Pennsylvania 18201
 5
     TAKEN ON:                   January 18, 20_ _
 6                               2:00 p.m.

 7   QUESTIONS BY:               Mr. Just T. Fax, Jr.
                                 Knight,Day & Fax
 8                               2300 Indictment Road
                                 Erie, Pennsylvania 18201
 9
     ALSO PRESENT:               Mr. C. King Truth, Attorney
10
                                 Mrs. Annie Rooney
11
     REPORTED BY:                Ima Verbatim
12

13
                        TELLING WILLINGLY,
14
     having been first duly sworn by the reporter, testified on her
15
     oath as follows:
16

17                        EXAMINATION

18   BY MR. FAX:

19   Q    Let's get your full name down for the record.

20   A    Telling Willingly.

21   Q    Mrs. Willingly, let me first introduce myself and tell

22   you why we're here and what we are doing.

23        My name is Just T. Fax, Jr., and I'm a lawyer.  I will

24   be asking you questions.  You have been put under oath, and

25   the court reporter here will be writing
```

FIGURE 19.7
First Page of Unsworn Statement (several statements in same case bound in a single cover)

```
 1

 2                  S T A T E M E N T S   O F:

 3                  CUT M. UPP, M.D.
                    NURSEM TEW HEALTH
 4                  JENTILLE THERAPY
                    DELIGHTFUL RECOVERY
 5

 6

 7        Taken on Wednesday, May 22, 20__, in the offices of

 8   C. A. Malpractice, M.D., West Slicem General Hospital, 7843

 9   Traction Street, New Orleans, Louisiana, at 10:00 a.m., before

10   Lively Digits, Court Reporter.

11

12

13                    *  *  *  *  *  *  *

14

15   APPEARANCES:

16                        TRYING A. CASE, ESQ.
                          123456 Contingency Circle
17                        New Orleans, Louisiana 70112

18   ALSO PRESENT:        MAY PAY MUNEE,
                          Representative, Liberal Insurance Company
19

20

21

22

23

24

25
```

FIGURE 19.8
Statement Certificate

1
2
3
4   C E R T I F I C A T E
5
6   I, LIVELY DIGITS, Certified Shorthand Reporter
7   in and for the Parish of Jefferson, State of Louisiana,
8   do hereby certify that the foregoing statements
9   consisting of _____ pages were reported by me in machine
10 shorthand and transcribed (by me) (under my personal
11 direction and supervision) and are a true and correct
12 transcript, to the best of my ability and understanding.
13   I hereby certify that I am not of counsel,
14 not related to counsel or the parties hereto, and am in
15 no way interested in the outcome of this matter.
16
17
18   _____
19   LIVELY DIGITS
                            Certified Shorthand Reporter
                            Parish of Jefferson
20   State of Louisiana
21
22
23
24
25

SECTION C

Chapter 20

Reporting a Typical Deposition: General Information

A *deposition* is a method of taking the sworn testimony of witnesses or parties to a litigation before trial. It is usually conducted in the presence of attorneys who have notified all parties involved about the deposition. The main purpose of a deposition is for discovery, to determine what the facts are concerning a litigation, but they may also be read at the time of trial in place of the presence of a witness.

Depositions are taken by notice or by agreement between the parties. Witnesses at a deposition are sworn to tell the truth, and their oath or affirmation carries the same weight and effect as if they were testifying in court. Depositions follow the Federal Rules of Civil Procedures, particularly Rules 26 through 31.

Although a deposition is usually conducted for one deponent, more than one person may be deposed at a deposition. Almost anything imaginable can be discussed at a deposition. The material covered is as diverse as the material covered at a civil or criminal trial. This chapter will take you step by step through a typical deposition.

Before the Deposition

Before the reporter shows up to take the deposition, several important preliminary items need to be taken care of. For example, the reporter needs to know where to go, to have the proper equipment in good working order, to know what to do at the deposition, and to know how to end the deposition and where to send the transcript and the invoice.

Obtain Directions

First, the reporter needs to know where to go and how to get there. Plan your route of travel, especially if you are unfamiliar with the location and have never been there before. If you are working for a freelance agency, the firm will tell you the best way to go to the deposition location. If you are freelancing on your own, you may have to ask for directions. Make sure that you know what time the deposition starts so that you can arrive on time.

When traveling to office buildings or locations that are new to you, obtain directions from a reliable source before you leave. Map out your route and find out where the nearest parking garage is located so that you do not have to spend time looking for a parking space.

Most reporters will also leave for their destination with plenty of time to spare in case of unforeseen circumstances. You will want to allow time for unforeseen traffic congestion, no parking spaces, or getting lost. Arrive at the deposition 20 to 30 minutes before the deposition begins.

Be Prepared

The reporter should have a basic checkoff sheet containing a list of items and supplies that are necessary for reporting. Occasionally, run through the checkoff sheet to be sure that all items are available.

Items needed for the deposition include the following:

1. A shorthand machine that is in good working order; make sure that the battery is charged, the machine inked, and everything is in top condition. Some reporters carry a spare shorthand machine in their car in case of emergencies.

2. If you use realtime, a laptop computer that is adequately charged and has enough storage space on the hard drive or enough disk space.

3. Electrical chargers in case the batteries on your shorthand machine or computer suddenly die. Also, an extension cord in case an outlet is not near where you are set up to take dictation.

4. Shorthand paper, at least one pad for every hour of dictation. If the deposition is scheduled for three hours, take three packs of paper, plus an extra one in case it is needed. Some reporters leave an extra box of shorthand paper in the trunk of the car.

5. Extra ribbon, shorthand machine ink, and diskette if the shorthand machine records to disk.

6. A pen and pencil, stapler and staples, paper clips, rubber bands, a note pad, and other miscellaneous office supplies.

7. Exhibit marking equipment, including a stamp and ink pad, labels, tags, string or ties used to attach tags to items, small baggies, envelopes, and other miscellaneous items used to mark or hold exhibits.

8. The reporter's worksheet or information sheet.

9. A supply of business cards that contain your name or the name and address of your agency.

10. Other items that may be needed to perform your duties as a professional freelance reporter.

Pertinent Information

If possible, the reporter should get as much information as he or she possibly can concerning the deposition beforehand. Some items of information are more important than others, but an effort should be made by the office manager making the original contact or the court reporter to get at least the basic information. The following items will be helpful:

1. Date, time, and place of deposition

2. Title of action, including caption and venue

3. Names of attorneys and whom they represent

4. Name of people to be deposed

5. Approximate length of time to schedule for the deposition

6. Copies of pleadings, including complaint and answer

7. Any extra information, such as the nature of the case, when the case is going to trial, and so on

At the Deposition

The reporter should introduce himself or herself to the office receptionist and state the reason why he or she is there—to take the deposition in the matter of Jones v. Smith. Make sure that you arrive well ahead of the starting time.

Get a Copy of the Pleadings

The wise reporter will ask the receptionist for a copy of the pleadings if they have not already been obtained. The complaint and answer will give the reporter a wealth of information concerning who the attorneys are, who the parties to the suit are, and all factual information surrounding the suit.

Set Up Equipment and Await the Arrival of Attorneys

The reporter should ask whether the room where the deposition is going to be held is available so that he or she can begin setting up the equipment. Once inside the room, the reporter should choose the best possible chair to sit in, making sure that it is in a good location for hearing and seeing what is going on.

As the different attorneys enter the room, the reporter should greet each with a handshake and exchange business cards. The business cards of the lawyers are used to verify the information contained in the pleadings concerning the names of counsel representing the parties to the action. If different lawyers are present from the same firm, it should be noted on the appearance portion of the reporter's worksheet.

Stipulations and Oath

When the attorneys and witnesses are seated and ready to begin the deposition, reference is usually made to the stipulations. Make sure that everyone present understands what the "usual stipulations" are or, if they are put into the record, make sure that you record and transcribe them into the record. Make sure that you understand the concept of stipulations as outlined in Chapter 21.

Before the first question is asked of a witness, make sure that he or she has been sworn in. Usually, the court reporter, as a notary public, swears in or affirms the witnesses. Make sure that you have memorized and can accurately pronounce a suitable oath as outlined in Chapter 21.

Examination and Exhibits

Once the oath is administered, the attorney who has called the deposition begins questioning the witnesses. Although most reporters and freelance agencies transcribe all testimony of witnesses at depositions as EX-AMINATION, some agencies use the headings DIRECT EXAMINATION when questioning occurs by the attorney who called the witness and CROSS-EXAMINATION when the opposing attorney questions the witness.

The testimony and any colloquy should be recorded just as any other verbatim transaction. Exhibits will be marked for identification only, because they cannot be received as evidence at the depositions. Most agencies and reporters mark exhibits as Deposition Exhibits, Plaintiff's Deposition Exhibit, or Defendant's Deposition Exhibit.

The reporter's worksheet should be filled in appropriately with the names of witnesses, the counsel conducting the examination, the numbering of exhibits marked for identification, who offered them, spellings of proper names, and unusual terminology.

Question Certification

During the deposition, if a question is asked and the attorney for the witness instructs the witness not to answer the question, the question may require certification. This subject will be explained in detail in Chapter 21.

Stopping Witnesses and Attorneys

If a witness begins to speak too rapidly or says something that is not understandable, the reporter must stop the witness and ask him or her to repeat what was not recorded. In most cases a polite "Excuse me, would you repeat what you just said?" or "I'm sorry, I didn't hear what you said, would you repeat that?" will suffice.

The reporter should use discretion when asking an attorney to slow down, keeping in mind that the integrity of the record is at stake. If you need to ask lawyers to repeat something, be courteous and avoid phrases such as "I did not get that" or "You are going too fast." Simply ask them to repeat their last question because you did not hear it.

Off-the-Record Discussions

If an attorney asks to go off the record to discuss something, make sure that the other attorney has agreed to going off the record. Let the attorney know that you are not recording what is being said by taking your hands off the machine and, in some cases, standing up. This method ensures that the attorneys realize that they cannot go back on the record until you are seated at the machine with your hands on the keyboard.

Parentheticals

Deposition reporters should have a clear understanding of when and how to use parentheticals as outlined in Section B of this handbook. Parentheticals involve marking exhibits for identification, reading back questions, recording off-the-record discussions, and inserting various question-and-answer parentheticals that will be used during most depositions.

Correct Spellings

The spellings of names and technical terms can be verified during the deposition by a polite request; however, do so during a break in the testimony or at the end of the hearing. Counsel do not like to be repeatedly stopped to spell every difficult word that is used during dictation. By using the pleadings wisely, you will already be aware of about 75 percent of the terms, phrases, and names that may be used during the deposition. You can ask about the other 25 percent after the deposition if you need to.

At the End of the Deposition

At the conclusion of the deposition, obtain all information regarding the billing, signing, and delivery of the deposition. Some of this information may have already been obtained in the stipulations made at the beginning of the examination.

Deposition Exhibits

Some attorneys expect the court reporter to keep and maintain all exhibits introduced for identification and then to include them in the transcript. Other attorneys keep their own exhibits and present them at the time of trial. The court reporter must ask at the end of the deposition whether the exhibits should be part of the record or whether the attorneys will keep them. If the attorneys are going to keep their own exhibits, make copies of the exhibits for reference while completing the transcript.

Retroactive Oath

If at some point during the deposition you discover that you forgot to swear in a witness, ask the attorneys if they would like to have the witness sworn in at that point. Most attorneys will agree, in which case you will use a retroactive oath that states that everything the witness has said *has been* the truth and that everything he or she says from now *will be* the truth.

Delivery Time

The court reporter needs to know whether the deposition is needed right away or whether the usual delivery time will be sufficient for the lawyers. One question that might be asked at this point is whether a trial date has been set for the litigation. Some attorneys may request an expedited copy or an immediate copy, in which case you should inform the attorneys of the rate charged for such service.

Special Requests

The court reporter should determine whether attorneys would prefer to use any of the litigation support services that your agency may offer: for example, ASCII files, keyword indexing, electronic modem delivery, or immediate rough copies. Such services require special fees, and the reporter should be able to quote the prices or have a rate sheet available for the attorneys.

Signing of the Deposition and Filing of the Original

If the signature of the deponent has not been waived, the reporter may inquire whether he or she should obtain the signature of the witness, or if the completed deposition should be sent to the attorney for the deponent so that he or she can obtain the required signature.

In the same manner, if the filing of the original has not been waived, the reporter may need to get the signed deposition back and file the transcript with the clerk of the court.

Charges and Invoicing

Attorneys usually note on the record any unusual circumstances about who is to be billed for the cost of the transcript. If nothing is said by the time the attorneys are ready to leave, you may need to inquire as to who will cover the cost of the deposition.

Invoicing and payments vary from lawyer to lawyer. Some attorneys agree that the lawyer who called the deposition is responsible for all costs. Other attorneys maintain that they should be charged only for their own examination. Still other attorneys split the cost down the middle. Make sure that you find out who is going to pay for what and that the proper invoice is included with each copy of the transcript.

Proofreading the Final Copy

The court and realtime reporter should feel a certain amount of pride in every transcript that he or she produces. Each transcript is a testament of his or her ability to record the spoken word and transcribe it in proper format. Transcripts should be proofread carefully for errors in transcription, format errors, proper spellings of names, and so on.

Things to Consider When Deposition Reporting

The next two chapters will explain some of the more specific items that the freelance court reporter needs to be concerned with in reporting depositions and other freelance work.

Chapter 21

Deposition Reporting: Things to Consider

Freelance Office Appointment Book

Every freelance agency, large or small, has an appointment book from which all initial calls from clients are penciled in and assignments are given to reporters in the firm. Most large firms have an office manager or receptionist who handles all incoming telephone calls.

Some reporting agencies use a computer software program that manages and schedules all appointments. Essentially, it is a computerized calendar that keeps track of the reporters, their assignments, their clients, the progress of a transcript, and the delivery and receipt of payment.

Preparation for Reporting Assignments

The reporter, whether official or freelance, is responsible for making sure that he or she is always ready. This means that the reporter should carry at least two extra floppy disks, three or four packs of paper, and a spare ribbon and, in some cases, have a spare shorthand machine handy in case something happens to the regular machine. Some reporters carry a manual machine writer as a spare, just in case something happens to the power and all computers are down. In either event, the reporter still has the ability to write and then transcribe later. In addition, a reporter needs to have ink, pens, pencils, a writing pad, paper clips, rubber bands, a stapler, and various exhibit writing items as discussed in Chapter 13.

Reporters need to dress comfortably but look sharp! You should look like a professional who is doing a professional job. Arrive for court or the deposition at least 20 to 30 minutes early.

In the case of deposition work, when you arrive at the appointed place, identify yourself to the secretary or legal assistant who greets you. She or he is a very important person to you. Give the office manager one of your business cards and explain that you are to take the deposition scheduled. If you are reliable, trustworthy, do good work, and make a good impression, the law firm may ask for your services again.

Eventually, you will be ushered into the deposition room, where ordinarily you will meet the attorney who hired you or his or her designate and his or her client or clients. Sometimes opposing counsel and the witnesses are also present at the beginning, although the custom is for each client to confer with his or her attorney separately before coming together in the deposition room.

Identify yourself to these people and give your business card to each attorney. Ask each counsel present for his or her business card, and mark on each card whom the lawyer is representing, that is, the plaintiff or defendant. If an attorney does not have a business card, write the name, address, telephone number, and whom he or she represents carefully on your information sheet.

If you do not have a venue, style or title, case number, and the name of the individual to be deposed from the notice, ask for a copy of the pleadings or a paper with this information. Any information that you can gather before the actual deposition will be helpful in noting appearances, witnesses, spellings, and special names that may arise during the deposition. All this information can usually be obtained from the office manager who greets you when you first enter the place where the deposition is being held.

Be sure that you note on your information sheet any extra people, such as insurance adjusters, family members, co-counsel, and representatives of parties to the suit, and list them on the appearance page when the deposition is transcribed. The worksheet and appearances are discussed in detail in Chapter 8.

Counsel will often ask you where you want to sit and what kind of chair you prefer. Request to be seated near the witness and beside or across from the questioning attorney. You must be in a good position to see both of them and particularly to hear them well. If the witness murmurs or whispers, move closer to the point where you can hear everything well. The record must be complete, and you must do whatever is necessary to secure such a record. You cannot be too timid and be a good reporter.

If possible, look for a straight chair with no arms unless such an item is not readily available in the office. In this case, you should do the best you can with whatever is available. Do not make an issue of petty things, or the next time depositions are to be scheduled, a different reporter or firm will be requested.

In any event, make sure that you are comfortable and that you can hear and see well, and do not feel intimidated. You are responsible for getting an accurate record.

The Deposition Worksheet

Chapter 8 dealt with the preliminary things necessary for an official reporter. This chapter touched upon the worksheet or information sheet that needs to be filled out by reporters before they begin a job. The items mentioned in the court reporting worksheet are the same for the freelance reporter with some minor differences.

Review Chapter 8 and note the different parts of the worksheet: heading, appearances, exhibits, witnesses, local abbreviations, spelling of proper nouns, designation of counsel and court, special instructions, and number of copies to be invoiced.

An example of a deposition worksheet is given in Figure 21.1.

How to Report Deposition Stipulations

As noted in Chapter 8, *stipulations* are agreements among counsel and the court as to certain things that occur at the beginning of a deposition. At the beginning of a deposition, when all parties to a litigation are gathered, the first thing that one attorney usually says to the other is "Usual stips?", to which the opposing attorney will usually respond "Okay." Usual stips means the *usual stipulations*. This phrase refers to the procedural ground rules that the attorneys will follow in taking the deposition. These stipulations are included in the transcript. A sample stipulation page is shown in Figure 21.2.

Some attorneys expect the reporter to know what the usual stipulations are; others will want to dictate them for the record so that absolutely no question will arise about what the attorneys are agreeing to. If you do not know what the usual stips are, ask that they be given.

If the stipulations are dictated, they may be read from a sheet of paper by an attorney. If they are read into the record, be prepared to write quickly, because items read into the record are often read at a fast pace. If possible, obtain a copy of the paper that the attorney may be reading from to verify the stipulations for your transcript.

If the attorneys are relying on you to insert the usual stipulations, you should ask the office manager or another reporter at your agency or firm for a copy of what has been included with other transcripts as the "usual stips."

FIGURE 21.1
Deposition Worksheet

```
                    DEPOSITION WORKSHEET

REPORTER _____
DATE _____ JOB NUMBER _____
CASE NUMBER _____
VENUE _____

                         Style
_____
_____
                         -vs-
_____
_____

PLAINTIFF'S           Witnesses           DEFENDANT'S
_____      _____
_____      _____
_____

                      Appearances
_____      _____
_____      _____
_____      _____

    EXHIBITS          COPIES OF EACH

WAIVE SIGNATURE           (   ) PURSUANT TO AGREEMENT (   )
SIGNATURE ANY TIME BEFORE       PURSUANT TO NOTICE    (   )
  TRIAL                   (   ) USUAL STIPULATION     (   )
SIGNATURE BEFORE FILING   (   )
COMMISSION                (   )

BILLING TO PLAINTIFF:
    ORIG & _____ OF _____
    ORIG & _____ OF _____
    ORIG & _____ OF _____
BILLING TO DEFENDANT
    ORIG & _____ OF _____
    ORIG & _____ OF _____
    ORIG & _____ OF _____

SPELLING, REMARKS, AND ARBITRARY FORMS:
```

FIGURE 21.2
Sample Stipulation Page

```
 1              S T I P U L A T I O N S

 2

 3        IT WAS STIPULATED AND AGREED by and between

 4  Counsel for the respective parties that notice, time,

 5  and all other statutory prerequisites incident to the

 6  taking and return of said deposition, including notice

 7  of filing, *(as well as the signing of same by the witness)

 8  are hereby waived; that same may be taken at the time and

 9  place set forth, and when reduced to writing and returned

10  into court, may be used by either party upon the trial

11  of said cause, said deposition, however, to be subject to

12  all other legal objections, which need not be reserved

13  at the time of taking the deposition, but may be urged

14  at the time of trial the same as if the witness were

15  present, testifying in person.

16

17  _____

18  *Add the following if the signature of the witness is

19  required, deleting the material between parentheses above:

20

21        IT WAS FURTHER STIPULATED AND AGREED by and between

22  Counsel that the said witness shall read and sign the

23  deposition before filing.

24

25
```

Usual Stipulations

Usually, counsel for the respective parties will stipulate that written notice of taking the deposition be waived, especially if they have previously agreed to the time and place of the taking of the matter. They also may stipulate that notice of filing be waived, which means that the reporter does not have to notify the attorneys when the original is filed with the appropriate clerk. Common stipulation forms are shown in Figures 21.3 and 21.4. The form in Figure 21.4 is of the checkoff variety; only those stipulations that apply to a particular deposition are checked off and included within the deposition.

Other usual stipulations are as follows: Objections are waived until the time of trial, except as to the form of the question; the signature of the witness or witnesses is waived; and the Notice of Taking and Notice of Filing are waived.

If any of these stipulations do not apply, then, during the deposition itself, an attorney may object for any reason; at the conclusion of the deposition, after the transcript has been produced, the witness must read and sign it before a notary public, and the original is filed with a notice to the attorneys.

Usual stipulations also means that the depositions may be used for all purposes contemplated under the statutes of the state or federal rules governing U.S. district courts.

FIGURE 21.3
Common Stipulations Form

STIPULATIONS (Insert proper numbers.)

IT IS STIPULATED AND AGREED by and between counsel for the respective parties hereto that this deposition is taken pursuant to the paragraphs below, number _____.

(1) That the deposition of the witness named in the caption hereto may be taken at this time and place before the herein named notary public of _____ County, State of _____; time notice, and the issuance of a commission being waived; and that the said deposition or any part thereof, when so taken, may be used on the trial of this case with the same force and effect as if the witness were present in court and testifying in person;

(2) That the necessity for the witness to read and sign this deposition is waived;

(3) That the necessity for preserving objections at the time of taking is waived, and that any and all legal objections to this deposition or any part thereof may be urged at the time same is sought to be offered in evidence on the trial of this cause;

(4) That this deposition may be filed with the clerk of the court prior to reading and signing of same by the witness; provided further, however, that the witness shall read and subscribe to same at or before the time of the commencement of the trial;

(5) That the witness shall read and sign this deposition before a notary public prior to the time of filing same with the clerk of the court; and/or

(6) That the necessity for preserving objections at the time of taking is waived and that any and all legal objections to this deposition or any part thereof may be urged at the time same is sought to be offered in evidence on the trial of this cause; except, however, that objections to the form of the questions and/or responsiveness of the answers must be made at the time of taking or else such objections are specifically waived.

FIGURE 21.4
Common Stipulations Form

(Check applicable stipulations for inclusion in the record.)

_____ 1. It is hereby stipulated and agreed by and between counsel for the respective parties that the deposition of the above-named witness may be taken on behalf of the (plaintiff – defendant) at the time and place set forth herein before the notary public herein mentioned and be reported by _____, a competent shorthand reporter and disinterested person, and thereafter reduced to printed form under (his/her) direction;

_____ 2. That all objections as to notice of time and place of the taking of this deposition are expressly waived;

_____ 3. That all objections except as to the form of the questions are reserved to the time of trial;

_____ 4. That this deposition, when transcribed, may be used for all purposes contemplated under the Rules;

_____ 5. That the reading of this deposition to, or by, the witness and the signing thereof by the witness are hereby expressly waived;

_____ 6. That it is hereby expressly stipulated that the signature of the witness shall be subscribed to the transcript of this deposition in the presence of a notary public; and/or

_____ 7. That in the event this deposition is not corrected and signed by the witness at the time of trial, reasonable opportunity having been given to do so, it may be introduced by either party with the same force and effect as though signed.

Dictated Stipulations

The attorneys may dictate other stipulations to the reporter. If the attorneys do not discuss stipulations at the beginning of the deposition and you have no opportunity to secure them at the outset, do not assume that they apply. Just inquire tactfully at the end of taking the matter whether any stipulations are to be included in the transcript. An example of dictated stipulations is shown in Figure 21.5.

Any special instructions that the attorneys give to you are very important. Make sure that you understand them thoroughly so that you do not make an irrevocable mistake in producing the transcript.

In some cases, the discussion about signing the deposition by the witness may take place at the conclusion. In some states, the attorney for any party may state on the record that the signature is waived. Be sure to include this statement in your notes.

Where Stipulations Are Placed in the Transcript

Deposition stipulations are usually placed at the beginning of the transcript itself. In most freelance firms, the title page is the very first page of the transcript. This page is usually not numbered, unless for some reason the computer software package only allows numbering to start with page 1 on the title page. The appearance page that contains the names and addresses of the attorneys and whom they represent is usually the second page; the index of witnesses and exhibits may be found on the third page; and the stipulations may be placed before the body of the transcript. In some states, the stipulations are placed at the end of the examination of the deponent by the attorneys.

FIGURE 21.5
Dictated Stipulations

```
1          MR. VELTA: May it be stipulated, counsel,

2     that the deposition of John Doyle is being

3     taken here on the 12th day of February, 1998,

4     pursuant to agreement, and may be used in the

5     cases of S. E. Jensen v. John Doyle, Eva

6     Jensen v. John Doyle, and also in the case

7     brought by John Doyle against both of the

8     Jensens, for all purposes which are

9     contemplated by the Rules of Civil Procedure

10    for the District Courts of the State of

11    Minnesota, for discovery purposes, and that

12    all formalities as to signing and filing of

13    the deposition may be waived?

14         MR. GALLAGHER:  Just one thing:  That

15    does not contemplate use of it in case of the

16    inability of the person to be in Court, does

17    it?

18         MR. LUNDQUIST:  As I understood it, you

19    said in regard to discovery only.

20         MR. VELTA:  I guess I did.  I stand

21    corrected.

22         MR. LUNDQUIST:  That stipulation is

23    satisfactory with me.

24         MR. BLATTI:  It may be so stipulated so

25    far as we are concerned.
```

How to Administer Oath and Prepare Witness Setup

Chapter 9 dealt with administering the oath, witness setup, and speaker and examination identification as these subjects relate to trial reporting. Some of the information presented in that chapter is relevant to their application to freelance reporting; therefore, you may want to review that chapter at this time.

The Notary Public

In some states, in order to administer the oath to a witness, one has to be a notary public. A *notary public* is an officer whose duty is to attest to the genuineness of legal instruments so that they can be used in courts of law. A notary acts in a ministerial rather than in a judicial capacity, and a notary public may not practice any form of law. You should check with the clerk of court or your county clerk to learn the necessary requirements for becoming a notary public in your county. Most reporters become notary publics because of the service that they can provide to judges and attorneys and because they may be required to swear in witnesses.

In most states, notaries can act in different counties within the state in which they are appointed. However, a notary from one state may not practice within another state without a stipulation noted on the record between the attorneys.

Each state has different requirements to meet for becoming a notary. In most states a person must be of legal age and a resident or citizen of the state in which the commission is to be granted and cannot have a criminal record. Usually, notaries are appointed by the secretary of state.

The information that you need to become a notary may be obtained from the county clerk. You will complete a form, and you may be required to take a test based on the duties and responsibilities of the notary. You will also be required to pay a fee, both for the test and for the commission, if you pass the test.

The duties and responsibilities of a notary public are not to be taken lightly. In some states a person appointed as a notary public must execute a bond with a solvent surety company. The company must be acceptable to the secretary of state and be authorized to do business in the state. The bond is to ensure faithful performance of the duties of the office.

Each notary public should keep a book of records of all acknowledgments of instruments taken before him or her and any fees collected for services rendered as a notary.

The notary is required to sign his name in the proper place on documents that he is attesting to and to key, print, or stamp his or her name, county and state, number, and date of expiration. Most notaries have a rubber stamp made that contains the information needed for the notary signature.

Some statutes also say that each notary public must provide a seal of office that conforms to the state laws. Some legal documents require that the notary affix his or her seal to the document. In some states, the custom is to inscribe the name of the notary public on a metal or rubber notary seal. Verify the custom and protocol for your county and court before you become a notary.

Reporter's Oath Used at a Deposition or Statement

An example of a typical oath that a reporter would use at a deposition or statement is as follows: "Do you solemnly swear that the testimony that you are about to offer regarding the cause hereinunder consideration shall be the truth, the whole truth, and nothing but the truth, so help you God?"

As noted in Chapter 9, if a witness cannot swear because of religious or personal beliefs, an acceptable affirmation may be used in place of the oath, for example, "Do you solemnly affirm that the testimony that you are about to offer regarding the cause hereinunder consideration shall be the truth, the whole truth, and nothing but the truth? This you do under the pains and penalties of perjury?"

The setup of the witness within the transcript is the same as outlined in Chapter 9. For review, a typical witness setup as it may appear in a deposition is presented here:

JOHN S. FLINTROCK,

called as a witness in his own behalf, having been duly sworn, testified as follows:

EXAMINATION

BY MR. ATTORNEY:

Q: Mr. Flintrock, please tell us your full name and address for the record.

How to Designate Speakers and Types of Examinations

The method used by a reporter to designate the speakers and to note the type of examination may be used at any trial, hearing, deposition, statement, or other legal matter where specific shorthand outlines are used to make such designations. A review of Chapter 9 at this time will be helpful.

How to Report Deposition Parentheticals

Relevant deposition parentheticals are reported in the same manner as they are in regular court reporting as outlined in Chapter 10. The basic guideline followed in the setup of parentheticals within a transcript is to indent the entire material contained between the opening and closing parenthetical three tabs in. Some agencies also indent the parenthetical five spaces from the right margin.

Some relevant parentheticals that may appear during a deposition are those that relate to off-the-record discussions, marking and receiving exhibits, reading back the last question and answer, and some descriptive one-word parentheticals, as outlined in Chapter 10.

Examples of these parentheticals are as follows:

(An off-the-record discussion was held.)

(Deposition Exhibit No. 5, a documented dated May 17, 2001, was marked for identification.)

(The last question and answer were read back.)

How to Report Objections

The deposition reporter is responsible for getting a verbatim record of all objections that are made during a deposition, as well as the response and counter-responses that may follow the initial objections. While most attorneys will waive all objections during a deposition, except as to the form of a question, attorneys may still object to certain evidence being presented during the proceeding. Refusal by a witness to answer a question based on the objection of his or her attorney may lead to what is called *certifying the question*.

How to Certify a Question

The *certification* of a question usually take places during a deposition or examination before trial where no judge is present. *Depositions* are discovery proceedings whereby a witness is subpoenaed to appear before an attorney to answer questions under direct- and cross-examination. The witness is sworn in by a notary public, who is usually a court reporter. The oath that the witness takes has the same force and effect as does a courtroom oath.

The testimony that is given under oath can be used in a court of law at the time of trial. Anything said is assumed to be the truth. If a witness later testifies in court and changes his or her story as to the facts, then he or she will be held accountable as to why the facts were changed. In other words, the witness has been impeached.

The deposition process usually begins with a recitation of stipulations that are agreed to by the attorneys involved. Among the stipulations may be the agreement that the attorneys will reserve all objections to questions until the time of trial. One exception is that attorneys may reserve the right to object to the form of the question. When an attorney objects to the form of the question, he or she is objecting to the way it was asked and requests that the attorney rephrase the question.

During the testimony given at a deposition, an attorney will sometimes ask a question of a witness and that witness's counsel will instruct his or her client not to answer the question. Such an instruction usually leads to an argument between the attorneys, eventually ending in a request for the reporter to "certify the question" or "cite the question."

When an attorney requests the reporter to *certify the question,* it means that the reporter will extract it from the deposition by transcribing it on a certification page containing the venue, the name of the deponent and reporter, and the objectionable portion. This certification page will then be taken to the judge who has jurisdiction in the matter and he or she will rule on whether the question has to be answered. If the question has to be answered, the attorneys will gather everyone together to continue the deposition or to answer the questions that required certification.

The certification of a question can take two different forms. One is an *immediate certification,* and the other is a *certification after the fact.*

Immediate Certification

When one of the attorneys at a deposition refuses to continue the deposition until the question is answered, an immediate certification may be required. If certification is requested, the deposition will be concluded with the stipulation that it will be reconvened after the judge has ruled on the certified question. The reporter is responsible for producing a copy of the certified question and presenting it to the lawyers, who will take it to the judge for a ruling. A certification of questions is shown in Figure 21.6.

Most reporters use a word-processing software package on their computers to prepare the certification and print it on their printer. Some reporters have a *template* file that contains several forms that can be filled in with various information. One of these forms may be the *certification form* for questions at depositions.

Certification after the Fact

Ordinarily, certification of a question prepared during a deposition is not possible, because judges are not usually available to make an immediate ruling. The normal procedure is to continue with the deposition, with objections and requests for certification being made from time to time. The reporter is responsible for noting the requests for certification within his or her notes and on the information sheet. When the deposition is transcribed, a separate certification of the required questions will be completed and included with the depositions. The Certification of Questions form is usually inserted under the front cover of the deposition.

In essence, the certified questions are not answered at the time of the deposition and are left blank. In fact, some attorneys will ask that a blank line be inserted in the place where the answer should be, with the stipulation that, if the judge requires the witness to answer, it can be inserted within the blank lines. The attorneys also have the option of reconvening the deposition and having the witness answer the question before a court reporter.

An additional example of a certification page is shown in Figure 21.7.

FIGURE 21.6
Certification of Questions

(a)

```
1      IN THE DISTRICT COURT OF DOUGLAS COUNTY, MINNESOTA

2                   FIFTH JUDICIAL DISTRICT

3

4    ANNA JUDITH PETERSON,        I
                                  I
5              Plaintiff,  I
                                  I
6      -vs-                       I         CIVIL NO. 696,137
                                  I
7    NILES G. ROWAN,              I
                                  I
8              Defendant,  I

9              CERTIFICATION OF QUESTION

10     I, Neaton Correct, a court reporter and Notary Public

11   in and for Douglas County, Minnesota, hereby certify that

12   pursuant to Notice dated January 10, 20__, duly served, the

13   deposition of ARTHUR ASHBY was taken before me commencing at

14   2:30 P.M., Monday, January 26, 20__, at the offices of

15   Jenkins & Barlow, Attorneys at Law, 419 Sycamore Street,

16   Linwood, MN, 55005, and that certain oral questions were

17   propounded and certain answers given; and certain questions

18   were propounded which were not answered, as follows:

19   Q    (By Mr. Stanton) Who, besides Nancy, could you name

20   by name as being Richard's closest friends?  Who are

21   his close classmates?

22           MR. MILLER:  That doesn't have anything to

23        do with this case.  You don't have to answer

24        that question, Arthur.

25   Q    (By Mr. Stanton) Would you care to answer it?
```

(b)

```
1        MR. MILLER: I told him not to answer it, and

2      he is going to do what I told him.  This is not a

3      fishing expedition.  If you think it is a relevant

4      question, you can have it certified.

5        THE WITNESS:  Upon instructions from my

6      counsel, I refuse to answer that question.

7        MR. STANTON:  I think the Judge is in his

8      chambers here today.  Mrs. Reporter, please

9      certify the question, and we will find out

10     whether the witness has to answer or not."

11     WITNESS MY HAND AND SEAL OF OFFICE, this, the 26th day

12   of January, A. D. 20__.

13

14   _____
                      NEATON CORRECT, Notary Public
15                    Douglas County, Minnesota
                      My Commission expires 6/30/__

16

17

18

19

20

21

22

23

24

25
```

FIGURE 21.7
Certification of Questions

(a)

```
1          IN THE DISTRICT COURT OF HARRIS COUNTY, TEXAS

2                    157TH JUDICIAL DISTRICT

3    HUBERT HAGOOD,              I
                                 I
4                 Plaintiff,     I
                                 I
5         -vs-                   I    CIVIL NO. 433,449
                                 I
6    MAGNOLIA PETROLEUM COMPANY, I
     ET AL.                      I
7                                I
                  Defendant,     I
8

9               CERTIFICATION OF QUESTIONS

10       I, Ima Nifty Writer, a court reporter and Notary Public

11   in and for the County of Harris, State of Texas, do hereby

12   certify that on the 28th day of May, 20__, beginning at the

13   hour of 3:30 P.M., in the offices of Davis & Johnson,

14   Attorneys at Law, 421 Maple Street, Houston, TX  77001,

15   there appeared before me one HUBERT HAGOOD for the purpose

16   of having his oral deposition taken.

17       Certain oral questions were propounded and certain

18   answers given, as shown in the transcript of the deposition

19   of HUBERT HAGOOD filed in the above-captioned cause, and

20   certain questions were propounded which were not answered,

21   as shown in the transcript of the deposition of HUBERT

22   HAGOOD, as follows:

23   Beginning at page 49, line 11:

24   Q    (By Mr. Harmon) I just wondered, since you, apparently,

25   were there at that time.  Did it appear to you that it
```

(b)

```
1    wasn't safe to be trying to load the drums onto the

2    boat from that platform there?

3    A    Well --

4    Q    I mean, did you think that he ought not to have been

5    asking you to do the work in that way?

6    A    Well, actually, I didn't feel it was my place to do it.

7    Q    I realize that.

8    A    Naturally, it was a little dangerous, it appeared at

9    that time, but I guess to him and to me that was the

10   only way to do it.

11   Q    Did it appear to you then that that was a reasonably

12   safe way to do it?

13       MR. McDERMOTT:  Wait a minute.  You are

14   going into matters of opinion.  I think you ought to

15   interrogate him on facts.

16   Q    (By Mr. Harmon) I want to know whether you thought at

17   that time it wasn't safe to be doing that.

18       MR. McDERMOTT:  I am going to instruct him

19   not to answer that.  That calls for an opinion and his

20   conclusion, and I don't think it's a proper question.

21   If I am wrong, I am willing to submit it to the

22   Judge, but I don't think that it is a proper

23   question.  I think this is to be a

24   factual deposition and not matters of opinion.  I

25   am perfectly willing, however, to submit it to the
```

(c)

```
1        Judge if you want an answer.

2            MR. HARMON:  I would like an answer.  May we

3        ask the reporter to certify it?

4            MR. McDERMOTT:  Why, yes.  If the Judge

5        thinks it's proper, he will surely answer.

6    Beginning at page 56, line 24:

7    Q    (By Mr. Harmon) Do you feel that the place where you

8        were doing your work was at least reasonably safe?

9            MR. McDERMOTT:  That is, again, an opinion.

10       I am going to instruct him not to answer.  Please

11       confine your questions to facts, not opinions.

12           MR. HARMON:  I would just like to know

13       whether he thought at that time that it was safe

14       to be trying to work there.

15           MR. McDERMOTT:  I still think it calls for

16       an opinion, and the jury will be called upon to

17       answer that question.  I am not going to let him

18       testify to it unless the Court says that it is a

19       proper question.

20           MR. HARMON:  Certify the question, please.

21

22       _____
         IMA NIFTY WRITER, Notary Public
23       Harris County, Texas
         My Commission expires 6/30/__

24

25
```

How to Mark and Handle Deposition Exhibits

Review Chapter 13 to familiarize yourself with the techniques used by the freelance reporter to mark exhibits during a deposition.

It is the responsibility of the freelance reporter to make sure that all exhibits are accounted for within the record and, in some cases, to maintain the exhibits to be included with the original transcript. The freelance reporter should ask the attorneys if they would like copies of the exhibits included with the deposition. In addition, make sure that there is complete understanding among all parties present at the deposition as to who will keep the exhibits.

How to Read Back at a Deposition

In most instances, the material to be read back at a deposition will be questions and answers in close proximity to any objections that were made during the deposition. Most readback situations will be immediate in nature; however, there may be times when the deposition reporter will have to read portions of testimony that may have been given minutes or hours or even days before.

A review of Chapter 14 will help to refresh some of the readback techniques that the freelance reporter should use in any readback situation.

Chapter 22

The Deposition Transcript: Transcribing, Invoicing, and Delivery

The production of the transcript for a deposition follows the same general pattern as that for any court document. A review of Chapter 15 will provide an outline of the main parts of the transcript, including the title pages, appearances, stipulations, index, body of the transcript, and certification page.

What was said in Chapter 15 regarding the professional appearance of the court transcript holds true for deposition transcripts. In most cases the document will be handled by lawyers, judges, and other court personnel, all highly professional people, and they expect a quality document that is accurate and presented professionally.

Deposition Transcripts

The preparation of deposition transcripts may involve obtaining witness signatures in addition to making copies and delivering the final transcripts. These procedures are presented in this section.

Reading and Signing the Transcript

Transcripts from a deposition may require the deponent, the person who gave the testimony under oath, to read the document and then sign it. Such reading and signing may require some extra work on the part of the court reporter.

If the attorneys have not stipulated that the signature and filing of the deposition are to be waived, you must obtain the signature of the deponent, the person who gave testimony. Lawyers normally discuss the reading and signing of the deposition in advance with their clients and instruct them on what to do.

Expert witnesses more frequently choose to read and sign their testimony than do laypersons because of the technical nature of their testimony, and they want to make sure that what they said was conveyed properly.

Getting the witness to read and sign the deposition is sometimes time consuming, and the reporter has to make sure that he or she obtains the signature in plenty of time for the billing, filing, and delivery of the copies. The procedure for reading and signing the original of a deposition varies greatly from state to state. Lawyers usually stipulate that the signing of the original deposition may take place before any notary public, which means that the signature may be witnessed before a notary public other than the court reporter who took and transcribed the deposition.

If reading and signing are required, a form letter should be prepared and sent to inform the witness's attorney that the original deposition is available in your office, ready for the client to read and sign. If you receive no response from the first letter, a second letter may be necessary. First and second letters to an attorney announcing the availability of a transcript for a witness's signature are shown in Figures 22.1 and 22.2. Occasionally, counsel will agree that you can send the original deposition to the witness for signature when it has been completed, although this procedure is usually reserved for an expert witness. In such a case, the original of the deposition should be sent by certified mail, return receipt requested, and a letter should accompany the transcript. The reporter should keep a copy of all correspondence, receipts, and the deposition itself. Sometimes the lawyers may agree that the original should be sent to the office of one of the counsel for signature. Letters regarding sending an original transcript are shown in Figures 22.3 and 22.4.

If a witness does not read and sign the deposition before the transcript needs to be filed, it is not your fault. You have done everything you can to get the witness to read and sign the document. If the witness will not sign the deposition, attorneys may stipulate that, if the witness has not appeared by a certain number of days before the trial, the reporter shall file the original of the deposition. The deposition will have the same force and effect as though it were read and signed by the witness. Some states have statutory laws governing such circumstances.

The freelance reporter should mark on his or her desk calendar when depositions, statements, or interrogatories are due to be filed and when the signature needs to be received in order to file it on time. The calendar should be checked every day, looking at the week ahead to see whether a polite telephone call might be necessary to remind a deponent to read and sign the document.

When a witness comes to your office for the reading and signing, provide a quiet area for the deponent to read the deposition. You should instruct the witness that no questions or remarks of either counsel may be changed, but the deponent's answers may be corrected if any errors are found.

No matter how careful a busy reporter may be, occasionally undetected errors occur within a transcript. For example, such words as "your analysis" for "urinalysis" or "curb" for "curve" will appear. Sometimes,

FIGURE 22.1
Form Letter Informing Witness That Original Deposition Is Ready

```
              LIGHTNING DIGITS REPORTING SERVICE
                    1492 Accuracy Avenue
                     Newton, ME  10574

                                  Telephone 207/555-5478

                 May 22, 20__


Mr. Ila Counsellem
123 Disputations Boulevard
Newton, ME  10574

        In Re:  Cornpone Investment Corporation
                  v. Abner Yokum
                No. 614,384

Dear Mr. Counsellem:

      The deposition of your client, Mr. Jubilation T.
Cornpone, is now ready for signature as provided for in
agreement between counsel at the taking of the deposition
on May 20, 20__.

      Will you please ask Mr. Cornpone to stop at our
offices at his earliest convenience between the hours of
8:00 A.M. and 5:00 P.M., Monday through Friday, to sign the
transcript of his testimony.

      Thank you very much.

                      Yours very truly,

                      LIGHTNING DIGITS REPORTING
                      SERVICE


                      _____
                      SPEEDY FINGERS

sf:ik
C:  Mr. Fighting Chance
```

FIGURE 22.2
Second Letter

```
              LIGHTNING DIGITS REPORTING SERVICE
                    1492 Accuracy Avenue
                     Newton, ME  10574

                                  Telephone 207/555-5478

                  June 6, 20__


Mr. Ila Counsellem
123 Disputations Boulevard
Newton, ME  10574

        In Re:  Cornpone Investment Corporation
                  v. Abner Yokum
                No. 614,384
                Our Reference No. 64-102

Dear Mr. Counsellem:

      The deposition of your client, Mr. Jubilation T.
Cornpone, still remains in this office unsigned.

      Will you please inform us what you want done with the
original transcript, as it is our understanding that this
case will be coming up for trial during the week of June 10,
20__.

      Thank you for your immediate attention to this matter.

                      Yours very truly,

                      LIGHTNING DIGITS REPORTING
                      SERVICE


                      _____
                      SPEEDY FINGERS

sf:ik
pc:  Mr. Fighting Chance
```

FIGURE 22.3
Letter Accompanying Original Deposition

```
                    STRICTLY VERBATIM & ASSOCIATES
                          Certified Reporters
                        Legalistic Jargon Avenue
                        Butcherville, FL 33745

                                          Telephone:  561/555-2345

               November 29, 20__

I. L. Choppem, M.D.
1459 Malpractice Lane
Butcherville, FL 33745

         In Re:  Marianne Maimed v. I. L. Choppem, M.D.
                 Civil No. 131,313

Dear Dr. Choppem:

The original transcript of your deposition taken before the
undersigned officer on November 25, 20__ is enclosed so that you
may read and subscribe to it.

After reading the deposition, please sign it on page 121 on the
line provided.  If you have any corrections to request, please do
not make these on the printed pages of the transcript, but enter
them on the sheet in the very front of the deposition that is
entitled "Reference Sheet," indicating thereon the page number,
line number, and desired corrections, and reason for making same.
If you use this sheet for corrections, please date and sign it at
the very bottom.

After signing your deposition, please use the enclosed addressed
envelope for returning it to this office.  The proper postage has
already been affixed to this envelope.

Please return the deposition so that it will arrive in this office
not later than December 31, 20__.

Thank you very much for your cooperation in this matter.

                                  Very truly yours,


                          By:_____
                          Hunt N. Peck, Staff Reporter

HNP:ir
c:  Ms. Liz Pending
    Suit N. Progress, Esq.

Enclosure
```

FIGURE 22.4
Letter to an Attorney for Obtaining Signature

```
                 GETTING ITT DOWNE & ASSOCIATES
                        Court Reporters
                        Verbatim Lane
                     Tranquility, MO  89006
                   Telephone (417) 555-1578

                 October 29, 20__

Thomas Tryingwell, Esq.
Tryingwell & Winning
Attorneys at Law
4837 Civil Practice Avenue
Tranquility, MO  89006

         In Re:  Deposition of Larry Libelous
                 Civil No. 789-80 - Our Job No. 9,998

Dear Mr. Tryingwell:

In an effort to provide better service to all counsel of record, we
have retained custody of the original deposition of Larry Libelous.

Please have Larry Libelous read the enclosed deposition copy.  If
changes are made, please indicate on the enclosed sheet(s) the
change, page number, line number, and reason for the change, using
Number "1", "2", or "3" as the reason for the change.

A line is provided on each correction sheet for Larry Libelous's
signature.

Please have the witness sign each correction sheet.

If no corrections are needed, please have the witness sign the
appropriate paragraph on the return form letter to Getting Itt
Downe & Associates.

Upon receipt of the signed correction sheet(s) and the
appropriately signed paragraph in the return form letter, we will
then notify opposing counsel of any changes, affix the correction
sheet(s) and signed return letter to the original deposition, and
file the original with the Court.

Thank you for your cooperation in this matter.

                                  Very truly yours,


                          BY:_____
                          EZEE WRITER, CSR
                             Staff Reporter

Enclosures
```

too, a transcriber's or notereader's transposition of letters or mishearing may be overlooked in proofreading, such as the common error of "now" for "not," which gives the opposite meaning, or "the Untied States," or "impcat" for "impact."

Any deponent is permitted to correct any errors that he or she claims are present in a reporter's transcript. In some jurisdictions, corrections are made directly on the original deposition and initialed by the witness, but more frequently they are listed on separate sheets, called *errata sheets, addendum sheets,* or *correction sheets,* provided the witness at the time of reading and signing. In some jurisdictions, the witness may add a statement at the end of the deposition listing claimed errors and what he or she considers to be the correct answers. Two examples of different correction forms are shown in Figures 22.5 and 22.6.

If any changes in the deposition are made by the witness, be sure to notify all counsel who ordered a copy as well as the clerk of the court. This notification is usually done in the form of a certificate. The original of the certificate is enclosed with the original of the deposition. Figure 22.7 shows a signature sheet accompanying a transcript. Remember that the proper procedure to follow in your jurisdiction may vary and that you should always be guided by the protocol within your own court and agency as to how you will handle corrections. A sample witness certificate is shown in Figure 22.8.

In many states, such as Texas, no certificate is required preceding the witness's signature. Immediately following the last line of the deposition, the reporter adds the signature line, which must be on the same page as the end of the last testimony or colloquy. This line is followed by the *jurat* of the notary public before whom it is signed. Neither the signature nor the jurat should appear on the deposition if signature is waved. A sample signature page used in states in which a certificate is not required before the witness's signature is shown in Figure 22.9. The *jurat* is the place at the bottom of a legal document where the maker signs his

FIGURE 22.5
Correction Form

```
          If any corrections to your deposition are necessary, indicate
them on this sheet of paper, giving the change, page number, line
number, and the reason for the change.

          The reasons for making changes are:

              (1)  To clarify the record;
              (2)  To conform to the facts; or
              (3)  To correct major transcription errors.

Page number          Line number                    Reason for change

Change_____ to _____

Page number          Line number                    Reason for change

Change_____ to _____

Page number          Line number                    Reason for change

Change_____ to _____

Page number          Line number                    Reason for change

Change_____ to _____

Page number          Line number                    Reason for change

Change_____ to _____

Page number          Line number                    Reason for change

Change_____ to _____

Page number          Line number                    Reason for change

Change_____ to _____

Page number          Line number                    Reason for change

Change_____ to _____

                              _____
                              SIGNATURE OF DEPONENT

Figure          Correction Form
```

FIGURE 22.6
Correction Form

```
 1          IN THE DISTRICT COURT OF PINELLAS COUNTY, FLORIDA

 2                       135TH JUDICIAL DISTRICT

 3
     SUEMM GOODE,            )              CIVIL NO. 14,589
 4                          )
            Plaintiff,  )              Requested Corrections
 5                          )
        -vs-                )              to the Deposition of
 6                          )
     PENNY ANTE,            )              SUEMM GOODE
 7                          )
            Defendant.  )
 8

 9          I, Mae King Munee, officer before whom the deposition
     of Suemm Goode was taken on the 15th day of August, 20__,
10   do hereby certify that I was requested by the deponent
     therein to indicate the following desired corrections,
11   subject to which he subscribed to the within transcript of
     his deposition.  I have entered these requested corrections
12   on the face of the appropriate pages of the original transcript
     in pen and ink and have initialled the corrections therein
13   inserted by me.

14
     PAGE      LINE       CORRECTION
15
      10         7        Change "now lines in New Orleans" to read
16                        "now lives in the Orient."  Reporter
                          misheard deponent's words.
17
      20        13        Following "my son," omit the period and
18                        add the words "and his two daughters may
                          have gone along."  No reason stated for
19                        correction.

20          IN WITNESS WHEREOF, I have hereunto affixed my official
     seal of office and signature this 20th day of August, 20__, at
21   Pine Key, Pinellas County, Florida.

22

23                                    _____
                                      MAE KING MUNEE, CSR
24   (Imprint notary                  Notary Public in and for the
     seal over signature.)            State of Florida at Large
25                                    My Commission Expires 4/30/__
```

FIGURE 22.7
Signature Sheet

```
              PLEASE SIGN THE APPROPRIATE PARAGRAPH WHEN
              MAKING RETURN OF CORRECTION SHEETS TO
                   GETTING ITT DOWNE & ASSOCIATES

TO:   GETTING ITT DOWNE & ASSOCIATES
      Verbatim Lane
      Tranquility, MO  89006

      I have read a copy of my deposition.

      Upon receipt of the enclosed signed sheet(s), you are hereby
authorized to file the original of my deposition, as corrected.

      SUBSCRIBED AND SWORN TO BEFORE ME on this the_____ day of
_____, 20__ .

                              _____
                              Notary Public in and for
                              _____County,_____
                              My Commission expires:_____

* * * * * * * * * * * * * * * * * * * * * * * * * * * * *

TO:   GETTING ITT DOWN & ASSOCIATES
      Verbatim Lane
      Tranquility, MO  89006

      I have read a copy of my deposition.

      Upon receipt of the enclosed signed sheet(s), you are hereby
authorized to file the original of my deposition, as transcribed.

      SUBSCRIBED AND SWORN TO BEFORE ME on this the_____day of
_____, 20__.

                              _____
                              Notary Public in and for
                              _____County,_____
                              My Commission expires:_____
```

```
 1              MR. QUESTIONING:  That is all the questions
 2    I have at this time.  Thank you.
 3              MR. HARDNOSE:  I have no questions at this
 4    time.
 5    STATE OF MINNESOTA
 6                      ss.          CERTIFICATE OF WITNESS
      COUNTY OF DEERWOOD
 7
 8         I, HEDGE N. EVADE, hereby certify that I have
 9    read the foregoing transcript of my deposition taken
10    February 3, 20__, at approximately 10:00 A.M., at Byron
11    Minnesota, pursuant to the applicable Rules of Civil
12    Procedure, and that the foregoing 178 pages of transcript
13    are in conformity with my testimony given at that time,
14    (with the exception of any corrections made by me, in ink,
15    and initialed by me).
16
17                  _____
                           HEDGE N. EVADE
18    STATE OF MINNESOTA
19    COUNTY OF DEERWOOD
20         SUBSCRIBED AND SWORN to before me, the undersigned
21    authority on this the 8th day of February, 20__.
22
23
                     _____
24                         NEATLY WRITING
                           Notary Public in and for
                           Deerwood County, Minnesota
25                         My Commission Expires 7/31/__
```

```
          MR. SMITHERS:  That's all.  Thank you.

          THE WITNESS:  You're welcome.


              _____
                         THE WITNESS

THE STATE OF TEXAS

COUNTY OF HARRIS

     SUBSCRIBED AND SWORN to before me, the undersigned
authority, on this the ____ day of _____, 20__.
              _____
                   SARA N. DIPITY
                   Notary Public in and for
                   Harris County, Texas
                   My Commission Expires 7/31/__


(BUT when the witness affirms, the jurat will read in every

instance:)

THE STATE OF TEXAS

COUNTY OF HARRIS

     SUBSCRIBED AND AFFIRMED before me, the undersigned

authority, on this the ____ day of _____, 20__.


              _____
                   GETTEM RIGHT
                   Notary Public in and for
                   Harris County, Texas
                   My Commission Expires 7/31/__
```

or her name. The notary public then signs, attesting to the fact that the person who signed (the maker) appeared before the notary at the time and place stated in the paragraph.

If a witness totally refuses to sign the deposition, you should notify the attorney who hired you and let him or her know what has occurred. The attorney will usually advise you to file the original document with a cover letter or certificate explaining the circumstances and send a copy of the letter or certificate and proper billing to the other attorneys involved.

Invoicing and Delivery of Deposition Transcripts

Most court reporting agencies have an office manager who sends out all invoices along with the transcripts. Invoices should contain the firm name, address, and telephone number. If you are sending the bill for yourself, it must contain your Social Security number so that the payer can notify the Internal Revenue Service of payments made to independent contractors.

Several computer software programs will generate client bills and keep a record of when they were paid. One of the most frustrating aspects of reporting is the collection of bills that remain unpaid after a lapse of time. Although most attorneys are very prompt in paying for the services that they employ from court reporting agencies, some wait until they are paid by their clients before they pay the court reporting agency. In some cases, payment may never be made.

The amount charged for services varies from agency to agency, depending on a great many factors, including the number of pages and the time between the hearing and the delivery of the completed transcript. Also, any litigation support services need to be properly billed.

Some firms have as many as 10 or 12 different options from which attorneys can choose to have the transcript signed, sealed, and delivered. This chapter discusses three major delivery options and then looks at realtime as a method of delivering a completed transcript.

The three main types of delivery are *normal* or *ordinary copy, expedited copy,* and *daily copy. Ordinary copy* is delivery of the completed transcript within five business days to two weeks from the date of the deposition. Although some agencies might consider five days a quick turnaround time, taking more than two weeks to get the completed transcript to the client is unconscionable for any firm.

Expedited copy is usually considered as having the transcript delivered within three business days. Therefore, if a hearing were held Monday morning, the transcript would be in the hands of the attorney on Thursday.

Daily copy usually implies that the transcript will be delivered by 9:00 a.m. on the day following the hearing. However, some firms offer a "daily rush" copy that would ensure delivery by 9:00 p.m. on the same day of the hearing, or a "daily split rush" copy that would deliver the morning session by 5:30 p.m. and the afternoon session by 9:00 p.m.

Immediate copy is another alternative of daily copy and is a more viable option with realtime reporting. *Immediate copy* means delivery of a completed transcript at the end of the hearing or deposition; however, portions of the transcript may be delivered on an hourly basis. Daily copy used to involve a team of reporters and transcribers who coordinated their work schedules so that one reporter reported while the other dictated his or her notes; and, while all this activity was going on, transcribers produced a copy of what was previously dictated so that a constant flow of reporting, dictating, transcribing, and editing occurred.

Realtime has changed the face of immediate copy so that now an instant copy can be produced. If a reporter does not have access to a scopist or editor on site, then the copy produced may be called a *rough copy.* Some attorneys are willing to sacrifice accuracy for time and purchase the *rough copy* with the stipulation that some errors may appear in the transcript and that it is not a fully edited version.

Some reporters vary their charges based on the number of pages that are to be transcribed. The following is a table of charges that a reporting firm might use when charging clients for various deliveries.

Number of Pages	Ordinary Copy	Expedited Copy	Daily Copy	Rush Copy	Rush-split Copy	Immediate Copy
1–100	Regular fee	+10%	+20%	+30%	+40%	+50%
101–200	Regular fee	+20%	+30%	+40%	+50%	+60%
201–300	Regular fee	+30%	+40%	+50%	+60%	+70%
301–400	Regular fee	+40%	+50%	+60%	+70%	+80%
401–500	Regular fee	+50%	+60%	+70%	+80%	+90%

The fees are based on every 100 pages, and the percentage increase is based on the total charge for ordinary copy. Applying the chart to a specific example, if the regular fee is $3.00 per page and the transcript is 250 pages in length, the actual charges would conform to the following schedule. Keep in mind that these fees are fictitious and are used only as an example and that reporting firms vary widely in the fees that they charge for individual services.

Type of Delivery	Regular Fee Plus Percentage ($)	Total Charges ($)
Ordinary copy	750 (250 pages × $3.00/page)	750
Expedited copy	750 + 225 (30% of total)	975
Daily copy	750 + 300 (40% of total)	1050
Daily rush copy	750 + 375 (50% of total)	1125
Daily rush-split copy	750 + 450 (60% of total)	1200
Immediate copy	750 + 525 (70% of total)	1275

In addition, realtime rough copy might be charged at a flat fee with the stipulation that the final copy will be sent when it is completed, with the additional fee based on the number of pages. Also, reporting firms may apply additional amounts for keyword indexing, ASCII copies, and so on. Your bill should accurately reflect the fees contracted. When you or your agency receive payment, the account for the billing should be clearly marked "paid." If you are working as an independent contractor, you must keep a record of all monies that you receive as income, as well as all expenditures that you make in producing that income.

An *attendance fee* may be charged for depositions, statements, or interrogatories. This may also be called an *appearance fee* or a *per diem rate*. The normal practice is to charge a flat fee for the reporter showing up at the hearing. If no witnesses or no transcripts are required, the client is billed for the attendance fee. If witnesses are involved and the amount charged is more than the attendance fee, the fee is waived and the cost of the transcript will be the only fee charged. This practice varies from agency to agency and from state to state. Remember to follow the protocol for your agency within your particular circumstances.

Delivering the Copies and Filing the Original Deposition

Before delivering or filing any deposition, be sure that you obtain the signature of the witness if it has not been waived. You will also want to be sure that all original deposition exhibits are bound within the transcript or into the back of the original deposition and that copies of the exhibits are included within each copy of the deposition.

If any certified questions or errata sheets are included, make sure that they are bound within the transcript. Also, make sure that the title page, appearances, index page, and the body of the transcript are in good order and that you have signed the certification at the end of the deposition attesting to the fact that you have completed the work to the best of your ability. Your invoice or the invoice of your agency should also be included as a part of the delivered transcript.

If the original of the deposition must be filed with the clerk of the court within the jurisdiction of the matter, the reporter should place the original of the deposition and exhibits inside a large manila envelope. The outside of the envelope should contain the case number, venue, title, deponent, date taken, costs, and by whom paid. Some states require a notarized certificate to accompany the envelope, while others require the notarized signature of the reporter on the envelope. The original documents are then delivered to the clerk of the court, and copies are delivered to the appropriate attorneys.

If the deposition is to be hand delivered, have the person receiving it sign and date a receipt that identifies the transcript by case title and number. If it is to be mailed, place the sealed envelope inside another envelope containing the proper name and address of the receiver, as well as a proper return address. When mailing the deposition, use the method that is best for your purpose: the U.S. Postal Service's priority mail or express mail, Federal Express services, or UPS overnight delivery. Whatever method you choose, make sure that you register and/or certify the envelope and that you require a return receipt. Most agencies will also insure the contents of the package to at least cover the invoice.

Chapter 23

How the Deposition Transcript Looks

Although deposition transcripts may vary from agency to agency, they all follow the same guidelines that have been outlined in this handbook. A sample of a deposition is included here. The next ten pages will give you a general idea of what the deposition transcript looks like. Note that a break in the transcript is noted in the page numbering for the transcript.

Note the different parts of the transcript, the stipulations, the witness setup, the Q and A format, the colloquy format, the certificate page, and so on.

```
 1   STATE OF NEW YORK


 2


 3   SUPREME COURT                    |        COUNTY OF MONROE


 4   - - - - - - - - - - - - - - - -


 5   Computek Systems, Inc.,


 6                              Plaintiff,


 7


 8      -against-                        Index No. SC199800734


 9


10   Master Computer Consultants,


11                              Defendant.


12   - - - - - - - - - - - - - - - -


13   Deposition of HEATHER A. HIGBY held in the law offices of
     Roscoe, Paul & Brothers, Attorneys at Law, 92 Hampton
14   Boulevard, Belmonte, NY 12345, on the 7th day of September,
     2002, commencing at 2:05 P.M.

15


16   REPORTED BY:   Melissa A. Cosgrove, RPR
                    Notary Public and Shorthand Reporter

17


18                  Expert Reporting Service
                    288 Professional Building
19                  Alfred, NY 14802
                    Telephone (515) 555-5555
20                  Fax (515) 555-5151
                    expertreporting@technet.net
21                  www.expertreporting


22


23


24


25
```

EXPERT REPORTING SERVICE
Alfred, NY

```
 1                    A P P E A R A N C E S

 2

 3   APPEARANCES:     Roscoe, Paul & Brothers, LLP
                      Attorneys at Law
 4                    92 Hampton Boulevard
                      Belmonte, NY 12345
 5                    by John T. Roscoe, Esq.
                      Attorney for Plaintiff
 6
                      Linda Kay Osgood, P.C.
 7                    Attorney at Law
                      15 Main St.
 8                    Belmonte, NY 14814
                      Attorney for Defendant
 9
     ALSO PRESENT:    Anthony T. Clarke, Esq.
10                    Clarke & Clarke
                      Attorneys at Law
11                    2218 Lake Street
                      Olean, NY 14432
12                    Attorney for noninterested third party

13                    John R. McDaniel, Esq.
                      Roscoe, Paul & Brothers, LLP
14                    92 Hampton Boulevard
                      Belmonte, NY 12345
15
                      Susan J. Simpson
16                    Continental Insurance Company
                      223 East Highland Ave.
17                    Rochester, NY 19283

18

19

20

21

22

23

24

25
```

EXPERT REPORTING SERVICE
Alfred, NY

SECTION C

I N D E X

WITNESSES

Heather A. Higby   Page

EXHIBITS

REQUESTS

EXPERT REPORTING SERVICE
Alfred, NY

SECTION C

```
 1                    S T I P U L A T I O N S

 2         It is stipulated and agreed among counsel for the

 3    respective parties that this Examination Before Trial be

 4    held pursuant to the provisions of the Civil Practice Law &

 5    Rules;

 6              that the presence of a Referee is waived;

 7              that the filing of the deposition is waived;

 8              that the witness may be sworn by a Notary Public;

 9              and that all objections, except those as to form, are

10    waived until the time of trial.

11

12

13

14

15

16

17

18

19

20

21

22

23

24

25
```

EXPERT REPORTING SERVICE
Alfred, NY

SECTION C

1　　　　H E A T H E R   A.   H I G B Y, having been called as

2　a witness, being duly sworn, testified as follows:

3　　　　　　　　　　　　EXAMINATION

4　BY MR. ROSCOE:

5　　　Q　Good afternoon, my name is John Roscoe. I'm

6　representing Computek, as you probably already know.　Let

7　me begin by explaining to you that if you don't understand

8　any of my questions, simply tell me that you don't understand, and

9　I'll rephrase it or try to make it more clear for you. If

10　you didn't hear me, tell me you didn't hear me so that I can

11　repeat the question. All your answers have to be verbal

12　because the reporter can only get what you say, try not to

13　nod or shake your head.

14　　　Now, if all of that is agreeable to you, Heather, let

15　me ask you to state your full name for the record.

16　　　A　Okay. My name is Heather A. Higby.

17　　　Q　What is your address?

18　　　A　County Route 5, West Amity, New York.

19　　　Q　Would you tell us your date of birth, please?

20　　　A　Yes. My birth date is 8/15/79.

21　　　Q　Would you tell me a little bit about your

22　education, where you've gone to school, what degrees you've

23　earned, and so forth?

24　　　A　Well, I didn't go any further than high school. I

25　graduated from Lincoln High in 1997.

1   the top of my head I don't know which ones are debited and

2   which ones are credited.

3   Q   Do you know how the hourly rates are computed and

4   how they are debited and credited when the computations are

5   different for each client?

6   A   Could you repeat that? I'm sorry.

7   MR. ROSCOE: Would you read it back, please?

8   (The last question was read back by the

9   reporter.)

10   BY MR. ROSCOE:

11   Q   Can you answer that question?

12   A   Do I know how the computations are debited and

13   credited?

14   Q   Yes.

15   A   If you mean, do I know how the program works, no,

16   I don't know.

17   Q   Do you know what account, if any, should be

18   debited and credited?

19   MS. OSGOOD: That's been asked and answered.

20   Go ahead.

21   A   I said that I could give you the names of the

22   account, but I'm not an accountant. I'm not a trained—I

23   don't know which has a normal debit and credit. There are

24   two accounts in my chart of accounts, and I know that they

25   are used. I don't know how the program runs. It doesn't

EXPERT REPORTING SERVICE
Alfred, NY

1   bookkeeping?

2   A   Yes, I did. I worked for two other companies.

3   Q   Would it be fair to say that you have an extensive

4   knowledge of accounting and bookkeeping procedures on how to

5   run a business?

6   MR. ROSCOE: Object to the form of the

7   question as leading and suggestive.

8   MS. OSGOOD: Go ahead and answer that

9   Heather.

10   A   Yes. I would say that I am a competent bookkeeper

11 and accountant for a small business.

12   MS. OSGOOD: Nothing further.

13   MR. ROSCOE: Just one more question, Heather.

14   EXAMINATION

15 BY MR. ROSCOE:

16   Q   Heather, how many years have you been working with

17 computers?

18   A   Oh, maybe the last year or so is when I really got

19 involved with it.

20   Q   Would you consider yourself a competent computer

21 operator?

22   MS. OSGOOD: I object to the form of the

23 question as being argumentative and beyond the scope of this

24 examination, and I instruct my client not to answer that

25 question. Counsel, you're stepping on grounds that

EXPERT REPORTING SERVICE
Alfred, NY

1   are not to be considered at this deposition, and you know

2   it.

3   MR. ROSCOE: I know nothing about any grounds

4   for questioning, and I think I have a perfect right to ask

5   that question, and I have a perfect right to have it

6   answered.

7   MS. OSGOOD: You have no right to ask that

8   type of question. Heather, don't answer it.

9   MR. ROSCOE: Reporter, would you please

10 certify that question, and we'll see who's right or not. I

11 have nothing further until we can get that question

12 answered.

13   (The deposition was concluded at 3:00 P.M.)

14

15

16

17

18

19

20

21

22

23

24

25

SECTION C

EXPERT REPORTING SERVICE
Alfred, NY

1

2   W I T N E S S   S I G N A T U R E

3

4   STATE OF NEW YORK |

5   COUNTY OF MONROE |

6

7   I have read the foregoing record of testimony taken at

8   the time and place indicated on the title page, and I do

9   hereby acknowledge it to be a true and correct transcript

10   thereof.

11

12   _____
                                          Heather A. Higby

13   Subscribed and sworn to
     before me this _____ day

14   of _____, 20_____

15   _____

     Notary Public

16

17

18

19

20

21

22

23

24

25

EXPERT REPORTING SERVICE
Alfred, NY

```
 1                          C E R T I F I C A T E

 2     STATE OF NEW YORK            |

 3     COUNTY OF MONROE             |

 4          I, Melissa A. Cosgrove, RPR, notary public and
       shorthand reporter do hereby certify that the matters set
 5     forth in the caption to the foregoing deposition are true
       and correct; that the witness, Heather A. Higby, appeared
 6     before me at the time and place set forth; that said witness
       was first duly sworn to by me to tell the truth, the whole
 7     truth, and nothing but the truth, and thereupon proceed to
       testify in said cause; that the questions of counsel and the
 8     answers of said witness were taken down stenographically by
       me and thereafter reduced to transcript format by computer-
 9     aided transcription under my direction; and that the
       foregoing 26 pages comprise a true, complete, and accurate
10     transcript of the testimony given and proceedings had during
       the taking of said deposition to the best of my ability.
11
            I further certify that I am not a relative or employee
12     or attorney or counsel of any of the parties hereto, nor a
       relative or employee of such attorney or counsel, nor do I
13     have any interest in the outcome or events of
       the action.
14
            WITNESS MY HAND AND SEAL OF OFFICE, this _____ day
15     of _____, 20_____.

16                              _____
                                Melissa A. Cosgrove, RPR
17                              Notary Public # _____
                                County of _____
18                              My commission expires _____

19

20

21

22

23

24

25
```

EXPERT REPORTING SERVICE
Alfred, NY

Section D

Captioning Reporting and CART

Chapter 24

The Working Environment of the Captioner

One of the most popular career choices in the field of court and realtime reporting is the area of captioning. The captioner uses the skill of the court reporter and the technology of the realtime writer and applies his or her own specialized methodology to perform a very useful service in today's world.

This section of the handbook describes the different aspects of captioning and how they relate to the total picture of court and realtime reporting.

Different Captioning Jobs

Captioners are known by a variety of titles. Among these are, *closed captioners, realtime captioners, stenocaptioners, steno interpreters, broadcast captioners, broadcast stenocaptionists, teleconference captioners,* and *CART providers.*

While all of these different titles belong to the same general category of captioning, there are distinctions that should be appreciated. Just as the term court reporter is an all-encompassing term that includes many different types of reporting jobs, so, too, reporters who are referred to as a captioners often perform a variety of tasks.

To simplify the issue, the titles mentioned above can be placed in three different categories: broadcast captioners, steno interpreters, and CART providers. It is important to note that, while there may be a distinction in titles as outlined here, captioning agencies, those firms that employ captioning reporters, will offer an array of services that cover the entire range of captioning.

Broadcast Captioners

Broadcast captioners are those reporters who are employed to report television programs; however, their duties may entail other types of captioning jobs. The broadcast captioner can work from a remote location (hundreds or thousands of miles away) or can work on site for a company.

Most broadcast captioners work for a company that has been contracted by a television station to caption their local or national shows. Most of the television shows that are broadcast are news, weather, sporting events, political elections, and other live stories.

Broadcast captioners write in realtime using the same type of shorthand writer that the court and realtime writer use; however, the software is slightly different from standard realtime software. The software used by captioners is designed to interface with the television encoders that allow the captioning to appear on televisions.

The captioned realtime is translated by the software into English and then sent to the television broadcast station and automatically encoded into what is called *line 21* of the television broadcast signal. The captioned words are then viewed on televisions equipped with a decoder.

Captioners use special format symbols that represent a new speaker or a new story. These format symbols are the angle brackets >>. Whenever a new person speaks, the broadcast captioner uses two brackets; whenever a new story begins, three brackets are used. For example,

```
>>BOB: MY NAME IS BOB VILA AND
I WELCOME YOU TO OUR SHOW FOR
TODAY. OUR GUEST TODAY IS MASTER
CARPENTER NORM ABRAM.
>>NORM: HELLO BOB! TODAY'S SHOW
LOOKS GREAT.
```

Only one or two lines show at a time, and they scroll off the screen as the next line is generated. Viewers can see when speakers change by watching the format symbols. New stories are formatted in a similar way, using three brackets >>>.

```
>>DON: BUFFALO BEAT COLORADO
IN THE SUPERBOWL.
>>>THIS JUST IN. FIRE AT THE
FRANKLIN FACTORY.
```

If you have ever watched a television program being captioned live by a broadcast captionist, you may have noticed a mistake here or there in the translation. While broadcast reporters attempt to be 100 percent accurate, errors may pop up because of unfamiliarity with terms that are not defined in the writer's dictionary. This is both understandable and acceptable by viewers.

Broadcast captionists provide closed captioning both on line and off line. Online captioning is live closed captioning, while offline captioning is writing a program at any time and making the captions a part of the program for later presentation as a package. Offline captioning is also referred to as open captioning, because it is viewable by anyone who watches the program and special decoders on television sets are not necessary.

Steno Interpreters or Stenocaptioners

In the category of steno interpreters, we can place captioners who perform the service of realtime captioning in most other public and private settings. Their services can be beneficial to people who suffer from any type of hearing impediment.

The services of steno interpreters are used in educational settings as an assistive technology for hearing impaired students. The school district or a college or university employs the steno interpreters to caption classes for students who need their services. Depending on the number of students, the steno interpreter will project what is being said onto a laptop computer screen for a single student or onto a large-screen television for many students to view.

Steno interpreters are used in church settings to caption worship services for members of a particular congregation who could not otherwise participate because of their loss of hearing. In some churches, large screens are located on the sides of the sanctuary and the captioner is an integral part of the service as he or she records every prayer, song, sermon, or hymn that is said or sung.

Live theater productions, plays, movies at movie theaters, and musical concerts are all examples of where steno interpreters are used to caption performances for the hearing impaired.

In addition, steno interpreters are used in business or office situations, particularly in captioning telephone conferences among business associates in different parts of the nation or world. The steno interpreter captions everything that is said, and then the captions are broadcast anywhere in the world via modem, Internet, and the World Wide Web. This assistive technology is also referred to as Web broadcasting.

Steno interpreters are used in courtroom settings to assist judges, lawyers, and witnesses who can benefit from this assistive technology.

The list of job situations where steno captioning can be used goes on and on, impeded only by a lack of vision or a fear of the new and untried. Steno interpreting or steno captioning is becoming one of the fastest growing areas of the realtime captioning profession.

CART Providers

Communication Access Realtime Translation (CART) is a specific service offered by some captioning agencies that is a step beyond broadcast captioning and stenocaptioning. In its broadest sense, CART is captioning; however, the reporters who offer CART services are specifically trained in dealing with issues that may arise in the captioning environment. CART providers are sensitive to the needs of the hearing impaired. Very often, they have training in the area of writing for the deaf or hard of hearing.

CART services include the recording of lectures and classroom discussion for individuals who may not be able to participate in class; accompanying a hearing impaired person at various social events, including religious services, entertainment events, and so on; and recording live audio- or video-streamed Webcasts on the Internet.

Information on the services of the CART provider can be found at their Web site www.CARTWheel.cc. This site also contains helpful links for those wishing to know more about CART.

A good summarization of what CART is all about can be found in "The CART Provider's Manual," prepared by the National Court Reporters Association's Task Force on Marketing Communication Access Realtime Translation. This manual is available on line at http://cart.ncraonline.org/manual/index.html.

THE CART PROVIDER'S MANUAL[*]

Updated May 2001
prepared by the

National Court Reporters Association

Task Force on Marketing
Communication Access Realtime Translation (CART)

INTRODUCTION

Communication Access Realtime Translation (CART) is a word-for-word speech-to-text interpreting service for people who need communication access. Unlike computerized notetaking or abbreviation systems, which summarize information for consumers, CART provides a complete translation of all spoken words and environmental sounds, empowering consumers to decide for themselves what information is important to them. CART consumers include people with hearing loss; individuals with cognitive or motor challenges; anyone desiring to improve reading/language skills; and those with other communication barriers. The Americans with Disabilities Act (ADA) specifically recognizes CART as an assistive technology that affords effective communication access.

---

[*]This manual is copyrighted by the National Court Reporters Association and is reprinted here with permission.

A CART provider uses a steno machine, notebook computer, and realtime software to render instant speech-to-text translation on a computer monitor or other display for the benefit of an individual consumer or larger group in a number of settings: classrooms; business, government, and educational functions; courtrooms; religious, civic, cultural, recreation, or entertainment events. A CART provider is sensitive to the varying needs of consumers and has had training in conveying a speaker's message, complete with environmental cues. This expertise distinguishes a CART provider from a court reporter in a traditional litigation setting.

NCRA's Registered Professional Reporter (RPR) designation is nationally recognized and at this time is considered a requisite for CART providers. Attainment of the Certified Realtime Reporter (CRR) designation is recommended.

I. Professionalism

A. Sensitivity

The CART provider has general knowledge about "capital D" Deaf culture, and understands that the preferred communication mode of a person with a hearing loss differs depending on whether that individual identifies himself as Deaf, deaf, late-deafened, or hard-of-hearing. Generally, CART consumers are individuals who have developed a hearing loss postlingually (i.e., after the acquisition of language).

There is a certain etiquette required when communicating with CART consumers. A CART provider should acquire training in communication techniques through court reporting association seminars, disability agencies, sign language courses, etc. Membership in organizations such as the Association of Late-Deafened Adults, Self-Help for Hard of Hearing People, and the National Association of the Deaf is recommended.

CART trainees may be present at an assignment with a CART provider to gain on-the-job experience only after the CART provider secures the consent of the consumer or client.

CART is often provided in personal settings such as medical appointments, church meetings, funerals, programs such as Alcoholics Anonymous, and even such things as police interrogations. Personal settings can be highly charged. Self-discipline, self-motivation, and the ability to manage stress and control emotions are important traits of a CART provider.

Additionally, projecting CART to an audience helps to educate others about CART technology and its uses. The CART provider should maintain a positive attitude when responding to questions.

At all times the CART provider should dress appropriately for the setting of the assignment. For example, business attire on a college campus may not be necessary and may make the consumer feel conspicuous.

The CART provider should be aware of the role of the sign language interpreter. Very often an interpreter will be present to serve deaf/hard-of-hearing individuals who prefer using sign language, or to voice for a non-oral individual. It should be stressed that the CART provider and interpreter work as a team, never in competition.

B. Staying In Role

A CART provider's role is to facilitate communication. The CART provider will at all times stay in role and perform in a manner appropriate to the situation. A CART provider should decline any invitation or suggestion to comment, interject, advise, respond to inquiries, or in any way become involved in the assignment outside the role of CART provider. If necessary, the CART provider should politely explain the necessity to stay "in role."

A CART provider may be asked to step out of role to answer questions about the service, to demonstrate equipment during a break, or to schedule future dates. Deviations from role should be the exception and should be discouraged, but may occur with the approval of the CART consumer.

The CART provider must exercise discretion in situations which may warrant interrupting the proceedings to ensure the integrity of the CART translation. Care should be taken not to call undue attention to the consumer or oneself.

C. Impartiality

The CART provider must be fair and impartial to each participant in all aspects of CART and be alert to conflicts of interest. Such circumstances may include, for example, an assignment involving a participant who is a close friend, family member, or business associate.

Any potential conflict of interest or inability to be impartial shall be disclosed by the CART provider. Failure to do so may make it difficult to prove oneself unbiased if challenged.

D. Confidentiality

Courtesy and discretion are required of the CART provider at all times. A casual word or action may betray a consumer's confidences or violate a client's privacy. Confidentiality of the consumer's information and privacy of the person must be maintained.

E. Professional Development

The CART provider should keep abreast of current trends, laws, literature, and technological advances relating to the provision of CART service.

II. Skills

The following categories outline the minimum foundational skills necessary for rendering proficient and professional CART service. Sensitivity training as described above is required.

A. Preparation

The CART provider works closely with the consumer, meeting coordinator, classroom teacher, or other appropriate individual to obtain all terminology inherent to the assignment and must research literature (curricula, syllabi, synopses, scripts, texts, meeting agendas, conference programs, and organization or company Web sites) to create a job dictionary and enhance the master dictionary.

Speaker identifiers are entered into the job dictionary prior to the commencement of any assignment. Generic usage (i.e., >> SPEAKER:) is recommended for an unidentified speaker. CART training addresses speaker identification in various settings.

Before providing CART service, one needs to establish a clear understanding of who is hiring the CART provider and whether an electronic file of the roughly edited text with disclaimer is to be preserved. The contents of the computer file may be deemed proprietary and should not be distributed without proper authorization. If providing the file, one should also establish a clear understanding of whether all participants have been informed that an electronic file of the roughly edited text with disclaimer will be preserved and who is entitled to receive a copy of said file.

It is recommended that the following language be inserted at the beginning and end of each file:

> "This text is being provided in a rough draft format. Communication Access Realtime Translation (CART) is provided in order to facilitate communication accessibility and may not be a totally verbatim record of the proceedings."

To aid communication with CART consumers and meeting planners, it is desirable for a CART provider to have a TTY, fax machine, and/or e-mail. A CART provider should also know how to use the telephone relay system to contact a CART consumer.

B. Realtime Writing

The CART provider writes conflict free, includes punctuation, and sustains accuracy for long periods of time. Discrete outlines for prefixes, suffixes, and root words are the foundation of precise writing and word building. Consistency in writing steno outlines leads to accuracy, increasing readability. Word-boundary problems (i.e., *contractor/contract or*) must be resolved.

Although RPR speeds are considered a requisite, a reserve of shorthand speed allows the CART provider time to add job defines and fingerspell. It is essential that the CART provider can create and retain realtime job defines "on the fly."

A foolproof number system is necessary. There are many systems and styles of writing that permit accuracy in numbers. The CART provider should be able to write numbers to translate as words (nine), Roman numerals (IX), cardinal numbers (9), and ordinal numbers (9th).

Fingerspelling (writing words letter by letter) is essential. In order to differentiate between initials, words that are spelled out by a speaker, and acronyms, the CART provider should utilize discrete spelling alphabets. Fingerspelled words should always translate with the appropriate spacing.

C. Dictionary Maintenance

Knowledge of the contents of one's dictionary is crucial. Due to high frequency of occurrence, names, terms, and places related to current events and culture must be entered into the dictionary regularly. Dictionary maintenance and development [are] an ongoing process. A qualified realtime writer continually adds and modifies steno outlines, and the dictionary must be updated constantly.

D. Software/Computer Knowledge

The CART provider must operate a Computer-Aided Transcription (CAT) program and understand its realtime translation and display functions. It is important to learn to troubleshoot and solve hardware, software, and other technical problems.

In order to meet consumer preferences, the CART provider must know how to activate upper/lowercase, colored backgrounds, enlarged text, and other display options.

During realtime, the phonetics table may be used so that untranslates do not appear in steno. The phonetics table should be customized to the steno theory used by the CART provider.

When appropriate, the CART provider is able to furnish the computer file of the session text as requested. Ideally, a rough-edit process should remove any untranslates and glaring mistranslates before the text is delivered.

Simultaneous display is a function of the computer. Not all computers support simultaneous display. A CART provider must know how to switch between the notebook's LCD screen and the external device (i.e., television monitor, projector). Turning off or blocking the external device display while making job defines is recommended.

E. Language Comprehension

Knowledge of grammar, punctuation, sentence structure, spelling, vocabulary, high-frequency colloquialisms, and slang is crucial. The CART provider must listen for continuity, sense, and detail of the proceedings, anticipating and preventing errors in translation.

III. Location Setup

A. Positioning

Room setup considerations include lighting and positioning for line of sight to overheads, slides, blackboards, and other media displays. Coordination with sign language interpreters, speakers, audiovisual technicians and other ancillary workers is important.

B. Display Options

The options for display should be discussed and arranged with the CART consumer before the assignment. A single consumer may prefer a large-screen projection display to allow for more participation with the group as a whole. A CART provider should demonstrate various display options such as different font sizes and colors for the consumer's selection.

C. Films and Videotapes

Films and videotapes are shown frequently in classrooms and other settings. Uncaptioned films need to be realtime translated. Some suggested tokens are:

>> MAN:
>> WOMAN:
>> VOICE:
>> NARRATOR:
>> CHILD:

Televisions made after June 1993 have built-in decoder chips for display of captions. Some videos and television programs are already captioned, so it is helpful to know how to turn on the caption feature.

D. Seating

For comfort and stress reduction, it is sometimes necessary to locate a suitable chair. One without an attached desk is preferable. The CART provider may need to take a portable stand for the computer.

E. Access to Electricity

It is important to carry an extension cord, a surge protector, and a 3-to-2 ground cord adapter. For everyone's safety, securing electrical cords with duct tape or gaffer's tape is recommended.

IV. The Legal Setting

CART may be provided in a court or deposition proceeding for a litigant, juror, judge, attorney, witness, or other participant. The court reporter for a trial or deposition and the CART provider perform different functions. For example, a CART provider may accompany a consumer into the jury room or into confidential discussions with attorneys.

Additionally, when providing communication access, the CART provider must include parentheticals to describe environmental sounds (i.e., alarm ringing), laughter, or anything that detracts attention from the proceeding. Necessary synonyms may be used to assure effective communication. The synonyms and environmental sounds would not ordinarily appear in an official certified verbatim transcript.

The CART provider should discuss with the judge and attorneys his or her role as an interpreter before the proceedings begin and agree on a method of interrupting if the CART provider cannot hear or understand a speaker.

A clear understanding should be established regarding who is hiring the CART provider; the role played by the CART provider in assisting with communication as opposed to the role of the Official Reporter of Proceedings in providing a verbatim record; the fact that no roughly edited electronic file is to be produced; and the need to preserve the unedited text file with disclaimer (as suggested previously) in accordance with statute or court order, or for a period of no fewer than five years.

In a confidential setting (i.e., legal discussions, jury deliberations, attorney/client discussions), the CART provider should delete all files immediately after the assignment unless requested not to do so, or ordered by the Court.

A CART provider should refrain from working in the dual capacity of Official Reporter of Proceedings and CART provider. However, when no other option exists, the role performed is that of the Official Reporter of Proceedings.

V. Broadcast Captioning

While broadcast captioning falls under the CART umbrella in its broadest sense—communication access—it is considered a separate specialty. The software, hardware, and technical knowledge base will not be addressed in this document. See www.ncraonline.org for additional references.

VI. Remote CART

When providing remote CART, the provider is in one location and the consumer is in another. The CART provider is usually listening to a voice via the phone line, writing on the steno machine, and transmitting the text to the other location. This is particularly helpful in areas where there is a lack of CART providers. Special technical training and support [are] necessary when providing this service. For equipment requirements, see Remote CART below.

VII. Equipment

It is important to keep current with rapidly advancing technologies in order to meet consumer preferences. The following is a listing of the displays known at this time for CART.

The CART provider should furnish and know how to operate all equipment necessary for BASIC DISPLAY. Asterisked items are recommended but not required. A backup steno machine, computer, and software key should be readily available.

A. Basic Display

- Stenotype machine with realtime cable
- Notebook computer
- CAT/realtime software
- Text-enlarging software
- Diskettes*
- Extension cord
- Surge protector with indicator light
- 3-prong to 2-prong ground cord adapter
- Duct tape or gaffer's tape for taping down cables
- Additional realtime cable
- 25-foot realtime cable*
- Notebook computer tray/tripod*
- Equipment case with wheels*
- Chair (make arrangements)*
- Infrared/FM listening device*

B. Advanced Display

The additional equipment necessary for the following displays can be furnished either by the CART provider or the hiring party. In all cases, before accepting an assignment to display with external monitors or equipment, the CART provider must establish and test hardware and software compatibility.

COMPUTER MONITOR DISPLAY

• Splitter box for additional monitors

• 25-foot monitor cables

• Multi-line block or digital sharing device* (for interactive realtime)

TELEVISION DISPLAY

• Digital signal converter (computer to television)

• Coaxial cable to "daisy chain" multiple TV monitors

PROJECTION SCREEN DISPLAY

• LCD plate and projector or combination unit

• Projection screen

• Extra projector light bulbs (must know how to replace)

L.E.D. DISPLAY

• L.E.D. message boards in various sizes and colors for indoor use

• L.E.D. message board for outdoor use

ENCODED DISPLAY (CLOSED-CIRCUIT SITES SUCH AS CONVENTIONS OR CLASSROOMS)

• Captioning software (requires training)

• Encoder or character generator

• Camera

• BNC cables

• Null modem cable and/or modem

REMOTE CART

• Telephone line(s)

• Voice/data modem (for use with single phone line)

• Special microphone (for speaker)

• CAT software which supports Remote CART

• Communication software (computer to computer)

VIII. Compensation

The CART provider will request compensation for services and ascertain particulars of billing/payment in a professional and judicious manner. Details regarding payment for CART service, rates, and rough-edited diskettes should be arranged in advance.

IX. Getting Started

Court reporters interested in getting started as CART providers should review the content available in the CART Special Interest Area on NCRA's Web site and participate in the CART Reporting section of NCRA's Online Forum. If you have additional questions, contact NCRA's Member Services and Information Center at 800-272-6272 or msic@ncrahq.org.

Chapter 25

Terminology and Legislation

The topic of captioning requires an appreciation and understanding of the terms and definitions particular to this genre of reporting. Some of the terms mentioned in this chapter have been defined in Chapter 24. Inclusion of these terms here is not a redundancy, but rather an opportunity to apply their meaning to the entire picture of captioning reporting.

Some Basic Terms

ADA   The Americans with Disabilities Act was passed in 1990 to protect the rights of individuals with disabilities as defined in section 504 of the Rehabilitation Act of 1973. The law covers an array of national mandates that attempts to make the lives of individuals with disabilities more productive and useful in American society. A comprehensive presentation on the ADA can be found at http://www.usdoj.gov/crt/ada/adahom1.htm.

ALDA   Association of Late-Deafened Adults.

Assistive technology   In the area of court and realtime reporting, captioning, and providers of CART, assistive technology refers to the use of any technological device to assist any individual with a disability. CART assists people who could not otherwise participate in educational, entertainment, and social events by allowing a disabled individual to actively communicate with all parties involved. Captioning is an assistive technology in the sense that its services may act as the "ears" of hearing impaired individuals.

CAPD   (central auditory processing disorder)   Applies to individuals who may have problems concentrating in classroom situations.

Captioners, Realtime Captioners, Stenocaptioners, Steno Interpreters, Broadcast Captioners   Titles for the role of a highly trained court reporter who can provide the service of realtime writing or translation in a variety of environments.

CART   Communication Access Realtime Translation is a service provided by court and realtime reporting agencies or captioning agencies. This service includes the use of a realtime reporter who is specially trained to assist a hard of hearing individual communicate in an otherwise silent world. CART providers record in realtime all verbal exchanges and note what each person says with special formatting symbols. In addition, parenthetical notations regarding environmental surroundings are noted.

CAT Computer-Aided Transcription refers to any application or use of the computer to help the court/realtime reporter or captioner produce a transcript or a record.

Closed captioning The act of recording via realtime methodology words, conversations, events, broadcasts, seminars, meetings, and other social gatherings into printed text that will appear on a computer screen or on television sets, depending on its application.

ESL English as a second language. In the captioning arena, people unfamiliar with the English language can use captioning to read words and hear their pronunciation to help them to learn English.

Line 21 The part of the broadcast signal located on all television sets that displays the captioned textual material.

NAD National Association for the Deaf.

NCRA, RPR, CRR The National Court Reporters Association (www.ncraonline.com) is a professional organization of court and realtime reporters and captioners. The NCRA acts as a benchmark by gathering and disseminating information relative to the field. The NCRA offers a variety of examinations for practicing reporters, including the Registered Professional Reporter (RPR) test and the Certified Realtime Reporter (CRR) test. Complete definitions of these tests can be found on the homepage for NCRA.

Offline captioning Closed caption that is done "after the fact." The text of the captions is written or created and then transferred to a videotape before broadcast and distribution.

Online captioning Live captioning of an event as it happens.

Open captioning Captions that have been decoded and made a part of the television picture, like subtitles in a movie. The captions cannot be turned off but are a permanent part of the movie or video projection.

Realtime The act of writing on a computerized shorthand writer that is connected to a computer and having the English words appear instantly on the computer screen for viewing and printing.

Remote access In realtime and captioning technology, the ability of a realtime reporter to caption events in one location and have the translation transmitted back to a home site for encoding and broadcast.

SHHH Self-help for hard of hearing people.

Simulcasting Broadcasting an event via more than one media, for example, radio and television at the same time or radio and Internet at the same time.

>>SPEAKER The special formatting symbol used by captioners to denote a new speaker when closed captioning.

>>>STORY The special formatting symbol used by captioners to denote a new story when closed captioning.

Television Decoder Circuitry Act of 1990 Mandated that after July 1993 all televisions manufactured for sale in the United States must contain a built-in caption decoder if the picture tube is 13 inches or larger.

TTY/TDD This device is a simple keyboard that connects to a telephone through an acoustic coupler that allows two people to communicate via their keyboards. Messages are typed back and forth. TTY is an abbreviation for teletypewriter, also referred to as text typewriter. TTD is an abbreviation for telecommunication display devices or telecommunication devices for deaf persons.

Voice-to-print (text)/speech to print (text) Any of the various methods used to convert spoken words to a textual format. Realtime reporting is a method used in voice-to-print technology.

Webcasting Live captioning of an event that allows the textual translation to be simulcast over the Internet via the World Wide Web.

Legislation Pertaining to Captioning

Many laws have been enacted to protect the rights of all individuals and to eliminate discrimination based on physical handicaps.

The Telecommunications Act of 1996

The Telecommunications Act of 1996 addresses the issue of closed captioning for video programs. Recent changes in the act are presented next.

SEC. 305. VIDEO PROGRAMMING ACCESSIBILITY. Title VII is amended by inserting after section 712 (47 U.S.C. 612) the following new section: "SEC. 713. VIDEO PROGRAMMING ACCESSIBILITY."

"(a) COMMISSION INQUIRY.—Within 180 days after the date of enactment of the Telecommunications Act of 1996, the Federal Communications Commission shall complete an inquiry to ascertain the level at which video programming is closed captioned. Such inquiry shall examine the extent to which existing or previously published programming is closed captioned, the size of the video programming provider or programming owner providing closed captioning, the size of the market served, the relative audience shares achieved, or any other related factors. The Commission shall submit to the Congress a report on the results of such inquiry.

"(b) ACCOUNTABILITY CRITERIA—Within 18 months after such date of enactment, the Commission shall prescribe such regulations as are necessary to implement this section. Such regulations shall ensure that---
"(1) video programming first published or exhibited after the effective data of such regulations is fully accessible through the provision of closed captions, except as provided in subsection (d); and
(2) video programming providers or owners maximize the accessibility of video programming first published or exhibited prior to the effective date of such regulations through the provision of closed captions, except as provided in subsection (d).

"(c) DEADLINES FOR CAPTIONING—Such regulations shall include an appropriate schedule of deadlines for the provision of closed captioning of video programming.

"(d) EXEMPTIONS—Notwithstanding subsection (b)---
"(1) the commission may exempt by regulation programs, classes of programs, or services for which the Commission has determined that the provision of closed captioning would be economically burdensome to the provider or owner of such programming;
"(2) a provider of video programming or the owner of any program carried by the provider shall not be obligated to supply closed captions if such action would be inconsistent with contracts in effect on the date of enactment of the Telecommunications Act of 1996, except that nothing in this section shall be construed to relieve a video programming provider of its obligations to provide services required by Federal law; and
"(3) a provider of video programming or program owner may petition the Commission for an exemption from the requirements of this section, and the Commission may grant such petition upon a showing that the requirements contained in this section would result in an undue burden.

"(e) UNDUE BURDEN—The term 'undue burden' means significant difficulty or expense. In determining whether the closed captions necessary to comply with the requirements of this paragraph would result in an undue economic burden, the factors to be considered include---
"(1) the nature and cost of the closed captions for the programming;
"(2) the impact on the operation of the provider or program owner;
"(3) the financial resources of the provider or program owner; and
"(4) the type of operations of the provider or program owner."

The Decoder Circuitry Acts of 1990
BILL TEXT Report for S. 1974
As finally approved by the House and Senate (Enrolled)
S.1974

One Hundred First Congress of the United States of America
At the Second Session. Begun and held at the City of Washington
on Tuesday, the twenty-third day of January,
one thousand nine hundred and ninety

An Act To require new televisions to have built-in decoder circuitry.

Be it enacted by the Senate and House of Representatives of the United States of America in Congress assembled.

SHORT TITLE

Section 1.

This Act may be cited as the "Television Decoder Circuitry Act of 1990."

FINDINGS

Sec. 2.

The Congress finds that—

1. to the fullest extent made possible by technology, deaf and hearing-impaired people should have equal access to the television medium;

2. closed-captioned television transmissions have made it possible for thousands of deaf and hearing-impaired people to gain access to the television medium, thus significantly improving the quality of their lives;

3. closed-captioned television will provide access to information, entertainment, and a greater understanding of our Nation and the world to over 24,000,000 people in the United States who are deaf or hearing-impaired;

4. closed-captioned television will provide benefits for the nearly 38 percent of older Americans who have some loss of hearing;

5. closed-captioned television can assist both hearing and hearing-impaired children with reading and other learning skills and improve literacy skills among adults;

6. closed-captioned television can assist those among our Nation's large immigrant population who are learning English as a second language with language comprehension;

7. currently, a consumer must buy a TeleCaption decoder and connect the decoder to a television set in order to display the closed-captioned television transmissions;

8. technology is now available to enable that closed-caption decoding capability to be built into new television sets during manufacture at a nominal cost by 1991; and

9. the availability of decoder-equipped television sets will significantly increase the audience that can be served by closed-captioned television, and such increased market will be an incentive to the television medium to provide more captioned programming.

REQUIREMENT FOR CLOSED-CAPTIONING EQUIPMENT

Sec. 3.

Section 303 of the Communications Act of 1934 (47 U.S.C. 303) is amended by adding at the end thereof the following:

"(u) Require that apparatus designed to receive television pictures broadcast simultaneously with sound be equipped with built-in decoder circuitry designed to display closed-captioned television transmissions when such apparatus is manufactured in the United States or imported for use in the United States and its television picture screen is 13 inches or greater in size."

PERFORMANCE AND DISPLAY STANDARDS

Sec. 4.

(a) Section 330 of the Communications Act of 1934 (47 U.S.C. 330) is amended by redesignating subsection (b) as subsection (c), and by inserting immediately after subsection (a) the following new subsection:

"(b) No person shall ship in interstate commerce, manufacture, assemble, or import from any foreign country into the United States any apparatus described in section 303(u) of this Act except in accordance with rules prescribed by the Commission pursuant to the authority granted by that section. Such rules shall provide performance and display standards for such built-in decoder circuitry. Such rules shall further require that all such apparatus be able to receive and display closed captioning which have been transmitted by way of line 21 of the vertical blanking interval and which conform to the signal and display specifications set forth in the Public Broadcasting System engineering report numbered E-7709-C dated May 1980, as amended by the Telecaption II Decoder Module Performance Specification published by the National Captioning Institute, November 1985. As new video technology is developed, the Commission shall take such action as the Commission determines appropriate to ensure that closed-captioning service continues to be available to consumers. This subsection shall not apply to carriers transporting such apparatus without trading it." (b) Section 330(c) of such Act, as redesignated by subsection (a) of this section, is amended by deleting "and section 303(s)" and inserting in lieu thereof, "section 303(s) and section 303(u)."

EFFECTIVE DATE

Sec. 5.

Sections 3 and 4 of this Act shall take effect on July 1, 1993.

RULES

Sec. 6.

The Federal Communications Commission shall promulgate rules to implement this Act within 180 days after the date of its enactment.

Speaker of the House of Representatives.
Vice President of the United States and President of the Senate.

FCC DISABILITIES RIGHTS OFFICE (DRO) CLOSED CAPTIONING RULES
Closed Captioning

Closed captioning is a technology that provides visual text to describe dialogue, background noise, and sound effects on television programming. As of July 1993, all television sets with screens 13 inches or larger sold in the United States must have built-in decoder circuitry that allows viewers to display closed captions on their sets. In 1996, Congress passed a law requiring video program distributors (cable operators, broadcasters, and satellite distributors) to phase in closed captioning of their television programs. Viewers may select to watch closed captions through their remote controls or on-screen displays. The new law does not require captioning of home videos or video games.

BENEFITS OF CLOSED CAPTIONING

Closed captions provide a critical link to news, entertainment, and information for individuals who are deaf and hard of hearing, enabling these individuals to be part of the cultural mainstream of our society. For individuals whose native language is not English, English language captions have also been used to improve comprehension and fluency in this language. In addition, studies have shown that captions have helped children learn to read, and have improved literacy skills.

NEW PROGRAMMING

All English language programming, which was first shown on or after January 1, 1998, must be captioned over an eight-year period, by 2006. The Federal Communications Commission (FCC) has set benchmarks to meet this deadline. These benchmarks measure the amount of programming that must be captioned each calendar quarter (every 3 months) and are as follows:

2000: 450 hours of programming per channel per quarter
2002: 900 hours of programming per channel per quarter
2004: 1350 hours of programming per channel per quarter
2006: 100% of all programming, with some exemptions

PRE-RULE PROGRAMMING

Programming first shown before January 1, 1998, is called pre-rule programming. Seventy-five percent of this programming must be captioned by 2008 under the following schedule:

2003: 30% of programming per channel per quarter
2008: 75% of programming per channel per quarter

SPANISH LANGUAGE PROGRAMMING

Because captioning is fairly new to Spanish language program providers, the FCC has provided a longer time period for compliance by these programmers. All new Spanish language programming that was first shown after January 1, 1998, must be captioned by 2010. The following schedule applies to Spanish language programming shown after January 1, 1998:

2001: 450 hours of programming per channel per quarter
2004: 900 hours of programming per channel per quarter
2007: 1350 hours of programming per channel per quarter
2010: 100% of all programming, with some exemptions

For programming first shown before January 1, 1998, the following schedule applies:

2005: 30% of programming per channel per quarter
2012: 75% of programming per channel per quarter

EXEMPTIONS

There are some exemptions to the above captioning rules (for both English and Spanish language programming). For example, captioning is not required for:

• Programs which are shown between 2 a.m. and 6 a.m. local time;
• Locally produced and distributed non-news programming with no repeat value (*e.g.*, parades and school sports);
• Commercials that are no more than five minutes long;

- Instructional programming that is locally produced by public television stations for use in grades K-12 and post secondary schools (only covers programming narrowly distributed to individual educational institutions);

- Programs in languages other than English or Spanish;

- Programs shown on new networks for the first four years of the network's operations;

- Public service announcements under 10 minutes, unless they are federally-funded or produced; and

- Video programming providers with annual gross revenues under $3 million (although such programmers must pass through video programming that has already been captioned).

In addition, a video programming provider or distributor may ask the FCC for an exemption for specific programming if supplying captions for that programming would result in an undue burden for the provider or distributor.

REAL-TIME VS. ELECTRONIC NEWSROOM CAPTIONING TECHNIQUE

Real-time captioning typically uses stenographers to convert the entire audio portion of a live program to captions. Electronic newsroom captioning technique (ENCT) creates captions from a news script computer or teleprompter used for live newscasts. Because only material that is scripted can be captioned with this technique, breaking news, sports and weather updates, and live field reports are typically not captioned when ENCT is used. As of January 1, 2000, FCC rules have not permitted the four major national broadcast networks (ABC, CBS, Fox, and NBC), television affiliates of these networks in the top 25 television markets, and national nonbroadcast networks (*e.g.*, cable) serving at least 50% of the total number of households subscribing to video programming services, to count live news programming using ENCT toward their captioning requirements. Rather, these networks and affiliates must provide real-time captioning for live news programming in order for it to count toward meeting the FCC's captioning schedules. Other programming distributors and providers, however, are permitted to use ENCT for live programming to meet the captioning mandates.

EMERGENCY PROGRAMMING

In addition to captioning, the FCC has issued specific rules requiring television programming distributors to make televised emergency programming visually accessible to persons who are deaf and hard of hearing. Emergency information is information that is intended to further the protection of life, health, safety, or property. Examples include, but are not limited to, hazardous weather situations such as tornadoes, heavy snows, hurricanes and earthquakes, and dangerous community situations such as the discharge of toxic gases, widespread power failures, civil disorders, and school closings.

In order to provide access, information about emergency programming may be closed captioned or presented through an alternative method of visual presentation, including open captioning, crawls, or scrolls that appear on the screen. Where emergency information is provided by a means other than closed captioning, it must not block the program's closed captions. The information provided visually must include critical details regarding the emergency and how to respond. The FCC's rules on emergency programming are effective for all such programming, i.e., there is no phase-in period for implementation and there are no exemptions as there are for the captioning mandates.

DIGITAL CAPTIONING

The FCC has released new rules adopting technical standards for the display of closed captions on digital television (DTV) receivers. These rules, which go into effect on July 1, 2002, will require DTV receivers to enable consumers to control the print type, color, size, and background of captions.

COMPLAINTS

If you wish to file an informal complaint for failure to provide closed captioning or access to emergency programming, you may send the complaint to the Disabilities Rights Office (DRO), FCC, Consumer Information Bureau, 445 12th Street, SW, Washington, DC 20554. In addition to sending a letter, you may contact the FCC by other reasonable means, including: facsimile transmission, 202-418-2839; phone 202-418-7096 (voice) and 202-418-0189 (TTY); e-mail fccinfo@fcc.gov; audio-cassette recording; and Braille. The complaint should include:

- The name of the video programming distributor against whom the complaint is alleged;
- The date and time of the alleged violation; and
- Details about the problem so that the distributor may correct or otherwise respond to the complaint.

You should include the name of the programmer (*e.g.*, News Channel 13) in addition to the name of the distributor (*e.g.*, ACME Cable of Maplewood). The FCC's DRO can provide informal dispute resolution to obtain compliance with the rules. However, the Cable Services Bureau (CSB) is responsible for handling formal actions needed to enforce the closed captioning rules. FCC rules require formal complaints for violations of the captioning rules to be sent first to the video program provider (the local television station, cable operator or satellite service) before they may be brought to the FCC. Although you are encouraged to bring formal complaints for violations of the emergency rules to the video program provider, you are not required to do so. If you do wish to file a formal complaint for a violation of either the captioning rules or the emergency programming rules, send it to: FCC, Cable Services Bureau, 445 12th Street, SW, Washington, DC 20554; phone 202-418-7096 (voice) and 202-418-7172 (TTY); e-mail CSBINFO@fcc.gov, and fax 202-418-1195.

For more information on the FCC's captioning rules and requirements, go to www.fcc.gov/cib/dro, and click on closed captioning.

SECTION D

Chapter 26

A Day in the Life of a Captioning Reporter

Just as in freelance reporting, the captioning reporter may be involved in a variety of job scenarios. And, just as in the freelance area, the individual reporter needs to take into consideration many things when working for a firm or agency.

The Captioning Industry

Usually, caption reporters are hired by large captioning corporations who specialize in closed captioning. These firms may hire individuals as independent contractors or as employees. They may also hire reporters to work on site at their office locations or the captioning reporters may work remotely.

Large captioning agencies or corporations usually secure their clientele by bidding for contracts, which are let from national or local television stations. For example, if television station TV4U wishes to have all their news, sports, and special live events captioned, they may let out a bid to all the companies who would like to have their business. For the purposes of discussion, let's say that EZCaption wins the bid. They now find themselves responsible for captioning many hours of live television and are in need of captioning reporters, who they then hire to fill these positions.

The captioning industry is competitive in the sense that the more jobs that an agency has, the more reporters they are going to hire to complete these jobs. Some captioning agencies may hire their captioners as either part-time or full-time employees; some may hire them as independent contractors.

Beginning reporters should research the history of a captioning company that they believe they want to work with. They should inquire about their training period, their benefits, whether the company can guarantee a certain number of hours per week, their scheduling practices, and so on. If possible, beginning reporters should try to talk with current or past employees of agencies that they might want to work for.

Equipment and Office

The captioner needs a certain amount of equipment to perform his or her duties as a closed captioning reporter. Most agencies outline the equipment that the reporter needs at the very beginning and make sure that their employees are capable of doing the work.

If a captioner is working on site, most of the technical equipment for encoding and transmitting the closed captioning will be provided by the company. However, if a captioner is working remotely, he or she will need to have a computerized writer with proper cable connections, two computers, two television sets, headphones, and direct access via modem or cable to the employing agency; the latter may require a separate phone line. The two television sets are necessary if the reporter wants to see the television program live, without captions on one screen, and the direct feed with captions on the other screen.

If a reporter is working in a home-office environment, it is important that a suitable environment exist. Preferably, the reporter's office should be in a private location—a separate room or basement office, for instance, adequate desk space for the reporter to work on; computers and monitors set up with ergonomic factors taken into consideration; proper heat, light, and ventilation; and, generally, a comfortable working environment.

Captioning: Four Different Perspectives

The following information is extracted from interviewing four captioning reporters who are currently working in different areas. The captioners who participated in an Internet interview were the following:

Monette Benoit (MB) is a Certified Shorthand Reporter, Registered Professional Reporter, Registered Merit Reporter, Certified Realtime Reporter, and a Certified Reporting Instructor. She owns and operates her own publishing company that produces and markets educational products for court reporters. She formed the American Realtime/Captioning Service (ARTS) in 1993 in San Antonio, Texas; she is an ADA consultant and CART provider. Monette has also written articles for *The Journal of Court Reporting*, many of which can be found on line at www.ncraonline.com.

Kelly DeVito (KD) has been a broadcast captioner for many years with a large captioning corporation. Kelly works both on site and from a remote location for her corporation. Kelly has also captioned teleconferences for large companies.

Ellen Oakes (EO) worked briefly as a freelance reporter, including both court and deposition work. Her realtime experience is with a large captioning corporation; however, Ellen works in a location about a thousand miles from the company that she works for and sends her live, realtime data back to the station via modem.

Traci Walker (TW) also works for a large captioning company, but has also worked as a freelance court reporter for many years. Traci has a broad range of experience that has covered many years as a reporter in many different areas. She was instrumental in helping to form a student-training program for recent graduates of court reporting who want to enter the captioning field.

Question 1: What is your name and current position or title?
MB: Monette Benoit, CART provider
KD: Kelly DeVito, stenocaptioner
EO: Ellen Oakes, Closed Captioner
TW: Traci Walker, Real-Time Captioner

Question 2: How do you learn about job assignments that you are called on to do?
MB: The CART asignments, requests that I receive, come from sign interpreters with whom I have developed professional and personal relationships, consumers (Big D—Deaf, little D—deaf, oral deaf, late deafened, hard of hearing). The majority of requests are word-of-mouth from prior work experiences and also involve community events where my work has been viewed, displayed.

KD: We get a monthly schedule that is posted on the Internet from our company.

EO: Our company provides us with a schedule that will post the various broadcast jobs that we do.

TW: All of the captioners for our organization receive a schedule that will list the names, jobs, hours, and so on, for each individual reporter

Question 3: How do you designate different speakers when captioning?

MB: I use the standard "banks" that I learned in school, and those that I used in court and on depos. The main speaker is always EUFPLT and the others are designated [by] a different bank, which I global into my job dictionary prior to each job. Classroom CART has banks for male student, female student, professor, etc. Church services have banks for priest, parishioners, cantor, sign interpreter, etc.

KD: For a new speaker, I use >>, and for a new story, >>> is used.

EO: >> designates a different speaker, >>REPORTER: designates the news reporter who is speaking.

TW: Two or three arrows are used for speakers.

Question 4: What types of jobs might you be called on to do?

MB: I began learning CART in a corner of a church with my screen turned down. I advanced forward with my work and displayed to a large screen next to the priest each Sunday. I wrote masses, meetings, baptisms, confirmations, international speakers, international events with prayer, Latin songs, deaf choirs, wedding vows. I have written PTA meetings, seminars, national, state, and international conventions, an international Lutheran convention with 28,000 teens, a parade, one year of Latin at a university, government meetings, telecourses for placement skills, funeral services. Health care classes, retirement parties, defensive-driving courses, county commissioner meetings. I CARTed an evening at a "dude" ranch with music and roping lessons for the SHHH, Self-Help for the Hard of Hearing. Each job is different; each audience is different. I love it!

KD: Most of the jobs we do are news programs. We have done "Family Feud" and "Spin City" in the past. We also caption baseball, basketball, and football games. With new technology we are captioning football games that allow captions to go to a hand-held pager that a hard-of-hearing person holds in his or her hand. They can then "listen" to the sportscasters while at the stadium! We caption city council meetings, National Geographic shows, and we are now doing teleconferences via the Internet.

EO: I caption news programs, World Harvest (religious) programs, sports broadcasts, and some precaptioned tapes.

TW: My main job is to caption the nightly news on television for my company; however, I have also done a lot of sports events.

Question No. 5: What technology do you use in your captioning or CARTing?

MB: Technology for CART, I believe each reporter needs to prepare for each job—most of the work is advance prep work. We need to write over 99 percent accuracy. We need to fingerspell, stitch words together. We need to have the speed for sustained writing and multiple speakers.

KD: The technology used for captioning is the same used in any realtime situation—computer, writer hooked to computer, software, etc. My company does the technical encoding and things like that.

EO: For captioning, these are the tools needed: two computers, one for prescripting and the Internet, and one for actual captioning; external modems for each computer; two phone lines, one for audio and one for captions to be sent; specialized captioning software; a shorthand machine hooked to computer to write in realtime.

TW: Captioning software, writer, computers, modems, et cetera.

Question 6: When you begin an assignment, are there some preparations that you need to make before you begin to write?

MB: I always try to introduce myself to the speakers, consumers, convention planners, if possible. I always request all bios (biographies). Bios are a necessity. I hunt for job-specific terms and request national magazines, anything to further help me to assist my consumers. I have globals for "speaking Latin" and for "speaking Spanish."

KD: On a majority of stations we do, we have access to their newsroom. Here, we can go in and script the entire show. I can get in an hour ahead of time and write exactly what is going to be on the anchors' teleprompter. I then leave myself 15 minutes before the show to do a quick edit of my work. When the show starts, I continuously hit a button on my computer keyboard, punching out the show that I have just written. If they have breaking news, or go to weather or sports (which are not scripted), I can go back to my steno machine and fill in the gaps.

EO: Yes. If the station provides prescript, you need to prepare that, which includes dialing up to the station's newsroom and typing out the show. If the station does not provide prescript, you need to access their Web site and record unfamiliar words and names into your dictionary to be prepared for the show. Just before beginning to write, you must dial into the proper encoder and dial into the audio line for the station you're captioning.

TW: Yes. Download scripts from television station, input names, spellings into dictionary relative to broadcast.

Question 7: During an assignment are there special precautions that you must be aware of while captioning?

MB: If a captioner, CART provider is broadcasting, the FCC requires that specific words (cuss words) are not permitted. I have a stroke for "(bleep)." I also have the most common "cuss" words dashed out within my main dictionary. In case someone says a term and I hit the stroke, it will come up as a bleep. If a cuss word needs to come up on the screen, I fingerspell it. If I am CARTing to a screen, I fingerspell it, if it's an adult audience and part of the speaker's presentation. If I am writing for teens and families, I will dash the term/word. Each job is different

KD: One of the biggest things to look out for is swear words. I have deleted them all from my dictionary and if one comes up, I fingerspell it as not to create some controversy.

EO: Yes. Each station has different ways of captioning. For instance, some stations have captions at the top, others at the bottom. Others caption the entire show at the bottom and have their weather captioned at the top. There are two different encoders we use, so you must be sure to dial into the right one. Also, you must pop your name at the beginning of each show and company info at the end.

TW: Yes, we have to be careful of spellings, homonyms, and the positioning of the caption on the screen.

Question No. 8: Once a job is complete, any special precautions that must be done?

MB: First, I pack my equipment. I actually have a chart for all the wires and cables. Many times I have been so tired or distracted that I have left equipment at the job. I always enter main dictionary terms if I think the term may come up again and it's not in my dictionary. The dictionary is the key—it is always a work-in-progress in mastering our CART skills.

KD: When a job is complete, even though I don't need to make a transcript, I edit the file to look for words that didn't translate correctly or were not in my dictionary. I also read my paper notes every day as well.

EO: You must be sure to hang up from the encoder connected to the station.

TW: Be sure to hang up the phone connection to the station.

Question No. 9: Can you give some examples of where realtime writing is used other than broadcast reporting?

MB: I strongly believe that wherever language is spoken and/or muttered, professional court reporters, captioners, and CART providers can provide verbatim records. I write for brain injured people, people re-entering the work force, individuals with physical challenges and/or limitations. We can share our skills anywhere.

KD: Realtime is also used for teleconferences. Also for the football games using the realtime, close-captioned pagers. Churches often will ask for a congregation to be captioned for their hard-of-hearing churchgoers. Hard-of-hearing students are starting to use realtime reporters to sit next to them in class and transcribe lectures for them. This takes work on the reporter's part, as they have to read textbooks in advance to get a sense of the terminology going into the lecture.

EO: Computer Integrated Courtrooms and new-age courtrooms.

TW: In the classroom, CART, conventions, meetings, et cetera.

Question No. 10: Briefly describe your working environment.

MB: Most of my work is performed on site, away from my office/home. I do 99 percent of the prep work before each job. Remote CART enables CART providers and consumers to work with new technology. Learn the CART ropes before you remote CART.

KD: Home office: I have my desk with two computers, a printer and audio equipment on it. My machine is on the floor in front of me. I have a TV also in front of me, always with the captions on! I have a mess of resource books including Rand McNally's "ZipCode Finder," and four books by M. Monette Benoit all geared to captioning and reporting, among others.

EO: I work in a home office, which is a 10×10 room with a corner desk and another big desk with shelves attached. I have windows above my desk, looking out at nature, filing cabinets filled to the brim, and my favorite lamp to enhance the lighting.

TW: I have an office in the basement of my home. I have three computers, desk, chair, three phone lines, fax machine, and backup of everything.

Question No. 11: Briefly describe a typical day in the life of a captioner, real-time writer, CART provider.

MB: There is really no "typical" day for a CART provider since each assignment is different. I have addressed this issue in many past articles that can be found in the *Court Reporting Journal* on-line at www.ncraonline.com.

KD: At this time, my daily schedule looks something like this! 2:45 a.m.—Wake up, stretch out, grab a class of water and a coke. 3:00 a.m.—Start looking for material that's going to be on my show this morning. Either using the station's newsroom or their Web site. 4:00–7:00 a.m.—Caption the early morning news from Houston, Texas. During this time I will do all kinds of research on the Internet to get the spellings of names that come up over and over, street names, etc. 7:00–9:00 a.m.—Go back to sleep!! 9:00–10:30 a.m.—Prepare for and caption my 11:00–11:30 show. 11:30 a.m.–2:00 p.m.—Do whatever I want, errands, work around house, go to gym, play with dogs, whatever! 2:00–3:00 p.m. I usually edit old files during this time. 3:00–5:30 p.m.—Prep for and complete my 4:00–5:30 show. At this point, I'm done for the day, shut down my computer, and struggle to stay up past 9:00 p.m.

EO: I usually have my first show around 5:00 or 6:00 p.m., but begin scripting or preparing about an hour ahead of time. Sometimes I'll have an early-morning, two-hour show, followed by evening news. I'll work until about 7:00 or 8:00 p.m. and have a break until my 11:00 p.m. show, which I prepare for starting at 10:00 p.m. I'll work ten days in a row followed by four days off.

TW: I work an early shift. I get up, prep by dialing into the newsroom computer for each show, write the show, and then edit the file afterward. Sometimes I caption seven or eight hours a day, possibly going to seven different locales across the United States.

Chapter 27

How the Captioned Job Looks

Most jobs that are captioned are not transcribed into a hard-copy format. The are viewed instantly, read on the screen, and then gone. However, most reporters save a file containing the captioned information and, in some cases, a hard copy may be desired. CART providers who caption classroom lectures may have requests for a hard copy of the notes or for an ASCII (floppy disk) copy.

As with the other two areas of reporting, officialships and freelancing, the captioning reporter or CART provider may be called on to do a variety of jobs. A sampling of some captioned broadcasts appear on the next few pages. Notice the use of the special symbols for new speaker identification >> and >>> to indicate a new story. Also, notice the all-capped format that would appear as white letters on a boxed black background, a line at a time.

You may notice an error or two in the realtimed notes—that's okay—captioners make mistakes.

PITTSBURGH WITH A SLIM LEAD ON
JACKSONVILLE.
DETROIT LOOKING FOR THEIR
FIRST WIN.
DENVER OVER WASHINGTON, 10-0
IN THE THIRD.
AND CHICAGO LEADS THE
BUCCANEERS IN TAMPA, 21-9 IN
THE THIRD QUARTER.

THE WILD HAVE BEEN SHUTOUT AT
HOME IN CONSECUTIVE WEEKS.
WE WILL HAVE HIGHLIGHTS
TONIGHT AT 10:00.
CONGRATULATIONS TO DALE
EARNHARDT.
>>> VIKINGS TOMORROW NIGHT.
WE WILL HAVE MORE ON THE
EMOTIONS FOLLOWING THE KOREY
STRINGER RETIREMENT CEREMONY
AT 4:00.
>> NOT BAD.
>> NOT BAD.
>> 40 YEARS, IT'S STILL KIND
OF MOIST!
>> KINDA.
>> OPERATIVE WORD!
>> I BET.

MOVE.

I HOPE THAT WILL LEAD TO MORE
RAPID PROGRESS ON THE
DIPLOMATIC FRONT.

>> REPORTER: ON THE MILITARY
FRONT, THE TALIBAN IS HOLDING
ONTO KANDAHAR.

U.S. OFFICIALS SAY THEY WILL
GET THEM THERE AND THEY'RE
CONFIDENT OSAMA BIN LADEN WILL
BE FOUND.

>> THE KEY HERE IS TO STRIP
AWAY HIS PROTECTION AND LOOSEN
THE GRIP OF THE TALIBAN.

AND BEGIN TO MAKE IT UNSAFE
FOR HIM TO BE WILL N LARGE
PARTS OF THE COUNTRY, WE'RE
TIGHTENING THE NET.

>> REPORTER: AND AFTER A
FIVE-YEAR SILENCE ORDERED BY
THE TALIBAN, KABUL TELEVISION
IS BACK ON THE AIR.

>> I'M HAPPY, YOU KNOW.
I THINK LIFE IS NOW ENJOYABLE
FOR ME.

>> REPORTER: TONIGHT IN KABUL,
RESIDENTS WHO STILL HAD

>>> TODAY MARKS THE END OF AN
AMAZING HIGH SCHOOL FOOTBALL
CAREER THAT ENDED THE WAY
TYLER EVANS HOPED IT WOULD.
HE SHATTERED RECORDS BY
THOUSANDS OF YARDS, BUT RANDY
SHAVER SHOWS US, HE WANTED
SOMETHING THAT HAD LITTLE TO
DO WITH INDIVIDUAL MARKS AND
EVERYTHING TO DO WITH THE
TEAM.
[MARCHING BAND SOUNDS]

>> REPORTER: ON A DAY
DEDICATED TO MINNESOTA'S HIGH
SCHOOL FOOTBALL STARS. . . .
SOME BURNED BRIGHTER THAN
OTHERS.
>> NO. 5, HE'S FAST, RUNS
HARD, HARD TO BRING HIM DOWN,
VERY STRONG RUNNER.
THEY'RE QUICKER TO GIVE CREDIT
TO HIS FALCON TEAMMATES FOR
TYLER'S SUCCESS.
WITH PILL {JER}.
— PILLAGER.

[SCREAMING AND CHEERS]
>> I'M REALLY PROUD OF HIM.
HE'S VERY THANKFUL FOR WHERE

ON TV WHEN WE COME BACK.

>>> NOW, TOM BROKAW IS A —
HAS A LOOK AT WHAT'S COMING
UP.
>>> TONIGHT, WITH BULLETS
FLYING, MARINES HIT THE GROUND

RUNNING IN AFGHANISTAN.
>>> ALSO, HOW A JANITOR
AVERTED A POSSIBLE MASS KERR.
NEXT.

>>> THERE IS MORE NEWS COMING
YOUR WAY AT 7:00.
DAVID HAS A PREVIEW OF THE TOP
STORY.
>> REPORTER: WE'RE SEEING
STRONG REACTION AROUND THE
COUNTRY, INCLUDING HERE IN
SOUTH CAROLINA TO THE NEWS
THAT A MASSACHUSETTS COMPANY
HAS CLONED A HUMAN EMBRYO.
IN RESPONSE, A STATE
LEGISLATOR WILL INTRODUCE A
BILL THAT WILL BAN CLONING
RESEARCH HERE IN SOUTH
CAROLINA.
AT 7:00: WE'LL HAVE MORE
ABOUT THE PROCEDURE AND

THE 2-A GAME FEATURES THE BULL
{DOGSZ}.
THEY HAVE WON 29 STRAIGHT
GAMES!
THEY TOOK IT ALL LAST YEAR.
THEY'RE A PERFECT 14 AND 0
THIS SEASON, LOOKING TO REPEAT
AS 2-A STATE CHANNEL SHOPS.
>> — — CHAMPIONS.
>> WE NEVER LOOKED AT IT THAT
SERIOUSLY.
IT'S BEEN OUR GOAL, STATE
CHAMPIONSHIP.

A LOT OF PEOPLE TALK TO US
ABOUT IT, BUT WE'RE NOT
FOCUSES — — FOCUSED ON THE WING
STREAK.
>> EVERY TEAM IS OUT TO BEAT
US, SO WE CAN'T COME OUT AND
JUST PLAY NOT HARD.
WE GOTTA COME OUT EVERY WEEK
AND PLAY HARD.
>> REPORTER: HERE'S THE
WINNER FOR THIS WEEKEND, THE
4-A DIVISION 2 GAME FRIDAY
AT:00 WITH THE TIGERS FACING
THE BULLDOGS.
THE 11 A.M. GAME FOR THE 2-A
TITLE.

BEGINNING WITH THE CURRENT
READING AS OF 6:00 THIS
EVENING: 72 DEGREES.
MY GOODNESS!

MOSTLY CLEAR SKIES AT THE
MOMENT.
THE DEWPOINT IS 66, 82 PERCENT
HUMIDITY.
OUR HIGH TODAY WAS 75 AT
COLUMBIA METRO WITH A MORNING
LOW OF 62 AND 64.
WE GOT A LITTLE BIT OF RAIN
THIS MORNING, A HELP DOWNPOUR
FOR SOME OF YOU, 2/10 OF AN
INCH THE MAJORITY.
72 HERE AND ORANGEBURG.
GRANNY, GOOD EVENING!
66 IN SUMTER, 67 IN NEWBERRY
AND IN GREENVILLE, MID-60S.
THIS MORNING, WE STARTED WITH
LOW CLOUDS, GIVING WAY TO
PARTLY SUNNY TO CLEAR
AFTERNOON AND NOW WE'RE
WATCHING A VERY POWERFUL STORM
THAT'S CENTERED IN THE HEART
OF THE COUNTRY.
AS LONG AS THIS RULES THE MAP,
WE WILL HAVE SEVERAL SPOKES OF
ENERGY COMING THROUGH, THE

RESUME OR COVER LETTER, LOG
ONTO WISTV.COM.
WE HAVE JOB TIPS FOR YOU.
AND CLICK JOB LINK, PROVIDENCE
HOSPITAL.
MANAGEMENT POSITIONS ARE OPEN
NOW.
WE HAVE AN ACCOUNTANT
EXECUTIVE POSITION OPEN HERE
AT WIS.

YOU CAN FIND OUT ABOUT THAT
AND MORE AT WISTV.COM.
>> THANK YOU.
MADE A COUPLE OF THE MISTAKES
MYSELF.
THEY'RE EASY TO CORRECT.
>>> TURNING BACK TO WEATHER
NOW.
>> BEN TANNER HAS THE FORECAST
AS HE ADD MYERS THE STATE
CHRISTMAS TREE.
>> TAKE A RIDE, THIS IS WHAT
YOU'LL SEE, A GORGEOUS CEDAR
TREE, ABOUT 30 FEET TALL.
WE'RE LIVE AT THE STATE HOUSE
WITH THE FORECAST.
WE'LL TALK ABOUT A BIG COOL
DOWN FOR THE WEEKEND.
STAY WITH US.

WE FOUND A {LOOLT} — LOT OF
PEOPLE HAVE GOOD INTENTIONS,
BUT ONE WRONG MOVE COULD COST
YOU THE JOB.

>> CAN I HELP YOU?
LOOKING FOR A JOB TODAY, SIR?
>> REPORTER: THE CROWD AT
THIS RECENT JOB FAIR SHOWS
JUST HOW COMPETITIVE THE JOB
MARKET IS TODAY.
10,000 PEOPLE HERE LOOKING FOR
JOBS.
>> ONE OF THE MISTAKES IS
PEOPLE AREN'T PREPARED FOR THE
JOB SEARCH.

>> REPORTER: STEPHANIE BERRY
HAS RAN A RECRUITING COMPANY
SINCE 1995 AND SAYS MISTAKE
NO. 1: A RAMBLING RESUME.
>> THE RESUME IS SUPPOSED TO
PERK THEIR INTEREST ENOUGH
THAT THEY WILL CALL YOU FOR AN
INTERVIEW.
>> REPORTER: THE WINNING
RESUME IS ONE PAGE LONG,
CONTENT TAIL {YORD} TO THE JOB
WITH A COVER LETTER.
MISTAKE 2: A LOT OF PEOPLE

TEST TEST.1
>>> A SCIENTIFIC BREAKTHROUGH
OR MORALISTIC NIGHTMARE COME
THROUGH? 4
>> THE CLONING OF AN EMBRYO
PITS SCIENCE AGAINST RELIGION
OVER WHO SHOULD CONTROL
HUMANITY. 8
>>> HELLO. 9
I'M DON SCOTT.
>>> I'M KELLYE LYNN.
A CONTROVERSIAL ANNOUNCE WILL
BY RESEARCHERS.
IN TODAY'S4""HEALTHWATCH""
MASSACHUSETTS SCIENTISTS SAID
THEY'VE CLONED A HUMAN EMBRYO
FOR THE VERY FIRST TIME, WHICH
COULD BE BENEFICIAL TO THOSE
SUFFERING1FROM PARKINSON'S
DISEASE, DIABETES OR
PARALYSIS.1
>> REPORTER: AFTER
SUCCESSFULLY CLONING THE FIRST
HUMAN EMBRYO, DR. WEST SAYS
HIS COMPANY, ADVANCED CELL
TECHNOLOGIES HAS NO INTEREST

Section E

Helpful Information for the Reporting Profession

Chapter 28

Ethics of the Reporting Profession

Ethics are a set of moral guidelines by which one conducts one's personal life and business practices. Ethics may be predefined by certain religious or cultural standards. Our personal ethics are formed by past events in our own lives and by the influences of those who have been responsible for our upbringing.

Some ethicists have said that ethics are a responsibility or duty that individuals have toward each other, while others say that ethics are a matter of personal choice. Ethics can be expressed or implied; that is, they can be written or understood. Most professions, including court reporting, have developed a code of professional ethics that governs the way that they do business.

The National Court Reporters Association (NCRA) has developed a list of professional ethics that serve as a guide for members of the organization. In addition, a set of guidelines for professional practices have been established by the NCRA. These guidelines are discussed in this section.

The Preamble to the Code of Professional Ethics and General Guidelines for Professional Practice is presented with permission from the National Court Reporters Association. It reads as follows:

CODE OF PROFESSIONAL ETHICS

PREAMBLE

The Committee on Professional Responsibility (COPR) was established in 1985 as the successor to the Committee on Ethics. In 1979, COPR presented its recommendations to the convention in the form of the Code of Professional Responsibility, Enforcement and Disciplinary Procedures, and Professional Practice Objectives, which were adopted by the convention. The President charged COPR in 1985 to review the Code and to evaluate its various sections. Following that charge, COPR revised the Code for brevity and clarity, and the Code was changed to Code of Professional Conduct. In addition, COPR established Mediation Procedures for the Membership in an effort to resolve amicably matters in dispute arising out of the Code of Professional Conduct, and changed the title of the Enforcement and Disciplinary Procedures to Complaint Procedures. In

1992, the President charged COPR again with the review and updating of the Code and the Standards of Professional Practice. As a result, COPR recommended (1) certain revisions to, and the retitling of, the Code as the Code of Professional Ethics; (2) certain revisions to the Complaint Procedures; (3) the corresponding change of COPR's name to the Committee on Professional Ethics (COPE); (4) the change of the title of the Standards of Professional Practice to the Guidelines for Professional Practice; and (5) the separate publication of the mediation procedures and transcript format guidelines from the Code, the Guidelines and the Complaint and Advisory Opinion Procedures. Although the mediation procedures and transcript format guidelines are still in effect, COPR believed that separate publication serves to streamline and direct proper focus to the Code, the Guidelines, and the Complaint and Advisory Opinion Procedures. From 1994 to 2001, the Committee on Professional Ethics (COPE) recommended additional changes to the Code, including expanding the Guidelines for Professional Practice, Sections I, II and III. In 1999, the Board charged the CART (Communication Access Realtime Translation) Task Force with the duty of creating ethical guidelines for that sector of the profession and COPE to review those guidelines before acceptance by the Board. As a result of that review, Section I now covers the General Guidelines for the reporter making the official record; Section II covers the Guidelines for the Realtime Reporter in Legal Proceedings; Section III covers the Guidelines for the CART Provider in a Legal Setting; and Section IV covers the Guidelines for the CART Provider in a Nonlegal Setting. In addition, during this time period, changes were made to the Complaint Procedures, Advisory Opinion Procedures, and Transcript Format Guidelines.

The mandatory Code of Professional Ethics defines the ethical relationship the public, the bench, and the bar have a right to expect from a Member. The Code sets out the conduct of the Member when dealing with the user of reporting services and acquaints the user, as well as the Member, with guidelines established for professional behavior. The Guidelines for Professional Practice, on the other hand, are goals toward which every Member should strive. Members are urged to comply with the Guidelines and must adhere to local, state and federal rules and statutes. It should be noted that these guidelines do not exhaust the moral and ethical considerations with which the Member should conform, but provide the framework for the practice of reporting. Not every situation a Member may encounter can be foreseen, but fundamental ethical principles are always present. By complying with the Code of Professional Ethics and Guidelines for Professional Practice, Members maintain their profession at the highest level.

CODE OF PROFESSIONAL ETHICS

Court reporters who join the National Court Reporters Association (NCRA) do so with an understanding of and agreement to adhere to its code of ethics. This code of ethics is presented here:

A Member Shall:

1. Be fair and impartial toward each participant in all aspects of reported proceedings, and always offer to provide comparable services to all parties in a proceeding.

2. Be alert to situations that are conflicts of interest or that may give the appearance of a conflict of interest. If a conflict or a potential conflict arises, the Member shall disclose that conflict or potential conflict.

3. Guard against not only the fact but the appearance of impropriety.

4. Preserve the confidentiality and ensure the security of information, oral or written, entrusted to the Member by any of the parties in a proceeding.

5. Be truthful and accurate when making public statements or when advertising the Member's qualifications or the services provided.

6. Refrain, as an official reporter, from freelance reporting activities that interfere with official duties and obligations.

7. Determine fees independently, except when established by statute or court order, entering into no unlawful agreements with other reporters on the fees to any user.

8. Refrain from giving, directly or indirectly, any gift, incentive, reward or anything of value to attorneys, clients, witnesses, insurance companies or any other persons or entities associated with the litigation, or to the representatives or agents of any of the foregoing, except for (1) items that do not exceed $100 in the aggregate per recipient each year, or, (2) pro bono services as defined by the NCRA Guidelines for Professional Practice or by applicable state and local laws, rules and regulations.

9. Maintain the integrity of the reporting profession.

10. Abide by the NCRA Constitution & Bylaws.

GUIDELINES FOR PROFESSIONAL PRACTICE

In addition to the professional ethics, members of the National Court Reporters Association are expected to abide by the Constitution and Bylaws of the NCRA. The Association has also established certain "Guidelines for Professional Practice" that lay the framework for the working environment of professional court reporters.

The following is a reprint with permission of the professional practice guidelines for court and real-time reporters.

GENERAL GUIDELINES FOR PROFESSIONAL PRACTICE

SECTION I—COURT REPORTER

The Court Reporter is the official reporter/officer creating the verbatim record of a proceeding. Common sense and professional courtesy should guide the Member in applying the following Guidelines.

In making the official record, a Member should:

A. Accept only those assignments when the Member's level of competence will result in the preparation of an accurate transcript. The Member should remove him or herself from an assignment when the Member believes the Member's abilities are inadequate, recommending or assigning another reporter only if that reporter has the qualifications required for such assignment.

B. Prepare the record in accordance with the transcript-preparation guidelines established by statute or court order, by local custom and usage, or when not so established, in accordance with the NCRA's recommended transcript format guidelines.

C. When sending a substitute reporter, ensure that the substitute is qualified to report the proceeding.

D. Preserve the shorthand notes in accordance with statute or court order, or otherwise for a period of no less than five (5) years through storage of the original paper notes or an electronic copy of either the shorthand notes or the English transcript of the notes on computer disks, cassettes, backup tape systems, or optical or laser disk systems.

E. Meet promised delivery dates whenever possible, make timely delivery of transcripts when no date is specified, and provide immediate notification of delays.

F. Strive to become and remain proficient in the Member's professional skills.

G. Keep abreast of current literature, technological advances and developments, and participate in continuing-education programs.

H. Assist in improving the reporting profession by participating in national, state, and local association activities that advance the quality and standards of the reporting profession.

I. Cooperate with the bench and bar for the improvement of the administration of justice.

J. As part of the reporting profession's commitment to the principle that reporting services should be available to all, members are encouraged to provide pro bono services, when requested through qualified legal assistance organizations providing free legal services to the indigent. Such participation should be in accordance with the basic tenets of the profession: impartiality, competence, and integrity.

SECTION II—REALTIME REPORTER IN LEGAL PROCEEDINGS

A realtime reporter in this setting is a court reporter using realtime skills and equipment to provide verbatim on-screen translation for use in a legal proceeding. A clear explanation and understanding of the realtime reporter's role is necessary among all parties to the proceeding.

The realtime reporter in legal or other proceedings will normally be the official reporter/officer creating the verbatim record and assumes a separate role from that of the CART Provider who performs realtime translation as an aid to communication for people who are deaf or hearing-impaired. The realtime reporter must firmly establish the role for which he or she has been engaged.

Common sense and professional courtesy should guide the Member in applying the following Guidelines. In legal proceedings, a Member acting as a realtime reporter should:

A. Establish, if possible, before beginning a realtime reporting assignment, a clear understanding of who will require realtime services.

B. Accept assignments using discretion with regard to skill, setting, and the consumers involved, and shall accurately represent their qualifications for realtime reporting.

C. When possible, acquire information and materials in advance to prepare a job dictionary.

D. Know the software and hardware system used and be able to do simple troubleshooting.

E. Strive to further their knowledge and skill through participation in workshops, professional meetings, interaction with professional colleagues and reading of current literature in the field, and to achieve realtime certification on a state or national level.

F. A disclaimer and/or order form should be transmitted as a cover sheet or cover sheets with each uncertified rough draft transcript stating that the uncertified rough draft transcript cannot be quoted in any pleading or for any other purpose and may not be filed with any court. A copy of the disclaimer and/or order form should be retained by the court reporter.

SECTION III—COMMUNICATION ACCESS REALTIME TRANSLATION (CART) PROVIDER IN A LEGAL SETTING

A Communication Access Realtime Translation (CART) provider in a legal setting performs realtime translation as an aid to communication for people who are deaf or hearing-impaired. Common sense and professional courtesy should guide the Member in applying the following Guidelines. When CART is provided in a trial or deposition setting, special legal requirements may apply. When providing CART in the nonlegal setting, follow the guidelines set out in Section IV.

In providing CART service, a Member should:

A. Accept assignments using discretion with regard to skill, setting, and the consumers involved, and accurately represent the provider's qualifications for CART.

B. Establish a clear understanding of: 1. who is hiring the CART Provider; 2. the role played by the CART Provider in assisting with communication as opposed to the role of the Official Reporter of Proceedings in providing a verbatim record; 3. the fact that no roughly edited electronic file is to be produced; and 4. the need to preserve the unedited text file with disclaimer in accordance with statute or court order, or for a period of no less than five years.

C. Refrain from working in the dual capacity of Official Reporter of Proceedings and CART Provider at the same time. When no other option exists, the role to be performed is that of the Official Reporter of Proceedings, and all present are entitled to read the display screen of the Official Reporter, which does not include the content and spirit of the speaker, as well as environmental sounds, that would normally be provided by the CART provider. Disclosure must be made to the court and all parties, including the person requiring interpretive services, of this limitation.

D. Acquire, when possible, information or materials in advance to prepare a job dictionary.

E. Know the software and hardware system used and be able to do simple troubleshooting.

F. Strive to achieve, as nearly verbatim as possible, 100% accuracy at all times.

G. Include in the realtime display the identification, content, and spirit of the speaker, as well as environmental sounds (except under circumstances described in C above).

H. Refrain from counseling, advising, or interjecting personal opinions except as required to accomplish the task at hand.

I. In a confidential setting (i.e., legal discussions, jury deliberations, attorney/client discussions), delete all files immediately after the assignment unless otherwise requested to do so, or ordered by the Court.

J. Cooperate with all parties to ensure that effective communication is taking place.

K. Preserve the privacy of a consumer's personal information.

L. Familiarize oneself with the provisions of NCRA's "The CART Provider's Manual," these Guidelines, the General Guidelines for Professional Practice, and any updates thereto.

M. Keep abreast of current trends, laws, literature, and technological advances relating to CART.

SECTION IV—COMMUNICATION ACCESS REALTIME TRANSLATION (CART) PROVIDER IN A NONLEGAL SETTING

A Communication Access Realtime Translation (CART) provider in a nonlegal setting performs realtime translation as an aid to communication for people who are deaf or hearing-impaired. Common sense and professional courtesy should guide the Member in applying the following Guidelines. When providing CART in the legal setting, follow the guidelines set out in Section III.

In providing CART service, a Member should:

A. Accept assignments using discretion with regard to skill, setting, and the consumers involved, and accurately represent the provider's qualifications for CART.

B. Establish a clear understanding of: 1. who is hiring the CART provider; 2. whether an electronic file of the roughly edited text with disclaimer is to be preserved; 3. if yes, whether all participants have been informed that an electronic file of the roughly edited text with disclaimer will be preserved; and 4. who is entitled to receive a copy of the electronic file.

C. Acquire, when possible, information or materials in advance to prepare a job dictionary.

D. Know the software and hardware system used and be able to do simple troubleshooting.

E. Strive to achieve, as nearly verbatim as possible, 100% accuracy at all times.

F. Include in the realtime display the identification, content, and spirit of the speaker, as well as environmental sounds.

G. Refrain from counseling, advising, or interjecting personal opinions except as required to accomplish the task at hand.

H. Cooperate with all parties to ensure that effective communication is taking place.

I. In confidential nonlegal settings (i.e., medical discussions, support groups), delete all files immediately after the assignment unless otherwise requested not to do so.

J. Preserve the privacy of a consumer's personal information.

K. Familiarize oneself with the provisions of NCRA's "The CART Provider's Manual," these Guidelines, and any updates thereto.

L. Keep abreast of current trends, laws, literature, and technological advances relating to CART.

SECTION V—GUIDELINES ON PROVIDING UNCERTIFIED ROUGH DRAFT TRANSCRIPTS

The National Court Reporters Association realizes that in some cases, court reporters are providing uncertified rough draft transcripts, in either paper or ASCII form, to parties involved in litigation either in the courtroom or deposition setting. The National Court Reporters Association suggests the following guidelines be used when providing such services. These guidelines are intended to aid a court reporter when providing uncertified rough draft transcripts. Generally speaking, uncertified rough draft transcripts are provided by court reporters who use realtime translation, but other court reporters are also providing uncertified rough draft transcripts as well. These are not mandates, but rather guidelines by which a court reporter may determine the propriety of his or her conduct in relation to the litigants, their counsel, the court, allied professions and the public.

The principal objective when a court reporter provides an uncertified rough draft transcript of proceedings is to aid in the administration of justice by rendering a valuable service to the litigants, their counsel, and the court.

1. A court reporter providing an uncertified rough draft transcript should perform the task undertaken by him or her in a professional manner, observing all laws, rules, and orders of the court relating to the proceeding.

2. A court reporter providing an uncertified rough draft transcript should keep informed of technological and other advances and improvements in the skills and methods of his or her profession and strive constantly for self-improvement.

3. A court reporter providing an uncertified rough draft transcript should not perform any service under terms or conditions which will compromise, in any way, his or her impartiality or the exercise of good judgment and skill, or which will adversely affect the fair and impartial portrayal of the proceeding. Court reporters should offer comparable services to all parties in a litigation proceeding.

4. An uncertified rough draft transcript should not include a title page, appearance page, certificate page, any mention of the swearing in of a witness (in depositions), footer with firm name or reporter name or CSR #, index page, line numbers starting with 1 for each page, borders around the text on each page, or time stamping.

5. An uncertified rough draft transcript should include a header or footer on each page stating "Computer uncertified rough draft transcript only." A brief disclaimer such as "uncertified rough draft transcript" should be included in the body of the text occasionally. An uncertified rough draft transcript provided on paper should be printed on colored paper, with the words "Uncertified rough draft transcript" hand stamped on each page. If provided on diskette, the diskette label should be similarly hand stamped, and the label should be a different color than those used on diskettes containing the text of certified transcripts. Uncertified rough draft transcripts should be provided in condensed format only. Page numbers may be included, but line numbers should be absolute, not starting with 1 for each page.

6. A disclaimer and/or order form should be transmitted as a cover sheet or cover sheets with each uncertified rough draft transcript stating that the uncertified rough draft transcript cannot be quoted

in any pleading or for any other purpose and may not be filed with any court. A copy of the disclaimer and/or order form should be retained by the court reporter.

7. Where possible, all untranslated steno strokes and conflicts should be resolved before an uncertified rough draft transcript is provided to any party. An unedited transcript should not be provided without resolving untranslated steno strokes and conflicts if the untranslated rate is 1.0% or higher.

8. Only court reporters who possess the capability of providing a substantially readable transcript should attempt to provide an uncertified rough draft transcript.

9. Minimum writing skills: conflict-free writing (software with automatic conflict resolution is recommended); untranslates of one percent or less; standard punctuation included; and speaker identification defined.

These are suggested guidelines. If your current writing skills do not meet these guidelines, don't let it stop you. Remember, you have a chance during breaks or on-the-fly to define untranslates and resolve conflicts. It is recommended that you not supply counsel with a rough draft ASCII disk or printed transcript until these minimum standards are met.

However, you may be able to provide the disk or uncertified transcript to them later that day or the next day.

_____

Chapter 29

Professionalism, Associations, Testing, and Continuing Education

Members of every profession have developed certain expectations regarding the way in which its members conduct themselves. Additionally, they form associations and networks to enhance and educate members. This chapter discusses what makes a reporter a professional and some of the professional organizations that court reporters may join.

Professionalism

Professionalism is the quality of having high standards that one follows in his or her career, and the ability to work with great skill in one's occupation. A professional is distinct from an amateur in many respects. Ten qualities that differentiate the professional court reporter from the neophyte are as follows:

1. A professional court reporter is conscious about doing a good job and will not be satisfied with shoddy or half-hearted work.

2. A professional court reporter makes sure that every job is covered with a competent court reporter and that he or she arrives at the scheduled time.

3. A professional court reporter dresses appropriately for the job, taking into consideration the protocol of the situation.

4. A professional court reporter produces a transcript when called for that is accurate, reliable, neat, and on time.

5. A professional court reporter charges a fair and honest price that takes into consideration the training, overhead, equipment, time, and expertise of the reporter and that allows him or her a nominal profit.

6. A professional court reporter keeps abreast of the changes within the profession by attending conferences and workshops that keep the reporter informed about the profession.

7. A professional court reporter keeps his or her equipment up to date and in top operating condition, making sure that it is always operating at peak performance.

8. A professional court reporter keeps his or her mind and body in good health, and does not become dependent on drugs or alcohol to function.

9. A professional court reporter treats all clients in a fair, impartial, and unbiased manner.

10. A professional court reporter does not give in to threats of obsolescence for the profession, but works diligently with associations and organizations to help to build up the profession by speaking highly of its benefits and attempting to recruit others into the profession.

Court Reporting Associations

The national and the state court reporting organizations do an excellent job in helping to maintain the dignity and respect of the profession of court reporting. All court reporters should strive to maintain that dignity and respect by becoming active members of their local and national associations.

The national organization is very helpful in answering any questions about the career of court and real-time reporting. It has been very vocal in helping to combat the onset of lesser quality reporting through the use of electronic recording devices, and it remains as a national clearinghouse and spokesperson for the profession of court reporting.

The address, telephone number, e-mail address, and Internet address for the National Court Reporters Association are NCRA, 8224 Old Courthouse Rd., Vienna VA 22182-3808, 800-272-NCRA (6272). The e-mail address of NCRA is msic@ncrahq.org. If you wish to visit the Web site for NCRA, you can use either address: http://www.ncraonline.com or http://www.verbatimreporters.com

In addition, most states and the provinces of Canada have local associations that carry out the work of the national organization. The state associations are important advocates in their own rights in upholding the professional qualities of the field of court and realtime reporting.

The mailing addresses and telephone numbers for these associations can be found by contacting the NCRA by letter, telephone, e-mail, or the Internet.

Perhaps one of the most important aspects of the national and local associations is their commitment to the future of courtroom reporting and their dedication to helping to produce reporters who are going to be "guardians of the record."

One of the most important steps a reporter can make in his or her career is to join and actively participate in the national or local professional association dealing with court reporting.

Testing and Continuing Education

The matter of testing to prove the competency of court and realtime reporters is a subject that is worth discussing because, in a very real sense, the skills of the court and realtime reporters are tested every day. Although the subject may seem quite direct and straightforward, it tends to get more complex as one looks at the variety of tests and examinations given in many different situations. To compound the issues, some states require testing in one situation and not another, and other states do not require any testing at all.

For the purposes of this chapter, three different types of examinations or tests that may be administered are discussed. These tests are (1) individual agency tests, (2) individual state tests, and (3) national examinations.

Individual Agency Tests

Most private organizations or court reporting agencies test court reporters who wish to work for them by administering their own examination. These examinations may consist of a grammar or punctuation test, a simple mathematics test, a spelling test, and a dictation test for which the notes or transcript are examined for accuracy. Some agencies may administer a realtime test.

Although not required, some agencies rely on the scoring of these individual tests for placement within their organizations. All freelance reporting agencies do not administer a test; some do, and some do not. Some agencies will recognize or require a national certification, such as the Registered Professional Reporter (RPR) designation as a prerequisite for being employed by their agency.

The makeup, administration, and scoring of individual agency tests are up to the person in charge of the reporting agency, and they vary from agency to agency and person to person. Some are very involved examinations that test many aspects of the potential employee, and some may be very informal testing situations in which the employer will look only at the notes of the prospective reporter.

Individual State Tests

The different tests offered within a state may be divided into tests for freelancing and tests for official reporters. Passing the state examinations may include the issuance of a professional certificate that will *certify* the reporter.

In some states, passing a test or the resulting certification are required to work as either a freelance or official court reporter. Some states require only the passing of a test to work as an official reporter, that is, a reporter for a specific court or governmental agency. States that require certification to work in the court system administer what is called a Certified Shorthand Reporter (CSR) or Certified Courtroom Reporter (CCR) examination within the state. In most cases, the passing of the certification test in one state does not carry over to another state. In other words, they are not reciprocal.

Currently, 28 states and two Canadian provinces require certification to work in some official capacity as court reporters. The tests offered for certification vary, but most contain a written-knowledge test and a speed test. The written-knowledge portion usually contains a number of questions pertaining to medical and legal terminology, English usage, legal procedures, and transcription. The speed portion may contain literary, jury charge, and two-voice material or, in some cases, four-voice material, all dictated at various speeds.

National Examinations

The National Court Reporters Association (NCRA) serves as a testing agent for court reporters throughout the United States and the world. This organization offers a series of professional examinations for court reporters, administrators, instructors, and evaluators of their approved programs. Some of the tests are recognized as standards for hiring and promotion by some freelance agencies, as well as by official courts.

One of the most highly regarded national examinations is the Registered Professional Reporter (RPR) exam that is offered by the NCRA. This examination offers a written-knowledge portion (WKT) containing 100 multiple-choice questions on various aspects of court reporting. The skills portions of the test contains five minutes of literary dictation at 180 words a minute, five minutes of jury charge dictation at 200 words a minute, and five minutes of two-voice dictation at 225 words a minute. If you pass one or more sections of the test (WKT, Literary, Jury charge, or Two-voice), you do not have to retake that portion when you take the test again. However, all four sections eventually must be passed in order to be awarded the RPR.

Two other court reporting examinations that the NCRA offers for court reporters are the Registered Merit Reporter (RMR) and Certified Realtime Reporter (CRR) exams. The RMR is an advanced-level reporting examination offered to those who have passed the RPR. The written-knowledge portion of the exam contains 100 multiple-choice questions dealing with court reporting. The speed portion is given at 200 words a minute for literary material, 240 words a minute for jury charge, and 260 words a minute for the two-voice material. All transcription must be passed with at least 95 percent accuracy. This test can be taken in sections to allow practicing for one portion at a time.

The CRR contains three parts that deal with realtime reporting. The first part is the proper setting up and operation of realtime equipment. The second part is writing in realtime for five minutes on straight-matter material at speeds ranging from 180 to 200 words a minute. The third part is converting a realtime file to an ASCII text file for grading.

In addition, the NCRA offers a number of other examinations for reporting professionals:

- Registered Diplomate Reporter (RDR)
- Certified Manager of Reporting Services (CMRS)
- Certified Reporting Instructor (CRI)
- Master Certified Reporting Instructor (MCRI)
- Certified Program Evaluator (CPE)
- Certified Legal Video Specialist (CLVS)

A description of certification tests required by individual states, as well as the different examinations offered by the NCRA, can be found on the Internet at their www.ncraonline.org addresses.

A Final Word about Testing

At some point in every student or reporter's life, the fact must be faced that a test of some sort is imminent. Tests are necessary in order to promote and advance ourselves in the field and to keep us on our toes.

If you are a student and facing testing situations daily, you should make every effort to put forth your utmost in every class. You should attend every class every day. You should practice with integrity, setting aside a specific place and practicing at a specific time every day. You should separate study time from practice time; study time is used for "book learning," and practice time is used for writing, reading, and transcribing.

Your study time should be divided into separate portions for each subject: English, legal terminology, medical terminology, and so on. Your practice time should be divided into practicing for accuracy and practicing for speed. You should read back 99.9 percent of everything you take down and transcribe at least 50 percent.

In reading back, circle any errors in your notes and make a mental note of words that are giving you problems. Even if you are using realtime, you can still read your notes by invoking the software command to show your notes. Practice the words that made you hesitate to overcome the hesitation.

For court reporters who are preparing for agency, state, or national tests, take the time to prepare correctly. If possible, obtain copies of previous examinations that will simulate what the questions and speed portion will be like. Practice speed tapes a little above the required speed. Practice transcribing the required speeds. Above all, relax and do not give up. Have confidence in your ability.

A number of good books, study aides, and various materials are available on the market for those preparing to take tests. The NCRA publishes a catalog of materials, and vendors advertise their practice aids in the *Journal of Court Reporting*, the publication of the NCRA.

Continuing Education

In a very real sense, the education of a professional never ends. He or she is constantly striving for ways to increase his or her knowledge and to keep pace with the changing role of the court reporter in an ever-changing technological environment. The truly professional court and realtime reporter takes seriously his or her role and does everything possible to maintain the necessary skills and knowledge. Court reporters who are licensed or certified within a given state may be required to complete courses for continuing education to maintain their licensure or certification. In addition, almost all certification tests offered by the NCRA require earning a certain number of continuing education credits within a given time.

Continuing education credits are offered for attendance at local, state, and national court reporting conferences, workshops, and seminars. A growing trend has been to offer continuing education credits for court reporting courses taught over the Internet or through distance learning.

NCRA continuing education points are offered in specific areas of knowledge pertaining to the field of court reporting, and points can be earned within each area. Once a reporter has passed a test, 30 continuing education credits must be earned over a period of three years. These points can be earned in the area of technology, academics, language, business, reporting, general, and professional. For information on continuing education opportunities offered through the NCRA, consult their Web site at www.ncraonline.com.

All court reporters should take seriously their role as "guardians of the record" and attempt to pass all pertinent tests and examinations that they have an opportunity to take. They should continue their education through completing courses and seminars that will grant them continuing education points.

SECTION E

Chapter 30

Research for the Record, Internet Research, Citations of Authority

Someone once said that success in this life is not measured by how much one knows, but rather by whether a person knows where to look for answers to questions. The ability to research and find the correct answer to questions that arise when transcribing is a very important quality that every court reporter should strive to acquire.

Whether it is as simple as looking up the definition of a word or double-checking the reference to a legal citation, the reporter has to be sure that what he or she records and transcribes is correct. Of course, no one can possibly know everything, but your ability as a reporter will be judged by how well you can research specialized material in the interest of a truly verbatim transcript that accurately portrays what a technical or medical expert intended to convey.

You will find that words that sound alike have two totally different meanings, and they must be used in their correct context. For example, the "coaming" on a ship is different from "combing" the hair, and the "culling" of witnesses is much different from the "calling" of witnesses.

Some students may have difficulty comprehending the amount of research that may go into a transcript in the reporter's search for total accuracy, but a good reporter will go to extreme lengths to be absolutely sure that everything in the transcript is true and accurate.

Although most reporters have a cadre of friends and acquaintances who are experts in the field of medicine, education, and so on, all reporters have a ready reference library of books and sources that they can turn to for answers to questions that may arise.

A Court Reporter's Reference Library

Reference books that a court reporter may find helpful in researching for the record are listed in this section. Make sure that you always obtain the most recent edition for any of the references listed, because differences always occur between older and newer editions. Most of the books can be found in the reference sections of bookstores. Many of the books are available on CD-ROM for computer-based research. Most computer applications can be run within some court reporting software programs.

Unabridged Dictionaries

Webster's Third New International Dictionary, Unabridged (Merriam Webster, Inc., Springfield, MA)
The Random House Dictionary of the English Language (Random House Publishers, New York, NY)

Desk Dictionaries

Webster's Tenth New Collegiate Dictionary (Merriam Webster, Inc., Springfield, MA)
Funk & Wagnall's New College Dictionary (Funk & Wagnall, New York, NY)
Webster's New World Dictionary of the American Language (Merriam Webster, Inc., Springfield, MA)
The American Heritage Dictionary, College Edition (Houghton Mifflin, Boston, MA)

Topical Dictionaries

The Dictionary of Cultural Literacy (Houghton Mifflin, Boston, MA)
Biology Dictionary (National Book Co., Portland, OR)
Webster's Dictionary of Synonyms (Merriam Webster, Inc., Springfield, MA)
Dictionary of American Slang (Pocket Books, New York, NY)
Webster's New World Dictionary of Computer Terms (Simon & Schuster, New York, NY)
Hack's Chemical Dictionary (McGraw-Hill Book Co., New York, NY)
The Dictionary of Scientific Terms (D. Van Nostrand Co., Inc., Princeton, NJ)
Construction Dictionary (National Association of Women in Construction, Greater Phoenix, Arizona, Chapter 98)

Legal References

Black's Law Dictionary (West Publishing Co., St. Paul, MN)
Law Dictionary (Barron's Educational Series, Inc., Hauppage, NY)
Ballentine's Law Dictionary (The Lawyers Cooperative Publishing Co., Rochester, NY)
Cochran's Law Lexicon (Anderson Publishing Co., Cincinnati, OH)
"Blue Books" Legal Directories (Legal Directories Publishing Co., Dallas, TX)
Legal Procedures for Court Reporters and Paralegals (Prentice Hall, Upper Saddle River, NJ)
A Uniform System of Citation (Harvard Law Review Association, Cambridge, MA)
Using Law Books (Kendall/Hunt Publishing Co., Dubuque, IA)
West's Law Finder (West Publishing Co., St. Paul, MN)
Introduction to the Criminal Justice System (Harper & Row, New York, NY)
Paralegal's Litigation Handbook (Institute for Business Planning, Upper Saddle River, NJ)
The Deposition Handbook (National Court Reporters Association, Vienna, VA)
Federal Rules of Civil Procedures and Title 28, U.S. Code, Judiciary and Judicial Procedure (West Publishing Co., St. Paul, MN)

Medical References

Gray's Anatomy (Running Press, Philadelphia, PA)
Taber's Cyclopedic Medical Dictionary (F.A. Davis Co., Philadelphia, PA)
Dorland's Medical Dictionary (W.B. Saunders Co., Philadelphia, PA)
Blakiston's New Gould Medical Dictionary (Blakiston Co., Philadelphia, PA)
Stedman's Medical Dictionary (Williams & Wilkins Co., Baltimore, MD)
Mosby's Medical and Nursing Dictionary (C.V. Mosby Co., St. Louis, MO)
Webster's Medical Desk Dictionary (Merriam Webster, Inc.)
The New American Medical Dictionary and Health Manual (New American Library, New York, NY)
The American Medical Association Guide to Prescription and Over-the-Counter Drugs (Random House, New York, NY)
Learning Medical Terminology (C.V. Mosby Co., St. Louis, MO)

Mastering Medical Language (Prentice Hall, Upper Saddle River, NJ)
Physician's Desk Reference (Medical Economics Books, Montvale, NJ)
The Merck Index (Merck & Co., Rahway, NJ)
The Pharmacist's Guide to Products and Prices (American Pharmaceutical Association, Washington, DC)
The Reverse Medical Secretary (Medical Economics Books, Montvale, NJ)
Medical Acronyms & Abbreviations (Medical Economics Books, Montvale, NJ)
The Surgical Word Book (W.B. Saunders Co., Philadelphia, PA)
A Word Book in Pathology and Laboratory Medicine, (W.B. Saunders Co., Philadelphia, PA)
Medical Terminology (Prentice Hall, Upper Saddle River, NJ)

In addition, the reporter should make every effort to obtain various medical directories of doctors, dentists, anesthetists, nurses, physical therapists, psychologists, and psychiatrists issued by state medical societies.

Encyclopedias

Encyclopedia Britannica (Encyclopedia Britannica, Inc., Chicago, IL)
Columbia-Viking Desk Encyclopedia (Viking Press, New York, NY)
Lincoln Library of Essential Information (Frontier Press, Buffalo, NY)
Grolier Encyclopedia (Grolier Society, New York, NY)

Grammar and Punctuation References

The Creative Writer's Phrase Finder (ETC Publications, Palm Springs, CA)
Encyclopedic Dictionary of English Usage (Prentice Hall, Upper Saddle River, NJ)
Court Reporter's Language Arts Workbook (Prentice Hall, Upper Saddle River, NJ)

Other Useful References

Hammond's Ambassador World Atlas (C.S. Hammond & Co., Maplewood, NJ)
World Atlas (Rand-McNally, New York, NY)
Encyclopedia Britannica World Atlas (Encyclopedia Britannica, Chicago, IL)
Bartlett's Familiar Quotations (Little, Brown & Co., Boston, MA)
The Home Book of Quotations (Dodd, Mead & Co., New York, NY)
Roget's International Thesaurus (Thomas Y. Crowell, New York, NY)

Miscellaneous

The Holy Bible (King James and American Standard versions)
Complete Works of Shakespeare (Doubleday, Garden City, NY)
Lyall's Guide to the Languages of Europe (David McKay Co., Inc., New York, NY)
Word Mysteries and Histories (Houghton Mifflin, Boston, MA)
Who's Who In America and Who's Who Series (A.N. Marquis Co., Chicago, IL)
The Congressional Directory (Superintendent of Documents, GPO, Washington, DC)
The Encyclopedia of Etiquette (Crown, New York, NY)
Business Etiquette Handbook (Prentice Hall, Upper Saddle River, NJ)
Barron's Weekly Market Analysis
Dun & Bradstreet Ratings and Reports
Moody's Manuals
The Wall Street Journal

The Hotel Red Book (American Hotel Association Directory Corp., New York, NY)

The Kelley Blue Book—Automobile Market Report (Kelley Blue Book Co., Costa Mesa, CA)

Robert's Rules of Order, rev. ed. (William Morrow & Co., New York, NY)

N.W. Ayers & Sons' Directory of Newspapers & Periodicals (N.W. Ayers & Sons, Philadelphia, PA)

The United States Directory of Post Offices, Publication No. 26 (Superintendent of Documents, GPO, Washington, DC)

Kelly's Directory of Merchants, Manufacturers, and Shippers (Kelly Directories Ltd., London, England)

Reference Manual for the Office (South-Western Educational Publishing, Cincinnati, OH)

The Science–Engineering Secretary (Prentice Hall, Upper Saddle River, NJ)

Thomas' Register of American Manufacturers (Thomas Publishing Co., New York, NY)

The Foundation Directory (Russel Sage Foundations, New York, NY)

Also, the reporter should obtain all local and state maps, telephone directories, local statutes, and so on.

The Internet

One of the most useful resources for finding valuable information is the Internet. Using any of the search engines that are accessible on most browsers, one merely has to insert a word or phrase to search the Internet for a list of references pertaining to a particular topic. Some common search engines are the following:

Alta Vista   www.altavista.com
Excite   www.excite.com
Webcrawler   www.webcrawler.com
Lycos   www.lycos.com
Google   www.google.com
Infoseek   www.infoseek.com
Yahoo!   www.yahoo.com

Meta-Engines, engines that use more than one source for searching the World Wide Web, are the following:

Inference Find   www.inference.com/ifind
Internet Sleuth   www.isleuth.com
Ask Jeeves   www.askjeeves.com
ProFusion   www.designlab.ukans.edu/profusi
Dogpile   www.dogpile.com
Locate   www.locate.com

Encyclopedic sources can be found at the following addresses:

Britiannica   www.eb.com
Grolier's Multimedia Encyclopedia   www.gi.grolier.com
Infopedia   www.mecc.com
Web Seeker   www.bluesquirrel.com
WebCompass   www.quarterdeck.com
World Book Multimedia Encyclopedia   www.worldbook.com
Microsoft Bookshelf and Encarta   www.microsoft.com

Some excellent library sources are the following:

Library Spot   www.libraryspot.com
Bookwire   www.bookwire.com

The Library of Congress   www.lcweb.loc.gov
New York Public Library   www.nypl.org

On-line reference books:

www.atlas.com
www.reference.com
www.dictionary.com
www.webster.com
www.itools.com/lang

Reporting Legal Citations

A *legal citation* is a reference made by a lawyer to a specific law or statute. It may also be a reference to a previous case that he or she has researched and found to be similar to the case being tried, particularly one that will help to bolster the case at hand. In this chapter, the legal citations have been divided into three broad categories. They are federal and state code books, appellate decisions, and legal indexes.

Attorneys who enter citations into the record sometimes read the material very rapidly. Reporters who record the citation reference in their notes can look up the actual citation, check the accuracy of their notes, or fill in any parts that they might have missed during the rapid exchange. Reporters, therefore, should understand the meaning of the codes used in legal citations.

Federal Codes

The Constitution and every law that the Congress of the United States passes are published in a set of books called the *United States Code.* The laws are systematically arranged under subject headings, called *titles,* and then into sections and subsections. The titles are arranged alphabetically and given a number. No matter how many separate statutes are placed under one title and how many books those statutes may fill, the title number remains the same. The *United States Code Annotated* contains, in addition to the text of the statutes, references to decisions rendered in particular states.

Whenever a lawyer refers to the United States Constitution and its amendments, they are cited as follows: *U.S. Const. art. I, sec. 9* or *U.S. Const. amend. XIV.*

The *United States Code* and *United States Code Annotated* are cited by lawyers as follows: *28 U.S.C. 2254* or *28 U.S.C.A. 2254.* The 28 is the title number and is always placed first; 2254 is the section number. If a subsection number is in the citation, it is added as follows: *28 U.S.C.A. 2254b.*

State Codes

Each state has its own method of compiling and codifying its laws. The following is a list of the accepted methods of citing them:

CITATIONS FOR STATE STATUTES AND CODES

State	Title	How Cited
Alabama	Code of Alabama, 1940	Code of Alabama, Title 10, Sec. 101
Alaska	Administrative Code	Alaska Statutes, Title 10, Chapter 10, Section 10
Arizona	Arizona Revised Statutes Annotated	RSA Sec 10-101
Arkansas	Arkansas Statutes Annotated (1947)	Ark. Stats. (1947) Sec. 10-101
California	Deering's California Code (Code of Civil Procedure)	CCP Sec. 101
Colorado	Colorado Revised Statutes, 1953	101-10-1, C.R.S. '53

Connecticut	General Statutes of Connecticut Revision of 1949	Conn.G.S. 1949 Sec.101
Delaware	Delaware Code Annotated (1953)	10 Del. C. Sec. 110
Florida	Florida Statutes Annotated	F.S.A. Sec. 101
	Florida Statutes, 1953	Florida Statutes, 1951, Sec. 101
Georgia	Georgia Code Annotated	Ga. Code Ann. Sec. 10-1010
Hawaii	Revised Statutes	Hawaii Revisal Statutes
Idaho	Idaho Code	Idaho Code, Sec. 101
Illinois	Illinois Revised Statutes, 1951	Rev. Stat. 1951 Ch. 10, Sec. 101
	Smith–Hurd Illinois, Annotated Statutes	Smith–Hurd Anno. St., Ch. 10, Sec. 101
	Jones Illinois Statutes, Annotated	Jones Ill. Stat. Anno., Ch. 10, Sec. 101
Indiana	Burns Indiana Statutes, Annotated, 1933	Sec. 10-1011 Burns Ind. Stat. Ann. 1033
Iowa	Code of Iowa	Code of Iowa, 1954, Sec. 110.10
Kansas	General Statutes of Kansas, 1949	G.S. 1949, Sec. 101
	1951 Supplement to General Statutes 1949	G.C. 1951 Supp., Sec. 101
Kentucky	Kentucky Revised Statutes	KRS 101.090(1)
	Kentucky Civil Code	Civil Code, Sec. 101
Louisiana	Louisiana Revised Statutes of 1950	R.S. 10:101
Maine	Revised Statutes of Maine, 1954	R.S. of Maine 1954, C. 10, Sec. 11
Maryland	Flack's Annotated Code of Maryland, 1951	Md. Code (1951), Art. 10, Sec. 101
Massachusetts	Massachusetts General Law	G.L. (Ter.Ed.) C. 10 Sec. 101
Michigan	Michigan Statutes Annotated	Stat Ann. Sec. 10.101
	1948 Compiled Laws of Michigan	C L 1948, Sec. 10.101
Minnesota	Minnesota Statutes 1953	Minn. Stat. 1953, Sec. 101.10
	Minnesota Statutes Annotated	M.S.A. Sec. 101.10
Mississippi	Mississippi Code, 1942, Annotated Miss.	Code, 1942, Ann., Sec. 101
Missouri	Missouri Revised Statutes, 1949	R.S. Mo. Sec. 101
Montana	Revised Code of Montana of 1947	RCM 1947, Sec. 10-101
Nebraska	Revised Statutes of Nebraska, 1943	Sec. 101, R.S. Nebr., 1943
	Reissue Revised Statutes of Nebraska, 1943	Sec. 101, R.R.S. Nebr., 1943
Nevada	Nevada Compiled Laws, 1929	NCL 1929, Sec. 1010
	Nevada Compiled Laws, Supplement 1953	NCL Supp. 1953, Sec. 1010.10
New Hampshire	1955 New Hampshire Revised Statutes Ann.	RSA 101.1
New Jersey	Revised Statutes of New Jersey	N.J.R.S. 10:101-10
New Mexico	New Mexico Statutes Annotated	1953 Comp., 1-1-10
New York	McKinney's Consolidated Laws of New York	(Corporation) Law, Sec. 101
North Carolina	General Statutes of North Carolina	G.S. 10-101
North Dakota	North Dakota Revised Code of 1943	Sec. 10-1010 of NDRC 1943
Ohio	Ohio Revised Code, 1953	O.R.C. Sec. 1110.10
Oklahoma	Oklahoma Statutes Annotated	10 O.S. 1951 Sec. 101
Oregon	Oregon Revised Statutes, 1953	ORS 11:010
Pennsylvania	Purden's Pennsylvania Statutes	10 P.S. Sec. 101
Rhode Island	General Laws of Rhode Island of 1938	Gen. Laws 1938 c. 1, art. 10 Sec. 101
South Carolina	Code of Laws of S.C., 1952	1952 Code, Sec. 10-101
	1952 Code Supplement	1952 Code Supp. Sec. 101
South Dakota	South Dakota Code of 1939	SDC 10.1010(10)
Tennessee	Tennessee Code Annotated	Code, Sec. 10-101
Texas	Vernon's Texas Statutes, Annotated	Vernon's Ann. Civ. St., art. 1010
Utah	Utah Code Annotated, 1953	UCA 1953, 10-10-1
Vermont	Vermont Statutes, Revision of 1947	V.S., 47, Sec. 1010
Virginia	Code of Virginia, 1950	Code, Sec. 10-101

Washington	Revised Code of Washington	RCW 10.11.101
West Virginia	West Virginia Code of 1955	Code Sec. 1010(2)
Wisconsin	Statutes of Wisconsin	Section 101.10(1) Stats. of Wis.
Wyoming	Wyoming Compiled Statutes, 1945	WCS 1945, Sec. 10-1010

Sometimes the laws of another state will be cited. If the name of the state does not appear in the citation, it should be added. For example, if the document is to be filed in Texas and a Louisiana statute is cited, it should be La. R.S.9:103. However, if the document were filed in Louisiana, the citation would be R.S.9:103.

All individual state statute books are kept up to date by means of supplements, which are printed annually and inserted into special pockets in the binding of the back cover of the books. They are often called *pocket parts*.

Appellate Decisions

Whenever a judge sits in a judicial proceeding and renders a decision, the decision is recorded for the proper guidance of the courts in deciding future cases. Each appellate court has a reporter who is responsible for seeing that the decisions are published at regular intervals. These publications are called the *official reports* and the following is a list of the official state reports:

CITATIONS FOR OFFICIAL REPORTERS

Title	*Citation*
Alabama Reports	Ala.
Alabama Appellate Reports	Ala. App.
Arizona Reports	Ariz.
Arkansas Reports	Ark.
California Appellate Reports	Cal. App.
California Appellate Reports, Second Series	Cal. App. 2d
California Reports	Cal.
California Reports, Second Series	Cal. 2d
Colorado Reports	Colo.
Connecticut	Conn.
Delaware Reports	Cited by name of reporter
Delaware Chancery Reports	Del. Ch.
Florida Reports	Fla.
Idaho Reports	Idaho
Illinois Reports	Ill.
Illinois Appellate Court Reports	Ill. App.
Iowa Reports	Iowa
Kansas Reports	Kan.
Kentucky Reports	Ky.
Louisiana Reports	La.
Maine Reports	Me.
Maryland Reports	Md.
Massachusetts Reports	Mass.
Michigan Reports	Mich.
Minnesota Reports	Minn.
Mississippi Reports	Miss.
Missouri Appellate Reports	Mo. App.

Montana Reports	Mont.
Nebraska Reports	Neb.
Nevada Reports	Nev.
New Hampshire Reports	N.H.
New Jersey Equity Reports	N.J. Eq.
New Jersey Reports	N.J.
New Jersey Superior Court Reports	N.J. Super.
New Mexico Reports	N.M.
New York Appellate Division Reports	N.Y. App. Div.
New York Miscellaneous Reports	N.Y. Misc.
New York Reports	N.Y.
North Carolina Reports	N.C.
North Dakota Reports	N.D.
Ohio Appellate Reports	Ohio App.
Ohio State Reports	Ohio St.
Oklahoma Reports	Okl.
Oklahoma Criminal Reports	Okl. Cr.
Oregon Reports	Ore.
Pennsylvania Reports	Pa.
Pennsylvania Superior Court Reports	Pa. Sup.
Rhode Island Reports	R.I.
South Carolina Reports	S.C.
South Dakota Reports	S.D.
Tennessee Reports	Tenn.
Tennessee Appeals Reports	Tenn. App.
United States Reports	U.S.
United States Court of Appeals, District of Columbia	U.S. App. D.C.
Utah Reports	Utah
Vermont Reports	Vt.
Virginia Reports	Va.
Washington Reports	Wash.
Washington Reports, Second Series	Wash. 2d
West Virginia Reports	W. Va.
Wisconsin Reports	Wis.
Wyoming Reports	Wyo.

As can be seen from the chart, not all states have an official reporter to list citations, so they rely on prepublished citations that are produced and printed by designated publishing companies. West Publishing Company publishes the decisions of all the federal and state courts by means of a system called the *National Reporter System.*

A list of the separate sets of reporters, the courts they cover, and the abbreviations in citing them are as follows:

CITATIONS FOR THE NATIONAL REPORTER SYSTEM

Title	Courts Covered	Citation
Supreme Court Reporter	United States Supreme Court	S.Ct
Federal Reporter	United States Circuit Courts of Appeals	Fe.
	U.S. District Courts	
Federal Reporter, Second Series	U.S. Courts of Appeals	F.2d
	U.S. Court of Customs and Patent Appeals	

Federal Supplement	U.S. District Courts, U.S. Court of Claims	F. Supp.
Atlantic Reporter	Connecticut	Atl.
Atlantic Reporter, Second Series	Delaware, Maine, Maryland, New Hampshire, New Jersey, Pennsylvania, Rhode Island, Vermont	A.2d
New York Supplement	N.Y. Court of Appeals	N.Y. Supp.
New York Supplement, Second Series	Appellate Division of the Supreme Court, Miscellaneous Courts	N.Y.S.2d
Northeastern Reporter	Illinois, Indiana	N.E.
Northeastern Reporter, Second Series	New York, Massachusetts, Ohio	N.E.2d
Northwestern Reporter	Iowa, Michigan	N.W.
Northwestern Reporter, Second Series	Minnesota, Nebraska, North Dakota, South Dakota, Wisconsin	N.W.2d
Pacific Reporter	Arizona, California	Pac.
Pacific Reporter, Second Series	Colorado, Idaho, Kansas, Montana, Nevada, New Mexico, Oklahoma, Oregon, Utah, Washington, Wyoming	P.2d
Southeastern Reporter	Georgia, North Carolina	S.E.
Southeastern Reporter, Second Series	South Carolina, Virginia, West Virginia	S.E.2d
Southern Reporter	Alabama, Florida	So.
Southern Reporter, Second Series	Louisiana, Mississippi	So.2d
Southwestern Reporter	Arkansas, Kentucky	S.W.
Southwestern Reporter, Second Series	Missouri, Tennessee, Texas	S.W.2d

Some of the *Reporters* are designated "Second Series." The designation is for numbering purposes and indicates that the numbers of the volumes have started over with number 1. Care should be taken that the 2d is added when so dictated. For example, 32 Fed. and 43 F.2d are two separate books.

Each week West publishes the decisions in paperbacks called *advance sheets*. These are mailed to lawyers subscribing to the service. When enough decisions have accumulated to fill a bound volume, they are published and mailed to the subscriber. The page numbers of the advance sheets correspond with the page numbers of the permanent volumes.

Cases in *Reporters* are cited as follows:

Black v. White, 124 S.W.2d 357 (Tex.Ct.app. 1967)

Black v. White is the style of the case; that is, the plaintiff versus the defendant. The 124 is the volume number; S.W.2d is the abbreviation for *Southwestern Reporter, Second Series*; 357 refers to the page number; the material in parentheses signifies that the Texas Court of Appeals rendered the decision in 1967. Showing the court rendering the decision is necessary only if the citation itself does not show it. For example, adding S.Ct. in parentheses would not be necessary because the citation 52 S.Ct.321 indicates that it is a Supreme Court case.

Sometimes notes are added to indicate the history of the case. The following are some of the frequently used abbreviations found in these notes:

Abbreviation	Meaning
aff'd	affirmed
aff'g	affirming
app.	appeal
cert.	certiorari
cor.	correct
den.	denied
juris.	jurisdiction
n.r.e.	not reversible
prob.	probable
rev'd	reversed
rev'g	reversing
w.o.j.	want of jurisdiction
w.o.m.	want of merit

If more than one citation is given, they are separated by semicolons.

The *U.S. Reports* prior to Volume 91 carried the name of the *Reporter* in the citation, and they should be cited that way. The following are the names of the old *Reporters*, the corresponding *U.S. Reports* volume numbers, and the way they should be cited:

CITATIONS FOR UNITED STATES REPORTS

Volume	No. of Volumes	Reporter	Citation
1 U.S. to 4 U.S.	4	Dallas	1 Dal. 10
5 U.S. to 13 U.S.	9	Cranch	1 Cranch 10
14 U.S. to 25 U.S.	12	Wheaton	1 Wheat. 10
26 U.S. to 41 U.S.	16	Peters	1 Pet. 10
42 U.S. to 65 U.S.	24	Howard	1 How. 10
66 U.S. to 67 U.S.	2	Black	1 Black 10
68 U.S. to 90 U.S.	23	Wallace	1 Wall. 10

Some law book companies publish only selected cases. Two examples of these reporters and the way they are cited are as follows:

American Law Review: *Black v. White*, 1967 A.L.R. 123 (U.S. Ct.App.)

Law Reports Annotated: *Black v. White*, 1967 L.R.A. 123 (U.S. Ct.App.)

Indexes

Another source for references that lawyers use in preparing their cases is legal indexes. *Corpus Juris Secundum* and *American Jurisprudence* are legal encyclopedias that are arranged alphabetically by subject matter and have an index. They are cited as follows:

12 Am.Jur. *Contracts Sec.* 74 (1938)

88 C.J.S. *Trial Sec.* 192 (1955)

A set of books that is also invaluable to the lawyer is *Shepard's Citations*. It is a list of cases with cross-references to other decisions on the same subject matter, plus notes as to the final outcome of the case. Lawyers call the use of these books "shepardizing a case," and they are referring to the necessity of checking *Shepard's Citations* to make sure that a decision has not been reversed by a higher court before they use it in their argument.

Chapter 31

Finding Employment

Whether working as a freelance reporter for an agency, an official court reporter, a self-employed reporter, or a realtime reporter in some other capacity, finding employment or changing jobs may be necessary. The purpose of this chapter is to offer some general information on looking for the right job, preparing a résumé, writing a letter of application, and surviving a job interview.

The Job Search

Whenever one seeks employment, whether for the first time or when moving from one position to another, it is important to conduct *a job search*. A job search can be defined as the active solicitation of possible employment, limited to a specific geographical location, and using the skills and qualifications of the searcher to the fullest possible extent.

The goal of the job search is to find a place to work that is both challenging and rewarding and that satisfies the needs and desires of the applicant. The job search leads to writing a résumé and a letter of application, which in turn leads to an interview, with the ultimate result of getting hired.

The following five guidelines will help you to conduct a job search:

1. You should attempt to answer this question: "Where do I want to work?" First, set the geographical location of where you want to work. Talking about moving to Atlanta, Georgia, or Los Angeles, California, to work is one thing; doing something about moving is quite another thing. That is, actively searching out the names, addresses, and telephone numbers of places where you can work in those areas requires not only time and effort, but also a firm commitment.

   In defining where one wants to work, limit the location to one or possibly two different locations. You can then concentrate on specific areas of interest.

2. Once the geographical location of where you want to work has been defined, ask, "Do I want to work as a freelancer or an official reporter, or do I want to work in some other capacity as a court reporter?" The type of work that you want to do is going to be very important in terms of applying to places of employment. However, keep in mind that the type of work that you choose to do may be limited by the certification required or your experience.

3. Once you have determined where you want to work and the type of work that you want to do, the next important step is to compile a list of places where you can work. For example, if you have determined

that you want to work for a large freelance agency in St. Louis, Missouri, then you need to devote your energies to finding the names of freelance agencies located in that city.

A listing of possible employers within a given city can be prepared from a local telephone directory and by looking in the yellow pages under "reporters," "freelance reporters," "court reporters," "shorthand reporters," "stenographers," or "realtime writers." Another valuable source for court reporting listings is the National Court Reporters Association, which publishes *Reporter's Source Book* that contains a directory of reporters and agencies by city and state.

4. After listing several possible places of employment within a given location, the next step is to evaluate these places. Your evaluation should consider the following items:

    (a) Do they have openings?

    (b) Do they offer full- or part-time employment?

    (c) Are reporters considered employees or independent contractors?

    (d) What are the benefits?

    (e) How much work can they guarantee?

    (f) Will you be able to make a living working for this agency or court?

    (g) How many other reporters are in the firm or agency?

    (h) What type of boss will you be working for?

    (i) Will you be required to buy expensive computer equipment and software?

    (j) Are there any other personal considerations that you feel are necessary in making your decision?

You will also want to talk to people who know something about the firm or agency, for example, former employees or people who currently work at the agency. Then, after taking these factors into consideration, you should number your possible places of employment, starting with your best choice first.

5. Now that you have actively searched out the best possible places of employment, you can send a résumé and letter of application with the goal of obtaining an interview. Keep in mind that once an interview is granted and you are offered a position at more than one agency, you may have to reevaluate your list of possible places of employment to make a final determination and acceptance.

The Résumé

A *résumé* is a summary of one's experience, education, and qualifications for a particular job. Résumés may be prepared in a variety of fonts and styles, especially with access to desktop publishing tools and word-processing software. A sample résumé is shown in Figure 31.1.

Some software programs will do an excellent job in helping you to develop your own résumé. Many résumé services or employment referral agencies can create and produce a first-class résumé and letter of application for you. The following items are guidelines that you should consider in developing your résumé:

1. Print your résumé on good quality bond paper, at least 20-pound weight. If color paper is used, select a soft pastel shade, off-white, or gray color, avoiding bright neon colors.

2. Use a laser, ink jet, or bubble jet printer that produces only the best quality print.

3. The résumé should be proofread at least three separate times by three different people. The finished résumé should be error-free.

4. The top of the résumé should contain important information about who you are and where you can be located, including your address, telephone number, fax number, and e-mail address.

5. Headings used within the résumé should include, at the very least, your education and training, experience and past employment, speed tests passed or certificates earned, organizations and associations, and references (or state that they are available upon request).

6. All items listed in the résumé, including your education and experience, should be listed in chronological order with the most recent first. In other words, if you are currently working, list your place of

FIGURE 31.1
A Sample Resume

Tyadra Rene Svorinson

89923 Memorial Park Apartments
Lincoln, NE 68557

Home Phone 212-555-5555

SUMMARY

I am a highly motivated well-qualified graduate of one of the best known court reporting programs in the State of Nebraska. I am anxious to put my skills to work and prove my ability as a freelance court reporter.

WORK HISTORY

1995 – present | Computer Input Specialist with Datatron Corporation. Working part time, three nights a week, I was responsible for inputting statistical data into the computer archive systems to maintain current records for future use.

January 2000 – May 2000 | Court Reporting Intern with various freelance agencies. Working as a student intern, I was responsible for learning how to write, read back, transcribe, put together a transcript, bill, and deliver the transcript.

EDUCATION

Wellington County Community College, Associate in Applied Science, Court and Realtime Reporting, May 2000, graduated with highest honors

Lincoln Senior High School, Regents Diploma, 1990

COURT REPORTING SKILLS

- Two-voice material at 230 words per minute for 5 minutes with 97 percent accuracy
- Jury charge material at 210 words per minute for 5 minutes with 98 percent accuracy
- Literary material 190 words per minute for 5 minutes with 95 percent accuracy
- Familiar with all major court reporting software programs
- Able to write realtime using my own dictionary and any CAT software program

AWARDS RECEIVED

- Dana-Warner Memorial Scholarship for two years of college expenses
- Thelma T. Bell award for outstanding senior
- Traci Watkins award for outstanding court reporting student
- Presidential High Honors Society

REFERENCES

Available at interview

---

employment followed by your other past job experiences in reverse order. Follow the same procedure for your education.

7. References should either be included on the résumé or, if "available upon request," a separate list of references that includes their professional titles, addresses, and the phone numbers should be prepared. People used as references should give their approval.

8. The résumé should be printed on 8½-by-11-inch paper and, preferably, be one page in length.

9. The résumé should never include information that is false or stretches the truth. Only actual information should be used.

The Letter of Application

The letter of application should be completed with one thought in mind—gaining an interview. Once your foot is in the door with an interview, you have an opportunity to show the prospective employer why he or she should hire you. A letter of application is shown in Figure 31.2.

Like the résumé, the letter of application should be neat and attractive, as well as concise and to the point. The following items should be taken into consideration when completing the letter of application:

1. Always address the letter to a specific individual within a firm or agency. If you do not know a name to address the letter to, find out by doing some research.

2. Double-check the spelling of the person's name and the name of the agency or firm.

3. Use the same quality paper used for the résumé, preferably the same type of paper.

FIGURE 31.2
Sample Letter of Application

May 24, 2000

Ms. Pamela J. Smith, CSR
E-Z Reporting Service
29 Washington Avenue
Great Lakes, NE 68577

Dear Ms. Smith:

A mutual acquaintance of ours, Mr. Arthur Byrd, District Attorney for the County of Wellington, has informed me that your agency is in need of competent, qualified court reporters. I believe that I have the qualities that you are looking for in a beginning reporter and would like to apply for a position as a freelance court reporter with your agency.

I recently graduated from Wellington County Community College with an associates degree in court reporting. While at Wellington I was able to maintain a 3.75 grade point average out of a possible 4.0, which allowed me to graduate with honors.

In addition, I was able to work part time as a computer input operator and maintain a family. I think you will see that I am highly qualified, extremely motivated, and ready to work.

Perhaps one of the most meaningful courses I took at Wellington was my internship course, which allowed me to work for 80 hours with a number of freelance agencies. I found the experience both challenging and rewarding.

My résumé is enclosed. I am anxious to have an interview with your agency so that I can show you some of the skills I have acquired while attending Wellington.

Please call me at your earliest convenience to arrange an interview.

Sincerely,

Tyadra Rene Svorinson

Tyadra Rene Svorinson
89923 Memorial Park Apartments
Lincoln, NE 68557

4. Avoid common phrases and cliches in writing the letter and avoid the use of the pronoun *I*.

5. The first paragraph should identify the particular job that you are seeking and how you learned about it.

6. The second paragraph should provide your qualifications for the job without restating everything that is on the résumé.

7. The third paragraph should explicitly state your intentions, that is, why you are writing the letter. For example, it should state why you are applying for the job of freelance reporter.

8. The last paragraph should bring the matter to closure, but open the door for an interview. Reference should be made to the résumé and your availability by telephone or letter.

9. Always have your letter proofread three different times by three different individuals and, most importantly, sign the letter.

The Job Interview

The ultimate goal of the letter and résumé is to secure a job interview during which you will have an opportunity to meet your possible employer. Although some people look on the interviewing process as a terrifying experience, it is actually a wonderful opportunity for you to present yourself and demonstrate what you know. The job interview can be a great deal of fun, if you go at it with the right attitude.

Here are some beneficial tips to follow at your interview:

1. Make sure that your appearance is commensurate with the employment that you are seeking. Dress conservatively, comfortably, and compatibly with the given dress code for the firm or agency.

2. Go to the interview alone. Do not bring along a friend, fiancé, spouse, parent, or child. Greet the interviewer with a firm handshake and let him or her open the discussion.

3. Behave appropriately. Do not chew gum, smoke, swear, use slang words, tell off-color jokes, or act rude.

4. Answer all questions honestly; be brief in your answers, but make sure that you answer all questions completely. When possible, use personal experiences and stories to illustrate your points.

5. When asked about past or current employment, be honest, but do not put other people down. Avoid a negative attitude and do not complain.

6. When asked about a starting salary, be honest; let them know what you require in order to live.

7. When asked about your capability as a reporter, be honest. Do not exaggerate your ability, saying that you can write 250 words a minute when you can only write 225. Most likely they will ask you to prove what you claim you can do.

8. Be prepared for a test by bringing your machine and paper. If invited to take a test to verify your speed and other qualifications, always accept the invitation. Never decline taking a test with the excuse that you forgot to bring your machine or that you have no steno paper.

9. If you state that you can write in realtime, be prepared to do so. Know how to hook up your steno machine to the computer and how to edit any untranslated or mistranslated words.

10. Have a good answer ready when asked why you want to work for their firm or what you have to offer them. Know something about the agency by doing some research. Employers are impressed by the fact that you took the time to find out something about their agency.

11. Relax, smile, and be yourself. Whatever the outcome of the interview, be polite and professional.

Most likely, the interview will end with the comment that they will contact you within a week or 10 days. Make sure that you follow up your interview with an immediate thank you letter before you receive final word from them. In some cases, this letter may sway the employer to offer you a position. If a position is offered, accept or reject it within a timely fashion so that others will have the opportunity to interview for a position with the firm or agency.

Chapter 32

The Office Environment

Court and realtime reporters work in many different situations. Sometimes they will sit all day looking at a video terminal; some days they will write on their shorthand machine for hours and hours; and, at other times, they may work under very stressful circumstances. In this chapter, we will discuss some concerns that court reporters may have to deal with in these situations. In addition, the general working environment of the court reporter is discussed.

The Office

Those who work in an official capacity will probably find themselves working in an office that is located close to the court to which they are assigned. In some cases, the reporter has a private office; in others, a number of cubicles or working areas may be arranged within a large general area. In any event, the main purpose of the office is to go to a place where work can be accomplished.

Therefore, the office must be arranged in a way that supports getting things done in the most productive way possible. The desk should be clutter free. The computer, printer, monitor, and keyboard should be easily accessible. The chair should be comfortable. Ample file and storage space for supplies and documents should be available. The telephone should be within easy reach for answering or making calls. Wires, extensions, and cords should be located so that they will not cause a hazard when moving around the office.

Those who work for a freelance agency will find that their office situation may not always be the most desirable. In some instances, offices may be a "space" or a "cubby hole" within a large room. In other cases, the reporter's "office" may consist of a desk, a chair, and a computer workstation. To a certain extent, the freelancer who works at home has an opportunity to choose what his or her own office environment will be like.

No matter what the situation, official reporter, freelance agency reporter, or self-employed reporter, certain factors should be considered in helping to develop the most productive working environment. When environmental factors are considered to produce a safe and secure working place, it is called *ergonomics*.

Ergonomics integrates the use of space, furniture, equipment, light, color, sounds, temperature, and other factors in the workplace to meet the needs of the workers to help them to be as productive as possible.

Office Furniture and Space

The office itself should be adequate to hold the furniture necessary to get the job done. The court reporter needs to have a desk from which to work. Preferably, the desk should be separate from the computer workstation. The desk should have a large working surface that is kept free of clutter, has plenty of drawer space, and is of sturdy construction.

The computer workstation should have a table top that is adjustable to a height of 24 to 32 inches. The monitor and keyboard platform should be movable so that they can be adjusted to the individual worker. A sufficient lighting fixture should be used as well as a copyholder placed in a position that reduces eyestrain. The chair should be comfortable, have a good solid back support, be movable, and be adjustable to a height between 15 and 22 inches.

Besides the desk and workstation, the court reporter's office needs to have adequate file cabinets to store and retrieve documents, forms, and files. Most court reporters have a locking file cabinet that is fireproof or fire retardant.

Shelving is a big consideration in any working environment. Without adequate shelves objects are put into places where they will accumulate unnecessarily. Shelves should be securely attached to walls so that they will not fall down. Every reporter's office should have a bulletin board for important notices or information. In addition, a large calendar may be used to mark appropriate court or deposition dates.

Enough electrical outlets are needed so that computers, lights, shorthand machines, air conditioners, and so on, can all be plugged in. Extension cords should be avoided, and power strips should only be used when the electrical amps used do not exceed the maximum allowed. In other words, avoid overloading the circuit by plugging too many pieces of equipment into a power strip.

Office Color, Light, and Temperature

Scientists have proved that the color of an office or workplace has a direct effect on a person's productivity. Color affects our emotions, moods, and attitudes in the workplace. Although bright colors tend to overstimulate the mind and soft colors tend to make a person sleepy and less productive, very often neutral shades offer a relaxing environment that is neither too stimulating nor too relaxing.

In addition, proper lighting is essential for doing productive work. Natural sunlight is preferred; however, more often than not, artificial lighting must be used to illuminate an office. Overhead lights are adequate to brighten an entire office; task lighting is preferred for individual workers. Task lighting involves the use of a dedicated light fixture that shines directly onto the work area. Lights should be placed in a position where they will not cast shadows on the work area.

Temperature, air quality, and ventilation all work together to make the office environment safe and productive. Proper heating and air conditioning are important for worker morale and health.

Health Issues for Court Reporters

As in any job or profession, several occupational risks are involved in court reporting. Over half of the disorders reported to the Occupational Safety and Health Administration (OSHA) are estimated to be connected with ergonomic issues. For the court reporter, these risks include repetitive motion injuries (carpal tunnel syndrome), back-related problems, vision strain, and stress-related problems.

Repetitive Strain Injuries

Keyboarders, court reporters, and pianists, those who repeatedly use their fingers, wrists, and forearms to employ the same type of movement over and over again, are sometimes susceptible to carpal tunnel syndrome. *Carpal tunnel syndrome* is the result of the compression of the median nerve that passes from the forearm, through the wrists, to the palm of the hand. It occurs when the muscles of the arms and hands are overworked or overstrained. Carpal tunnel syndrome is also called *median nerve entrapment* and can develop in other parts of the body, including the neck and shoulder areas.

Some symptoms that may point to the onset of carpel tunnel syndrome are pain or burning in the wrist area, pain in the shoulders or wrists while sleeping, loss of the sense of touch, dropping objects that you would normally not drop, and tingling or numbness in the fingers.

A variety of treatments for the injury are used; each depends on the severity of the injury. Treatments include lightweight splints, injections, exercise, and surgery. A new form of treatment called *myofascial re-*

lease therapy has proved very successful and does not involve the use of surgery or drugs. Preventive measures should also be considered.

Many ergonomic devices can be used by keyboarders and court reporters that will help to alleviate pain and sometimes even prevent injury. Among these devices are cushioned wrist pads for the keyboard, tripods that tilt in for the shorthand machine, and special gloves or wrist supports that can be worn while working.

As with all injuries, one should consult a qualified physician for proper diagnosis and treatment.

Back-Related Problems

Court reporters and those who sit in a sedentary position for long periods often suffer from persistent back pain. These back problems are usually the result of poor posture when sitting or standing or from sitting in chairs that do not offer proper back support.

Court reporters should be keenly aware of their sitting and standing positions, making sure that they follow all the good-posture rules. Some of these rules include standing or sitting as straight as possible, not slouching, and using proper back support when sitting.

Court reporters should be aware of any onset of pain in the back area and immediately consult a physician or chiropractor for diagnosis and treatment of any back injuries.

Vision Strain

Court reporters use the sense of sound and sight to a great extent. Very often physical problems are directly related to problems in seeing. A good eye exam by a qualified optometrist will usually detect any problems with vision.

In addition, court reporters who work in front of computer monitors are susceptible to eyestrain that may lead to blurred vision or headaches. A good eye-to-monitor range is 18 to 22 inches, looking down at the monitor at a 30-degree angle. The computer terminal should be adjustable and allow for tilting of the monitor slightly downward.

Stress-Related Problems

Court reporting can be a very stressful occupation for many reasons. In most instances, court reporters are constantly doing something, either writing or transcribing; they have deadlines to meet; and they have the constant pressure of maintaining their speed and accuracy.

Sometimes physical problems, such as carpel tunnel syndrome, back problems, or vision problems, can lead to psychological problems that need to be dealt with by a professional.

Because reporters are under a great amount of pressure, they need to make sure that they take time off for relaxing. Court reporters should never forego their vacation time or fail to get the proper sleep and rest necessary to rejuvenate their minds and bodies.

Most successful court reporters take time to engage in some activity that is totally divorced from their everyday occupation; in other words, they have a hobby that they enjoy doing in the evenings, on weekends, or whenever they get some spare time. Usually, their hobby involves some physical activity since they are engaged in such a sedentary occupation. Some reporters enjoy tennis, golf, jogging, or hiking; others enjoy reading, writing, painting, or working on a computer.

Beginning court reporters need to be warned against the dangers of substituting drugs and alcohol for proper health, diet, sleep, and exercise. Any signs of abuse in this direction should be dealt with immediately by consulting a professional.

Upon reflection, most of the cases that a reporter deals with are "bad news" cases involving rape, murder, death, abuse, and so on. Eventually, this constant bombardment of negativism can lead to a negative attitude toward people as a whole. The court reporter needs to be able to release these feelings by following some sort of tension-releasing hobby.

Always Consult a Professional

Consulting a qualified person in any of the areas where problems may occur is important for court reporters. Court reporters need to be in tip-top shape, mentally, physically, and emotionally. Someone once said that a successful court reporter surrounds himself or herself with five good people. The first is a good friend or confidant who may be a spouse or partner; the second is a member of the clergy, a pastor, or a counselor; the third is a good financial advisor or accountant; the fourth is a good general physician who can diagnose and refer you to specialists; and the fifth is a good lawyer.

Chapter 33

The Court System in America

Before we look at the job description of an official reporter, we need to know the makeup of the judicial process in the United States. Briefly, the court system in the United States can be divided into two broad categories, federal and state. The Judiciary Act of 1789 created the U.S. Supreme Court and established a system of federal courts of inferior jurisdiction, leaving to the individual states the right to establish their own judicial systems, subject to the exclusive jurisdiction of the federal courts.

Federal Court Structure

The federal court system (Figure 33.1) was developed originally so that the national government would not have to depend on state courts to carry out its laws. Eventually, federal courts came to have exclusive jurisdiction over criminal matters involving violation of federal law.

United States Supreme Court

The highest court in the United States is the Supreme Court. The Supreme Court hears cases that have been previously tried and appealed, and no further appeal is allowed as a result of its decisions. The Supreme Court consists of a chief justice and eight associate justices. The power of the United States Supreme Court to review the decisions of state courts is limited to lawsuits that involve a federal question. However, the Supreme Court has the power to declare unconstitutional any federal or state statute that is contrary to the United States Constitution. Only about 10 percent of the cases that apply for review by the Supreme Court are declared worthy of being heard.

The United States Supreme Court is the only court created by the United States Constitution. Its jurisdiction is varied and usually of an appellate nature. In most instances, the United States Supreme Court may decide whether it will hear a particular case. Once a decision has been made in a trial court and in an appellate court, the losing party may petition the Supreme Court for a *writ of certiorari,* more commonly called a *writ of review.*

The United States Supreme Court is obligated to hear some cases that come to them on appeal, bypassing the courts of appeal. Also, in some instances the Supreme Court has original jurisdiction, such as when states incur disputes over boundaries. It is a trial court in this instance, because it has original jurisdiction over disputes between states.

FIGURE 33.1
Federal Court Structure

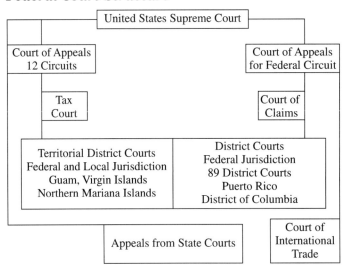

United States Courts of Appeals

The United States is divided into twelve judicial circuits; that is, eleven judicial circuits and the District of Columbia Judicial Court. Each circuit has a federal court of appeals. These courts have no original jurisdiction. The court of appeals is the court of last resort in the federal court system. Cases may be appealed from the court of appeals to the United States Supreme Court.

United States District Courts

The United States is divided into judicial districts, and the federal district courts are courts of record. Legal actions that involve an interest and a right of the government of the United States are tried in federal courts. All other litigation that is less than international in scope is tried in the state court system.

District courts are the trial courts of the federal court system and have original jurisdiction, exclusive of the state courts, in all criminal offenses against the United States. They have broad jurisdiction over civil actions arising under the U.S. Constitution and federal laws. They also have original jurisdiction of civil actions exceeding $10,000 that arise under the Constitution, laws, or treaties of the United States.

Special Federal Courts

Special federal courts are called *legislative courts*. These courts include the Claims Court, the Court of International Trade, the Tax Court, and so on. These courts have special jurisdiction as implied by the name of the court.

Individual State Courts

Each state has the authority to create its own courts, and these are hardly uniform. Most state court systems consist of a supreme court, or court of last resort; an intermediate appellate court, usually called the *court of appeals;* trial courts of regional jurisdiction where suits are commenced; and inferior or lower courts such as *probate courts,* also called *surrogate's court,* and other specialized courts (see Figure 33.2).

Usually, a case is first brought and tried in a trial court and appealed to higher courts of appellate jurisdiction until it reaches the state's highest appellate court or, finally, the United States Supreme Court.

Most states are divided into circuits, or districts, with a court for each; and all state courts operate independently from one another and from the federal government.

FIGURE 33.2
Basic State Court Structure

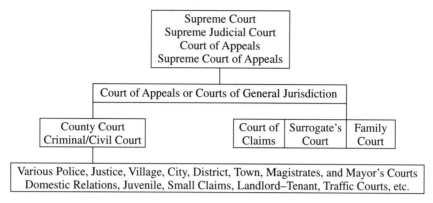

Most state supreme courts, or courts of last resort, have appellate jurisdiction over all controversies arising in state trial courts unless the state has an intermediate court of appeals. Each state has only one supreme appellate court.

All but five states use the designation Supreme Court for their court of last resort. In Maine and Massachusetts, the highest court is called the *supreme judicial court;* in New York and Maryland, it is called the *court of appeals*; and in West Virginia, the *supreme court of appeals.*

State Trial Courts

This tier of trial courts hears important matters—felony trials in which the defendant may be sentenced to a long prison term and civil suits that usually involve over $1,000. Such courts are generally located only at the county seat. In some states several counties share a single court or judge who normally sits in one county and then visits the other counties for short periods each year. Judges of these courts are always lawyers and normally serve for relatively long terms. All jury trials in state courts are heard in these courts, although most cases are heard by the judge alone or are settled out of court.

These superior courts are the highest state courts of original jurisdiction. In some states these courts are called *circuit courts, district courts,* or *courts of common pleas.* In New York, however, the highest state court of original jurisdiction is called the *supreme court.* These courts have general jurisdiction over civil, criminal, and equity matters. Their jurisdiction often extends to two or more counties. They have appellate jurisdiction over cases originating in the lower courts, such as municipal, justice, and small claims courts, in addition to being the court of original jurisdiction.

In some states these courts have separate departments that have jurisdiction over special matters, such as matters of law or equity. They may have separate civil and criminal divisions. The state trial courts are courts of record.

State Lower Courts

Lower courts include those whose proceedings are directly subject to appeal review by a higher court, such as municipal courts, justice of the peace courts, small claims courts, city courts, traffic courts, police courts, justice courts, magistrate's courts, recorder's courts, village courts, mayor's courts, town courts, and so on.

All lower courts have limited jurisdiction. In criminal cases they are generally restricted to misdemeanors, preliminary hearings, or inquiries in felony cases. In civil actions their jurisdiction is over cases involving small amounts of money.

Generally, lower courts are not courts of record; but in many jurisdictions, examining trials are fully reported verbatim to bind defendants over to the superior court. Full-time reporters fill these positions in larger cities. In some hearings held in courts not of record, attorneys for defendants may retain freelance reporters to record and transcribe the proceedings to assist in the preparation of the case before the trial court.

Justice of the Peace Courts

Where the office of justice of the peace still exists, the cases usually involve minor criminal and civil matters such as traffic fines, local ordinance violations, and suits involving small amounts of money. In many states these functions have been limited to minor matters, and a professional magistrate or judge has been installed to hear criminal and civil suits.

In most states, courts of minor jurisdiction do not hold jury trials; all matters that come before them are settled by the presiding officer alone. If a jury trial is requested and permitted by law, the case must be transferred to another court.

Section F

The Technology of the Reporter

Chapter 34

Hardware and Software Considerations, CAT, and Litigation Support

Today's court and realtime reporters require modern, up-to-date equipment in order to deliver the full array of services that are required in today's computerized world. This chapter will touch on the hardware and software issues that need to be considered in court and realtime reporting. In addition, some ancillary services that modern court and realtime reporters can offer their customers will be discussed.

Hardware and Software

Computers have significantly affected all aspects of a reporter's work. They are used for organizing and running the office, scheduling appointments, billing and invoicing, delivery of transcripts, transcript production, and a variety of other tasks.

The computer equipment that a reporter uses is similar and, in many cases, the same as computers used both in other professions and in the home. When discussing computer systems, it is useful to speak in terms of hardware and software and input and output devices.

Hardware refers to the different types of physical equipment that make up the computer system. Typical hardware includes a monitor or screen, the computer processing unit (CPU) that contains the memory and disk drives, a keyboard, mouse, modem, fax, and printer. For the court reporter, the shorthand machine is also considered a hardware device that is an integral part of the computer system when it is connected to the computer with special cables to allow for writing and translation on the computer.

The various pieces of hardware can be further divided into input and output devices. Anything that deals with putting data into the computer system is considered an input device. The keyboard, the joystick, the mouse, the disk drives, and the shorthand machine are all considered input devices. Pieces of equipment that help to produce a workable copy of the data that was input into the computer are called output devices. The screen, the printer, and the modem are considered output devices.

Software refers to internal or external programs that are run on the computer system. Typical software programs include word-processing programs, spreadsheet applications, and, for the court reporter, computer-aided transcription programs.

The technology of computers is rapidly changing. Modern computers contain more memory, run faster, and are less expensive than earlier models. And, more than likely, the trend will be for even faster and less expensive computers in the future.

It is important for the court reporter to keep abreast of the changing technology in the field of court reporting because it directly affects different tasks that the court reporter performs when taking down dictation and producing an accurate record.

Reporters should be aware of the basics of operating systems, the different sizes of memory, and the common computer terms that are used when talking about memory, disks, storage, and other common concepts. The reporter should also be familiar with what their particular software application can do in terms of computer-aided transcription.

Computer Basics

The court and realtime reporter needs to take a number of things into consideration when considering the purchase of a computer for business and work.

Most modern-day applications of court and realtime reporting require the use of a personal computer or laptop computer. The personal computer (PC) is a larger, more stationary unit that will usually remain in the office or at home. Work can be generated on the PC by using a CAT system of writing and reading, as explained later. Some courts use PCs that are a permanent part of the court setup; the judge, attorneys, and court reporter all have a personal computer with a monitor. As the court reporter writes what is being said, the judges and lawyers have access to an instant transcription as it appears on their screens.

A notebook or laptop computer is used when portability is needed. The notebook computer allows the realtime reporter to bring everything with him or her, set up, and begin realtiming. Some court reporters use notebook computers in their courts and freelance reporters often take their laptop computers with them on their jobs. CART providers (Communication Access Realtime Translation) use notebook computers because they are often called on to provide realtiming on a one-on-one basis for the hearing impaired. CART technology is explained in greater detail in Chapter 35.

Computers save information in a number of places within the central processing unit. One of the main storage areas is the hard drive. The hard drive of a computer can store information in the form of software programs, applications, and computer operating systems. If a court and realtime reporter is using a specialized software program to write in realtime, the hard drive is the place where this application and all its subsequent files are stored.

Hard drive space is now measured in gigabytes. A gigabyte (GB) is approximately 1 billion bytes. A byte is a set of bits that represents a single character in the computer's memory. There are 8 bits in a byte. Hard drive space is also measured in megabytes (a million bytes of information). As computers advance in speed and capability, their storage capacity increases. The next generation of computers will store memory in terms of terabytes (a trillion bytes of information). When purchasing a computer for court and realtime reporting, one should consider purchasing a unit with enough hard-drive space for many large files.

The speed at which a computer processes information is measured in megahertz. One megahertz is 1 million complete cycles per second and is used to measure transmission speeds. Some older computers have processing speeds of 200 MHz or more, but modern computers now have speeds of 800 MHz and greater. Some computers can process information at the speed of 1000 MHz, which is referred to as a gigahertz (GHz).

The microprocessor is the heart of the computer. In PCs, the most common microprocessor used is the Pentium generation of processors. Microprocessors perform many operations using instructions that are integrated into each chip, but software programs can also tell the processor to do specific instructions.

Other things to consider when purchasing a computer are the modem and modem speed, the type of browser to be used, and the ability of your computer to handle video, graphics, sound, and other multimedia peripherals and programs.

The court and realtime reporter's shorthand writer is cabled to the computer via a parallel port located in the back of the computer. These communication ports are measured in terms of the number of pins in each connect. Common pin configurations are 25-pin and 9-pin connectors. Most shorthand writers use a common cable to connect the writer to the computer. Parallel-port technology is now being replaced by the USB interface. USB stands for Universal Serial Bus and is a computer standard designed to eliminate the guesswork in connecting all types of peripherals to a PC.

If your computer comes with a USB port and not a regular 25-pin communications port, and your writer has a 25-pin cable, you may have to use a USB port adapter. Some of the newest computerized shorthand writers are now coming equipped with a USB port as well as a standard 25-pin port, making them adaptable to almost any computer.

Every computer has an operating system (OS), which is the software that actually communicates with the computer's hardware. Without an operating system, the computer would be worthless. The OS allocates memory, processes instructions, accesses disks, communicates with the drives, allows the peripherals to function, and acts as the user interface.

Developers write programming commands within operating systems to make computers operate as they are supposed to. Windows® and all the different versions are examples of operating systems.

For a computer to process the commands that are written within an operating system or program, the computer uses a memory bank called ROM (read-only memory). ROM is a storage chip containing programmed instructions that the computer uses when it boots up. In PCs, the instructions that are read by a computer are read from a small program called BIOS (basic input/output system). BIOS instructions are read before any other software programs are loaded into memory.

ROM memory is permanent and cannot be changed. Once ROM is activated, all software programs and computer applications rely on RAM (random-access memory). RAM is a temporary storage place where a computer can read common instructions to common programs that run on your computer. Rather than accessing the hard drive for specific program instructions, accessing RAM is much quicker. The more RAM that you have on your computer, the more data that can be loaded from the hard drive into the RAM, helping to speed up your work.

It is a fact that computers are outdated within a very short period of time after purchasing; however, thankfully, most software manufacturers make their programs adaptable to a number of computer operating systems and configurations.

It is best to consult an equipment manufacturer or a software vendor for specific information regarding what the needs are for your specific computer applications. A minimum computer system for a realtime writer might include the following:

1. Pentium generation or higher microprocessor
2. Minimum 10 gigabytes of hard drive space
3. Minimum 128 RAM or higher
4. Minimum 500 MHz or higher processing speed
5. Windows98, or ME
6. Video card, sound card, speakers
7. CD-ROM drive

In addition, it is a good idea to have Internet access via the most updated version of browser, such as Internet Explorer 5.0®; Windows 9x word-processing software such as Microsoft Word®; and e-mail accessibility with your own personal address and mailbox (make sure that your provider does not limit the size of documents that can be sent or received via e-mail).

Computer-Aided Transcription

The concept of CAT (computer-aided transcription) has been around since the early 1970s. It can be defined as the production of a transcript by using the technology of the computer. Like any technology, CAT has undergone many improvements and changes since its inception. Most court reporters use a computer in some aspect of their transcript production; some rely heavily on the use of computers, while others use computers to perform just the basic operations of keyboarding and printing.

The most basic from of CAT is typing one's notes into a standard word-processing software application, utilizing the spell-check features and other word-processing commands and then printing a final copy. In a very menial sense, the computer is used simply as an input, storage, and output device. Although this method of CAT is sufficient, it is time consuming in the sense that someone has to read and translate the shorthand notes and input them into the computer by typing them on the keyboard. There is a better and faster method.

The computer can be used to read and translate the shorthand notes when the notes are electronically recorded on a computer disk. Some computerized shorthand machines have the ability to write regular shorthand notes on paper and to record them to disk. Once a job is complete, the court reporter takes his or her disk, inserts it into the computer, and the computer will automatically translate the notes for the reporter.

The translation process requires a specialized software program that contains a shorthand dictionary that will translate shorthand outlines into English words. If any of the shorthand outlines are not in the dictionary or if the reporter makes an incorrect stroke in writing a word, the computer will not be able to translate the word. However, these untranslated words can be entered into a personal dictionary for correct translation to occur from that point on.

Once a transcript has been produced by the computer, someone must edit the screen output and translate any words that were not translated by the computer or make corrections to words that may have been mistranslated. Sometimes the original court reporter who took down the dictation edits his or her own job. Some reporting firms use a scopist to edit the reporter's work. A scopist is someone who is trained to read shorthand outlines and spot errors in punctuation or format. In a sense, they are editors or proofreaders who correct all errors in the transcript before final printing, signing, and delivery.

After the transcript has been proofread and all errors have been corrected, it is printed and delivered to the person or persons who ordered the transcript.

The CAT Cycle

Most computer-aided transcription software performs five basic functions that make up the CAT cycle: reading, translating, editing, saving, and printing.

Reading

The first step in producing a transcript using the computer is to have the computer read the shorthand notes. This reading step is nothing more than inputting the recorded notes, that is, the electronic signals that are captured on the disk or other magnetic media, into the computer. This step is usually accomplished by taking the disk from the shorthand machine and putting it into the computer and selecting the *read* option on the menu of the software program. As the computer reads the electronic signals, it prepares itself for the next step in the CAT cycle.

Translating

After reading the electronic signals that make up the shorthand notes, the computer translates them into their English equivalents. In other words, it converts the shorthand strokes into the words that it finds in its dictionary. Words that are not in the dictionary or words that it cannot translate because of misstrokes are called *untranslates* or *untrans*. A *mistranslate* occurs when the computer inadvertently translates different strokes into wrong words. These untrans and mistrans must be corrected, along with other format errors that may occur in the transcript.

Editing

The editing process usually involves two steps. The first is to correct the transcript for all untrans. Most CAT programs have a function key that will go from untrans to untrans and allow the scopist or editor to mark and define those strokes that were not translated by the computer. If the shorthand is "good" shorthand, that is, there are no errors in the strokes, the outline is put into the master dictionary so that, if the word is ever written again, it will be translated. Words that relate only to a particular case or job are defined and put into a special dictionary that may be used for related jobs. The second step in the editing process is to proofread the entire document for mistranslates, errors in format, and any other mistakes that need to be corrected before printing the document.

Saving

It would be both ludicrous and disastrous to spend hours translating and editing a job that may contain hundreds of pages and then to lose it or not have some way of preserving it. All software applications that do word processing have a feature that allows the computer to save the document to disk or to the hard drive.

Most court reporting software packages will automatically save a file to the hard drive, allowing the court reporter to copy or move them to $3\frac{1}{2}$-inch disks for external storage in the court reporting firm's archives.

Printing

The final step in the CAT cycle is to produce a hard copy of the document so that it can be delivered to the client along with the invoice. Most firms have high-speed laser printers capable of producing an original copy that will then be duplicated on the firm's copiers.

The CAT Dictionary

By providing a beginners dictionary or a dictionary build program, most CAT systems allow you to build your own personal dictionary that contains outlines for most of the common words used in translation. Students or reporters who already have their own dictionaries may be able to use them in CAT systems that are used by freelance companies. Most CAT systems are able to convert other dictionaries for use from one system to another system.

The dictionary is the heart of any court reporting shorthand software application, because the dictionary allows for the shorthand symbols to be translated into their English equivalents. In a very real sense, the translation process is the same that takes place when ones translate from a foreign language to English; the shorthand symbols represent the foreign language and are translated into the English by an "interpreter" or dictionary during the translation process.

Most theories taught by court reporting schools are able to use a series of strokes that allow for virtually no conflicts in writing. A conflict occurs when the same shorthand outline is used for two or more words. For example, the words *two, to,* and *too* all need a distinct and separate way of being written, even though they all sound the same. Many words in the English language sound the same, but have different spellings and different meanings.

Modern-day theories have addressed the issue of conflicts and have developed writing styles that eliminate any known conflicts. In addition, court reporting software manufacturers and representatives offer advice on how to build a dictionary that will help the translation process.

Most dictionaries used by reporters contain the outlines for the most common words that occur in particular writing situations, but they also have the ability to automatically form derivatives or endings of root words, even though they may not have been predefined into the dictionary.

Other CAT Features

Most CAT programs have a powerful spell-check application that can rapidly proofread hundreds of pages for spelling and format errors. Most court reporting software programs also have global capabilities for searching and replacing; index creation and keyword indexing; ASCII disk creation; modem and telecommunication capabilities; and other specialized features.

The software packages offered by court reporting companies are highly specialized applications designed to make the work of the court reporter easier and quicker. Over the years they have been perfected, with new and better options being offered with each new edition.

Litigation Support

Litigation support has been defined as any supplemental service that a court reporter or agency can offer to lawyers, judges, or other court personnel to help them in their pursuit of justice. Not all litigation support services are offered by every agency, but more firms are beginning to offer a wide variety of extras for their clients. Reporters and reporting firms charge more for these services because it costs more to offer them.

These ancillary services can be offered because of advances in modern technology. While not all court and realtime software programs offer all these features, most include them in their program packages.

Listed next are examples of some litigation support services that may be offered by court and real-time reporters.

Condensed Transcript

A condensed transcript is exactly what the words imply. It is a printed transcript that is reduced from its original size so that more than one page of the transcript can be printed on a regular $8\frac{1}{2}$-by-11-inch paper. To offer the service, a special software program is needed that will print the transcripts in condensed format. Most of the programs offer two, four, six, or eight pages of transcript on one or both sides of a regular-sized page. This means that one sheet of transcript could conceivably contain as many as 16 pages of transcript. Lawyers like this reduced-size transcript.

Keyword Indexing

An attorney will be interested in portions of the testimony where certain words occur over and over again. For example, in the direct examination of a defendant, the attorney who will be cross-examining may be interested in how many references were made to the word *gun* or *knife* in direct examination. Using keyword indexing, a court reporter can offer a printed page that lists the page and line number of every reference to the word *gun* or *knife*. The attorney can then turn to those pages for the context of chosen references.

Instant Viewing and Marking Capabilities

Using the technology of computer-integrated courtrooms, lawyers and judges can view a computer monitor that shows the printed transcript on the screen in realtime. While viewing the screen, an attorney can go backward within the transcript and search for words or important parts and then *mark* them or *cue* them on his transcript only. He can also pull in previous testimony on the same matter and even previous transcripts that pertain to the case at hand. This remarkable achievement is now in place in some more advanced courtrooms in the nation.

Different Print Options

Attorneys or clients can have a transcript printed in many different ways. Besides printing a hard copy in regular format or condensed format on transcript paper, attorneys can also have a Braille copy printed for the blind or visually impaired, an ASCII copy printed to disk to allow for downloading onto their own computers, or a copy printed in Spanish or any other foreign language.

Other Litigation Support Services

As technology advances in the world of court reporting, we will undoubtedly see an explosion in new types of services offered by court reporters to their clients, for example, instant translation services from one language to another, instant research of all available transcripts for words or activities, and bundling together transcripts from a variety of cases that relate to a particular circumstance. As a court reporter, it is important that you keep abreast of the changes that are taking place in the field and keep up with the most up-to-date services offered by reporters and agencies.

Chapter 35

The Technology of Transcript Production

This textbook has discussed aspects of court and realtime reporting and concentrated on CAT (computer-aided transcription) as the primary method of producing the transcript, with some references being made to realtime translation.

This chapter will discuss some of the other methods used by court and realtime reporting to produce an accurate record. Some of these technologies have proved to be very successful, some are experimental, and some are controversial. We begin our discussion with realtime translation and closed captioning.

Realtime Writing and Translation

Most freelance reporters and many official courts have been working with realtime technology for many years. Realtime translation is exactly what the words imply—translation of the spoken word into printed format as soon as it is spoken.

As technology becomes friendlier and easier to use, as prices decrease, and as court reporters keep abreast of the changes in their field, realtime reporting and translation are becoming the standard of the industry. More and more reporters realize the need to adapt to the changing technology of the field, and they are using the concepts of realtime writing in their everyday working environment.

To write and translate in realtime requires certain specialized equipment. This equipment includes, but is not limited to, the following:

1. A shorthand writer that is either hooked to a computer by cable or is capable of storing the shorthand strokes on a cassette tape, disk, or internal memory storage device.

2. The ability to read the electronic strokes into a computer that is equipped with specialized software to translate the strokes into their English equivalent.

3. A shorthand dictionary that is stored in memory that will translate the shorthand outlines.

4. A word-processing application within the software that allows for editing and printing of the translated textual material.

5. Monitors or computer screens on which judges, lawyers, and perhaps the jury can see the spoken word.

6. Various other peripheral equipment, such as high-speed printers and copiers, fax hookups, and modems to allow for instant translation and transmission.

Realtime setups can involve a very simple application, as when the reporter uses his or her laptop computer to display realtime translation, or they may be very elaborate and complex applications involving many PCs and monitors spread throughout a courtroom for instant viewing and interaction by lawyers, as well as transmission to other buildings in different locations.

Some realtime setups have a laser printer that prints rough-draft copies of the translated material. The rough drafts can be distributed to lawyers before the final copy with the understanding that it may contain untrans that will be edited before a final copy is printed out.

Realtime reporting is considered a necessity in today's court scenarios for a number of reasons. Here are some of the advantages of using realtime:

1. Realtime provides an instant transcript that is less expensive than daily copy and an instantaneous record.

2. Realtime means that both a hard copy and a computer diskette copy can be obtained. Sometimes the computer diskette copy is preferred to the printed transcript.

3. The computerized transcript can be sent to clients by modem using e-mail, by fax, or by FTP or other fast methods of document transmittal. This method of communicating is much quicker than the regular mails and can save money.

4. Instant readback in court situations is available by either looking at the screen and scrolling within the document that appears on the screen or by using an instant hard copy that can be printed in rough-draft format.

5. Realtime reporting offers a new dimension in terms of searching the record for key words or phrases. Some realtime applications are able to search the immediate record being reported and cross-reference it to other related documents.

Closed Captioning

Realtime writing and closed captioning go hand in hand. In a very real sense, realtime writing uses closed captioning, and closed captioning uses the technology of realtime writing. If any distinction can be made between the two technologies, it would be in the translation. Usually, realtime translation appears on a screen or monitor in printed transcript format, that is, question and answer format with colloquy set up, and so on. The realtime translation usually appears as 25-line-page format that can be scrolled backward and forward.

On the other hand, words that are translated when using closed captioning usually appear inside a box at the bottom of a televised picture. The text is usually limited to what the character on the television is saying and, once it appears, it disappears and cannot be retrieved or scrolled as in realtime. Closed captioning is used more for translation of programs or speeches for immediate reading by the hearing impaired.

One of the greatest services performed by a reporter today is that of the closed caption television writer, because television is one of the best means of mass communication, and hearing impairment affects millions of Americans, young and old.

Many captioning agencies provide coverage for a variety of news programs and prime time shows. Captions display television's auditory information in visual form. Similar to subtitles, captions translate spoken dialogue into printed words on a screen. They also identify speakers and indicate additional information, including sound effects and mood music. Captions can be synchronized with speech patterns and changes in camera angles to convey a sense of rhythm and pace to the viewer.

Closed captions are seen only on television sets equipped with special decoders. The American with Disabilities Act has made it mandatory for all television sets to be equipped with such decoders. Captions appear as white capital letters against a black background. These $\frac{1}{2}$-inch high letters are usually displayed at the bottom of the screen, although they are sometimes placed in other positions to identify speakers or to avoid interference with graphics or text. Musical notes accompany song lyrics.

Captioning can be either closed or open. Closed captioning takes place when the reporter writes what is being said either online or offline and the captioned materials appear on the screen; however, for the viewer to see the material, the television set has to be equipped with a receiver that can be controlled on a TV screen. Open captions appear on a screen regardless of whether a television is equipped to receive captioning signals, like subtitles that appear at the bottom of foreign language movies. Some television shows can be captioned off line, which means that they are not done in realtime, but captioned and then made a part of the program or movie.

Some captioners use a live scopist who immediately edits words that were mistranslated or untranslated during the captioning.

A person who plans to become a closed caption writer should have a wide knowledge of current events, a good vocabulary, familiarity with names, countries, foreign and national affairs, and have a good writing theory that has no conflicts and is readily translatable.

CART

Perhaps the best example of realtiming, closed captioning, and modern technology all working together can be found in what is called CART, or Communication Access Realtime Translation. Reporters who work in the field of CART are called CART providers. The concept of CART is stated in its name; that is, CART provides a method of accessing communications by using realtime translation. Communication is usually in the form of visual text for hearing impaired persons. CART providers record not only the spoken word, but also actions, sounds, and other interpretive directions that are necessary to paint an entire picture of the words that are portrayed on the screen.

For example, if there is laughter in the background, it is so noted; if someone screams while another person it talking, the captions include the notation that someone screamed. This reporting of words and action is what distinguishes the CART provider from court and freelance reporters who record only the spoken word.

Although CART was originally designed for use by the hearing impaired, it is also used by those who may need help in understanding the English language; those who are physically or psychologically challenged and need assistance in hearing words; and those who wish to improve their reading skills and linguistic abilities.

CART is an *assistive* technology in the sense that it aids and helps (assists) those who need help in understanding, hearing, reading, or interpreting the spoken word.

Much like the realtime reporter and closed captioner, the CART provider uses the computerized machine writer, a notebook computer, and specialized realtime software. CART providers work on a one-on-one basis with individuals in business settings or classrooms, or they can be set up in environments with larger TV screens for hundreds of people to "hear" the spoken words by seeing them on the screen.

Videography

Where stenography is the skill of recording in shorthand and photography is the skill of recording by picture, videography is the skill of recording by videotape. As a permanent method of recording events, it has its advantages and disadvantages, some of which will be listed in this section.

Many freelance agencies are offering the videotaping of testimony as a litigation support to their clients. In a very real sense, the videotaping of testimony offers a new dimension in transcript production, a dimension that may be advantageous at times and disadvantageous at others.

Successful use of the videotape occurs when it is used as a complement and supplement to the live court reporter, not as a replacement. Although widely used by lawyers and court reporting agencies to record depositions, it has not proved to be widely acceptable as the permanent means of recording hearing or trials involving many days of testimony.

In most jurisdictions that allow the videotaping of proceedings, it has been stipulated that the court reporter should be present in order to assure a quick and accurate record in case of electronic malfunction or for other reasons.

There are many excellent reasons for having a court reporter present to make a shorthand record at the same time that a videotape is being made; among them are the following:

1. Electronic malfunction may occur, or poor quality of videotape may result from a variety of reasons.

2. The printed transcript enables the Court to rule on potentially objectionable testimony without having to view the entire videotape.

3. Costs are saved when the technician has a printed transcript for editing purposes.

4. Producing a printed transcript from videotape is often difficult, slow, laborious, and expensive.

5. It is difficult to locate portions of videotaped testimony or colloquy in a hurry.

6. If a judge wants to review testimony, an operator or equipment may not be available to view the videotape.

7. Extraneous noises, such as the rustling of papers or moving of chairs, may block out the sound on a videotape, but the reporter can ask the witness to repeat an answer otherwise lost on the record.

Without a doubt, videotaping with a live reporter present offers a different dimension in terms of capturing an accurate record, and there are definite advantages and disadvantages.

Advantages of Videotaping

1. Videotapes can be viewed, rather than read, so long as the record is not too long, requiring hours of view time.

2. Videotaping gets all the physical gesture and motions that occur during testimony.

3. Videotaping gets sound and action for the record.

4. A printed record can be produced from the videotape, but the costs and time for producing the transcript from videotape need to be taken into consideration.

5. The training of a professional videotape technician requires less time than the training of a qualified court reporter.

Disadvantages of Videotaping

1. Viewers of videotapes can become easily bored after prolonged watching.

2. Searching for important spots in the videotapes is often difficult.

3. Malfunctions during videotaping can occur, including the picking up of excessive background noise, making them difficult to listen to.

4. Videotapes have a shelf life, which means that they are only good for a certain length of time; excessive use can also wear them out, causing breakage.

5. Videotapes must be protected from damage, such as magnetic fields and other factors that could destroy their contents.

6. Storage of videotapes can be a problem, as they require a great amount of storage space.

7. The production of a written transcript from the video is time consuming and requires additional expenditure.

8. Lengthy trials lasting two or three months pose problems, such as the quantity of videotapes needed, their cataloging and storage, viewing the entire record, producing a written transcript, and so on.

Applications of Videotaping

In specific instances, the videotaped deposition of a witness or videotaped proceedings may be preferred to the actual record, keeping in mind that the court reporter is also present at the videotaping to guarantee an accurate record. Reporting firms that offer videotaping of proceedings as a litigation support do so in the following situations:

1. Expert witnesses may have their depositions taken prior to trial. Videotaped testimony is then played back at the time of trial, saving the cost and inconvenience of bringing the expert in during the trial.

2. Doctors' depositions are taken for the same reason, and presentations of x-rays and slides may be shown more effectively through videotapes.

3. Demonstrative evidence can be presented showing laboratory experiments that would be impossible to perform in the courtroom.

4. Demonstrations of evidence showing disabilities of injured people in daily situations are shown effectively to juries.

5. Videotaping of places where accidents occurred or the scene of an arson may be used in place of a jury visit.

6. Some police departments videotape confessions and statements.

Most large court reporting firms now make it a standard practice to offer videotaping services as a litigation support for all depositions. Some firms have conference rooms set up with videotaping equipment, available for their clients to use at their convenience. Smaller firms may find it to their advantage to subcontract the videotaping of depositions. In either case, the court reporter is always present to preserve the record and ensure its integrity.

Forms Used by Videotape Technicians

Various specialized forms are required at videotaped depositions or proceedings. For example, an Opening Statement Form is read by the reporter at the very beginning of the recording. An example of this type of form is shown in Figure 35.1.

A specialized stipulation page may be used by the videotape technician to make sure that the parties understand the ground rules for making a videotaped deposition. This stipulation page spells out all the logistics of the taping and is agreed on by all parties before the videotaping begins. An example of this form is found in Figure 35.2.

The technician may also be required to fill in a certification page attesting to the length of the videotaping and the fact that he or she was the technician involved. An example of such a certificate is found in Figure 35.3.

Examples of title pages used for a videotaped deposition can be found in Figures 35.4 and 35.5.

A Final Note about Videotaping

Both competent reporters and trained video-production personnel are required to produce a good videotaped proceeding. The National Court Reporters Association offers seminars on videotaping in addition to a certificate program for Certified Legal Video Specialist (CLVS). The seminars and workshops offered by the NCRA are an excellent opportunity for reporters who use videotaping to gain invaluable knowledge regarding the logistics of videotaping.

Electronic Tape Recording

Electronic tape recording uses tape recorders to report the proceedings. The technology of electronic tape recording has changed remarkably over the past few years in order to keep pace with the complex needs involved in verbatim reporting. The standard one-track cassette tape recorder has given way to a multichannel system that records different voices on different tracks of the same tape. Modern sound-filtering microphones help to assure the quality of the sound.

However, given all the advances that have been made in audio sound recording, the system is still not as reliable and accurate as the modern-day court reporter who uses the computer to produce the transcript.

Very often, in their haste to find new, improved, and better ways of recording the spoken word, people tend to forget that a transcript has to be produced from the record, and it is in producing the transcript that the "marvels" of electronic tape recording tend to break down. The electronic tape recorder may do a good job in recording the spoken word, but production of the transcript very often requires more time and energy than the actual recording of the record.

FIGURE 35.2
Stipulation for Videotape Technician

(TITLE OF COURT AND CAUSE)

It is stipulated by and between the undersigned as follows:

1. That the deposition of _____, a witness produced by the _____, be taken at _____ o'clock ___.m. on _____, the _____ day of _____, 20___, at the office of _____ at _____.

2. That the deposition of said witness be taken in the usual manner, under Rule 30, Federal Rules of Civil Procedure (Section 2019(c) California Code of Civil Procedure), before _____, a qualified deposition reporter, and that the proceedings, including the swearing of the witness, be videotaped for use at the trial in lieu of reading the transcript of the witness's testimony.

3. The deposition reporter will take the stenographic record and will hire, control, and be responsible for providing an experienced camera operator for making the videotape.

4. The videotape shall be timed by a timedate generator that shall show continuously each hour, minute, and second of each tape.

5. The camera operator shall take an oath to record all proceedings accurately and completely, and certify as to the correctness and completeness of the videotape.

6. At the beginning of the deposition, the parties and counsel shall be shown in the visual portion of the deposition.

7. During the deposition the witness shall be recorded in as near to courtroom atmosphere and standards as possible. There will not be any procedures to give undue emphasis to any portion of the testimony. The camera shall focus as much as possible on the witness and the lawyer asking the questions. If it is not possible to do both, then the camera will focus on the witness.

(a)

FIGURE 35.1
Opening Statement Form

(Prior to opening the record, the video technician will give general instructions to all parties and the court reporter will secure the agreement the deposition is being taken under. After receiving the signal from the video technician to begin, the court reporter will read the following opening statement. Be sure to speak slowly and distinctly and with plenty of volume.)

AT THIS TIME THE DEPOSITION OF _____, A WITNESS PRODUCED BY THE _____, IS BEING TAKEN IN CAUSE NO. _____ STYLED _____ VS. _____ COMMENCING AT _____ O'CLOCK (A.M.) (P.M.) ON (DAY) _____, THE _____ DAY OF _____, 20___, AT THE OFFICE OF _____, LOCATED AT _____, IN THE CITY OF _____, COUNTY OF _____, STATE OF TEXAS.

THE COURT REPORTER TAKING THIS DEPOSITION IS _____ AND THE VIDEO TECHNICIAN OPERATING THE CAMERA IS _____.

WILL COUNSEL PLEASE STATE THEIR APPEARANCES FOR THE RECORD?

(After this statement is read, appearances are given. After this, the witness is sworn and the deposition begins.)

A Place for Tape Recorders

Tape recorders have their place. They are used successfully in very low profile situations where one or two people are speaking at controlled rates of speed. They can be used in situations that do not last more than an hour or two. And they are used very successfully for entertainment purposes.

They may also be a very effective means of recording the spoken word where all that is required is an audio transcript, in other words, where audio playback can be used instead of a printed transcript. Such is usually not the case in court cases involving many hours of testimony by various witnesses. The printed record is preferred over the visual or audio record. If a printed record is requested from the audio recording, the process involves listening to the tape, deciphering what is on the tape, and typing a transcript.

Most courts that have experimented with audio tape recording have been very dissatisfied with the quality of the transcript produced from the audio tapes, as well as the expense of having the transcript produced. Some courts thought that they would save money by eliminating the court reporter position and bringing in low-paying personnel to run tape recorders, but they forgot to include the cost of producing the transcript from the tapes, which proved to be very time consuming and expensive. The ultimate savings anticipated in using tape recorders over court reporters was virtually nil, and the resulting product was poor compared to the accurate record that the court reporter guarantees.

In one instance a hearing agency weighed the costs of using court reporters versus tape recorders and decided to save money by tape recording their proceedings. After the hearings were completed and it came time to produce transcripts, the quality was so poor and it would take so long to get the transcripts that the agency decided to contact a freelance reporting agency and have court reporters listen to the tapes and produce the transcripts using CAT technology.

FIGURE 35.2
(continued)

8. Each attorney and the witness shall be provided with an individual microphone.

9. The person operating the video camera shall give a two-minute warning before the end of each tape.

10. It shall not be necessary for the witness to view and/or approve the videotape.

11. At least one original videotape record must be made and shall remain in the custody of the deposition reporter until trial or until the Court has ruled on any objections and an edited copy of the original has been prepared for presentation to the jury, whichever shall sooner occur, at which time the original and the edited copy, if any, shall be filed with the Clerk of the Court and kept in a place suitable for preservation of magnetic tape.

12. Any party may purchase a duplicate original or edited tape from the reporter, at any time.

13. The deposition reporter shall be responsible for providing equipment and facilities to edit the tape and to play back and show the videotaped deposition.

14. Objections shall be ruled on in camera prior to showing the videotaped deposition to the jury. Any editing of the tape that becomes necessary as a result of the trial Court's rulings shall be done immediately after the in-camera hearing and prior to the presentation of the videotape deposition to the jury. Editing costs may be assessed against any party participating in the deposition as shall be determined by the Court.

15. For showing of the videotape deposition to the jury, the deposition reporter shall furnish a television screen at least 19 inches corner to corner, with a suitable stand.

(b)

FIGURE 35.2
(continued)

16. If the jury requests that any portion of the videotape deposition be read back, the court reporter shall read back from the stenographic record or from the edited transcript, as the Court shall direct.

17. Except as provided in Paragraph 14, only the stenographic record of the deposition shall be taxed as costs.

18. After time for appeal has expired, appeal has been concluded or settlement effected, the videotape shall, on request of _____, be delivered to him or, if no request is made in 60 days after such final determination of the case, then to the deposition reporter.

DATED this _____ day of _____, 20___.

_____

_____

(c)

FIGURE 35.3
Form for Videotape Technician

```
                          }            CERTIFICATE OF
                          }            VIDEOTAPE TECHNICIAN
                          }
                          }
           -vs-           }
                          }
                          }
                          }

    I, _____, VIDEOTAPE TECHNICIAN AND
NOTARY PUBLIC IN AND FOR THE COUNTY OF _____ OF
THE STATE OF TEXAS, DO HEREBY CERTIFY THAT I HAVE ACCURATELY TAKEN
THE VIDEOTAPE RECORDING OF THE DEPOSITION OF _____
IN THE ABOVE CAPTIONED MATTER, FURTHER STATING THAT THIS
DEPOSITION WAS TAKEN ON THE _____ DAY OF _____,
A.D. 20___, AT THE
_____
CONSISTING OF _____ TAPES AND, FURTHER, THAT THE TOTAL ELAPSED
TIME WAS _____ HOURS, _____ MINUTES, AND _____ SECONDS
AND THAT NO ALTERATIONS, ADDITIONS, AND DELETIONS WERE MADE
THERETO.



             _____
             NOTARY PUBLIC, _____ COUNTY, TEXAS
             MY COMMISSION EXPIRES JUNE 1, 20___.
```

FIGURE 35.4
Title Page of Videotaped Deposition

```
 1                    NO. 67-33572-75

 2   JOHN A. WALKER         )        IN THE DISTRICT COURT OF
                            )
 3      -vs-                )        TARRANT COUNTY, TEXAS
                            )
 4   INSURANCE COMPANY      )        67TH JUDICIAL DISTRICT
     OF NORTH AMERICA       )
 5

 6

 7

 8

 9

10

11

12        DEPOSITION OF WILLIAM ROGER BERNELL, M.D.

13               TAKEN FOR PLAINTIFF

14                   VIDEOTAPED

15

16

17

18

19

20

21   REPORTER:  GLORIA CARLIN, RPR, CP, CM

22   VIDEOTAPE TECHNICIAN:  DOUGLAS MORRIS, RPR

23   DATE:  FEBRUARY 18, 20__.

24

25
```

FIGURE 35.5
Title Page of Videotaped Deposition

```
 1                    NO. 67-33572-75

 2   JOHN A. WALKER         X        IN THE DISTRICT COURT OF
                            X
 3      -vs-                X        TARRANT COUNTY, TEXAS
                            X
 4   INSURANCE COMPANY      X        67TH JUDICIAL DISTRICT
     OF NORTH AMERICA       X
 5
                           - - -
 6
          ANSWERS AND DEPOSITION OF WILLIAM ROGER BERNELL, M.D.,
 7
     a witness produced on behalf of the Plaintiff, taken by
 8
     shorthand and videotape in the above styled and numbered cause
 9
     on the 18th day of February, A.D. 20>>, commencing at 2:00
10
     P.M., before Gloria Carlin, a Notary Public in and for Tarrant
11
     County, Texas, at the office of Dr. William Roger Bernell,
12
     M.D., located at 622 S. Henderson, in the City of Fort Worth,
13
     County of Tarrant, State of Texas, in accordance with the
14
     agreement hereinafter set forth and the accompanying Notice
15
     hereby attached.
16                         - - -

17
     APPEARANCES:
18
         For the Plaintiff:
19
             DUSHMAN, GREENSPAN & FRIEDMAN,
20           By:  Lowell E. Dushman, Esq.,
             920 Commerce Building
21           Fort Worth, TX  76102

22       For the Defendant:

23           STREET, SWIFT, BROCKERMEYER, BELL & WARD,
             By:  Richard E. Ward, Esq.,
24           515 Fort Worth Club Building
             Fort Worth, TX  76102
25
```

Advantages of Using Tape Recorders

Without a doubt, there are some advantages to using tape recorders. These advantages need to be taken into consideration in weighing the different alternatives.

1. Tape recording is quick and easy and requires very little skill.
2. The first stage of tape recording is relatively inexpensive, that is, the recording itself (this does not include the production of the transcript).
3. Modern tape recorders use different audio tracks to record different voices and filter out unwarranted sounds.

Disadvantages of Using Tape Recorders

Some of the problems encountered with using electronic tape recorders are the following:

1. Tape recorders sometimes fail during taping.
2. The transcript production from the recording is time consuming and expensive.
3. Audio tapes tend to wear out over time and lose their quality.

4. Audio tapes are subject to environmental factors, including smoke, pollution, static electricity, and magnetic fields.

5. Listeners may have a difficult time determining who is doing the speaking and excessive noise may compete with speakers.

6. Audio tapes have not perfected the use of realtime translation as live court reporters have.

A Final Note about Electronic Tape Recording

Courts and litigation proceedings that require a quick, true, accurate, and dependable record have not been satisfied with the results of electronic tape recording. Many advances have been made in the technology, but the bottom line remains that there are still many problems with electronic tape recordings. While it may offer a good alternative in terms of reporting the spoken word, it is not the best method.

After all the testing, researching, development, and experimentation have been completed, the most effective method of producing an accurate record remains the live court reporter coupled with the computer.

Voice-to-Print or Speech-to-Text

Voice-to-print technology can be defined as the ability to take the spoken word and have it instantly translated on a computer screen for editing or printing. The technology reduces the voice to electronic signals that are transmitted to the computer and then translated into printed text.

Voice-to-print technology has been around for many years. Large computer companies such as IBM have been experimenting with it for many years, trying to perfect the technology. Some companies have given up because of the many problems that are encountered. Some of these problems have been overcome with advances in technology, but some remain an obstacle for true voice-to-print to happen.

Problems Encountered with Voice-to-Print

1. One major obstacle is the ability for a computer to recognize different dialects as they are spoken. Dialects and accents usually are found in one group of people or one geographical area. For example, a person from Boston, Massachusetts, pronounces certain words differently than a person from East Paterson, New Jersey; and a person from the Bronx in New York City pronounces words differently than a person from San Diego, California.

2. Voice-to-print technology will only work for one person speaking at a time, and that person has to speak very clearly, distinctly, and precisely into the microphone, saying the words nearly the same way every time. Different inflections of words are sometimes not recognized.

3. Words that are mumbled, muffled, or slurred will not translate; in addition, background noises such as a chair scraping across the floor or an air conditioner being turned on will often mask out the words so that they are not translated.

4. Translation is limited to the words contained in the system's dictionary, although new words can be added.

Experiments in the technology continue. Current technology electronically photographs the user's voice, and the computer associates the dictated sounds with a set of keystrokes. The system compares the user's voice to electronic graphs stored in the system memory and keys the corresponding words.

Although some people say voice-to-print technology is still in its infancy, most developers feel as though the technology has gone as far as it possibly can. Any further development will require the use of computers using artificial intelligence to make decisions regarding what words to translate in different cases.

Voice-Recognition Technology and Voice-Activated Systems

Voice-recognition technology is different from voice-to-print technology. Voice recognition is the ability of the computer to recognize certain voice commands and to perform specific functions based on those commands. For example, to save a document that has been input into the computer, one merely has to pronounce the word *save* into the microphone and the document is saved without the need of pushing any function keys or ALT keys; the word *print* results in the document being printed.

Some of the same problems encountered in voice-to-print occur in voice recognition; for example, the voice commands have to be precise, they cannot be muffled or mumbled, and the computer is usually programmed to recognize only one voice. In some cases, if the speaker has a bad cold resulting in an "unrecognized" voice, the computer will not recognize the "new" voice.

Voice-recognition and voice-activated systems are similar. Voice-activated systems allow one to turn lights, televisions, radios, and so on, on or off with a simple command. Voice-recognition and voice-activated systems have a place in modern technology. They serve as a valuable tool for paraplegics or those who do not have the full use of their hands or arms. They can save time, as when the same one-word phrase is input into a computer for looking up pricing information or time schedules. They also serve as a great novelty item for the 21st century, that is, being able to have the computer do everything for us with a spoken command. However, their use is very limited in the field of courtroom reporting.

A Final Word about Voice-to-Print Technology

The costs of implementing voice-to-print technology may prohibit their use for some time in the future, but as the technology becomes more refined and more companies enter production, costs should decline. Currently, three or four software programs are available that provide the ability to print letters right from the user's dictation and recognize voice commands. The success of these programs has not been proved, and their use is very limited.

So many problems exist in securing a system that will differentiate between voices and apply the formats required in court reporting that many years of refinement will be required to make voice-to-print a viable instrument for reporting work. Not long ago, researchers predicted the "paperless office" of the 1990s, which never developed as fully expected or anticipated. The same can be said for some of the predictions for the 21st century regarding voice-to-print, voice-recognition, and voice-activated systems.

Voice Writing

A recent development (within the past five years) has been the use of a highly trained person in a court or legal setting who repeats everything that everyone says into a sound filtered mask that will only pick up what the speaker says (no extraneous noises). As the person speaks, he or she uses special edit commands that allow a speech-recognition engine to translate the words that are spoken into the desired format. In essence, a complete transcript can be "dictated" in realtime by one "reporter," who merely repeats everything that is said in the courtroom or legal setting. This technology, called *voice writing,* requires specialized equipment, as well as personnel who are trained in the art of "repeating" everything that is said.

Table 35.1 gives some of the pros and cons of realtiming using realtime writing (stenography) versus realtime voicing (speech to text). This material was contributed by a current CART provider and broadcast captioner, Elizabeth Maki, who has been reporting for many years.

Another current realtime writer, Chris Ales, who has investigated the aspects of both writing and voicing had this comment about voice writing: "Accuracy and translation rate depend on the amount of time invested in training the system . . . reporters must analyze the way they speak, practice every day, build their vocabulary, and work with their conflicts. This requires time and discipline."

There is no doubt about it, the technological development that is taking place in the field of court and realtime reporting is remarkable. We live in very exciting times in which the technology of tomorrow is being developed and tested today.

TABLE 35.1

A COMPARISON OF TWO DIFFERENT REALTIME TRANSLATION SYSTEMS

Realtime Writing (Stenography) *Pros*	*Realtime Voice (Speech-to-Text)* *Pros*
Keystrokes are conveyed to computer software for precise translation.	Shorter learning curve. The training time is accelerated.
Speech-to-text readability; text output occurs at a comfortable, manageable pace for viewers.	Reliable translation of words is improving.
For the skilled writer, additions can be made to dictionaries during realtime writing, thereby improving the reliability of proper name translations.	Accuracy and speed are improving, provided the reporter trained the system.
Formatting is achieved on the fly through keyboard macros. The keyboard macros are received in precise order with the words, and so they are executed at precisely the right location.	Letter-by-letter spelling and word-building capabilities, though currently not as reliable as stenotype, but constantly improving.
Letter-by-letter spelling formats provide reliable translation of words not housed in writer's dictionary.	Vocabulary builds at computer speed, rather than human speed.
Word building has reliable translation.	Technology builds on previous technology. Doesn't start at ground zero.
Interacts reliability with encoders for broadcast captioning work.	Equipment costs, although currently comparable to a stenographer's investment, will decrease as the number of users increases with use of mainstream software.

Cons	*Cons*
Equipment start-up costs are hefty.	Voice commands received by the computer search a look-up table dictionary for closest match. Reliability of translation depends on the reporter's training level.
The training period is lengthier than for voice.	For the newer realtime voice reporter, text will come out in paragraphs, rather than a few words at a time, thereby making the viewer wait for text, and then a large chunk will output to the screen. This makes it harder for the viewer to manage the information flow.
The attrition rate of students in training programs is higher.	Sometimes spoken words and spoken commands are misinterpreted for one another.
Students build their vocabulary or their dictionary at "human speed."	Vocabulary training or dictionary additions are made easily, but not while dictating live.
	Letter-by-letter spelling formats and word-building techniques are not yet perfected for a reliable translation.
	Designed for Windows-based program and will not run in DOS programs; currently will not interface with encoders for broadcast captioning purposes.

Chapter 36

Tomorrow's Technology: Computer Integrated Courtrooms and Beyond

An excellent place to start talking about the technology of tomorrow is with the technology being used today in some modern courtrooms. These technologically advanced courtrooms are called computer-integrated courtrooms or CICs.

Computer-Integrated Courtrooms

The computer-integrated courtroom makes available the wonders of computer technology to the judge and the trial lawyers in both the courtroom and the judge's chambers. This technology is being used in new courts with increasing frequency. Applications include realtime translation; courtroom litigation support; computer-assisted legal research using LEXIS, WESTLAW, and ABA/Net systems; document processing, including online exhibit copying; presentation applications; and other word-processing and desktop publishing functions.

A computer-integrated courtroom is a combination of hardware and software designed to accomplish specific tasks related to court trials and litigation proceedings. The precursor to the CIC was the TAC, or the total access courtroom, which attempted to make the courtroom accessible to all people with disabilities.

Courtroom 21

A CIC is a courtroom that uses the most modern, up-to-date, technological advances to enhance the justice system, for example, Courtroom 21, short for The Courtroom of the 21st Century Today. This is an international demonstration and experimental project that seeks to determine how technology can best improve all components of the legal system. Courtroom 21 is located in the College of William & Mary Law School in Williamsburg, Virginia, and is a joint project with the National Center for State Courts. Among other methods of recording the spoken word, it includes a computerized shorthand writer and realtime translation. The judge and lawyers have a computer monitor to view the transcript immediately. They can mark the transcript, refer to various portions of it, and even call in previous transcripts or court documents all at the same time.

Some technological advances include automatic video recording of proceedings using ceiling-mounted cameras with voice-initiated switching; realtime or recorded televised evidence display with analog optical disk storage; remote, two-way television arraignments; text, graphics, and TV capable jury computers; LEXIS legal research at bench and counsel tables; built-in video deposition playback facilities; information storage and presentation; and realtime court reporter transcription, including the ability for each lawyer to mark an individual computerized copy of the transcript for later use.

A complete description of Courtroom 21 can be found at the Web page http://www.courtroom21.net. This Web page describes in detail some alternative methods used in recording court proceedings, that is, some of the technological advances that were discussed in the previous chapter. This modern-day courtroom offers a variety of recording processes, something that will more than likely be the norm in all proceedings in the future.

Advantages of CIC

Some of the advantages of using a computer-integrated courtroom for the lawyers, judges, and jury are the following:

1. Review the testimony instantly by scrolling backward in the text to find testimony that has already been given. In addition, judges and lawyers can review objections and rulings.

2. Readback by the court reporter is virtually eliminated because of the ability to scroll within the transcript.

3. Review and compare previous testimony in other transcripts as well as perform other tasks simultaneously.

4. Perform a keyword search in any transcript for occurrences of an object, name, place, or date.

5. Access court and legal databases online to use in legal citations.

6. Cue, mark, or code points within a transcript that are pertinent to each individual lawyer.

7. Make electronic notes that will be helpful for cross- or redirect examination or for closing arguments.

8. Obtain disk copies as well as printed copies of a transcript in standard format or compressed format.

9. View and audio-sync testimony with the printed transcript.

10. View animated or videoed exhibits and presentations on screen.

Courtroom 2000

Another example of a computer-integrated courtroom is the Courtroom 2000 project being used in the New York State Supreme Court. The technology used in this courtroom is similar to the technology that was used during the infamous O. J. Simpson trial held in California.

Courtroom 2000 has 16 different computer monitors for use by the judge, the attorneys, and the jury. They are strategically located at the judge's bench, the jury box, the attorney's table, and the clerk's desk. The monitors are used not just for realtime display, but also for visual presentation of evidence on CD-ROM and for showing graphic and animated exhibits as well as expert testimony.

The courtroom is also equipped with PC docking stations, a computerized blackboard that will capture drawing or writings and put them into the record, integrated VCRs for the playing of expert testimony that was prerecorded, and a touch-screen monitor for use by the witness. In addition, video conference and closed captioning are available.

Tomorrow's Technology

The future of court and realtime reporting is linked to the technology of today. Here are 10 predictions, based on the technology of today, concerning the future of court and realtime reporting.

1. The technology of electronic tape recording will advance, but will not replace court and realtime reporters as the sole method of recording verbatim proceedings. Audio recording technology will have its own niche in recording proceedings.

2. Voice-to-print technology will advance, and it will be used in low-key situations where accuracy and dependability are not important. The technology of voice-to-print will use artificial intelligence to help

to decipher dialects and mumbling. Voice-to-print technology will be bolstered by the use of speech-to-text technology such as voice writing, where one person repeats what others say.

3. Voice-recognition and voice-activation systems will continue to be improved and will be used by physically disabled persons. The technology will also be used to perform certain functions and commands. Its application will not be used in court and realtime reporting except to perform certain functions by voice command, for example, editing and printing may be done by voice recognition. The technology will supplement the other technologies used by the court and realtime reporter.

4. Video recording will continue to be used as a viable method of recording events, but the technology will be coupled with a realtime writer.

5. The technology of court and realtime reporting will involve multirecording that will all be synchronized to produce a choice of transcript production. One court/realtime reporter, using one shorthand writer, will be able to write shorthand notes on paper tape, record the notes electronically on disk, and video and audio record the speaker on CD-ROM.

6. Enhanced evidence-capturing technology will allow documents, drawings, videos, depositions, and other multimedia presentations to become part of the total record of proceedings.

7. Instant translation will be available in any language, regardless of the speaker's language. Translation will also be available in Braille and as closed captioning for the visually and hearing impaired.

8. The speed of translation and transcript production will increase remarkably. Using artificial intelligence, all transcripts, regardless of the writer's errors, will be virtually error free; there will be no conflicts and no untranslates and, therefore, no editing. Realtime translation will be replaced by realtime transcription.

9. Fast input and transcription (FIAT), using the shorthand machine and a computer with appropriate software, will be used by business and industry as a viable alternative to the standard keyboard. Realtime teleconferencing and Internet/Web discussions will be realtimed for instant viewing via closed-captioning technology.

10. Transcripts will be produced on CD-ROM that will play back the visual and audio portions, as well as produce a printed transcript in one window of the screen. The CD-ROM will contain all evidence presented during the proceedings, all videos presented during the trial, and any other related cases that are pertinent to the matter. This enhanced packaged transcript on CD-ROM will become the standard of the court and realtime reporting industry.

A Final Word about Court and Realtime Reporting, Captioning, and CART

Without a doubt, the field of reporting is in an exciting and challenging transition stage. In a very real sense, the court reporters of today hold the future of their profession in their own hand. The court and realtime reporters, as well as the captioners and CART providers of tomorrow, need to work with a vision and imagination that will continue to enhance the ultimate goal of the profession.

This goal can be summarized in the following statement: to capture the spoken word and guarantee a true and accurate record that will serve as an assitive technology for those who can use their services and to preserve the record for posterity.

Index